RCUS. Bluck aqu

A Major London 'Minor':
the Surrey Theatre 1805-1865

Detail from Banks's 'Balloon View of London' (1851), looking south
(the Surrey Theatre is immediately below the Obelisk)

A Major London 'Minor':
the Surrey Theatre 1805-1865

William G. Knight

The Society for Theatre Research
1997

First published 1997
by
The Society for Theatre Research
c/o The Theatre Museum, 1e Tavistock Street, London WC2E 7PA

\- - - - - - - - - - - -

ISBN 0 85430 061 9

Set by Blot Publishing
9 Swan View, PULBOROUGH, West Sussex RH20 2BF

Printed by Plumridge & Co.
41 High Street, LINTON, Cambridgeshire

Contents

List of Illustrations

End-papers

Plates

Figures

Note. Southwark Local Studies Library is the source of playbills for the Surrey Theatre which are without citation in the list below. Grateful thanks are expressed for generous permission to reproduce these items from the library's collection.

Foreword

A Major London 'Minor': The Surrey Theatre 1805-1865

The routes leading to an interest in theatre history are as diverse as the subject itself and are by no means confined to the conventional path through the groves of academe. William Knight's history of the Surrey Theatre is a splendid case in point. The author did not embark upon his research until he had retired and then with the initial objective of producing a family history until his forbears' involvement with the Surrey Theatre took centre stage.

William Knight has drawn upon national and local archives, published and manuscript sources to create his account of the Surrey Theatre under the management, amongst others, of the Davidge family, thereby raising both the theatre and its manager G.B. Davidge to their deserved places in the annals of London's minor theatres.

The exigencies of publication have necessitated some editing of William Knight's typescript, but it has been the true intent of Frances Dann and her successor Derek Forbes to retain the author's distinctive style and approach.

It is my pleasant duty as Chairman of the Publications Sub-Committee to express the Society's appreciation to all concerned: to William Knight for entrusting his book to us, to Audrey Knight for her help and encouragement, to Frances Dann and Derek Forbes for their work as editors and to Leonie Forbes of Blot Publishing for her attentiveness and expertise.

Members of the Society for Theatre Research receive this volume in addition to the annual publications for 1995-6 and 1996-7.

Richard Foulkes
For the Society for Theatre Research

Kerschner
EIN FESTE BERG

A Major London 'Minor': The Surrey Theatre 1805-1865

Introduction

I never intended to write a history of the Surrey Theatre in the first place. My objective was, and still is, to compile a family history for private circulation, covering the period from 1570 to date. It just so happens that my great-grandfather Joseph Kerschner was manager of that great London 'Minor Theatre' in the 1840s and my great-grandmother and her mother were in the Surrey's chorus-line in the 1830s. Consequently I was putting the playbills under scrutiny for genealogical purposes and would be very satisfied to find a bill showing ancestors at the box-office *and* in the chorus on the same evening. The fact that Macready might be playing Macbeth that night, with Mrs Ternan as Lady Macbeth, was of only passing interest.

The idea evolved that if I turned my story upside-down, so as to make people like Macready more important than the box-office keeper, I would have a history of the Surrey – at least in part. By chance the family connection starts soon after the fire of 1805 destroyed the theatre and fades away just before fire destroyed the building again in 1865. The fires seem a fitting framework within which to cast my text. Perhaps someone else will write the story of the rebuilt Surrey Theatre after 1865.

Because this originated as a family history, obviously it is the people who are highlighted – their feuds, quarrels and loves, their performances and theatrical enterprise, their failures and successes. There is little about the size of the stage or the number of dressing-rooms. I do go somewhat outside my proclaimed range by including such details as I could find regarding the life and career of George B. Davidge before he took over the management of the Surrey in 1834. This is firstly because he is 'family' (my grandmother's uncle) and secondly, no-one else seems to have put together an account of his life. There is a better reason still. When Davidge was not actually appearing at the Surrey – which he did many times before he assumed its management – he was in strong competition with it as manager of the Coburg (now the Old Vic) just up the road. To explain why the Surrey did something it helps to know what its rival was doing.

Where I have been able to make up my mind as to their probability I have included pieces of oral tradition passed on to me by my father William Knight (1873-1956) and my uncle George Knight (1875-1971). I have kept scholarly apparatus to a minimum as I intended this work initially for a private readership and subsequently for a general one. There are no annotations. Where appropriate, brief citations are given in the text; full titles appear in the list at the end. In quotations from nineteenth-century sources, slight abnormalities (to us) of spelling and punctuation have usually been retained unamended and without remark. Inconsistency in the spelling and wording of play-titles in successive playbills and quotations etc. has not been corrected, so that, for example, *Llewellyn, Prince of Wales; or, Gellert the Faithful Dog* (Thomas Dibdin's title for his piece, according to Allardyce Nicoll) may be quoted in the text from the playbill as *Llewelyn, Prince of Wales; or, the Faithful Gelert*. The punctuation in titles such as the above has however been standardised.

Now for acknowledgements. Firstly to my wife Audrey for her work on finding and analysing playbills, and later proof-reading and indexing my work. Then to my colleague Sheila Frazer, both for her criticism of my literary style (I was abashed at the number of times the word 'incidentally' fell to her blue pencil) and for her suggestion which led to the 'Opera, Pantomime and Ballet' discussion being developed in one sequence rather than spread throughout the book. Also to Tom Ryan for sight of his doctoral thesis on Thomas Dibdin. We go hand-in-hand most of the way until we come to Dibdin's dramatisation of Smollett's novels, which I prefer to dispose of in two or three lines against the thirty-odd pages in the thesis. Next, thanks to Jane Moody, for her list of newspaper and magazine comments on Surrey matters. Then to Nicola Smith formerly of Southwark Local Studies Library who supplied the push to change this part of my work from family history to theatre history. As well as Southwark's, further resources helpfully consulted include those of the Minet Library (London Borough of Lambeth), the Guildhall Library (Corporation of London), the British Library and Museum, the Theatre Museum, the Bodleian Library (University of Oxford), the Garrick Club, the Public Record Office, and the National Portrait Gallery. Finally thanks go to all my friends in the Society for Theatre Research, particularly Frances Dann and Bob Flanagan who have added titbits of information at various times. I am grateful to you all.

William George Knight

Chapter One

In General; and the New Start (1806-09)

The Surrey Theatre was situated at the southern end of Blackfriars Road, then called Great Surrey Street, close to St George's Circus. At the time of writing (early 1990s), its site is a hole in the ground behind advertising hoardings, next to the disused Royal Eye Hospital.

It had been built as the Royal Circus by Colonel Temple West and opened, with Charles Dibdin senior as the first manager, in November 1782. After the Colonel's death in 1784 it was let by his widow, Mrs Jane West, to James Jones. He took into partnership his son-in-law John Cartwright Cross, who wrote many pieces for the theatre. At this stage the horses topped the bill, but the theatre was gutted by fire in 1799. The partnership managed to get things moving again but the financial burdens proved too much and a committee of five Trustees for the creditors tried to run the theatre. According to the *Memoirs* of the comedian Jacob Decastro: 'The first season they had the place it was burned down, on the 12th of August 1805. It was by the trust deed to have been insured for £6,000 but by some negligence or mistake, it was only for £3,000 and with that sum they commenced re-building a new theatre. On the following Easter Monday, it was opened with great spirit'. The theatre burnt down again in 1865. This story covers the period between these two fires.

Any history of the Surrey Theatre said to cover this period might give the impression of a continuity which hardly exists. Although the external fabric of the building was virtually unchanged, there were over the years three major configurations of the auditorium representing different ideas of the purpose of the theatre. In its 'equestrian academy' days the ground floor was a circus ring, with a vestigial stage used at times as a vantage point for spectators of the 'scenes in the circle'. At other times the ring was filled with benches and the stage became the place where entertainments were mounted. In the first fifteen years of this story these two settings alternated, depending on the purpose of different managers and lessees. In the late 1820s the stage predominated. In 1834 Davidge introduced a retractable stage so that the type of production could be changed overnight. It was thus that the Surrey could play *Macbeth* on stage one week and offer the use of the circle to Ducrow and his horsemen the next. The changes in the theatre's name in the early days indicated these changes in function: later it turned on the manager's whim. First it was 'The Royal Circus and Equestrian Philharmonic Academy', then 'The Royal Circus and Surrey Theatre'. Elliston dropped the Royal Circus appellation in 1809 and Jones and Dunn put it back again in 1816; in 1818 it was back to its name under Elliston, 'The Surrey Theatre'. Then it had a short spell as 'The New Surrey Theatre', preceding a return to 'The Surrey Theatre' until 1834, when Davidge made it 'The Royal Surrey Theatre'.

These changes of name, managerial ideas and interior layout, though, were less important in determining the Surrey 'character' than the changes outside its walls. At the beginning of the century, London stopped at the Surrey. At its doors there was the toll-gate, there were the green fields. True, there was some ribbon development along the Dover and Brighton roads, but behind these houses were the open fields. Indeed, a major necessity of an 'equestrian academy' was pasture for its horses and so without St George's Fields there would have been no Royal Circus. The same consideration determined the site of the Surrey's friendly rival, Astley's Amphitheatre, a short distance up the road towards Westminster Bridge.

Many of the buildings round St George's Circus were institutions from which a theatre could not draw an audience; the Indigent Blind School on the other side of the Circus was an obvious example. The 'Rules of the King's Bench' may not mean much these days or be recognised as a hindrance to theatrical management, but at that time there was a large area around the theatre where certain debtors were required to live, with attendance at theatres forbidden to them. In 1819 this area reached from the Elephant and Castle and up to the Borough, west along Webber Street and south roughly where Morley Street is now, to St George's Road, and eastwards to the Elephant again: that is, completely surrounding the theatre. There were also restrictions on the inhabitants of the nearby Philanthropic Reform Home and the Magdalene Hospital, otherwise the Home for Penitent Prostitutes. All these factors limited the Surrey's potential local audience.

This meant that customers had to be attracted from north of the Thames. Just as Westminster Bridge opened up Astley's to Londoners – who, at that time, would not have recognised those living on the Surrey side as being of their number – so did Blackfriars Bridge for the Surrey Theatre. As an inducement to visit the south bank, ticket agencies north of the river offered a pass to cross the bridges 'toll free'.

At the beginning of this period, there was nothing in the way of public transport. Either one was a member of society, and visited the Royal

Circus in one's own carriage – 'Coachmen to set down with their horses' heads towards the Bridge, and take up in the opposite direction' as the playbills advised – and occupied a box, or one came on foot and filled the pit and gallery. The middle-class playgoer was virtually unknown. A change in the habits of society later robbed the Surrey-side theatres of much of their box clientele. When the evening meal started later and lasted longer, performances starting at six-thirty were just not attended by people following this pattern.

From at least 1814 there was a livery stable at the back of the theatre, no doubt to accommodate those who arrived on horseback. In 1826 a coach was running nightly from the theatre to Deptford and Greenwich. In 1829, George Shillibeer introduced the first horse-omnibus service to London and by 1836 a nightly horse-omnibus service was operating from the theatre to Fleet Street, Holborn and Islington. One took a 'King William' or a 'Napoleon' to St George's Circus; numbered routes came much later.

By 1865 London had flowed out round the theatre, the railway had reached out from Waterloo to Wandsworth, Herne Hill and Norwood, and horse buses were running through to the new suburbs beyond. Within easy distance of the theatre were terraced houses with gardens and small detached houses, with larger detached houses no further than Brixton and Battersea. The middle classes had arrived but the green fields had gone: two good reasons why the circus declined and why there was a growing demand for cultural entertainment. Astley's could easily provide 'horse opera' and the Surrey provide melodrama; both could thrive without affecting each other's audiences: but there was now competition within a few minutes' walk of both of them. A new bridge, started in 1809, was not even finished, let alone named Waterloo Bridge, before the advantages of a new theatre at its southern end were foreseen and thus the Coburg, now better known as the Old Vic, came to be built. It opened in 1818 and it is hardly possible to write the history of the Surrey without considering what its main rival was doing at the time.

Another great difference between the beginning and end of this story is in the legal field: what could or could not be done at different theatres and at what time of year. This was not necessarily what actually was done. At times, blind eyes were turned; at others, legal proceedings were all the rage. At the beginning of the nineteenth century, three main legal problems faced Surrey managements.

Firstly, as F.G. Tomlins put it in his *Brief View of the English Drama*, published in 1840, 'any actor who performed in any kind of theatrical entertainment without special license from the crown, or without having a settlement in the place he performed, was deemed to be a rogue and vagabond'. John Palmer, who had been employed by the Royal Circus in 1789, was imprisoned under this head.

Secondly, the building itself needed a licence from either the Lord Chamberlain or from the local magistrates. By a quirk of jurisdiction the Coburg needed one from the Lord Chamberlain whereas the Surrey only needed one from the magistrates. Some theatres were licensed only for the summer, some only for the winter. The Adelphi Theatre, north of the Thames, had only a winter licence; so at times the company would come to the Surrey in the summer months and put on joint productions with the Surrey players.

The third legal restriction, however, was the greatest bugbear in the early years – the monopoly of 'legitimate' drama by the patent theatres, namely Drury Lane and Covent Garden and, in the summer, the Haymarket Theatre. Dialogue was not permitted on the stage of a so-called 'minor' theatre. The patentees were quick to issue writs if they thought their monopoly was being infringed. Consequently the minors were restricted to song and dance, mime and burletta, and attempted in many an ingenious way to circumvent the ban. Burletta included rhymed verse, agreed – but did it include blank verse accompanied by music? Well, yes. What about *The Beggar's Opera* with spoken dialogue between the songs? The answer was no, unless the dialogue was turned into rhymed couplets.

By the mid-1830s no-one was paying much attention to what the law strictly did or did not permit. As Tomlins commented in 1840:

> All the fierce endeavour to maintain the exclusive privileges only engendered an evasion of the law and deterioration of the art which is almost beyond cure. At present three theatres can alone perform any one of the productions of our fine regular drama, while the whole sixteen may perform *Jack Sheppard*.

This legal nonsense was swept away in 1843 when the monopolies were abolished by Act of Parliament. All the theatres operated thereafter on equal terms.

A good view of the theatrical life of London just before the 1843 Act is given by Tomlins. He begins with the minor theatres and must have had a strong feeling for the Surrey, as this is put at the head of the list:

> The Surrey Theatre has established, by its constancy to one class of sentiment and spectacle, a kind of standard, whereby may be represented certain dramatic performances, and 'a

> regular Surrey piece' is the stereotyped phrase for a drama which, in three acts, pourtrays the heroism of watermen below, and the constancy of housemaids above bridge; wherein characters, the most heavenly, are continually coming in contact with characters very much the reverse; where the British navy is in every other sentence declared to be the only perfection exemplified on earth.

But context is all. His fair description of the theatre in 1840 would be quite wrong for 1820 and earlier (when horsemanship dominated), 1830 (Shakespeare and English opera), 1850 (translations of Italian operas) or 1860 (translations of French plays). The Surrey changed its style as often as it changed its manager.

However, it is useful to have Tomlins's account of the Surrey's rivals in 1840 as a guide to the variety of entertainment available:

> The Victoria Theatre [earlier the Coburg] has suffered more vicissitudes than any other. Its performances have been of every kind and of every quality. Melodramas of the deepest dye and coarsest texture were once its staple commodity – when Turpin cut his horse's throat upon the stage, the fact was 'realised' by a quantity of red ochre.... Situated in one of the worst neighbourhoods, its audiences are of the lowest kind, and if the English Emperor or Empress should visit it, it would be necessary to imitate the Roman potentate, by drenching the audience with rose-water to neutralize certain vile odours arising from gin and tobacco and bad ventilation.

Of Astley's, he writes:

> Astley's Amphitheatre is a name at which the youthful heart bounds, and the olden one revives. Here there is no humbug about legitimate drama; it openly proclaims in its classic bills, 'Historical panoply, and the glorious emblazonment of deeds of chivalry and skill'.... Here we have the gauntlet thrown down for spectacle, and it is said and sincerely believed, to be the one great thing. This theatre is what it pretends to be – a place of amusement, and as such is respectably conducted and respectably attended.

These, then, are the Surrey's immediate rivals. As the visits of the Adelphi company to the Surrey have been mentioned,

> we will now cross the water, and step into the 'great minor', on the opposite bank of Old Father Thames – the Adelphi Theatre, where melodrame, with all her woes, maintains her

> empire. Here the wild and wonderful, amidst blue fire and sinking traps, give a terrible warning to the murderer and the felon; here 'horrors upon horror's head' are accumulated, and 'intense interest and excited feelings' are enkindled... by agonised partings and melting meetings; by frenzied fathers, mad daughters and remorseful wives.

These will be the especial treats for the Surrey audiences when the Adelphi shuts for the summer.

The Surrey Theatre was flanked by two public houses also built on Temple West's land, namely 'The Equestrian Tavern' (Watney's) to the south, and 'The Coal Hole', later 'The Flowers of the Forest' (Whitbread's) to the north. These were more than merely providers of their respective breweries' heady liquors during the intervals. At different times, they acted as manager's residence, box office and administration centre, quite apart from being the obvious venue for theatrical parties and celebrations.

One last topographical feature, the Obelisk. When writers had used up all their descriptions of the Surrey audiences as 'Surreyites', 'Surreysiders', the 'people on the other side of the water' and such like, they would use phrases such as 'the good people of the Obelisk'. This referred to a miniature 'Cleopatra's Needle' originally installed in 1771 at the centre of St George's Circus, just beyond the theatre. Blackfriars Bridge had been completed in 1765, the road to the Circus had been built up shortly after and the Obelisk showed on three of its faces the distances to Westminster, Fleet Street and London Bridge. It was moved a couple of hundred yards up Lambeth Road in 1905, to the road junction outside what is now the Imperial War Museum.

It is not easy to generalise about prices of admission over so long a period and to compare them with the weekly wage. What can be said for certain is that, apart from the early 1830s, when cholera hit London and theatre prices were halved to attract any sort of audience, the Surrey was usually filled to bursting. An evening's entertainment usually consisted of two major pieces and something – song, dance, juggling and the like – to cover the time required to change the scenery between the main pieces. The whole programme could run from six-thirty to midnight, even beyond, given the many mishaps in presentation ranging from collapsing scenery to inebriated actors. It became the custom to admit people at the half-way stage (planned for eight-thirty) at half-price; this in turn led to new plays being introduced at full price one week and at half price the next. It followed that a newspaper critic would only attend the first half of the evening and would miss any triumph or disaster happening in the course of the second piece – which, of course, he had reviewed the week previously. Thus many of the most revealing anecdotes in the memoirs of managers and actors are difficult to verify in the public prints.

There was a major exception to this custom. The pantomime was always the last item in the bills and if anyone thought he could go along at eight-thirty on Boxing Night and get in at half price, he was in for a rude awakening to the facts of Surrey life.

Our detailed chronicle starts when the five trustees opened the rebuilt theatre on Easter Monday 1806 ('Doors open Half-past Five, to begin at Half-past Six O'Clock'). Their policy was to present a mix of old favourites. For example, on 21 April 1806 there was *Cottage Courtship; or, Damon and Clara*, with Montgomery and Miss Johnston, followed by an equestrian performance by Makeen, Sutton and James, with Master Avery and, as Clown to the Horsemanship, Porter. Then came *The Mysterious Freebooter*. The evening ended with a pantomime by J.C. Cross, *The Sorceress of Strozzi; or, Harlequin Wanderer*, with music by William Ware. In the saloon and lobby, there were further attractions in the form of 'all Kind of Refreshments, Ices, Jellies, Fruit, Coffee, Tea &c'.

Cross also gave the trustees two new plays, *The Cloud King; or, Magic Rose*, produced on 30 June 1806 and *The False Friend* produced on 7 September, but they both had short runs. There was another pantomime on 28 July 1806, *The Flying Island of Laputa; or, Harlequin Gulliver*, which was probably also written by Cross, though it is not credited to him in Allardyce Nicoll's analysis of nineteenth-century productions (where it is listed in the 'Unknown Authors' section). It is also probably the pantomime shown in the engraving by Rowlandson and Pugin and published in Ackermann's *Microcosm of London* in 1810. The illustration is clearly of a pantomime – Harlequin and Columbine, Clown and Pantaloon are easily identified – and the on-stage scenery consists of a gigantic tea-pot, twice the size of the Harlequinaders, and a large cup and saucer, about half their size. I have some doubts concerning such an identification, firstly because Gulliver finds this size difference in Brobdingnag not Laputa and secondly because the backcloth shows normal-sized houses. On the other hand, I can trace no other pantomime at the Surrey before 1810 with a title suggesting that the size difference was relevant. But who expects pantomimes to be logical?

'Probably' is necessary in the narrative because so few playbills have survived for the early part of my period and there is not much in the way of alternative evidence. Cross published half-a-dozen of his plays but none of his pantomimes. A trawl through the items by 'Unknown Authors' in Allardyce Nicoll's *Nineteenth-Century Drama: 1800-1850*, vol. II, finds the names of seven plays and six pantomimes under this management.

One playbill which does survive, in the Theatre Museum collection, shows the departmental chiefs as at 24 May 1808. Saunderson is in charge of the orchestra; Marchbanks is named for scenery, Branscomb for machinery; Giroux is Ballet Master (with Miss Giroux as Columbine). Leading performers are Sutton (horsemanship), Hengler (slack rope), Hollingsworth as Harlequin, Bradbury as Clown. It will be seen that these people are still with the Surrey many years later. As for management style, one can simply say that the theatre lived up to its name of Royal Circus, Equestrian and Philharmonic Academy!

There was a forerunner of the Surrey's greatest run of all when Wilkinson sang Gay's ballad of 'Black-Eyed Susan' on 19 October 1808. However, as Decastro recounts, concerning the trustees: 'The mode or system adopted in its management did not succeed; the novelty of the thing wore off with them and they began to weary of their pursuit'.

On 18 February 1809 the trustees advertised that they were seeking a responsible person to whom to lease the Royal Circus. Robert William Elliston, of the Theatre Royal, Drury Lane, offered them his ultimatum, with complicated terms which loaded the dice in his favour come any contingency. This was just as well, as the day after agreement was reached Drury Lane burnt down. According to Decastro: 'Though the Trustees paid but a rent of £210 a year, we believe Mr Elliston paid them £2,000'. So the Trustees were not persuaded entirely by Elliston's mode of negotiation.

Chapter Two

'But was it the Same Elephant?' (1809-14)

Although from 3 April 1809 the Royal Circus was nominally under the control of Robert Elliston he seldom appeared there, spending more time on legal and political battles in an attempt to obtain a patent or licence to permit him to compete with the two major theatres. He acted at Bath, Bristol and Manchester, and in London at the Haymarket Theatre under George Colman.

> What do you all think of Elliston, the actor? I will tell you my opinion. He is one of the most mercenary, selfish creatures I ever met with. I once thought better of him; that was at the very beginning of our acquaintance. I had absolutely been in love with the man, ever since I accompanied my mother to witness his performance in the comedy of *The Honeymoon*. Elliston, in the character of the duke, appeared so very manly, so very gentlemanlike, so everything which a man ought to be to win a fair lady's heart, that I did not recover myself for more than a fortnight.

Thus the notorious Harriette Wilson in her *Memoirs,* but this infatuation did not last:

> I did not altogether like Elliston in *Wild Oats*. He made too many faces, and reminded me of the minor theatres, where grimace is in considerable request. Perhaps, also, since the time I fell in love with him in *The Honeymoon,* he was all the worse for having presided over a small theatre, as manager, for several years. He joined us after the play, and being tipsy, which is generally the case with him, I thought him very pleasant, although, as I have since discovered, there is not a heavier, more matter-of-fact, stupid companion on earth than Elliston, when he is sober.

(That's what managing the Surrey did to a man, according to London's most literary courtesan!)

In fact Elliston left most of the Surrey management to John Cross at first, and later to Thomas Dibdin. The theatre had some good players to sustain a programme of pantomime and burletta, and a good writer in John Cross. It was he who found a way of putting on in a minor theatre a piece normally within the monopoly of the patent theatres: he took *The Beggar's Opera* and set the dialogue as rhymed couplets, with a musical background. It was staged on 15 June 1809 and was a success. Cross then set about doing the same to *Macbeth*, this time relying heavily on mime, and had it on stage at the end of August. On this occasion, Elliston found time to play Macbeth. *The Morning Chronicle*, tongue in cheek, claimed that 'with the exception of the dialogue, the performance was almost exactly the play of Shakespeare'.

The Royal Circus ended its first season under Elliston in November. As his attempts to found a third 'major' had come to nothing, he set about removing the horse-ring and adapting the Royal Circus as a stage-orientated playhouse at the Obelisk, to be known as the Surrey Theatre. It opened in its new glory on Easter Monday, 23 April 1810, with Thomas Dibdin having 'the management of the Stage'. The departmental chiefs were Sanderson as the musical director, scenery by Marchbanks, machinery by William Branscomb (who was later to become one of the Surrey directors). John Cross was now dead but Mrs Cross had been found a place in the wardrobe, with Mrs and Miss Freelove. As well as Thomas Dibdin to write songs and pantomimes, there was Dennis Lawler who, for the season commencing 8 May 1811, wrote *Alfred the Great; or, England Invaded* and a piece based on Hogarth's 'Two Apprentices', *Industry and Idleness*.

Many of the company can still be found at the Surrey nearly forty years later. T.P. Cooke played an Abbot in the first piece and The Man in Brass Armour in the Lord Mayor's Procession which was the highlight of the afterpiece; he was playing nautical roles at the Surrey up to 1848. Thomas Ellar, a great harlequin and a partner of Grimaldi, the greatest clown, was merely Chip, a carpenter, in *Alfred the Great*; he was Harlequin in the Surrey pantomime of 1837.

The circus tradition was not easy to shake off. When the plot so required there was 'The Equestrian Department under the management of Mr Davis'. William Davis was one of the great names of equestrianism, ranking with Philip Astley and William Parker, and drew on their companies for his horsemen. For example in *Blood will have Blood*, staged on 26 July 1811, he deployed over twenty horsemen, including Peter Ducrow and his son, Andrew – later to become the 'great' Ducrow – plus William Parker's son and Elliston's nine-year-old son Henry. Also in the piece as one of the Sicilian ladies was Miss Jane Scott who, as Susan, was to chalk up hundreds of performances with T.P. Cooke as William in the Surrey's great hit some eighteen years later, *Black-Eyed Susan*.

SURREY THEATRE,

under the Superintendance of Mr. ELLISTON.
The Management of the Stoge by Mr. T. DIBDIN.

This present FRIDAY, the 26th of July, 1811,
PRECISELY AT A QUARTER-AFTER SIX.

Will be presented, 41st time, a New Grand & highly popular Hippodramatic Romance, with New Music, Scenery, Dresses, and extensive Embellishments, called

"BLOOD will have BLOOD!"

Or, the BATTLE of the BRIDGES.

The whole of the Melo-Drame and Poetry, written by, and produced under the Direction of, Mr. T. DIBDIN.
The Overture and Music composed by Mr. SANDERSON. The Scenery designed by Mr. MARCHBANKS, and painted by him, Mr. SMITH, and Assistants.
The Machinery invented and executed by Mr. BRANSCOMB. The Dresses by Mr. BRETT, Mrs CROSS, Mrs. SIMMONS, and Miss FREELOVE.
The Decorations, Armorial Ensigns, and Equestrian Caparisons, by Mr. SUTTON and Mrs. FREELOVE.
The Real Armour by Mr. MARRIOTT, of Fleet-Street.
The EQUESTRIAN DEPARTMENT under the Management of Mr. DAVIS.

CHARACTERS:

The Baron Polaski, Mr. S. SLADER. Sir Theodore, of England, Mr. HUNTLEY. St. Aubert, Peer of France, Mr. GIBBON.
Count Conrad, of Hungary, Mr. COOKE. Bertrand, the Baron's Confident, Mr. SMITH. Henry, 'Squire to Sir Theodore, Mr. FITZWILLIAM.
Antonio, and Bendetto, (Sicilians), Mr. DORMER and Mr. BARNARD. Ribeski, Butler to the Baron, Mr. G. GIBBON.
Provinski, Mr. PAYNE. Mysterious Monk, Signior RIVOLTA. Equestrian Spectre, Mr. DAVIS.
Leonora, Daughter of the Baron, Mrs. DITCHER. Paulina, her Attendant, Mrs. HATTON. Beatrice, and Lauretta, (Sicilians), Mrs. PEARCE and Miss SCOTT.
Alexina, Jacquelina, Mina, Florina, (Polonese Damsels), Miss HATTON, Miss GREEN, Miss DELY, and Miss JELLETT.

PRINCIPAL HORSEMEN:

Polish Knights,—Messrs. H. ELLISTON, DAY, DAVIS, BROWN, and DUCROW.
English Knights,—Messrs. ELLAR, BRADLEY, R. COOKE, DUCROW, Junr. and JENKINS.
Hungarian Knights,—Messrs. JOHNSON, TATE, CASTAY, SALTER, and LONDON.
French Knights,—Messrs. PEARCE, PARKER, BANKS, CHASE, HENRY, and SAUNDERS.
Heralds, Guards, &c.—Messrs ODWELL, BURDEN, DOYLE, CHESTER, CLANDFIELDS, &c.
Polish Ladies,—Mesdames, RIVOLTA, MAY, HIBBERT, DAVIS, Misses TAYLOR, GARCIA, FREELOVE, and DENT.

In the course of the Piece, among others, the following New Scenes will be introduced:
Interior of a Romantic Cavern on the Sea Shore;—View of the Castle of the Baron Polaski;
Rustic Bridge and Cascade;—Elegant Apartment in the Castle;—The Baron's Hall of Audience;
Grand Gothic Corridor;—Antique Banquet Room; State Bed Chamber;
Fortifications of the Castle, with its Works, Bridges, &c.
In Act I. a Storm & Shipwreck.—In Act III. a Grand Banquet & a Battle, with the Storming of the Baron's Castle.

To conclude with, 17th time, an entirely New Burletta, founded on Mr. T. DIBDIN's Comedy of "FIVE MILES OFF, or the FINGER POST," called

RIGHT of COMMON;

Or, How to get a Freehold.

The New Music composed by Mr. SANDERSON.

Farmer Flail, Mr. DORMER. *Kalendar,* Mr. DE CAMP. *Sordid,* Mr. G. GIBBON. *Edward,* Mr. HILL.
Laurence Luckless, Mr. GIBBON. *Andrew,* Mr. BANKS. *Spriggins,* Mr. S. SLADER. *O'Gimlet,* Mr. FITZWILLIAM.
Flourish, Mr. JOHANNOT. *Black Bob,* Mr. COOKE.
Dapper, Mr. MAY. *Robert,* Mr. H. ELLISTON. *Dick,* Master SALTER. *Bricklayer,* Mr. WILLIAMS.
Mrs. Prue, Mrs. PEARCE. *Mary Flail,* Miss HATTON. *Jenny,* Mrs. HATTON. *Laura Luckless,* Mrs. HIBBERT.

☞ The Public are respectfully informed, that Miss FERON will perform on SATURDAY in the Burletta of

TAG in TRIBULATION,

that Piece commencing the Entertainments of the Evening.

⁂ Tickets and Places for the Boxes may be had of Mr. BORAUER, at the Box-Office, from Ten till Four.——BOXES 4s. PIT 2s. GALLERY 1s.
The Doors to be opened at a Quarter-after Five; to commence at a Quarter-after Six precisely.——NO MONEY RETURNED.

Hartnell, Albion-Press, Bermondsey-Street, Southwark.

Of the other players in this piece, Johannet, Huntley, Payne and Edward Fitzwilliam were still with the Surrey several managements later. The programme can be considered a success, running for over forty nights.

In August 1811, horses and pageants were put to one side and an operatic mood took over. In these early days, it is not always easy to define what is and what is not opera. The terms of the licence excluded practically everything but music, and one might think that opera was the very thing for a minor theatre. But at that time the English ballad-opera held sway, not the through-composed operas to which we are accustomed today, and ballad-opera contained much dialogue between the songs. But dialogue was not permitted in a 'minor'. Elliston – or Thomas Dibdin – persevered with the genre and 1811 saw *Il Bondocani; or, the Caliph Robber* by Attwood and Moorhead (plus a bit pinched from Mozart), *Branksome Castle* by the Surrey's musical director Sanderson, and *Secret Springs*, a re-working of Thomas Dibdin's libretto for *The Cabinet*. In the following years, many English ballad-operas were similarly produced at the Surrey, re-written, renamed or furnished with new or additional music which was sometimes written for the occasion, sometimes borrowed from other composers.

This, then, was the nature of opera in Elliston's time. As most players, male and female, were expected to be able to sing, one finds the songs shared out amongst the regular company. There was no separate opera company.

Now we come to the elephant. At the start of the pantomime season on Boxing Night 1811, Covent Garden put on *Harlequin and Padmanaba; or, the Golden Fish* to include 'a real elephant, the first to appear on a British stage'. The same evening, at the Surrey, was announced

> A REAL ELEPHANT decorated in all the costly habiliments of the East, and is the FIRST ANIMAL of that description ever introduced to Public Notice on a British Stage. N.B. The Elephant (who is procured for SIX NIGHTS ONLY) is between Five and Six Feet in Height, is remarkable for its docility & beauty, and will be directed by a Child, attended by its Indian Keeper.

The wording of both notices is carefully chosen. One can read them as if Covent Garden and the Surrey introduced separate elephants simultaneously, or as if the same elephant appeared on both stages during the same evening.

The animal was – or the animals were – indeed the first to appear on any stage in this country; but Frost's *Circus Life and Circus Celebrities,* in connection with *Bluebeard* at Covent Garden in March 1811, says that:

> The elephant although docile enough, could not be induced to go upon the stage until one of the ladies of the ballet who had become familiar with the animal during rehearsals, led it on by one of its ears. This went so well with the audience that the young lady repeated the performance at every representation of the spectacle.

The trouble with this account is that I cannot find a Covent Garden playbill for *Bluebeard* or a review in the papers which mentions any elephant in that production. I rather think that Frost has confused the March 1811 Covent Garden *Bluebeard* (without elephant) with the 1813 Surrey *Bluebeard* (with elephant) and both with the Boxing Night performances of 1811. John Genest reviews the March 1811 *Bluebeard* at Covent Garden and expresses his disgust at the introduction of horses on that stage: 'In the first row of the pit the stench was so abominable that one might as well have sitten in a stable'. He would surely not have overlooked an elephant from that viewpoint.

The Times of 30 December 1811 says about Covent Garden's *Harlequin and Padmanaba:* 'The Elephant... evinces almost uncomplaisant dislike to the shoutings of the mob and the glare of the stage-lights'. So much was this so that, as *The Dramatic Censor* of December 1811 reports, the elephant 'appeared somewhat disposed to throw his human incumbrances from his shoulders'. As one of the 'human encumbrances' was Mrs Parker, as Columbine, this would clearly not do. So was this the occasion when a young lady of the ballet, one of the attendants on Columbine, saved the day?

Much depends on whether the elephant at the Surrey that night was the same one as at Covent Garden. If it was the same elephant, it is clear that 'the young lady of the ballet' would be needed just as much, if not more so, to persuade the elephant to face a Surrey audience. Unfortunately the Covent Garden and Surrey playbills are not sufficiently detailed to find a name common to both productions, and thus identify an 'Elephant Girl'.

But was it the same elephant? There was no Waterloo Bridge at that time, so to get an elephant from Covent Garden to the Surrey one would either go east along Fleet Street and across Blackfriars Bridge or west along the Strand and Whitehall and across Westminster Bridge. Then back again for the next night's performance, and so on for a week, according to the Surrey playbills. I can find no report of chaos on London's streets due to the elephant. It has been suggested that it had to be crated and drawn between theatres. I can go part-way with this idea – indeed, as far as the cobblestones go – but early prints of the area suggest that the road may not have been made up all the way. Indeed, one of the prints published by the Southwark Local History Library shows a bill-poster putting up an advertisement (which mentions the elephant) on the Obelisk itself. The scene is positively rural; the road is terrible!

The general view is that the Covent Garden elephant was named Chuny and was hired from Edward Cross's Menagerie in Exeter Change, on the north side of the Strand, within a couple of minutes' walk of Covent Garden Theatre but still a long way from the Surrey. However, the Surrey also hired animals from Cross, both before and after he had transferred his stock to the Surrey Zoological Gardens (between the Kennington and Walworth roads), only two minutes' walk away from the Surrey. So did Cross own two elephants? Even if he did not have access to land south of the river before he set up the Zoological Gardens, there was room to stable the beast at the back of the Surrey itself. If this is the answer, the problem of getting an elephant backwards and forwards across central London disappears.

Thomas Dibdin left the Surrey (temporarily, as it happens) at the end of the 1811 season and Elliston hired Samuel Russell of no. 8 Gray's Walk, Lambeth, to manage the theatre. It was as well to have someone local as Elliston lived on the other side of the river, off Oxford Street. Russell was a fine actor and often appeared opposite Elliston, who now seemed willing to give the Surrey-siders more of his attention. In his old age, Samuel Russell was given accommodation by a later manager of the Surrey, Davidge, in Bolwell Terrace, a row of houses Davidge had built. Russell, in fact, outlived Davidge who died in 1842, leaving Russell some money in his Will.

There was a benefit night on 10 March 1812 for Miss Green, the dancer. One of her guest-artistes was Henry Coveney, the father of two brilliant daughters, Jane and Harriet, who were seen at the Surrey over the next half-century. Another guest was Mr Flexmore, the father of Dickie Flexmore, destined to be one of the best harlequins to be seen at the Surrey when at his peak in the 1840s.

The evening ended with *Obi; or, Three-fingered Jack* played by Richard John Smith,who so much made the part his own that he was soon billed as Obi Smith. He too can be found at the Surrey thirty years later.

Drury Lane, rebuilt after the fire, re-opened in October 1812. Though Elliston was not able to secure its lease, he became its leading actor – and took some of the best of the Surrey company and the best Surrey pieces with him. On paper he was still lessee of the Surrey until March 1814 but did not act there in this period. Russell still managed it for him and hit a winning streak with a 'Grand Welsh Melo-drame: *Llewelyn, Prince of Wales; or, the Faithful Gelert'*, staged in June 1813. The melodrama and its faithful hound were still running in September, having had over seventy performances. The star? The dog, actually – Llewellyn only 'also'-ran! There were quite a few dog-dramas staged at this time up and down the country, of which *The Forest of Bondy* was another favourite at the Surrey. The plots would involve the dog saving a drowning child, or jumping on the villain, or leaping through the window of a burning cottage and generally being the melodramatic hero.

Clearly the Surrey meant little to Elliston, merely an address until Drury Lane was available to him again. He served it better when he returned after going bankrupt at Drury Lane in 1827. So much better did he then do that one is tempted to ask 'But was it the same Elliston?'

SURREY THEATRE.

FOR THE BENEFIT OF

Mr. RUSSELL,

will be produced THREE ENT[illegible] NEW PIECES, in each of which Mr. RUSSELL will *for that Night only*, perform principal Characters; with a variety of NEW SONGS.

On MONDAY, December 13th, 1813,

The Evening's Entertainments will commence with a New Burletta founded on the celebrated Comedy of

LAUGH WHEN YOU CAN;

Or, Female Constancy.

Mortimer, for that Night only, Mr. FAULKNER. *Gossamer*, Mr. RUSSELL.
Delville, Mr. HITCHENER. *Sambo*, Mr LEWIS. *Costly*, Mr. COVENEY.
Gregory, Mr. ELLER. *Bonus*, Mr. G. GIBBON.
Blackbrooke, Mr. BANKS. *Waiter*, Mr. COATES. *Servant*, Mr. REES.
Mrs. Mortimer, Mrs. BROOKES. *Miss Gloomly*, Mrs. PEARCE. *Emily*, Miss DELY.
Dorothy, Miss HOLLAND. *Chas. Mortimer*, Miss BODEN.

After which a New Burletta, in Two Acts, founded on the polite Musical Comedy of "SPRIGS of LAUREL," called

ORANGE BOVEN;

Or, the Embarkation for Holland!

Sinclair, ... Mr. GIBBON. *Lennox*, ... Mr. BARNARD. *Major Tactic*, ... Mr. MIDDLETON.
Captain Cruiser, ... Mr. HITCHINER. *Mary*, ... Miss DENT.
Nipperkin, ... by ...... Mr. RUSSELL.

In the course of the above Piece, the following Songs, Duets and Trios:
"A MAN OF A THOUSAND," by Mr. RUSSELL.
Love among the Roses," by Mr. Gibbon. "*I like each Girl*," by Messrs. Barnard & Gibbon.
"*Come my Soldier bonny*," by Miss Dent.
Trio, "*Tap beats the Drum*," Mr. Gibbon, Mr. Barnard, and Miss Dent.
"A GLASS IS GOOD AND A LASS IS GOOD," by Mr. RUSSELL.

The Evening's Entertainments to conclude with a New Grand Melo-Dramatic Spectacle founded on and called

BLUE BEARD;

Or, FEMALE CURIOSITY.

With New Scenery, Dresses, Decorations, &c. and all the Original Songs, Duets, Choruses, &c.

Abomilique, ... (Blue Beard.) Mr. SMITH. *Selim*, ... Mr. GIBBON. *Ibrahim*, ... Mr. G. GIBBON.
Shacabac, ... by ...... Mr. RUSSELL. *Hassan*, ... Mr. MAY.
First Spahi, ... Mr. COVENEY. *2d Spahi*, Mr. CHURCH. *3d Spahi*, Mr. LOCKE.
4th Spahi, Mr. REES. *5th Spahi*, Mr. BANKS.
Guards, ... Messrs. Coates, Williams, Hill, *Bradley*, &c. &c.
Fatima, ... Miss DONALDSON. *Irene*, ... Mrs. BROOKES. *Beda*, ... Miss DELY.
Turkish Women, Misses Dent, Jackson, and Mackey: Mesdames Boden, May, Rivolta, &c. &c.

SKETCH OF THE SCENERY, INCIDENTS, &c.

A MOUNTAINOUS COUNTRY, with the Grand March and Procession of

BLUE BEARD on his ELEPHANT.

And his Magnificent train over the Mountains to claim his intended Bride.—GRAND CHORUS OF TURKISH SOLDIERS.—Turkish Women and Children bearing Presents for FATIMA.

A MAGNIFICENT PALANQUIN, borne by Turkish Slaves ——After the Procession is formed on each side of the Stage, a GRAND CHORUS.——BLUE BEARD demands of IBRAHIM his Daughter in Marriage which being complied with, the Procession then returns with Acclamations to Blue Beard's Castle in the Mountains.

Abomelique and Fatima seated on a Superb Throne in the ILLUMINATED GARDEN.

THE ENCHANTED BLUE CHAMBER with Pictures of Blue Beard's murdered Wives.——Folding Doors which discover various Tombs, in the midst of which, Ghostly and Supernatural Forms, some in motion, some fixed.——In the centre a Skeleton leaning on a Tomb, whereon is written in Letters of Blood, "*The Punishment of Curiosity.*"

BLUE BEARD'S CASTLE, with Moat, Drawbridge, &c.——The CAVERN OF DEATH with a Skeleton and Tomb, and a Inscription of "*This Sepulchre shall inclose her who may endanger the Life of Abomelique.*"——A Fight in which Selim overcomes Blue Beard, who falls at the Foot of the Skeleton,——The Charm is broken, and the Skeleton immediately plunges a Dart into his Body, when they both sink in a Cloud of Sulphureous Fire, and Fatima is rescued from impending Fate by her faithful Lover Selim.

The whole of the Evening's Entertainments produced under the direction of Mr. Russell.

The New Music by Mr. Sanderson.—The Scenery by Mr. Smith and Amatgate.—The Machinery by Mr. [illegible]
The Dresses by Mr. Brett.—And the Properties by Mr. Sutton.

Tickets to be had of Mr. RUSSELL, at his house, No. 6, Gray's Walk, Lambeth Walk; and of [illegible] of the Theatre, where Places may be taken from Ten till Four. [illegible]

Doors opened at a Quarter-past Five; the Performance to commence at a Quarter-past [illegible]

Glendinning, Printer, Wine-Office Court, Fleet-Street.

Chapter Three

Hippodrama and Tightropes (1814-16)

In the gap of two years or so between Elliston leaving the Surrey in March 1814 after his first period of management and Thomas Dibdin arriving in May 1816, the lease was taken by Messrs Dunn, Heywood and William Branscomb with a view to returning the theatre to its 'Royal Circus and Equestrian' form. Hippodrama was not the only entertainment offered.

A.H.Saxon writes in *The Life and Art of Andrew Ducrow:*

> The 1814 season at the Circus was a memorable one, leading to a number of claims and stories which Ducrow himself seems to have recalled in later years. One of these relates to his repute as a ropedancer. 'At the Surrey, some years ago' [he would start], he wheeled a boy in a barrow on the rope, from the stage to the gallery, and (a much harder feat) back from the gallery to the stage! What the sensations of the gentleman were whilst *in transitu,* we can imagine better than describe, but on the second night he was *non est inventus.* Ducrow was obliged to ascend with an empty barrow, but judge of his amazement, when, on arriving at the gallery, he saw the aforesaid young gentleman, quietly seated, viewing the performances. Ducrow seized him, as Rolla does the child [holding him high with one hand], popped him into the barrow, and rolled him down at a brisk trot; the young gentleman being, as Shakespeare says, distilled almost to jelly by the act of fear.

Although I cannot trace Heywood, one of the three joint managers, on the Surrey playbills I see that Mrs Heyward (Heywood?) appeared in *Pizarro* on 24 January 1815 as Cora, the mother of the child saved by Rolla. James Dunn can be found in the box office, while Branscomb, as well as being in charge of the machinery, ran the Circus Coffee-house (otherwise the Equestrian Tavern) as did many a theatre-manager after him. Clearly the fortunes of the Equestrian Tavern, and of the Coal Hole on the other side of the Surrey, depended on a thriving theatre. Sadly the managers soon found that they had tightropes to walk of their own.

Of topical interest in the entertainments under the new management was the song 'John Bull on the Thames', not a boating song but a reference to the Frost Fair held on the frozen river at the beginning of 1814, the very last one to be held. It is relevant to slip in another bit of family history here. There is in the British Museum an engraving of the 'Frost Fair on the River Thames / As it appeared in the hard Frost, Feby. 4, 1814 between London and Blackfriars Bridges when the river was one sheet of Ice and Snow, and on which several trades and pastimes were carried on, / the above view was taken on the Spot at Bankside, Feby. 4'. The printer was my ancestor, George Thompson (grandfather of Joseph Kerschner, a later manager of the Surrey), and his copper-plate printing press is also shown on the ice.

One of the three managers, William Branscomb, died on 8 April 1815; his executor, Frank Honeyman, found it necessary to take a benefit at the Surrey to cover costs as late as 13 November. Shortly before this, on 11 September 1815 there was a benefit for T.P. Cooke (described as Stage Manager) which exploited Wellington's recent victory. Cooke played Richmond in *Richard III,*

> and, in the Battle of Boswell Field *[sic]*, Mr Cooke will be accoutred in a REAL FRENCH CUIRASS, Stripped from a Cuirassier, on the Field of Battle, at Waterloo and which bears the indenture of Several Musket Shot and Sabre Cuts.

At the end of the show, there was

> the Ascent of a Real Balloon To the Roof of the Theatre, which will there Burst, distributing to the Audience in the Pit... several REAL Lottery Tickets! The whole concluding with a Magnificent Exhibition of FIREWORKS made by Mr Southby.

A slump followed the end of the Napoleonic wars. Heywood went bankrupt. The surviving partner, James Dunn, and the widowed Mrs Branscomb (who lived only until mid-1816) went into partnership with James Jones, the man who had originally taken the lease of the Surrey from Mrs Jane West and had gone broke. He had shaken off his committee of creditors, and had been employed by Elliston at the Surrey in 1813 as riding master. Now he was back in the management seat (albeit shared with two others) – though not for long. His playbills for 19 February 1816 are headed:

> THE LAST NIGHT and Final Close of this Theatre. JAMES JONES begs to inform the Public in general, that in consequence of his not being able to obtain a Renewal of his Lease, which expires at Lady Day next, by reason of the Ground Landlord enhancing the present Rent of 200 guineas

> to £4,200 per Annum, although his Misfortunes, from the destruction of the said Theatre by fire, and the re-building the same on a more extensive and improved plan, at the enormous expense of £14,500, when there only remained 11 Years of the Original Lease, induced him to believe he should meet with a corresponding Liberality from such Landlord in return, upon his application for a Renewal of his said Lease; but having experienced the contrary without hope of Remuneration, and not having taken a Benefit for 8 Years past... he has fixed on the above-mentioned Night for that purpose, when he trusts he shall experience that Liberality and Patronage he has heretofore experienced....

His troubles were due to a bridge, of all things. It was clear that enhanced business would accrue to the Surrey once the new Waterloo Bridge, then a-building, was opened. This would give easy access from the West End, to complement custom coming from the City via Blackfriars Bridge. The ground landlord, Temple West, son of Colonel West and Mrs Jane West, calculated that this potential increase in income justified the twenty-fold increase in the ground rent about which Jones was complaining. At the expiration of the lease, the horses and much of the scenery, machinery, dresses and properties were sold by auction and cleared away. Jones, however, retained his portion.

Messrs Dunn and Jones decided that, rather than meet West's exorbitant demands, it was cheaper to build a new theatre of their own. They found a piece of Lambeth Marsh available. Their activities at the Surrey were licensed by the local magistrates and they hoped to be able to transfer that licence to their new venture. It seems, however, that they could not agree what sort of theatre should be built. Dunn, from his past experience, wanted a circus-ring; Jones, despite having been a riding master and the proprietor of the Pantheon Riding School in Blackfriars Road, wanted a dramatic establishment. They split. Dunn eventually made his way back to the Surrey (disastrously) while Jones advertised:

> PROPOSALS FOR THE ROYAL COBURG THEATRE
>
> Mr Jones (late proprietor of the Royal Circus, or Surrey Theatre), having agreed for a piece of land near the foot of Waterloo Bridge, on the Surrey side, for the purpose of building a theatre... proposes to dispose of a part by way of subscription.... The whole property in scenery, dresses &c., &c., at the Surrey theatre has been moved to this concern and the theatre is intended to open at Christmas next....

The Jones/Cross dynasty of the last chapter and this does not entirely disappear from the Surrey story in March 1816. Thirteen years later the playbills for 7 May 1829 would announce a 'Benefit for Mrs Cross, Widow of the late Mr Cross, and Daughter of the late James Jones, Founder of the Royal Coburg Theatre'. But was it the same 'Founder' of the Royal Coburg who had appeared on the Surrey bills just a few years before this? – on 19 September 1825, 'Vocal Music Mr J. Jones' and 'Duet, Mr J. Jones with Miss Tunstall'; and again on 3 September 1827, 'Divertissment with Mr J. Jones and Mlle. Rosyer'. It may have been the old man, yet the James Jones who appears in Davidge's will in 1841, along with others of the Surrey company, must be of the next generation. Such speculation may seem to be of the utmost insignificance but it illustrates the intricate web of family connections at the Surrey, where marriages were made and children and grandchildren introduced into the company. When my grandmother and my Uncle George went backstage at the rebuilt Surrey in the 1880s they were greeted by the manager, George Conquest, as family, not as visitors.

In early 1816, despite the Surrey being stripped to the bare walls following its closure in February, and despite the potential competition from the Coburg, Thomas Dibdin felt he could make the Surrey pay even on the new terms. He took a seven year lease of the theatre in May.

Chapter Four

Thomas Dibdin (1816-22)

For forty years the Dibdin family fortunes were entwined, not always successfully, with those of the Surrey. The two sons of Charles Dibdin the Elder, Charles born in 1767 and Thomas born in 1771, both wrote their memoirs at considerable length. As Thomas writes in his:

> My father was the first manager of the Royal Circus. I became manager for Mr Elliston when he new-named it the Surrey Theatre; again I managed it myself, and at this date [August 1826] my brother is director there.

In May 1816 Thomas was one of the joint managers of the Theatre Royal, Drury Lane, and also had a proprietorial interest in Sadler's Wells. He saw an advertisement inserted by Temple West, the freeholder, inviting bids for the lease of the Surrey and he liked the idea of being 'the first man in the village' rather than having fractional interests elsewhere. The Drury Lane management committee at first agreed, provided he did not act as the Surrey manager while his Drury Lane commitments continued. However, when he ascertained the terms of the Surrey lease he took against the idea, deciding to stick with Drury Lane. But Temple West had heard of Dibdin's tentative enquiries and took the initiative, as Dibdin recounts:

> Then Mr West came behind the scenes (on whose power of admission I know not) at Drury-Lane, and insisted I was the only man to whom he should like to let the theatre, because his father had built it that my father should manage it; that I should have it on liberal terms; and that the Circus should be itself again. He further represented that there was a new bridge from the Strand to the Obelisk in a very forward state, and that the treasures of El Dorado were brass tokens when compared to the wealth that awaited me in the county of Surrey.

Finally, all these arguments prevailed. He took the Surrey lease on 23 May 1816 (his wedding anniversary), and later sourly remarked that he:

> never made a better bargain than on the memorable 23rd. at Manchester in 1793, nor a worse than on this anniversary, when I took possession (as lessee) of the Surrey Theatre....

> My rent was one thousand a year; and Mr West was to have one third of the profits, without sharing in the risk to be run in obtaining them. The whole interior of the theatre required substantial repair: there was not a scene nor a frame to hang one on: the dressing-places and even stairs had been pulled down by the last tenants: there was not a chandelier nor a candlestick: the estimate of what it was to cost me to supply these deficiencies was about two thousand pounds; it cost me four, before I could draw up my curtain.

On the plus side:

> The house itself is, without exception, the best-constructed both for audience and actors in or near the metropolis: there is no part of the theatre from whence you may not see, nor any from whence you may not hear with the greatest facility: the audience part of the house is commodious, and as spacious, except in height, as either Covent-Garden or Drury-Lane: the stage, its offices, green-room, dressing-rooms, and wardrobes on the first scale of convenience.

Nevertheless, there was a lot to do:

> From the twenty-third of May till the first of July, I had to rebuild and furnish all behind the curtain; to remove the horse-ride; construct a pit; alter, re-imbellish and furnish all in front of it: twenty-eight new chandeliers, a new curtain, and in short, every thing essential was to be provided: a company, a band, painters and other artists, with stage carpenters to be engaged; and three new pieces, with comic songs, were to be written.

Dibdin details his company: twenty-two in the band, including Sanderson and Erskine, competent composers both; thirty-five actors and thirty-two actresses, including T.P.Cooke, Bengough, Davidge, John Kirby and Ridgway; Mrs Mountain, Mrs Glover, Mrs Fitzwilliam (though she was still Miss Fanny Copeland when Dibdin opened) and Miss Bence. He comments:

> I commenced with a company which, though labouring under the disadvantage of being almost all strangers to each other, performed on the first night with a precision often unattained in the 'great grand' theatres – in fact, they were all determined to do their best.

His playbills were headed 'New Royal Circus & Surrey Theatre'. He opened on Monday 1 July 1816 with three of his own works: a pantomime, *The House Warming; or, The Peasants' Pic-Nic*, in which Miss Tree, as

Columbine, introduced a solo on the flageolet; a ballet spectacular, *The Sicilian; or, The Prince and the Pirate;* and a dramatic romance, *Chevy Chace; or, The Warlocks Of the Border,* to include a 'Scotch ballet'. Another of his dramatic romances, *Who's the Murderer; or, A True Tale of the Twelfth Century,* was produced a fortnight later. In this, Davidge, later to manage the Surrey, made his first appearance on its stage. Also in the bill was Peters, the 'British Voltigeur', who performed 'many new and wonderful Feats of Balancing in Equilibrium on the Slack Wire'. Dibdin's next work, produced on 31 July, was *Slaves in Barbary; or, British Vengeance,* the piece ending with 'The Bombardment of Algiers' which capitalised on the recent punitive attack by a Royal Naval squadron under Rear-Admiral Lord Exmouth.

All these pieces were firmly within the field permitted to a minor theatre. There is no evidence here that Dibdin was a follower of Elliston and a deliberate challenger of the patent theatres' monopoly, though sooner or later he was bound to upset them.

On 26 August 1816 Dibdin staged the pantomime *The Dog and Duck; or, Harlequin in the Obelisk,* in which Miss Tree played Columbine, with Miss Worgman as Columbinetta, one of the Yarnolds as Harlequin, Davidge as Punch, John Kirby as Clown and Hollingsworth as Pantaloon. At this time, pantomime was not dominated by the clown. Though, elsewhere, Grimaldi had set this major change in motion, the Surrey was not quite ready for the innovation.

Pantomime at this time was not specifically a Christmas entertainment. Dibdin wrote *The Magic Grape; or, Harlequin Wine-Merchant* as the offering for Easter 1817. As an example of the 'friendly rivalry' that the Surrey had with Astley's Amphitheatre up the road, Dibdin also provided Astley's with *The Golden Axe; or, Harlequin Woodman* to open the same evening! The theatres were only ten minutes' walk apart, allowing Surrey-siders to revel in a double helping of pantomime's spectacle, comedy, music, dancing, topical comment, local jokes, special effects and elaborate stagecraft, with no time wasted on a logical plot or finely-delineated characterisations.

The playbills for Boxing Day 1817 announced that the theatre had been 'Improved by additional Warmth in the Interior; a neat Apartment in the lower Box Lobby for the Convenience of Visitors who wait for Half-price Admission; as also two Porticos with other added Accommodations at the Pit and Gallery Entrances'. The programme consisted of Garrick's *Christmas Tale,* complete with an enchanted garden, the castle of a sorcerer with a 'Fiery Lake which is converted into a Beautiful Fairy Region'. This was followed by a comic pantomime ballet and then the full pantomime *The Touchstone; or, Harlequin Traveller.* As well as Harlequin (Fitzwilliam), Pantaloon (Howell) and Columbine (Mrs Bryan), there were Pierrot (John Kirby) and Scaramouche (Master Doré) – echoes of the Italian commedia dell'arte – but no Clown. In later years, Kirby would take the clown parts again, as he had in *The Dog and Duck;* but for a while the Surrey preferred the old-fashioned style. Even four years later, when a Grimaldi-type clown had displaced Harlequin as the leading pantomime character at most theatres, Thomas Dibdin wrote *Three of Them; or, Harlequin Hum, Strum and Mum* which had a Harlequin (Ridgway), Columbine (Miss Adcock), and Pierrot (Wyatt) but had neither Clown nor Pantaloon. It took another management, and Grimaldi in person, to fix the part of Clown firmly on the Surrey stage.

Dibdin's narrative continues:

> The season at the Surrey had commenced very well but early in the autumn, an unprecedented succession of heavy rainy weather constantly inundated us to an excess, which (though we thus had literally an overflowing house every evening) kept everything in the shape of profit away from us. The succeeding winter months were still more severe: intense frost pervaded the metropolis; the poor were hourly crying out for food; and in one week I gave six charity benefits, which I grieve to say were very indifferently attended.

The great hit of the season was a burlesque based on Mozart's *Don Giovanni,* which Dibdin wrote in a couple of days after seeing the opera at the King's Theatre. It ran for more than a hundred performances. Dibdin also adapted four of Smollett's novels for the Surrey. Of these, *Humphrey Clinker* and *Roderick Random* were not exactly smash hits but they held their places in the bills for a respectable period.

Unlike some theatrical managers, Dibdin was in the good books of the law. He writes:

> On going to Kingston for renewal of my licence, accompanied by Mrs Dibdin, we were invited by the chairman of the Quarter Sessions and his lady to dine and remain at their residence till the next day; the magistrate was Mr Evance who paid a public compliment from the bench to the manner in which the Surrey Theatre had been conducted; which flattering testimony was repeated by the High Sheriff.

Sir Walter Scott (still anonymous at this time as 'The author of *Waverley')* had written a number of stories under the general title of *The Tales of My Landlord* . Dibdin based many a Surrey piece on these:

> Having engaged Mrs Egerton, that lady happily suggested that Madge Wildfire would be an eligible character for her debut, in case I felt inclined to dramatise the beautiful romance of *The Heart of Midlothian.* I procured the romance that evening; read, altered and adapted it to my stage and company by the Wednesday following; put it in rehearsal on Thursday; and on the succeeding Wednesday produced the melo-dramatic romance of *The Lily of St. Leonard's; or, The Heart of Midlothian* which was acted above one hundred and seventy nights in the space of nine months. Letters of congratulations flowed in from friends and strangers, and the character of St George's Fields seemed to have undergone a temporary change: carriages of the first nobility graced the road in nightly lines, sometimes double, extending from the theatre to Charlotte Street.

In fact, versions of this novel under a variety of titles such as *The Whistler* and *Effie Deans* continued to succeed on the Surrey stage for the next fifty years. 'Letters of congratulation' could also be found in the press. *The Theatrical Inquisitor* of January 1819 published such a letter, claiming that 'of all the old-established minor theatres, the Surrey is the only one which lays claim to rational approbation'.

When Mrs Egerton's engagement finished in March 1819 there was still mileage to be had from *The Heart of Midlothian.* Dibdin persuaded the young Fanny Copeland, so far only experienced in comic opera, to attempt the part of Madge Wildfire: 'Her reception in it was so deservedly enthusiastic, that I immediately added a pound per week to the salary we had agreed on for the season'. (Although Dibdin does not mention it in his memoirs, Mrs Dibdin took on the part of Queen Caroline at about the same time.) For this play:

> The theatre was frequently honoured by the patronage of several of the royal family; their Royal Highnesses the Duke and Duchess of Kent often distinguished me by their notice... and on each evening of their presence my house filled to an overflow.

For their visit on Friday 6 August 1819 Dibdin printed his playbills on satin, not only in honour of his distinguished guests, but also in anticipation of the additional custom their presence would attract. It was not, however, a moment for innovation as regards the content of the bill; *Melodrama Mad* played for the 41st time, and *The Heart of Midlothian* for the 101st.

Still raiding Sir Walter Scott, Thomas Dibdin 'produced in less than a fortnight from their publication, the tales of *Montrose* and *The Bride of*

Lammermoor both in one night' (5 July 1819) and adds that he had no reason to repent of his exertions. Possibly Sir Walter did have reason. Under the copyright laws of the time, he would get not a penny from these productions. Next was *Ivanhoe; or, The Jew's Daughter,* produced on 20 January 1820 with Sanderson's music. Ridgway, an excellent Harlequin and dancer, arranged 'the Action, Combats and Procession' and also played the 'Unknown Knight' (that is, Ivanhoe himself). There were fourteen scenes in the three acts, credit for painting which went to Wilson; there was credit also for 'Dresses by Mr Jones and Miss Freelove; the Armour, Banners and Decorations by Mr Morris and Mrs Freelove'. Morris, a valued sceneman, property-master and engineer of gas and water effects, had come over from Sadler's Wells, where the 'Aqua-drama' management of Thomas's brother, Charles Dibdin the Younger, had just folded. Later this 'very ingenious artist', as Charles described him, made his mark at Vauxhall Gardens. No doubt Morris contributed to the effect in *Ivanhoe* about which Thomas commented:

> Our tournament scene was numerously grouped with living actors, and a continuation of figures in painted and gilded perspective profile, so brilliantly executed, that to a deceived eye there appeared at least a thousand nobles, knights, guards and spectators on the stage.

This mastery of effect can also be seen when Thomas Dibdin staged *Douglas* some weeks later. He knew what a Surrey gallery audience expected and arranged for 'a very clever boy' to stand in for one of the leading ladies at the conclusion of the tragedy. By his 'good acting and fearless agility' the lady appeared 'to throw herself from a distant precipice into a boiling ocean', bringing down thunders of applause. This was a trick identical to one arranged by his brother Charles using the Sadler's Wells tank fifteen years earlier, which had excited such a 'stimulus to public curiosity,' says Charles in his memoirs, that it 'doubled the profits of the preceding Season'.

Thomas Dibdin received a letter dated 29 March 1820:

> Sir, An anxiety on the part of the proprietors of the two patent theatres of Drury-Lane and Covent-Garden, to avoid interfering with the entertainments of the public, has hitherto prevented them from enforcing the laws against the manifold infringements of their rights, which have so repeatedly taken place in performances at the Circus [that is, the Surrey]. But observing that those performances extend to 'entertainments of the stage' and therefore are not included in the license of the magistrates, which is confined to music and dancing, the proprietors are compelled, for the protection of their

> establishments, to give you this notice – that if you do not, in future, confine your performances strictly within the powers of your license, they will be under the painful necessity of having recourse to such measures as the laws have provided.

This was signed by C.W. Ward for Drury Lane and T. Harris for Covent Garden. As Dibdin was a personal friend of Harris's, he felt he could take a chance; but then Harris died and Dibdin had to watch his step for the rest of the year. It so happened that in early January 1821 *Kenilworth* had been published. Dibdin announced its dramatisation for the Surrey before he had even read it. Elliston, then managing Drury Lane, had been impressed with the success of the earlier 'Author of *Waverley*' transcriptions at the Surrey, and called on Dibdin to try to have *Kenilworth* first produced at Drury Lane. (I suspect that the threat in the letter of 29 March 1820 might have been used to exert a little leverage on the argument.) Being short of cash Dibdin agreed and had finished the dramatisation within five days. Elliston took ten days to set up a reading to the assembled cast, then decided firstly that there was no hurry to put it on, and later that he did not want it at all. But while Elliston dithered, the Adelphi obtained another dramatised version and mounted this at the end of January 1821. Dibdin sprang into action and in a fortnight had the scenery and dresses made, the cast rehearsed, and his version of *Kenilworth* produced at the Surrey.

A new writer, Edward Fitzball, now appeared on the scene. In the decades to come he was to write dozens of successes for the Surrey. In his *Thirty-Five Years of a Dramatic Author's Life* Fitzball records that he

> forwarded a melodrame to the Surrey Theatre called *Edda*. Tom Dibdin was the manager. It was accepted, and played many nights. I came to London with my wife to attend rehearsals, and see the representation of *Edda*. I shall never forget how astonished I was at the vast size of the theatre. I seemed to tread on air; there was an enchantment about it all, more than earthly. The kind, enlightened, facetious manager; the amiable manageress; the performers – I thought them scarcely inferior to demi-gods; the beautiful scenery; the exciting rehearsals! How enchanting! – what a delusion!
>
> One thing struck me as strange – Bengough and Clifford disputed about a phrase in the drama. One said it should be the 'mounting sun', the other the 'mountain sun', yet neither referred to me, the author. 'How is this,' I inquired aside of Mr Dibdin. 'My dear lad', was Dibdin's facetious reply, 'each is afraid that you should set him right.'

Edda; or, the Hermit of Warkworth was 'founded on Dr. Percy's celebrated Tale' and first appeared on 29 May 1820, with Bengough playing the Earl Osrick and Clifford playing the Hermit; Miss Taylor was Edda.

Soon the Surrey was being affected by and taking sides in the great political argument of the day: whether Queen Caroline should be crowned. The Prince Regent had formally separated from his wife, Princess Caroline of Brunswick, and when he succeeded to the throne as King George IV on 29 January 1820 he went so far as to order that no prayer for his wife as queen should be admitted into the Prayer Book. Dibdin reports:

> On the day Queen Caroline arrived from the Continent, the Surrey roads were so lined with people, that every friend congratulated me on the prospect of having the fullest house of the season: it was imagined that after Her Majesty had passed, many of the innumerable host, who had been expecting her all the afternoon, would go into the theatre to finish their half-holiday; but as many as could followed the Queen over the bridge, and those who did not go into public-houses, I presume went home. My receipts, instead of being the best of the season, were the worst of any night in the course of six years, being under fourteen pounds!!! which to a manager whose nightly expense was at least eighty guineas, caused me anything but the jubilee sensation.

When the coronation arrangements were being made Caroline insisted on being crowned at the same time. Not having this at any price, the king set in motion an investigation which he hoped would prove his wife guilty of adultery. It did not. The later arguments in Parliament turned on whether a queen-consort was crowned by usage or by law. The general public supported Caroline who did what she could to maintain such support.

Her first visit to a transpontine theatre was to the Coburg (later the Old Vic) on 26 June 1821. Such was the welcome given that the queen did 'a repeat performance' by visiting the Surrey. At the Obelisk 'a considerable multitude' hailed her on her arrival 'by loud cheers', as *The Times* reported on 9 July 1821. The proprietors in full dress received the royal visitor at the door and conducted her with all due state and ceremony to a box on the right-hand side of the stage. This had been sumptuously decorated with mirrors on the inside and hung on the outside with purple velvet on which the royal arms were embossed in gold. *The Times* went on to report the audience's enthusiastic reception of Her Majesty, and pointed up similarities between incidents in the plot of *The Heart of Midlothian* and the 'infamous investigation' instigated by George IV:

> How completely the public feeling went along with her Majesty on Saturday evening may be judged by the fact that this detached sentence of no importance to the drama, 'If it had been true, it could have been easily proved', was received with three distinct peals of applause.

Like sentiments elicited 'similar marks of satisfaction'. Later, the phrase 'This is the Queen's garden' was spoken by the actor with a hand pointing to the audience,

> conveying the idea that the Queen's chief delight was in the possession of the affections of the people; the pit immediately rose as by one consent, and gave three cheers.... The gallery signified their assent... by bursting into the most extravagant uproars of applause that we have ever heard, and the ladies in the boxes... showed it by... the general waving of their handkerchiefs. It lasted so long, that her Majesty at last rose and courtesyed her gratitude to the audience for the marks of affectionate esteem which they had bestowed upon her.

This show of support by people and paper did not help Caroline achieve her object. Twelve days later, she was refused admission to Westminster Abbey for the coronation. She died shortly afterwards.

Dibdin comments further on the Coronation arrangements:

> In common with all other theatres, I received an order to open the Surrey at the expense of the Crown and was paid three hundred pounds, which came most opportunely. We presented *The Two Gregories, Harlequin Hoax* and *The Seven Champions,* and when all was peaceably over, and the public had departed in excellent temper, a select party of us supped on the roof of the theatre, from whence we had a capital view of fire-works in various quarters of the town, and sang catches and glees to the astonishment of the passengers below, who, not being able to see us as we sat behind the parapet, and played bo-peep from among the chimneys, could not imagine from whence the voices emanated.

Despite such happy evenings, Dibdin was in trouble financially. He laments that 'Except on the night of Her Majesty's visit, when the receipts amounted to three hundred guineas, I did not receive half my nightly expenses'. He had hoped that the crowds coming for the Coronation would fill all the theatres, 'but they came not to see plays or pantomimes or melodrames, but to buy finery and sport it at the Coronation'. He looked for someone who would take the tail-end of his lease for a 'trifling consideration'. Watkins Burroughs decided to take on the Surrey and on 19 March 1822 Dibdin handed over control. He blamed his ill-fortune on the opening of the Coburg –

> a lamentable circumstance to both parties; it was the ruin of my incipient good prospects at an expense to itself of still greater magnitude. I lost nearly eighteen thousand pounds at the Surrey, and Mr Glossop senior assured me that he was twenty-seven thousand pounds minus at the Cobourg.

Dibdin was also aggrieved at the conduct of Temple West, to whom he owed rent. He records that:

> the very landlord who had followed me in Drury-Lane Theatre, night after night, seized and had appraised in his own favour, the scenes, wardrobes, chandeliers (for which latter alone I had paid five hundred guineas) machinery, piano-forte and even kettle-drums, together with all the furniture, dressing fixtures and every appurtenance, which had cost me between four and five thousand pounds, for the sum of thirteen hundred; and now enjoys an advance of rent for a furnished theatre, which, when I leased it, had to boast of only four bare walls.

Thomas Dibdin ended in the hands of the Court of Insolvency.

So why did he fail? In my view he tried to take the Surrey up-market, seeking the West End carriage-trade and neglecting the locals. In his memoirs Dibdin lists many dukes and 'other leading nobility' who had graced his theatre – was this the real cause of alarm for the patent theatres? He blames the Coburg for taking his trade but the Coburg did not attract the fashionable audiences and in any case was no better off financially, so the groundlings did not flock there. Certainly, in his final five years Dibdin failed to provide the Surreyites with their favourite diet, Shakespeare (however garbled) and Harlequin. Incredible as it may seem, there were no Christmas pantomimes from 1818 to 1821. In their place Dibdin offered 'spectaculars' with an Arabian Nights flavour, but this is not what 'the good people of the Obelisk' wanted. If they did not go to the Coburg, could Astley's have won their custom?

I think that, at heart, Dibdin was not competing with the Coburg and Astley's but with Elliston at Drury Lane. He had long wanted to manage Drury Lane, and was putting on 'West-End' pieces at the Surrey with better staging than Elliston's to show that he had the capability to run a patent theatre. Unfortunately for him, he never found a way of supplying West End quality at Surrey-side prices.

Chapter Five

Watkins Burroughs – and Others (1822-25)

When Thomas Dibdin was forced out by financial problems the Surrey Theatre was hired from March 1822 on a monthly basis by one of his actors, Watkins Burroughs. In his fifteen months as manager he kept Dibdin's company together with much the same repertoire, repeating many of Dibdin's past successes and, like Dibdin, missing out a pantomime at Christmas 1822.

Clearly he was not against pantomime in principle and indeed his first success was to engage Grimaldi, admittedly for one night only, on 26 March 1822 in *Harlequin and Mother Goose; or, The Golden Egg.* This was the piece which, at Covent Garden on Boxing Day 1806, had established Grimaldi as the standard by which all later clowns are judged. It was also the piece through which Clown was to become the principal figure in pantomime in place of Harlequin. *Mother Goose,* with its script by Thomas Dibdin and its music by William Ware, was revived many times and was still going strong at the Surrey sixteen years after its opening. The story opens in an English village square, where the Squire is about to marry Avaro's ward Colinette, who loves Colin, who saves Mother Goose from the ducking stool, who gives Colin the goose which lays the golden eggs, which persuades Avaro to choose a different son-in-law, so that he can get his hands (and his knife!) on the goose. Mother Goose upbraids Avaro, and effects the transformation scene:

> Thou avaricious, selfish, ingrate elf,
> Like other fools too cunning for thyself;
> Thy ward shall still perplex you by her flight –
> Lo! thus I change the lovers... Motley white!
> Thou too shall wander till this egg of gold,
> Which in the sea I cast, you once again behold.
> Stop, fool! – some recompense is yet thy due.
> *(To the Squire; changes him to Clown:)*
> Take that!
> *(To Avaro; changes him to Pantaloon:)*
> – while thou shalt wear my livery too.
> *(Gives Harlequin the sword:)*
> This gift receive; amend what's past,
> And guard it better than the last;
> Regain the egg, and happy be,
> Till then, farewell! – remember me!

Squire thus becomes Clown (Grimaldi), Avaro Pantaloon (Bartlett), Colinette Columbine (Miss Adcock) and Colin Harlequin (Ridgway). In the course of the pantomime Grimaldi sang 'Tippetywitchet' and 'Hot Codlins'; it would not have been Joey without those songs. Mother Goose herself was always played by a man – Mr H. Baker on this occasion – and had the last word with:

> Ye patrons kind, who deign to view
> The sports our scenes produce,
> Accept our wish to pleasure you
> And laugh with Mother Goose.

Although this prototype 'pantomime dame' dates from 1806 it was a long time before 'she' became an essential part of pantomime. This particular pantomime continued at the Surrey after Grimaldi's one-night-stand, with John Kirby – 'his 1st Appearance these 6 seasons' – as Clown.

There was an extraordinary pantomime staged on 15 July 1822, *The Three Fishermen; or, the Box, the Fish and the Genii* (and not extraordinary just because it did not have 'Harlequin' somewhere in its title.) There were, in fact, three of everything: three Fishermen, afterwards Harlequins (Ridgway, Ellar and Auld); three Magicians, afterwards Pantaloons (Blanchard, Bartlett and Brunton); three Lively Sprites, afterwards Clowns (Kirby, Paulo and Bradbury); and three Spell-bound Fairies, afterwards Columbines (the Misses Cooke, Lewis and Vallancey). Not quite the entire pantomimic strength of the metropolis but very nearly. There was never more than one of each on the stage in any one scene but by ringing the changes a fresh team could be thrown into the action without any need for a breather. There were only two scenes before the transformation, but eleven knock-about scenes followed. These included the comic policemen, the 'how to make a wheelbarrow' scene, Columbine shut up and Clown on guard, a 'Cutting, Bumping and Thumping Scene' which included a 'Patent Blunderbuss, invented to shoot round a Hay Stack'. All the traditional routines were there except one, which later became indispensible to Surrey pantomimes, namely the 'Splosh' scene. All that this required was a set of circumstances in which the characters could empty buckets of water over each other. One would have thought that a pantomime concerning 'Three Fishermen' would have had ample opportunity for a 'splosh', but apparently not. It may be that this routine had not yet evolved, or simply that after the transformation the Harlequinade lost the piscatorial quality of the opening.

This remarkable show ran twenty-four nights to Saturday 10 August 1822 and is surely unique in the history of pantomime. It had a sort of revival on 2 September for Blanchard's benefit night, under the name of *The House that Jack Built; or, Harlequin Tatter'd and Torn.* This consisted of eight scenes from *The Three Fishermen* plus a new scene, 'The Fives Court'.

On 5 September that year, again for one night only, was staged *The Death of Harlequin,* with Signor Paulo as Clown, Tom Ellar as Harlequin and Tom Blanchard as Pantaloon. I was tempted to identify this piece with that seen by the young Charles Lamb as recorded in one of his essays, 'My First Play': 'I saw the primeval Motley come from his silent tomb in a ghastly vest of white patch-work, like the apparition of a dead rainbow. So Harlequins (thought I) look when they are dead'. But such an identification is unsound, if only because Columbine was played by Mr Wyatt, so I fear that this must have been a skit on the original, despite the excellence of the rest of the troupe.

One achievement of Burroughs's régime was to engage the services of the playwright Edward Fitzball on a regular basis. Fitzball did not know Burroughs and had not kept up his links with the theatre. At a time when his main source of income was his employment in a London printing office, his melodrama *The Innkeeper of Abbeville; or, the Ostler and the Robber* was staged successfully in Norwich. By chance an actor from Norwich called at the printers, recognised the young author and asked why the new play had not also been taken up by the Surrey. Fitzball said he needed an introduction to the new management and records:

> 'You require no introduction', was the prompt reply. 'Send your piece which I saw, *The Innkeeper of Abbeville,* to the Surrey. Watkins Burroughs is too good a judge not to bring it out directly.' I thanked the stranger and did as he requested me. Watkins Burroughs did bring out the piece, it made a hit, ran upwards of a hundred consecutive nights.

Bengough played the innkeeper, Burroughs played Ozzrand, the ostler of the inn, and Miss Cooke and Mrs Pindar supplied the feminine interest. In January 1823 Fitzball had two of his plays in the Surrey repertory at the same time, with *The Innkeeper of Abbeville* supported by *The Three Hunchbacks; or, the Sabre Grinders of Damascus.*

The dramatisation of Sir Walter Scott's novels continued apace. As well as Ivanhoe and Fitzjames, Burroughs in his first year added to his repertoire Tressilian in *Kenilworth* and Lord Nigel in *The Fortunes of Nigel* (supported by Mr and Mrs Davidge as John Christie and Mrs Saddlechop). This last, staged in June 1822, was dramatised by Fitzball who writes that:

> Dibdin could dramatise a novel in a day or two. I was compelled to take a week!... Watkins Burroughs enacted the part of Nigel, Bengough the King, which on account of the Scotch dialect he was dreadfully afraid to undertake, and Buckingham was cast the part of the Miser. We had also Mrs Glover's two daughters, both very young and very pretty, as Margaret Ramsey and Mrs Christie, one of them having never made her appearance on the stage.

(We still find Mary Glover appearing at the Surrey twenty-odd years later.)

> The greatest confidence was placed in me by the manager.... As the vast scenes were pushed into sets, imperfectly painted, and the different costumes and properties were brought in, piece by piece, on the arms of the tailor or tailoress, to be approved of by the manager, I could scarcely believe myself of sufficient importance to be the agitator of all this mighty commotion....

Sir Walter Scott's works were then all the rage as we have seen. The enormous success achieved by Dibdin's *Heart of Midlothian* led many to suppose that any attempt by a young, inexperienced author to provide a 'follow-up' would be a failure. Fortunately for Fitzball they were mistaken. Nothing ever went off more smoothly. *The Fortunes of Nigel* was received with great favour and ran for ninety-six consecutive nights, bringing in a 'vast sum of money'.

An odd letter was published in *The Theatrical Observer* of August 1822. It starts with what may well be fair comment regarding the Surrey,

> which has done up many a prime fellow – Elliston feels queer about the shoulders when he thinks about it; and Tom Dibdin calls it *white* Surrey, and is glad he has washed his hands of it; while Mr Burroughs, no doubt, is of the opinion, that if a man has any money to lose, that is the best place in the world to get rid of it.

So far, an acceptable point of view, but the letter continues:

> At last, it seems, it has fallen into the hands of a most distinguished character – the boil'd beef man from the Old Bailey. I understand it is intended to hand round plates of beef and mustard between pieces, to be included in the price of admission.

Now the 'boil'd beef man from the Old Bailey' might have been one of the Glossops. Joseph Glossop Senior was a provision merchant, or tallow-chandler as his enemies would have it (leading his son to be ridiculed as 'the Lamplighter's Boy'). As reported by Dibdin, Glossop Senior lost nearly £27,000 from his theatrical investment in the Coburg; it is possible that he may have wanted to switch to the Surrey instead. Joseph Glossop Junior, the lessee of the Coburg, had to get out fast in 1822 one jump ahead of a warrant for his arrest for forgery, according to Winston's *Diary*, going abroad where by 1824 he was managing La Scala at Milan. If Glossops are in question here, the correspondent to *The Theatrical Observer* seems to be amalgamating the provision-merchant father with the forger-son sought by the Old Bailey. In any case no such take-over happened, if it was ever more than mud-slinging.

The customers of the Surrey had a change of entertainment between Fitzball's successes. In the week commencing 21 October 1822, Leaders of Horse Messrs. Adams and Woolford presented their equestrian melodrama, 'written by J.H. Amherst and produced under his Superintendance called *The Infernal Secret; or, the Invulnerable* preceded by Cherubini's grand Overture to *Lodoiska* with the Inimitable Performance of the Wounded Horse and the naturally Beautiful and sagacious PIE-BALD ASS! After which, an entirely novel Performance called *The Choreiakomite* by the Infant Prodigy, Miss A.Woolford (not 4 Years of Age)'.

This is the company, originally in competition with Andrew Ducrow, the great equestrian showman of Astley's Royal Amphitheatre in Westminster Bridge Road, which eventually merged with Ducrow's company. James Amherst wrote many of Ducrow's successes, such as *The Battle of Waterloo* and the spectacular *Siege of Troy,* always trying to integrate the feats of horsemanship and plausible dramatic action. Henry Adams was second only to Ducrow as a rider and the Woolford family added both skill and beauty to Ducrow's productions. Indeed, the Woolford family provided Ducrow with Louisa, his second wife.

When handing over to Burroughs Thomas Dibdin agreed to write 'a comic piece on the strangely popular plan of *Tom and Jerry*; it was in three acts, containing about forty songs, or rather chansonnettes, and, as I am informed, was particularly well received'.

So well received that Fitzball was asked to provide a sequel to be played in support of the Adams and Woolford horse-opera. He came up with *The Treadmill; or, Tom and Jerry at Brixton,* opening on 18 November 1822. The stories of Pearce Egan featured Corinthian Tom, Jerry Hawthorne and Robert Logic, Esq., who were turned into popular cartoon characters by Cruikshank. The stage version employed all twenty of the regular company, including Mr and Mrs Davidge, Paul Bedford, Richard

Lawrence, the two Misses Jonas and Miss Bence. A further version, *Tom and Jerry in France,* was mounted three weeks later, with 'Comic Song by Mr Davidge'. 'Tom and Jerry' turn up many times at the Surrey in various later adventures.

Fitzball was still working on Scott's novels. The dramatised version of *Peveril of the Peak* was staged in February 1823. Davidge played Sir Jeffrey Peveril, Burroughs played Julian Peveril, Mrs Davidge was Deborah Debbich. Also in the cast was one whose fortunes were linked with the Surrey over the next twenty-odd years – Miss Eliza Vincent. Fitzball recounts that she 'first appeared at the Surrey, as a precocious child, in an entertainment, written for her by the clever Moncrief. Her first appearance in the drama was in my *Peveril of the Peak* when she walked on the stage, as little Sir Jeffery Hudson, out of a fiddle-case'. The Moncrieff piece was probably *Zulico and Oriana; or, the Indian Boys,* staged on 28 August 1821. Eliza showed up again on 26 February 1822 with 'Dåncïng by Miss Ponder and Miss Vincent (her first Attempt). Pupils of Miss Adcock.' She also appeared on 11 August 1823 in the role of a Theban Child in Fitzball's *Antigone.* By January 1825 Eliza Vincent was being described on the playbills as an infant prodigy, 'the Little Pickle'. She delighted audiences as a charming soubrette at the Surrey in the 1830s and at the Victoria in the 1840s. By 1848 she was joint lessee of the Surrey and in the first half of the 1850s held the Victoria Theatre's management.

Miss Adcock, the dancing teacher just mentioned, was Columbine in the Surrey's *Harlequin and Mother Goose* of 26 March 1822 in which Grimaldi made a guest-appearance. She is a rare example of one of the Surrey's lesser-known names about whom we can give personal details. She was the daughter of actors who also appeared there. According to Pieter van der Merwe, who supplied this information, her Scottish mother was Mary Montford Campbell, daughter of Colin Campbell, seventh baronet of Auchinbrech. She eloped with the family tutor, Charles Robert Adcock, himself reputedly the son of a general. Disinherited, he and his wife joined the northern stage by 1791. Their children included Angelica Harriet, that is 'Miss Adcock' (who was known in the family as Harriet or 'Hal'), a younger daughter Rebecca (who was born in 1807 and until her marriage also acted occasionally as 'Miss R. Adcock'), and at least one son, George, who became an engraver. Both the girls were musical and the family as a whole were at the Surrey in 1823-4. No later than 1825 Rebecca became the second wife of Clarkson Stanfield (1793-1867), then a young widower with two children and well on the way to becoming the most celebrated theatrical scene-painter of the age. It was not a new acquaintance, as their families had acted together in the north from around 1812 and he had worked at the Coburg from its opening in 1818 before joining Drury Lane in 1822.

The dancer 'Mlle Angelica' at Drury Lane in the mid-1820s and noted in a letter of George Adcock as having a début at the Academy of Music at Paris in 1831 is likely to have been Harriet Adcock under a stage-name. Uncertain evidence does however invite the speculation that at some point Harriet's younger sister Rebecca (or some other person entirely) may have danced under the same name, perhaps after tuiton by Harriet, the prototype Angelica. We do know that Harriet later lived in Edinburgh as a 'Professor of Dancing'. She died unmarried there on 16 April 1858. Her age was then given as 54, implying a date of birth in 1804-5. This seems on the low side for someone who had 'pupils' at the Surrey in 1822 but is not unthinkable, particularly for the company's resident Columbine. Her father died on 30 December 1828, as has just come to light from a document offered in a dealer's catalogue; her mother died in 1847. Her sister Rebecca outlived Clarkson Stanfield and died in 1875.

At the Surrey in 1823 J.H. Amherst came back with two more pieces, *Will Watch* and *The Fatal Coral Reef*, which do not seem to be in his usual equestrian style. Indeed they look forward to the time when the Surrey becomes known as the 'home of nautical drama'.

When Burroughs took his benefit night on 27 February 1823 Mrs Fitzwilliam (Miss Copeland that was) appeared with him in Farquhar's comedy *Archer and Aimwell* (better known these days as *The Beaux' Stratagem),* there being 'in the Course of the Piece, the favorite Duett of Love's Catechism by Mrs Fitzwilliam and Mr Burroughs'. Mr and Mrs Davidge appeared in *The Husband of Two Wives* and virtually all the company in the 'Serio Operatic Burletta', *The Young Hussar.*

The season came to an end in the middle of March 1823, with the usual spate of benefit nights. Though he does not own up to it in his memoirs, I think that Fitzball dramatised yet another of the *Tales of My Landlord* by Sir Walter Scott under the title of *The Black Dwarf; or, The Wizard of the Moor* (or took over an anonymous version of 1817, *The Black Dwarf; or, the Reiver of Westburn Flat).* This was produced for Davidge's benefit and repeated for Bengough's on 17 March, which, also happening to be St Patrick's Day, called for Irish songs by Lawrence and by Miss Roberts.

Burroughs reopened for a month or two, but 24 June 1823 was 'positively his last appearance'. He had run out of capital and the lease passed to Llewellyn Williams, who ran the Globe Tavern in Fleet Street. This was not to be the last time that Watkins Burroughs trod the Surrey stage, though he had to wait a quarter of a century for his next appearance there.

Jacob Decastro, the comedian, had little good to say about the Burroughs régime. In his *Memoirs* he wrote that the Surrey under Burroughs displayed 'all the imbecility of a once vigorous constitution'. Admittedly Burroughs was not a Dibdin or an Elliston but there had been mixes of equestrianism and melodrama before and would be again, and Burroughs had attracted to his theatre talented artistes in both these fields. Could Burroughs be all that bad if Grimaldi, Blanchard, the Davidges, Bedford, Kemble, Adams, Woolford and Amherst were willing to work with him?

For the next two years Llewellyn Williams held the lease of the Surrey but does not seem to have run the theatre, probably being too busy with his inn. Fitzball says 'the Johnstones had taken it, with a Mr Delaforce' but does not identify these people. However, the leases of the Equestrian Tavern and the Surrey Coal Hole, on either side of the Theatre, were held by Mary Johnson (not Johnstone) and Samuel Delaforce respectively. They, more than anyone else, would not wish to have the theatre out of commission as most of their custom came from its patrons. On the other hand they would not have had the time or experience to run the theatrical business. I have not found any appointment of managers but subsequent playbills show that the persons with the most clout were Gallot and Auld. They can be found together at the Coburg, for example in *Bluebeard* in June 1822. It could be that Auld sized up the possibilities of the Surrey when he made his guest appearance in the 'triple pantomime' in July 1822. Several of the previous company stayed on, for example Tom Blanchard, Henry Kemble, Miss Adcock and Miss Jonas, while Fitzball was still the resident playwright with Sheppard at the box office and Erskine the Musical Director.

The Christmas pantomime in 1823 was *Fox and Goose; or, Harlequin The White Knight of Chess,* with Auld as White King/Harlequin, Miss Adcock as White Queen/Columbine, Henderson as Black King/Pantaloon and Hartland as Black Pawn/Clown. The playbills give a good example of the 'dark opening':

> The Pantomime opens in the Regions of the Evening Star, where Hesperus is discovered reclining. Night then descends attended by her Sprites claiming her dark Sovereignty; she summons Glimmer [Miss Vincent] to her presence, who tells her that she tarried on Earth to gather the nature of a dreadful quarrel which had taken place between the Black and White Kings of Chess.

An attempt was made to introduce a new 'art' form to the stage – prize-fighting! The playbills of 11 February 1824 indicated that: 'Langan, the Irish Champion, having been prevented by Accident from fulfilling his first Engagement, will positively Appear with Tom Reynolds, his Second, and display their peculiar Powers in the ART of SELF-DEFENCE!!!' Although there were further attempts to popularise this form of entertainment, it never really prospered. I get the impression that prize-fighters were less reliable in keeping their bookings than actors.

The triumvirate of publicans, Llewellyn Williams, Mary Johnson and Samuel Delaforce, evidently hoped to improve the fortunes of the Surrey by putting money into refurbishing it, as the playbills of April 1824 describe:

> THE DRESS CIRCLE OF BOXES Has been Re-built after the peculiar Fashion and Elegance of The Grand Theatre of San Carlos, at Naples, And is lined throughout with a New Sumptuous Figured and Burnished Gold Paper, manufactured expressly for the purpose. The Pannels in Front are Decorated with Massy Gold Ornaments, and Borders tastefully arranged, on a Ground of GENOA ROSE COLOURED VELVET. An entirely New Proscenium Drapery has been painted by Mr Walker, and is supported by Two immense richly carved COMPOSITE COLUMNS OF HIGHLY WROUGHT GOLD. The Ceiling has been Re-painted and Beautifully Ornamented, from which is suspended A New and Brilliant Glass Lustre! The GALLERY is now rendered the most commodious and convenient in Europe.

Ironically, after all this expenditure, the 'Re-modelled and Embellished' Surrey Theatre seemed to attract disasters. Fitzball gives a lively account of the production of his next work for the Surrey, *The Burning Bridge:*

> The opening scene was an orange grove, in which Mrs Young, and little Miss Young (afterwards the celebrated Mrs Honey) were discovered, the latter on a ladder, throwing the oranges, which she was gathering from a tree, into her mother's lap.... After a little interval, for a duet, between the ladies, 'Take, oh take this golden fruit,' Henry Kemble had to rush into the orange grove; in doing so, his long costly robes, becoming entangled with the set piece, pulled down with it, the orange tree excepted, every morsel of scenery on the stage, discovering only bare walls and flaring lamps.

Consternation in all departments! Actor, manager, author, and most of all – the poor scene-painter! Auld, then acting manager, rushed forward to address the almost-convulsed audience, as follows:

> Ladies and Gentlemen, the scenery has fallen down! (roars of laughter) Ladies and Gentlemen, honoured by your approval, if you will allow us to draw up – I mean let down the curtain, this piece shall begin over again, from the beginning (loud applause; curtain falls).

The scene was reset and within in a few minutes the curtain rose again, and all went smoothly to the end. The audience was in such an excellent humour that Fitzball mused whether it would not be a good idea, on the first night of a new and doubtful piece, to push all the scenery into the pit, 'by way of exciting the tender sympathies of the generous public'.

It was not necessary for the Surrey to repeat its catastrophes. It was perfectly capable of finding new ones, risking not only the lives of its actors but also the lives of those animals brought on as 'extras'. In the former category there was more trouble with *The Burning Bridge,* when it was not just the bridge that burnt. As Fitzball recounts:

> At the conclusion of the drama, a female spectre had to rise from a lake, surrounded by mist, which effect was produced by lamps, placed behind gauzes, surrounding the figure. When this cloud of gauzes had almost reached the ceiling, a breathe of air blew one of the folds across the lamp, and the spectre's dress was instantly in flames. Poor Leslie! for it was a gentleman who played the lady, immediately made an effort to dispossess himself of his unearthly garments, and in so doing, discovered to the amazed audience, that he/she was a Scotchman, with his kilt on, ready dressed for the afterpiece, *Waverly*. The effect was too ludicrous, notwithstanding the peril of the circumstances, for the audience to repress their uproarious mirth, which was very soon changed to compassion by Leslie, who was terribly frightened, jumping out of the machinery, an immense height from the stage, by which means he was, I am sorry to add, seriously injured, and never entirely recovered.

I have been unable to find any reference to Leslie in subsequent Surrey playbills, though whether he resumed his career at a less accident-prone theatre I have been unable to discover.

Yet another accident, though even in a play named *The Fire-worshippers* it had nothing to do with fire, concerned Gallot, who had to ride across the stage on a camel which was decorated with gorgeous trappings. They had just left the side scene when a large trap gave way under the immense weight of animal and rider. Again I call on Fitzball to report:

> In an instant the poor helpless creature lay crushed, with its neck broken, in an immense box; it was impossible to extricate him, except limb by limb, which, as he expired in the course of the evening, was the eventual result. For Gallot, he saved himself by his presence of mind, throwing himself off the camel's back, to a considerable distance, with the greatest dexterity. Notwithstanding this interruption, and the confusion it excited, the spectacle was very well received, although it went somewhat tamely....

Hardly 'tamely'. The play ends with the overthrow of Al Hassan, Gallot's role, 'who, for his Presumption, in attempting to extinguish the Sacred Fire' (and killing the Sacred Camel?) 'is struck by a Thunderbolt'. One can date this accident fairly closely from the playbills. That for Easter Monday, 19 April 1824, refers to a 'Hunting Procession... mounted on The Real Camel.' By Thursday 22nd there is no mention of any camel. Concerning the night in question Fitzball continues:

> The after-piece to follow, was a nautical melo-drama, called *The Floating Beacon,* in which Mrs W. Clifford, and Henry Kemble were to make their appearance; Gallot, also, had to sustain a most prominent part; and all this over the body of the poor dead camel.

Now what else could go wrong? Well, there are always the actors themselves. Fitzball again:

> All was proceeding smoothly – even the departed camel was forgot – when it was discovered that one of the principal actors could not, from a 'spiritual' cause, by any means remember a word of his part, and yet, was sufficiently obstinate – not infrequent in such attacks – to persevere in trying to perform his best. This, of course, like an inexperienced dancer in a quadrille, threw everybody else out. The hisses began, rage ensued. At length the curtain fell amid shouts of scorn and disapprobation.

The next performance, with the dead camel removed and the actor sober, went much better:

> The delinquent of the preceding night, had now studied his part, got more sober and less mellow in it, and was quite

> capable of suiting the word to the action. The result was, that this melodrama, with which the public, the night previously, had left the theatre in disgust, made so tremendous a sensation, that it ran the actual number of one hundred and twenty consecutive nights.

Later this year Llewellyn Williams withdrew from the Surrey before the end of his lease. The playbill for 29 November 1824 announced the 'Last Night of the present Management' with a pantomime *The Three Gifts; or, the Farmer and the Puddings*. Although again missing from the title there was a Harlequin, and a good one, Tom Ellar; with him were Signor Paulo as Clown and Tom Blanchard as Pantaloon – that is, the team for *The Death of Harlequin;* but now the Columbine was the dancer Mrs Searle, another whose pupils were often seen on the Surrey stage.

The new manager was already at hand. The pub next door, the Surrey Coal Hole, had been taken over by an ex-sailor, 'Francis Robert Honeyman for a term of 56 years from 23 June 1823 at a yearly rent of £130'. It was common and convenient to have the box-office run from a nearby pub, which would be open at all hours, and Frank Honeyman evidently acted as theatre treasurer. The earliest playbill I can trace with his name on it is for 28 February 1825 when he takes a benefit as Treasurer. Then the bill for Easter Monday, 4 April, headed 'New Proprietor' sheds more light: 'The Public are most respectfully informed, that Mr Honeyman (who conducted this Theatre, during the late Winter Season as Treasurer) having purchased of Mr Williams, the whole of his interest in the Lease and Property in this Theatre, he is now the sole Proprietor'.

Honeyman had thus been in the background for the previous few months even though not mentioned by Fitzball as his paymaster. He can be credited with three important additions to the company at this time: Bob Fairbrother as prompter and two of Fairbrother's daughters, the younger from 27 December 1824 and her older sister a month later. Charles Dibdin the Younger described them: '... the eldest a principal Dancer; a very clever, and what is much better, a very correct girl; she is now a principal dancer on the Caledonian Stage: her sister, as well conducted as herself, was also a dancer'. Later their brother Benjamin Smith Fairbrother also joined the company, first as prompter in his father's shoes and later in other administrative capacities. The Fairbrother name can be found associated with the Surrey for the next thirty years.

Frank Honeyman did not find it easy to run the Equestrian Tavern as well as the theatre. For the latter he sought an experienced manager. As will be seen, he did not get his first choice.

Chapter Six

Charles Dibdin (1825-26)

The new lease-holder tried to get Thomas Dibdin to come back and manage the Surrey for him. As it turned out Tom had just signed up with Sadler's Wells. Instead Honeyman engaged Tom's elder brother, Charles Dibdin the Younger, initiator of aquadramas, who had earlier enjoyed a period of nearly twenty years supervising the Sadler's Wells 'Water-Theatre' himself. In spite of a rather cool start the relationship between the two men proved happy and fruitful.

George Speaight's edition of Charles Dibdin's *Memoirs* gives a detailed and colourful account of his eighteen months as Surrey manager. In this chapter I can only quote a meagre selection of the wealth of good material it contains. Dibdin describes their first interview, at which Honeyman

> rather reluctantly, having been disappointed in his hope regarding my Brother, engaged me as his Acting Manager, Author, and Contriver; and on the same day, Easter Monday, April 4th 1825, Tom and I exchanged Posts of Command; he opened the 'Old Wells', and I opened the 'New Surrey'....
>
> The first meeting between Mr Honeyman and me, evinced a little hesitation on both sides; and our first addresses were equally laconic. His 'Glad to see you, Sir, you'll excuse me, but I'd much rather have seen your Brother'. Mine, 'Obliged to you, Sir, and I am sorry to see you Proprietor of the Surrey Theatre'.

At this stage Charles Dibdin was not optimistic concerning the Surrey Theatre, because neither his father, Charles Senior, nor his brother Thomas could make it answer. Nevertheless the abruptness of the meeting with Honeyman let them immediately into the nature of each other's dispositions and a good working arrangement was set up with little trouble. A salary was agreed. As regards 'manager's perks', Honeyman signed his name at the bottom of a sheet of paper and said, 'There's a Carte Blanche, fill it up how you please'. In fact, Dibdin never found it necessary to enter anything on the carte blanche during the whole of his engagement; they were always friendly and comfortable together. Charles Dibdin got down to work:

> I had just 14 days to arrange the Engagement of the Company; write three new pieces, and get them up.... Mr Honeyman gave me for my Stage Manager, Mr Gallot... [who] was also one of my principal Performers in tragedy, comedy, opera and farce. My Prompter was my old acquaintance, Bob Fairbrother... a veteran in the service of the Stage of more, I think, than 50 years standing, when he left it (in 1826). He had originally been a superior Mimist, and broad sword player.... I had many minor theatrical stars: Huntley, a tower of strength, altho' now a little dilapidated; Mortimer, Ridgway; Clifford; Vale, my buffo caricato, much 'beloved by all the Gods' and rather too much devoted to their service; Mrs Wm. Clifford, our 'Mrs Siddons'; and Miss Louis, our 'Fanny Kemble'.... Mons. Simon, from Paris, principal Dancer... with Mad. Simon (whom I have heretofore mentioned as Miss A. Kennedy...) who has continued at the Surrey ever since; and Mrs Searle, the very clever and popular Dancer, with several of her interesting little juvenile pupils, of which she has generally sufficient, to form a Ballet of themselves; and did form several very effective ballets with them during our Seasons; and when this Lady and her little pupils used to come to the Theatre en train, they always reminded me of a hen and chickens. Our Company Leader was Erskine (of whom my Brother makes such honourable mention) and our principal Scene Painter, Tompkins....

Dibdin then explains the half-price system, whereby a new piece would be mounted at the commencement of the evening at full price during one week, and at the latter part of the evening at half price during the following week. It was then withdrawn, to make way for more 'New Novelty', as one contemporary writer put it. This mode was 'death to an Author', because a piece was never long enough before the public to be judged a 'hit'.

One of Charles Dibdin's strong points was that, like his brother, he could work at top speed and could keep it up week in, week out. This suited the Surrey's demand for novelties. He summed up his first season thus:

> We had now been open 28 weeks, and I had produced 21 new pieces, chiefly of three Acts each, 8 of which were grounded on French plots, and the remainder British Manufacture; I considered therefore that I had provided a good stock of reserve for changing, during the remainder of my Management, which was to continue till Michaelmas 1826, when Mr H's term in the lease, expired....

NEW SURREY THEATRE.

Acting-Manager, Mr. C. DIBDIN. Stage-Manager, Mr. GALLOTT.

REVIVAL OF THE FATAL PRECEPT.

The Part of Kreitzner, (First Time) by Mr. ROWBOTHAM.
In consequence of the great Popularity of, and perpetual enquiries for, "THE COLONEL's COME," it will be performed during the Week at Half-Price,

A New Melo-Drame, and a New Musical Extravaganza will be immediately produced.

Composer and Leader of the Band, Mr. ERSKINE. *Ballet Master, Mr. RIDGWAY.*

MONDAY, OCTOBER 10th, 1825, AND DURING THE WEEK,

Will be revived the very favorite Melo-Drame, in Three Acts, *(written by Mr. C. Dibdin,)* Called, The

Assassin of Silesia!

Or, The Fatal Precept.

The Overture and Music composed by Mr. ERSKINE.—The Scenery by Mr. Tomkins.
Kreitzner, *a Man of Mystery, (First Time,)* Mr. ROWBOTHAM. Conrad, *his Son,* Mr. MORTIMER. Marceline, *his Infant Son,* Miss RICKY. Baron Strainsheim, *a Bohemian,* Mr. E. WHITE. Gurts, *an Hungarian Adventurer,* Mr. CLIFFORD. Ilenstein, *a Lawyer,* Mr. VALE. Weinburg, *Post-Master,* Mr. T. B. CLIFFORD. Intendant, Mr. LLOYD. 1st. Guard, Mr. TURNER. 2d. Ditto, Mr. BOULANGER. Josephine, *Wife of Kreitzner,* Miss LOUIS. Mrs. Weinburg, *(First Time,)* Madame SIMON.

In Act the Third, A BALLET, composed by Mr. Ridgway.

AN IRISH COMIC SONG BY Mr. BRYANT.

A favorite Ballet, composed by Monsieur SIMON, Called,

L'AMOUR EN CORSET;

Or, The Dandy in Distress.

The Overture and Music composed by Monsieur SIMON.
Monsieur Grenouillet, a retired Corset-Maker, Mr. BOULANGER. Puppy Grenouillet, his Son, the Dandy, Monsieur SIMON. Franquique, an English Sailor, in Love with Genevieve, Mr. RIDGWAY. English Sailors, Messrs. G. and T. RIDGWAY, TURNER, GOUGH, &c. Madame Minouflett, a Lady of Rotundity, Mr. HENNING. Genevieve, Madame Minouflett's Daughter, betrothed to Puppy Grenouillet, and in Love with Franquique, Mrs. SEARLE. Louisette, her Sister, Miss FAIRBROTHER. Peasant Girls, Misses Rountree, A. Fairbrother, Lancaster, Manning and Merritt. Misses Ricky, Billing, Foster and Phillips, (Pupils of Mrs. Searle,) will also Dance.

MONSIEUR GOUFFE,

IN THE

ISLAND APE

WILL PERFORM HIS MOST EXTRAORDINARY

Leaps, Features of Agility and Gymnastic Displays; Horizontal Balancings,

PARTICULARLY

One from the Top of a High Column, extending himself Horizontally by his Feet, and in that unprecedented Position lifting a Boy from the Ground, suspending him in the Air, and then supporting him on his Shoulders:

HE WILL CONCLUDE HIS PERFORMANCES BY

Running round the Fronts of the BOXES and GALLERY, supported only by minute Mouldings.

The Entertainments to conclude with, in consequence of the Repeated Enquiries after its Revival, the Popular Musical Extravaganza, *(written by Mr. C. Dibdin,)* Called,

The Colonel's Come

Or, LA FEMME SOLDAT.

Clairmont, *a Traveller incognito,* Mr. MORTIMER. Adolphus, *Captain of the Fifth French Hussars,* Mr. GALLOTT. Serjeant Sabre, *(1st. time,)* Mr. JONES. Cadet, *Waiter at an Inn,* Mr. VALE. André, *Ditto,* Mr. TURNER. Eliza, *La Femme Soldat,* Madame SIMON. *Madame Clairmont, Wife to Clairmont,* Mrs. SEARLE. Louisette, *a Servant at the Inn,* Miss TUNSTALL.

The Overture and New Music composed by Mr. Erskine.——The Scenery by Mr. Tomkins.
The Characters dressed by Mrs. Arts. The Dresses, by Mr. Lyon & Miss Freelove. The Machinery, by Mr. Keys. The Decorations, by Mr. Marvell.

Boxes 4s. Pit 2s. Gal. 1s. Doors open at Half-past 5, and begin at Half-past Six. Second Price at Half-past 8

☞Places and Private Boxes (which have been splendidly decorated and newly furnished) may be engaged by the Night or Season, on Application to Mr. PARKER, Box Book-keeper, at the Box Office, from 11 till 4; or of Mr. SAMS, Royal Library, St. James's Street.

Free Admissions for the Season, transferable, or not transferable, may be purchased by Application to Mr. G. Lewis, Treasurer, at the Treasury of the Theatre.

The Public are most respectfully informed, that Mr. MATSON's Coach calls Every Evening at HORNYMAN's Coffee House, to convey Passengers to Deptford and Greenwich.

[T. Romney, Printer, Lambeth.]

Ridgway, the harlequin, 'composed and got up' a new entertainment for Dibdin, *Juan Fernandez; or, The Island Ape.* This was based on the talents of John Hornshaw, better known as Mons. Gouffé, the Man-Monkey. The playbills promised that he will 'perform his most extraordinary Leaps, Features of Agility and Gymnastic Displays. He will conclude his Performance by Running round the Fronts of the BOXES and GALLERY, supported only by minute Mouldings.' He made his début at the Surrey on 18 July 1825 and appeared in many similar 'monkey plays'. These remained popular. After Hornshaw retired, a new 'Mons. Gouffé' appeared in 1837.

Dibdin continues:

> Our Summer Season [1825] approaching its close, the Proprietor took his Benefit on Monday October 31, on which Night I brought out for him, a New Melodrama, in three Acts (from the French) which I had previously written, called *Filial Love; or, the Prisoner's Daughter,* and a musical Extravaganza, called *The Figure of Fun,* which I wrote some years before; and my Brother wrote a song for this Night, called 'Honeyman's Hive, or a Swarm of Friends'. Grimaldi also sung for him, the last song ['Hot Codlins'] I ever wrote for him at the Wells, in 1819....

The summer season ended on 12 December 1825 after 198 nights. Dibdin immediately started to prepare for the winter season, due to open on 26 December.

As his brother had done before him, Charles Dibdin ignored one of the basic facts of Surrey life, for his preparations did not include a pantomime. Instead an extravaganza, *Crom-a-boo; or, The Ape and the Infant,* was offered to the audience. This, of course, featured 'Mons. Gouffé' and also another of the Fairbrother girls who later achieved fame and fortune in a different field – she became the morganatic wife of the Duke of Cambridge and mother of his children, the FitzGeorges.

Dibdin recounts how, when Mrs Searle 'seceded', a new ballet master, Hullin, came over from the King's Theatre with 30 juveniles. Among them were two especially clever infants, 'Mlle Angelina', sister of Miss Worgman and supposedly aged five, and 'Mlle Mélanie Duval' who 'although but 6 years of age (probably two more) played the difficult part of *La Fille mal Gardé* with a tact and precision... rarely seen exceeded by adults'. The infant rope-dancer, 'Mlle Sylvia Zaphora' (8 billed as 6), whose act followed *La Fille mal Gardée,* caused dismay to *The Times* (27 December 1825):

> It is not good to think by what inducements a chit of this insufficient age... can have been brought to balance herself and a long heavy pole upon the bottom rail of a chair, the head

> of which rests upon two bottles which rest upon the rope.... There is a society for looking after the fate of chimney-sweepers, and many other classes of wretchedness.... Here is a field for... the wars waged against the sins and vanities of the world by the church militant.

The 'church militant' does not seem to have bothered Dibdin. He continued with 'an operatic melodrama', *The Foresters; or Truth and Treason,* with music by Whitaker, and says that 'in this piece every effective performer in the Company was cast. The piece played six weeks; chiefly, I consider, owing to the beauty of the music'.

The winter season ended on 18 March 1826. Dibdin re-engaged Mrs Searle and her twenty juveniles, the imitator Buckingham and 'Ruffian Bradley' who was named 'not for his ruffianly manners, for he was a different description of Character – but from his able representation of that species of character, and the "desperate combats" he was celebrated for fighting'. For example, *Bruno the Black and the Knight Champion* was presented on 27 March 1826, when Bradley, as Bruno, a border chieftain and bandit, engages in 'Grand and Terrific Combat' with Ridgway, the Knight Champion. Dibdin also employed Mrs Ridgway, 'who without assuming merit, possessed much'.

He then tried his hand at ballad-opera by dramatising Hogarth's cartoons on the lines of *The Beggar's Opera*. This was not exactly a new idea either for the Surrey or for the Dibdin family, as a version of *Industry and Idleness* had been written by Lawler with Sanderson's music and produced at the Surrey in April 1811 under the direction of Thomas Dibdin. The present compilation included about thirty musical pieces, in the main 'borrowed' in true pasticcio style from popular tunes of the day but supplemented by songs composed by Whitaker. Two scenes were inserted at the request of the local police. One of these showed how a burglary was committed, so that householders in the audience should know how to guard their homes in future; the other showed how the police were able to arrest a thief in a public house where rogues gathered, in the hope that any young thieves in the audience might take warning. Dibdin accepted these insertions somewhat unwillingly; he did not fancy being associated with 'Crimewatch – 1826'! Nevertheless he staged his version as *The Apprentice's Opera* on Easter Monday, 27 March 1826.

There was another attempt to introduce prize-fighting as an entertainment in the first week of July 1826 with the 'Arena of Fancy', when Dick Curtis, the Pet of the Fancy, was in combat every evening with Young Dutch Sam. Unfortunately Jem Ward, who as Champion of England was the top attraction, failed to turn up.

Dibdin brought out his second Hogarthian opera, *The Rake's Progress,* on 10 July 1826. This contained twenty musical items. The piece was 'well performed' and played 'for many nights to gratified audiences'. A summer pantomime, *The Monster of the Glen; or, Harlequin and the Fairy Fanciful,* was produced on 17 July. The next item of note was staged on 11 September, a new *Paul Pry.* This nosy character, like 'Tom and Jerry', had a number of theatrical manifestations; Dibdin knew of two earlier versions. His was not a success. Nor was a subsequent charity benefit. In the 1820s these concessions were proving to be a far cry from such war-time boons as Sheridan's at Drury Lane on 2 July 1794 which had taken over £1,526 (the eighteenth century's largest single gross, according to *The London Stage Pt V)* for the dependents of those killed in the naval battle of 'The Glorious First of June'. Dibdin says of the benefit he allowed in 1826:

> On September 13... a Benefit Night was taken by a Society of Copper Plate Printers, in aid of a fund for assisting such of their fraternity as were out of Employ. The Benefit was not profitable, nor... did I ever know a Charity Benefit do otherwise than fail.... Those Benefits always inconvenienced us, we received barely the nightly expenses of the house for each; scarcely any produced profit; the majority occasioned loss; the persons concerned were always dissatisfied, and we were disgusted. After that Season, we declined giving Charity Benefits.

The collaboration between Honeyman and Dibdin ended on 28th September 1826 when Honeyman's lease ran out. He had no wish to enter a new lease on the terms expected by the Ground Landlord. Messrs. Dunn and Docker agreed to the advanced rent and re-opened the theatre – a short-lived venture as we will see.

Charles Dibdin summed up his own contribution as continual hard work, not just in writing tragedies and farces, but also 'Comic and other Songs, to be sung between the Pieces; for incessant exertion, and a perpetual succession of novelty and variety were indispensibly necessary for the welfare of the Theatre'. He was generous in ascribing a large part of his success to the Surrey Theatre itself:

> It is perhaps the best constructed Theatre in London, without exception, both for hearing and seeing; two paramount desiderata in a Theatre. It is, by the best Scene-painters, preferred to all others, for the advantageous exhibition of scenery; and there is certainly no Theatre in London, so well calculated to assist the voice of the Actor, or the Singer, the latter especially.

Charles Dibdin (1825-26)

Under the management of Messrs. Dunn and Docker an attempt was made to go back to the circus format, with J.H. Amherst, the experienced rider, writer and producer for the ring, as stage manager; B.S. Fairbrother, following the family tradition, remained as prompter. As Dunn had opted out of paying a lower rent ten years earlier and planned to build a new theatre, the Coburg, instead, why did he now think that he could make a go of the Surrey? My view is that he had seen what a success Andrew Ducrow was making at Astley's, just up the road, riding, as A.H.Saxon puts it, 'three horses abreast, standing with a foot on each of the outside ones. He then shifted his footing as he repeatedly made the animals change places'. But Astley's only had a summer licence, and in September 1826 Ducrow's company set off for Bath and Bristol. Dunn and Docker thus had a clear six months at the Surrey to try to capture Astley's customers and establish themselves before Ducrow's return. They failed, for Ducrow returned with even greater marvels, now riding five horses abreast.

Nevertheless the attempts by Dunn and Docker to bring the Surrey back to its equestrian days, though an ill wind as regards their own finances, blew someone some good. Davidge had embarked on his first managerial foray by leasing the Coburg from Easter 1826. He must have been pleased to find that, for a large part of his first year, he had no dramatic competition from the Surrey.

The celebrated MAN MONKEY, as Jocko,
Who will support himself horizontally upon ONE HAND on the Top of FOUR PINT GLASSES placed on each other, forming a Pyramid, with a Boy on his back; he will also support the weight of his body from a high column, raise a Boy from the ground, suspend him by his teeth, and then place him upon his shoulders; he will also place himself horizontally out on the Pole, &c.

A typical man-monkey act.
(Reproduced by kind permission from a playbill of 1826 in Hertford Museum)

Chapter Seven

Elliston (1827-31)

When the ground landlord of the Surrey Theatre, Temple West, advertised in May 1827 that the theatre was available for letting, Robert Elliston decided to have a second go at running it, even though he was still an undischarged bankrupt due to his failure at Drury Lane. It meant that matters had to be so arranged that his son, Charles Robert Elliston, was nominally the lessee, bearing the legal and financial responsibility. With nice ambiguity the playbills announced that the theatre was 'under the direction of Mr Elliston'. *The Times*, with a fine balance between reality and legal fiction, announced on 4 June1827 that the Surrey 'opens this evening under the immediate direction of the Messrs. Elliston'. So the answer to the question posed earlier – 'But was it the same Elliston?' – is 'Legally, no!'

In his four years running the Surrey until his death in July 1831, Elliston's extensive theatrical experience and vigorous personality had a strong shaping influence on the way the theatre developed. All his life he had campaigned for the minor theatres to be free to stage the 'legitimate' drama which was by law reserved in London for the patent theatres. Though he did not live to see the abolition of this monopoly in 1843, his campaigning had played a large part in bringing it about. In this sense, his most important influence on the Surrey took effect after his death.

For the first two months of his management Surrey Theatre playbills are rather thin on the ground. The earliest I have found is dated 14 July 1827. Perhaps he was having 'cash flow' problems and had to cut down on his advertising, yet it was in this field that he was meeting unexpected and unusual competition.

Elliston would have known that there are many ways of making money out of the theatre, and even more ways of losing it. He was now to find that an outsider could make money out of his theatre without his permission or his co-operation – and keep it up for four years.

The man with the bright idea was J.H. Cox, a printer, at first of 11 Lambeth Road, on the south side of St George's Circus. Elliston's early playbills were printed by G. Head of Wine Office Court, Fleet Street. They were of foolscap size (8 x 13 inches, that is about 21 x 33 cm), and were intended not just for display on hoardings and in shops but also for sale in the foyer as programmes. They would contain not only details of the evening's entertainments but also a 'coming shortly' section giving the names of the plays and of the leading players, perhaps for a week ahead.

Within a week or two of Elliston opening at the Surrey Cox had his version of the playbills on sale outside the theatre. In three months he seems to have driven the official printer out of the arena. Head was succeeded by Samuel Glover Fairbrother, of the Lyceum Printing Office, Exeter Court, Strand, who decided to try to scare off the opposition with the following announcement:

> Mr Elliston having very kindly assigned to me, as Printer to the Surrey Theatre, the right of selling the Bills at the Doors of the Theatre, and such right having been infringed upon by an unprincipled individual, who prefers depriving a fellow tradesman of his just emoluments, to the more slow but honest plan of gaining business and profit by fair means, the Public are hereby most respectfully cautioned against purchasing the spurious Bills of the Surrey Theatre, which are made to resemble, as much as possible, at a cursory glance, the genuine ones; but which, upon comparison, will be found, from omissions and general incorrectness, to be a gross fraud.
>
> Legal proceedings are about to be instituted against the individual above mentioned; in the meantime, the Public are respectfully apprised that the only genuine and authorised Bills of the Surrey Theatre, are those which have my imprint at the bottom.

Legal proceedings – yet what would be the charge? Cox's bills were not copies of either Head's or Fairbrother's; the style and layout were different, also his bills were on greyish paper whereas Fairbrother used a greenish-blue paper. There was no 'passing off' as Cox showed his name and address clearly on each bill. As far as I can make out, Cox compiled his bills, not from a current original but from the 'coming shortly' information. When a new piece was staged he could not show who was to take the minor parts, as these were not given in 'Coming Shortly'. Even when a regular piece returned to the bills he could not be positive that the same players would be engaged for the minor roles; he resorted to phrases such as 'other characters as before', and trusted to luck. In short, his were original compositions and not copies. When one thinks of the number of 'original compositions' staged at the Surrey which were based on the works of famous authors such as Sir Walter Scott without permission or remuneration, it is laughable to think that Fairbrother had any case at all.

In the early days, Cox did not date his bills but used the formula 'This present evening will be presented...'. By August 1828 Cox had moved to new premises at 14 Garden Row, off London Road, and so still within a few minutes' walk of the Surrey. He seems more confident and now dates his bills, even giving two days' programmes on one bill. There is however a hint of 'passing off', as his bills are now on a greyish-blue paper, close to Fairbrother's greenish-blue.

Elliston and Fairbrother made another attempt to frighten Cox. The playbills for 27 September 1830 stated: 'Every Playbill issued from a Theatre by the Proprietor is Copyright; such Copyright has been given to Mr S.G. FAIRBROTHER general Printer to this Theatre; and any infringement upon this right, will, in future, certainly be met by legal interference'. This is weaker than the threat first used, and when one sees that Cox had been running his operation for over three years by this time, one wonders what Elliston hoped to achieve by his words.

I have not found any of Cox's bills after the death of Robert Elliston. As Charles Robert Elliston continued as proprietor for another six months and S.G. Fairbrother as printer for many more years, I conclude that Cox's target was specifically Robert Elliston. As to Cox's reason for picking on him, could Cox have been an unsatisfied creditor in the 1826 bankruptcy? Certainly, Cox was not the official printer for Drury Lane, but he may have lost money in another way.

As to Elliston's repertory, basically he was reviving productions for the Surrey which had been successful during his other theatrical ventures. *The Times* said as much on 5 June 1827:

> Mr Elliston performed his old character – the Singles, in The Three and the Deuce – which will be recollected as one of his most popular efforts. He appeared stronger than when we last saw him at Drury Lane and was received with the welcome of an old favorite.... The acting of the manager alone, however, is a treat not often to be enjoyed at a minor theatre.

What Elliston also aimed for was a change of programme every night, thus giving the Surrey-siders what they wanted, namely variety. This does not imply a totally different programme every night. He had the ability to spot a winner, and would keep on a clear favourite indefinitely as the first (or full-price) piece, while ringing the changes on the other pieces night by night. Thus John Stafford's *Love's Frailties,* which received its first performance on 2 January 1828, was revived over and over again, clocking up over a hundred performances by March 1829. But this pales into insignificance when compared with the success of

Jerrold's *Black-Eyed Susan.* This was first staged on 8 June 1829 and achieved over two hundred performances in Elliston's lifetime, with over a thousand altogether.

When Elliston felt he had captured the Surrey audiences he obtained further variety by increasing the operatic content of the bill. One can detect the first signs of movement from the native ballad-opera towards the German and Italian works which were to oust them. This process spanned several managements and I have dealt with it more fully in the next chapter. The same applies to changes in the structure of pantomime and this, too, is discussed in that chapter.

An early success for Elliston was to engage the child prodigy Master Burke in various dramatic, comic and operatic roles. An outstanding one (or do I mean six?) was in *The March of Intellect* where Master Burke played Master Socrates Camelion 'A Youth of Parts', Mr Terence O'Leary 'from Killarney – with a NEW IRISH SONG, composed by Mr W. West', Signor Sardini 'from Italy – in which he will introduce an Italian Air, with Variations, on the Violin', Bluster Bubble Esq. 'from the Moon', Jack Ratline 'from the Binnacle Man of War – with a NAVAL HORNPIPE' and finally Napoleon Buonaparte 'from Elyseum'. All this at the age of nine!

The Times of 3 September 1827 reported:

> Indeed, we have seldom witnessed in performers of more mature age, a more accurate conception of their parts, or more complete knowledge of stage effect, than this child displayed throughout the piece.... Master Burke is described as between eight and nine years old; but his appearance, when off the stage, is that of a child even under those years.... He is... quite the child in his habits. On the evening we saw him, he came round to the boxes in front of the curtain, after his performance, and seemed as much delighted with the pantomime of Jack and the Beanstalk as if he had just entered a theatre for the first time in his life.

The Times report of 27 December 1827 shows how lucky Master Burke was at that first time of playing in a piece immediately before a pantomime, and how he could not bank on his luck holding:

> The entertainments for the holyday folk at this theatre, were the tragedy of Douglas, and, of course, a pantomime. The first went off almost in dumb show, and for any thing the audience heard of it, might as well been omitted. Not even the excellent acting of Master Burke, who played Young Norval, could fix the attention of the Gods for more than a passing moment, or quell their boisterous impatience for the legitimate amusement of the season – the new pantomime.

It was called *Harlequin and the Astrologer of Stepney; or, the Enchanted Fish and the Fated Ring. The Times* thought it a really clever production, most splendidly got up, which would have done honour to Covent Garden or Drury Lane.

Although *La Sonnambula,* as an opera by Bellini, did not reach the Surrey until May 1839, the story – as a play – was known to Surrey audiences over ten years earlier, as Fitzball relates:

> Apropos of the Sonnambula, I think this not a bad opportunity for telling a little anecdote respecting the first appearance of that somniferous lady in this country. She first walked the plank at the Surrey, in Elliston's time: an author then of no great celebrity, and still less experience, had got hold of the French ballet, and put language to it. Elliston, finding it very dramatic – and Elliston was an excellent judge – resolved to bring it out at his theatre; but finding also a great want of tact displayed, even in the language – for stage language should always be, like its scenery, a little over-coloured – applied to me to give it here and there what he called a 'touch up'.

Fitzball was somewhat reluctant to interfere with the work of another author but Elliston, putting on all his pomposity, told Fitzball to name his price. Still not relishing the employment Fitzball named a considerable sum, but Elliston instantly agreed to give it and was promised the work the following morning. At the time appointed Fitzball produced the amended script to Elliston. The manager, who was

> seated, like Cardinal Wolsey, in his chair of state, opened the leaves one after another. His eye brightened at every page; at length, at the scene where the Count goes out at the window, and where I had contrived to pop into his mouth a clap-trap, respecting what the man deserves who would be coward enough to take advantage of unprotected female innocence, Elliston smiled one of his George-the-Fourth smiles, and exclaimed, rubbing his hands, exultingly, – 'That will do, sir, that will do; now we shall bring them down!' Then, pointing with kingly dignity towards the mantelpiece, I found lying there, according to royal promise, the gold from the exchequer which was to requite my labour....

It is interesting to find 'clap-trap' used in its original sense of a trap to get the audience to clap.

Although Fitzball does not date his story, *The Spirit of the Hill; or, The Village Somnambulist* was first staged on 1 March 1828. It was produced by William West, with Erskine's music, and with Dibdin Pitt, Wynne, Mr and Mrs Vale, Mr and Mrs T.B. Clifford, and, as the Sleeping Beauty, Mrs Fitzwilliam.

Fitzball has another story about Elliston:

> I was one morning proceeding in the direction of the Surrey Theatre, where I met Elliston opposite the Riding School. He had a lofty, but a gracious way of stopping and speaking to you. It was always condescending, but never humiliating....
>
> 'So, sir,' he commenced, 'concocting, eh? Something imaginative floating in the air, eh? Why not write for the Surrey Theatre, eh?' This happened at a time when I had ceased to write for that side of the water, being more fully employed, and better paid, at the other legitimate theatres. 'Have you anything would suit us? – good enough for us, eh?'
>
> 'I have a melodrame,' I answered, 'called The Inchcape Bell!'
>
> 'Ah! The Inchcape Bell! – good! Come and read it to me: you may tomorrow morning.'
>
> Elliston was again enthroned in his chair of state, but looking unusually dull and drowsy, I thought. However, I commenced:
>
>> 'Act 1 – Scene 1. Exterior of an old-fashioned Public House on the sea coast, inscription over the door "The Inchcape Bell". An ancient castle on a distant cliff, &c.'
>
> Elliston nodded his head; it was not like a token of assent, or approbation; however, I continued to read:
>
>> 'Chorus of Seamen:
>> "Over the green and circling wave,
>> Warning the seaman from his grave,
>> When rocks sink deep, and billows swell,
>> Ding dong rings the Inchcape Bell –
>> Ding! dong!"'
>
> Elliston snored, fell almost out of his chair, and rubbed his eyes. I took no notice; but proceeded, stifling something like an indignant feeling under the sound of my own poetry:
>
>> '"Oft through the stilly midnight gloom,
>> Knelling the drowned wretch to his tomb,
>> Through forked flash, and tempest yell,
>> Ding dong rings the Inchcape Bell –
>> Ding! dong!"'

'Ding dong' produced little effect on the manager. It emerged that Elliston had had a bad attack of gout in the night, and had dosed himself to the eyebrows with laudanum. Fitzball read on for a while, and then sat silent. When Elliston showed signs of awakening, Fitzball had the bright idea of turning to the end of the script, and reading the final lines:

> "'Mother! mother! it is accomplished! You are avenged!" (Places dumb boy in Sir John's arms, and sinks exhausted with fatigue. Grand Tableau. End. Curtain falls.)'

Elliston looked vacantly around, commended the work (mainly unheard!) and suggested that Fitzball submitted it to the Coburg. Yet within a fortnight, Elliston was again asking Fitzball if he had anything to suit the Surrey. Fitzball, with tongue in cheek, replied:

> 'Yes, sir,' I replied, 'I have a nautical melodrame.'
>
> 'Nautical, eh? – good. What do you call it? Nautical! – the very thing. What is it, eh?'
>
> 'The Inchcape Bell, sir!'
>
> 'Excellent! the very sort of title to make out our bill. Let me have it to read directly, sir – this very evening.' My intended sarcasm was lost. He had utterly, not only forgotten the title of the piece, but every circumstance connected with it. I sent him the M.S., he read it at once, and produced it immediately. It ran eighty nights with the utmost approbation, and drew money.

After *The Inchcape Bell* Elliston's next great success was *Black-Eyed Susan; or, All in the Downs*. The way the piece came to the Surrey is no credit to Elliston. Up to the end of 1828, Davidge at the Coburg was employing Douglas Jerrold as his company dramatist and thought highly of him. Elliston at the Surrey had the same opinion and managed to lure Jerrold away from the Coburg. Although it was standard practice for the Surrey or the Coburg to engage performers from the rival theatre for short periods (for example the Coburg on 8 September 1828 had engaged 'Mr Wynne from the Surrey Theatre, his First Appearance'), Davidge thought it was going a bit far to have one of his salaried staff stolen from him, particularly a writer who might well have been given various plots to work up, and whose finished product might then be seen at the other place.

Davidge must have had a pretty good idea that Jerrold was at work on Gay's popular ballad of 'Black-Ey'd Susan'. The moment Elliston announced on 28 May 1829 that he would stage such a piece on 8 June at the Surrey, Davidge jumped in. The Coburg advertised for 1 June that 'This evening will be presented (1st time) an entirely new nautical melodrama called BLACK EYED SUSAN; or, the Lover's Perils.' As to plot, it had a pressgang, mutiny, storm, shipwreck, pirate's cavern, battle and rescue, finishing with 'A Nautical Triumph' and 'View of the victorious British Fleet lying at anchor'. While the Coburg was presenting its version as *Black-Eyed Susan*; *or, the Lover's Perils* in the first week of June, the Surrey was doing *King Lear, King Henry VIII* and *Virginius.*

Elliston was furious. When, a week behind Davidge, he staged *Black-Eyed Susan; or, All in the Downs* he fulminated in his bills:

> It will perhaps be necessary to state, that this Piece has been for some Weeks in preparation, and that its announcement was taken advantage of by another establishment, which, in pirating the title of Black-Eyed Susan has committed a contemptible and unprincipled infringement on Private Property.

This is, of course, utter rubbish: Elliston had no rights to the title of Gay's ballad; the full titles of the two pieces were different; the story-lines were different, as in place of shipwreck, pressgang etc. Jerrold had a wicked uncle, smugglers, coastguards, an amorous Captain and a court-martial.

In his introduction to the first published version in 1829 Jerrold himself admits:

> As to the title – 'Black-Ey'd Susan' – the writer trusts he may be pardoned for having compelled Gay to become sponsor to the present drama; well aware that as for any pertinance that may exist between the ballad and the piece, the latter might, with equal justice, have been called 'Blue-Ey'd Kate'.

Elliston did not see it this way. He – who had conducted the affairs of a Patent Theatre – upstaged by a mere newcomer to dramatic art, who had never even set foot on a 'major' stage! Intolerable! His playbills for the following week thundered:

> The only resource of a vain and ignoble mind, when detected in its obliquities is to fly to some notable blockhead (y'clept a friend) who, in endeavouring to apologise for the delinquency, contrives to string together a few periods of very bad English, and remarkable for nothing else, except gross vulgarity, and

> the absence of common reason. Nothing, however, can be so abhorrent to the feelings of the Conductor of this Theatre, than any collision, or association in an assumed rivalry, with the Coburg Theatre; he condescends while he castigates; and as this is probably the last time that he will ever be induced to drag that Theatre even into a temporary notice, by his observations, he assures the illustrious Charlatan of that classical and highly talented spot, that he shall leave him in the full and solitary enjoyment of his ingenuous machinations and contrivances for the decadence of the National Drama.

This is pure bombast. There was no need for Davidge, directly or indirectly, to apologise for an imaginary delinquency. Indeed Davidge could have pointed out that the Coburg might have a prior claim to the title in view of its pantomime, *Harlequin and Black-Eyed Susan*, staged there on 11 July 1825.

As it happens, Davidge's version, *Black-Eyed Susan; or, the Lover's Perils,* only ran a fortnight. Edwin Fagg penetratingly sums up: 'But it had not Mr T.P. Cooke'. Similarly, Douglas Jerrold: 'To the perfect acting of Mr T.P. Cooke is mainly attributable the prosperity of the production'. So Elliston could maintain the position that he personally had routed the competition from the Coburg, when the credit belongs to T.P. Cooke. Relations between the two theatres remained bad for twenty years.

Jerrold made little use of the ballad in the course of the action – merely as a chorus of sailors in the background in act two, scene three, and only the names William and Susan link ballad to play:

> All in the Downs the fleet was moor'd,
> The streamers waving in the wind,
> When black-ey'd Susan came aboard:
> Oh! where shall I my true love find?
> Tell me, ye jovial sailors, tell me true
> If my sweet William sails among your crew.
>
> William, who high upon the yard,
> Rock'd with the billow to and fro,
> Soon as her well-known voice he heard
> He sigh'd and cast his eyes below:
> The cord slides swiftly through his glowing hands,
> And (quick as lightning) on the deck he stands.

In his introduction Jerrold disclaims any attempt to write 'shiver my timbers' dialogue, but William's opening speech is so full of nauticalisms that it is excruciating to read. The story goes that while William is at sea his wife Susan lives with Dame Hatley in a cottage owned by Susan's wicked uncle, Doggrass, who is in league with the local smugglers, led by Tom Hatchet. Tom has his eye on Susan and says to an intermediary:

> *Tom:* I must marry Susan – she knows not you – you must swear that you were her husband's shipmate – that you saw him drowned. Susan now lives with old Dame Hatley; she has no other home; and if she refuse, Doggrass will seize the old woman's goods for long arrears of rent, and turn Susan adrift; then the girl has no chance left but to marry.

(Ah! but Tom, you don't know Susan as we know Susan: on to scene three.)

> *Susan:* Twelve long tedious months have passed, and no tidings of William. Oh! the pangs, the dreadful pangs that tear the sailor's wife, as, wakeful on her tear-wet pillow, she lists and trembles at the roaring sea.

(But William is safe in the Downs, where the Fleet is at anchor.)

> *William:* Ah, if my Susan knew who was here, she'd soon lash and carry, roused up by the whistle of that young boatswain's mate, Cupid, piping in her heart.... I have been piped up, roused from my hammock, dreaming of her, for the cold, black middle watch – I have walked the deck, the surf beating in my face, but Susan was at my side, and I did not feel it. I have been reefing on the yard, in cold and darkness, when I could hardly see the hand of my next mess-mate – but Susan's eyes were on me, and there was light.

(William goes on to explain that his captain, Captain Crosstree whose life he has saved in action, has promised to write to the Admiralty to get his discharge. However when Crosstree himself catches sight of Susan he too falls for her.)

> *Captain:* The wife of a sailor! wife of a common seaman! why, she's fit for an admiral. I know it is wrong, but I will see her again – and, come what may, I must and will have her.

(The plot thickens! Then it is unthickened when the coastguards arrest Tom Hatchet, the smuggler, leaving the captain to make his play that evening with Susan, who calls out for William.)

William: Susan, and attacked by the buccaneers – die! *(Strikes at the captain, whose back is turned towards him; he falls.)*

Captain: I deserve my fate.

All: The captain!

(Tableau! The curtain falls on Act Two. In the last act there is a court-martial. The captain is delirious with his wound and William will not call Susan to witness that she was being pestered by the captain. William is, of course, found guilty and sentenced to hang. At the last minute in staggers Captain Crosstree holding a letter from the Admiralty relating to William's discharge.)

Captain: ...'Tis here, dated back: when William struck me he was not the king's sailor – I was not his officer.

Admiral: *(perusing letter)* He is free!

But just how original is Jerrold's work? To me, there seems to be distinct likeness to J.C. Cross's *The False Friend; or, The Assassin of the Rocks,* staged at the Surrey on 7 September 1806. Compare the opening speech of Tom Hatchet, quoted above, with this from Cross:

Fitzhugh: Well said, old Rapine, don't you think me right!
I've master's orders here, in black and white,
And if her pride and haughtiness endures,
I'll turn the wheedling vixen out of doors.
Her daughter I've lov'd long and now am bent
That they shall starve, if they refuse consent.

A scroll is displayed, reading 'Mandeville orders Fitzhugh, if the Widow Wantley's Rent is not immediately paid, to distrain her goods'. The hero is William 'Billy' Surge, a sailor. He is put on trial for murdering his officer and disposing of the body. At the last minute the officer staggers on, wounded, and accuses Mandeville of attempting to murder him. Billy is freed, and marries the girl. True, the style is different; indeed, it shows how much the theatres' grip on dialogue had slackened in the intervening years. Nonetheless there is a marked similarity.

Erroll Sherson in his *London's Lost Theatres of the Nineteenth Century* gives a splendid example of the way incongruous items were dragged into performances to suit the particular talents of the leading actors and actresses. He recounts how the singer John Braham was at the Surrey in 1829,

> playing Henry Bertram in *Guy Mannering.* In the second act, Bertram is on a lonely heath in a wild part of Scotland, a storm of rain and lightning is in progress and he is very depressed at having lost his way. Turning to the wings, he sees a piano and a music stool! He exclaims:
>
> > Ha! What do I see on this lonely heath? A Piano? Who could be lonely with that? The moon will shortly rise and light me from this unhallowed place; so to console myself, I will sing one of Julia's favourite melodies.
>
> Sitting down to the piano, in the middle of the thunderstorm, he proceeds to sing, 'Is there a heart that never loved?'

I have been unable to find the corresponding playbill. At the Surrey 1829 was the year of the introduction of *Black-Eyed Susan*, which ran and ran, but Elliston did manage to fit in two productions of *Guy Mannering,* one with Foster and Mrs Waylett as Henry and Lucy Bertram, the other with Benson and Miss Somerville. There were also productions in 1828 with Benson and Miss Graddon and in 1830 with Hunt and Miss Somerville, but no trace of Braham anywhere. Indeed, when one looks at the Surrey playbill for 24 June 1839 one finds Braham appearing as Count Belino in *Devil's Bridge,* the opera written by Braham himself in conjunction with Charles E. Horn, and being announced as his 'first appearance in this Theatre'.

However, it does not really matter if Sherson is wrong about the date or the theatre or the opera, or all three– it's a good story and only too true in general terms. Even today, Sherson is in good company. For some years up to at least 1991 the Old Vic programmes contained a short history including the sentence, 'Its renaming as the Royal Victoria Theatre in 1833 prompted the young princess [Victoria] to come and see the famous actor Guy Mannering'. In the famous play *John Braham*, no doubt!

Also in 1829 Elliston was challenged by the Adelphi management when he attempted to stage Fitzball's *Flying Dutchman; or, The Spectral Ship* which had already been advertised for the Adelphi, where T.P. Cooke was engaged to appear. The Adelphi took legal action against this 'contemptible and unprincipled infringement of private property' (as Elliston had said about the Coburg's *Black-Eyed Susan; or, the Lover's Perils).* The Surrey playbills 'respectfully informed' the public on 7 October 1829 that

> in consequence of an application made by Messrs. MATHEWS, YATES and CUMBERLAND, to the MASTER OF THE ROLLS (who is at Brighton) they have succeeded at present in obtaining an INJUNCTION against the performance of THE FLYING DUTCHMAN at the Surrey Theatre. The Order having been served in the middle of this day, the Proprietor had no means of seeing HIS HONOR in time, to state his reasons.

Whatever legal activity Elliston set in motion behind the scenes, there is no doubt what he did before the scenery: he commissioned Jerrold to write a new play, *The Flying Dutchman; or, The Phantom Ship,* to be staged on 15 October. There must have been tremendous efforts to write, rehearse and stage this in a week – quite unnecessarily, as it turned out. As the Surrey bills for 16 October smugly announced:

> Injunction Refused! by the Master of the Rolls. A Mistake having occurred in some of the legal technicalities, necessary to confirm the Order for the Injunction, granted in consequence of the exparte Depositions made by Messrs Yates, Mathews and Cumberland, Mr Elliston found, on his arrival at Brighton, that no Injunction had been issued against his performance of what has been usually called THE ADELPHI FLYING DUTCHMAN.... The Master of the Rolls distinctly stated, as his opinion, that Messrs Yates and Mathews had not the slightest title to the exclusive right of performing Mr Edward Fitzball's Burletta of the FLYING DUTCHMAN.

The 'mistake in the legal technicalities' was fundamental. Apparently Fitzball had sold his work twice, as the Surrey bills of 26 October revealed:

> The Public are respectfully informed that the Proprietor of this Theatre has purchased Mrs JAMESON'S interest in the Copyright of the ADELPHI FLYING DUTCHMAN, as sold to her in Manuscript by Mr BALL in 1827.

At the end of October Elliston then mounted 'Fitzball's *The Old Flying Dutchman; or, The Phantom Ship* (as performed at the Adelphi)' and Jerrold's *New Flying Dutchman; or, The Spectral Ship* in the same week! Fitzball's play was revived many times; Jerrold's *Flying Dutchman* sank without trace.

In January 1830 the Surrey introduced three 'Juvenile Nights', offering the pantomime *A Apple Pie; or, Harlequin's Alphabet* together with T.P. Cooke playing three of his best-known roles in *Black-Eyed Susan, Sally in our Alley* and *The Pilot.* In passing it is worth mentioning that a future manager of the Surrey, Robert Honner, appears in the bills at this time, for example as Harlequin in *A Apple Pie.*

An old stager returned to the chorus-line in 1830, none other than Miss Eliza Vincent who had appeared as a child prodigy five years earlier and who would, with Shepherd in 1848, become lessee of the Surrey. She appeared mainly in opera, a soprano in small supporting parts, and was a Singing Witch in the 1831 *Macbeth.* She threw in her lot with Osbaldiston when he left the Surrey in 1834 and ten years later was in dramatic roles such as Desdemona.

In Elliston's first spell at the Surrey he had introduced dog-drama. He returned to this form of entertainment on 6 July 1827 with a brand-new piece entitled *The Grateful Lion,* starring 'Mr Wood's celebrated dog, "Bruin"'. A re-write of the Androcles story? Another new piece was staged on 1 December 1830, *The Greenwich Pensioner,* whose dog was played by 'Neptune'. Two other such pieces followed, again starring Neptune: Barrymore's *The Dog of Montargis; or, The Forest of Bondy* on 1 February, and *The Dog of the Convent; or, The Adventure on Mont St Bernard,* produced for the first time on Easter Monday, 4 April 1831. The fact that dog-dramas could be commissioned for the Surrey and introduced into a holiday bill shows how popular they were at that time.

By 1831, there was mounting pressure both by the managements of the minor theatres and by the public for the abolition of the privileges of Covent Garden and Drury Lane, especially that of the monopoly of presenting Shakespeare as written. Elliston was aiming as closely as he could to that standard and in quick order mounted *Macbeth, Henry VIII, Hamlet, Richard III* and *Othello* before his death on 8 July 1831. Shortly after that a Parliamentary Committee was set up to consider the situation. On the playbills for 5 January 1832 it was announced that a 'Petition to the House of Commons lies at the Box Office for Signatures' concerning 'a Bill to rescind such Acts as tend to impede... the Minor Theatres'. The Dramatic Performance Bill was introduced and passed the Commons in 1833; it failed in the Lords as it appeared to be an attack on the royal prerogative. Another ten years passed before the minor theatres were set free to present the standard repertory in competition with the former patent houses.

With the death of Robert Elliston his son Charles Robert Elliston, already the nominal proprietor, took command in the middle of the opera season. He let things run as no doubt his father had planned.

One piece put on ten days after the death of Elliston senior was *Black-Eyed Susan* – but with a difference! It appears there had been a bad case of multiple sex changes, so that William was played by Madame Simon (Agnes Kennedy that was) and Susan by Sam Vale, with the rest of the cast similarly affected. As the genuine Susan had already passed her 200th appearance, maybe someone thought that she wanted livening up; but no, the old girl was good for hundreds more performances yet.

D.W. Osbaldiston had been playing lead parts during Robert Elliston's lifetime, and was in several of the longer-running pieces which continued into young Elliston's spell of command. Osbaldiston had accumulated enough experience as an actor to feel confident he could succeed without the Elliston name, and so he offered to buy young Elliston out. When the Christmas season started on Boxing Night 1831 with *Old King Cole; or, Harlequin and the Fiddlers Three* Osbaldiston's name appeared as proprietor. It was not just a change of management. The very nature of pantomime – and opera – was changing.

London 21st Decr 1837

In consideration of the sum of Fifteen pounds which I hereby acknowledge to have received I do hereby assign and sell to George Bolwell Davidge of the Surrey Theatre his Exors Administr & Assigns all my interest right & title to an Opera called the Magic Flute.

And I do hereby agree that the same shall not be performed at any Theatre either in or out of London without the express consent of the said G B Davidge whose sole property it is —

And it is further agreed that the said Opera called the Magic Flute shall not be printed or published without the consent of the said G. B. Davidge —

W. T. Moncrieff

Witness

Lawrence

Davidge-Moncrieff contract for a translation of *The Magic Flute*
(Reproduced by kind permission of London Borough of Lambeth Archives Department)

Chapter Eight

The Changing Nature of Opera, Pantomime and Ballet

Opera, pantomime and ballet as experienced by British audiences in the first thirty or forty years of the nineteenth century developed in form so considerably that the old favourites were consigned to the history books, supplanted by the newcomers.

In the first case, the English ballad-opera with spoken dialogue between numbers gave way to the continental through-composed opera, leaving the odd curiosity such as *The Beggar's Opera* as about the only old-timer capable of holding the stage. Regarding pantomimes, is there anyone living who has seen a harlequinade? Yet it was that on which the original pantomimes were based. As for ballet, it was little more than an interlude while the scenery was being changed. Hence how did these art forms develop at the Surrey, so as to be recognisable today?

There is no indication that managers of the Surrey before 1827 gave any consideration to through-composed operas. It was not the fashion for British composers to write such things and there had been no opera company, particularly south of the river, with singers capable of tackling operas from other countries. Indeed at the Surrey there was little understanding until Elliston's second spell of management as to what might be available from the continent – and this applied to plays as well as opera.

Surrey patrons expected novelty and variety. One way in which Elliston sought to supply these was by increasing the operatic content of the Surrey bill, drawing on German and Italian work to supplement the native ballad-opera. All the same, if I were to say that the Surrey audiences saw *Der Freischutz* by Weber in November 1827 and again on 25 July 1831 and two Rossini operas, *Il Barbiere di Siviglia* on 14 June 1831 and *Là Cenerentola* on 7 November 1831, it would give the wrong impression. The operas did not appear quite as Weber and Rossini envisaged them: and I do not just mean that they were translated into English.

Appearing as the second half of a double bill with *Romeo and Juliet, Der Freischutz* was announced as 'a compilation from the published dramas upon this subject from the Pens of Messrs [Fitz]Ball, Soane and W. McGregor Logan, assisted by a Manuscript presented by Mr Phillips'.

Many characters acquired new names: the chief of these, Max and Agathe, become Rodolph and Linda; Aennchen becomes Rose. The forces of darkness are increased, for as well as Zamiel there is a Witch of the Glen (or in the 1831 production, Serpent Charmer and Fire Fiend). There is no doubt about the strong musical forces employed as these are listed in the playbills: eight violins, two tenors (that is, violas), five 'bassos', two oboes, two flutes, two clarinets, two bassoons, four 'cornis', two trumpets, three trombones and 'two on drums'. So it might have passed for the real thing. More importantly, it gave Surrey audiences the terrors of the 'Wolf's Glen' music, which made that associated with Purcell's and Shakespeare's witches seem tame.

There may have been an attempt with *Der Freischutz* to get close to the composer's intentions but *Cinderella* in 1831 was tackled differently. Here we have a piece 'written expressly for this Theatre' with the 'Whole of the Music selected from the Works of Rossini including the Grand Overture to *La Cenerentola*', but apart from Cinderella herself every other character's name has been altered, and opening and closing scenes involving Oberon and Titania have been added. Rossini, who had to alter Cinderella's slipper to a bracelet because the Italian censor would not permit a lady's ankle to be exposed on the stage, might have been pleased that the Surrey reverted to a 'little glass slipper' but there would not be much else to give him satisfaction. In fact the impression given by the playbill is that this was an English pantomime to which Rossini's music had been added in ballad-opera style; there is no sensing that this was a through-composed opera as Rossini left it. But as it notched up thirty-five performances in this form it must count as a success. On one evening it was coupled with the German lyric opera *The Nightingale and the Raven* by Weigl, so the customers were beginning to realise that the continent might have music to their taste.

The Barber of Seville received slightly more respectful treatment. The characters in the main retain Rossinian names: Count Almaviva is sung by Mr Hunt of the Theatre Royal Covent Garden and the English Opera company; Figaro is sung by Mr Latham of the Theatre Royal Drury Lane; and Rosina by Miss Somerville, the Agathe/Linda of the 1831 *Der Freischutz* and the Cinderella, which indicates that again a Rossinian contralto heroine has been supplanted by a soprano. Messrs Williams and Ransford take Dr Bartolo and Don Basilio respectively. When one tries to match up the vocal music as shown in the playbills with the libretto, it appears that the principals do not sing all of their music and the rest of the cast do not sing except perhaps as the chorus. Don Basilio's 'La calumnia' is missing and Berta/Marcellina's aria 'Il vecchiotto cerca moglie' appears in Rosina's mouth as 'An old man would be wooing'. The 'Buona Sera' quintet is missing. To make up for these losses, in act two Count Almaviva is given an aria 'Let Fame sound the Trumpet' which was actually written by William Shield and first heard at the Surrey several years before Rossini wrote his opera. If, therefore, the rest of the cast do not sing, I think we can assume that a through-composed opera has again been put into the form then acceptable to Surrey audiences, namely that of a ballad-opera, though admittedly with the same story line.

Other continental imports at this time were *The Swiss Family; or, Home! sweet Home!* and *Sylvana*, on 28 June and 2 September 1828 respectively. The music of *The Swiss Family,* as with *The Nightingale and the Raven,* was by 'Herr Weigl, Capel Meister to his Imperial Majesty the Emperor of Austria'. But now the Surrey demonstrated a novel way of producing opera. Elliston had engaged the child prodigy, Master Burke, in various dramatic and comic roles, and realised he could use the boy's musical talent in operatic productions. He set about finding other child prodigies,or at least singers who could pass for children; they would then perform on a set scaled down to their size. One of his other 'child prodigies' went on to scale the heights. In *The Swiss Family* the part of Emmelina was played by a Miss Coveney. This has to be Jane Coveney (at the age of four and a half!). She was also in *Die Nachtigal* which had at least forty-one performances, while her mother Sophia Elizabeth Coveney was appearing in opera by the main company at much the same time. The third offering by the Juvenile Company was Arne's *Artaxerxes* on 16 September 1828, though the presence of Miss Somerville in the cast suggests that the 'juveniles' had been somewhat strengthened.

In December 1832 when the juvenile opera was revived, Jane Coveney sang in Weber's *Oberon* and in a revival of the quasi-Rossini *Cinderella.* Both Jane and her younger sister Harriet can be found in Surrey productions twenty-five years later and were still going strong many years after that. Another child in *The Swiss Family* and *Artaxerxes* to reappear at the Surrey in adult roles was Miss Matley. In the juvenile opera she sang the Countess in Mozart's *Marriage of Figaro* in December 1833, with Jane Coveney as Susanna and Miss Vincent as Cherubino.

To bring these operatic adventures into new territory Elliston needed someone whose knowledge and experience went far beyond his own. He was well-rewarded in his choice of Jonathan Blewitt as Musical Director. This was a man who had studied with Haydn and was considered the foremost music teacher in Dublin, where he spent his early life. At the Surrey he set about providing a bridge between British and continental styles with a mix of balladised imports and his own compositions in the traditional form. He wrote the operatic romance *The Talisman* based on Sir Walter Scott's novel and produced it in April 1828. In May 1828 his operetta *Auld Robin Grey,* written in conjunction with Alexander Lee, was premiered. In September it was *Mischief-Making,* and in October *The Heart of Midlothian* (not to be confused with Bishop's 1819 version). As if all this were not enough, Blewitt also held the post of musical director at Sadler's Wells for part of this time.

Having sampled German and Italian opera the Surrey had a look at a different repertoire. On 2 December 1828 the bills announced 'a new musical piece founded on French Operetta *La Vieille*... with the original music of Mons. Fétis under the title of *Love in Wrinkles; or, My Old Woman'.* This reached the stage in January 1829. Francois Fétis in fact considered himself a citizen of Belgium, then part of Holland, rather than French. For the true French sound one has to wait until 11 February 1832 when *Abou-Ali-Ben-Aliki* received its first hearing in this country at the Surrey. It was based on *Le Calife de Bagdad* by 'the French Mozart', Boieldieu, and adapted by Barham Livius (one of the courtesan Harriette Wilson's little friends).

Elliston's operatic offerings by other composers included Shield's *Rosina,* presented in the July of 1827. This can still hold the stage today (at infrequent intervals) and is obtainable on records. In November Elliston staged *The Slave* and in the next year Planché's *Clari,* both operas set by Bishop. These have disappeared from view, but one tune from *Clari* is still to be heard – 'Home, Sweet Home'.

There followed a quartet of pasticcios: *The Haunted Tower* by Storace and others, Isaac Bickerstaff's *Maid of the Mill* set by Samuel Arnold, *Love in a Village* by Thomas Arne (and no less than sixteen other composers) and Storace's *No Song, No Supper.* Although revivals of *The Apprentice's Opera, Love in a Village* and *The Slave* managed to squeeze in whenever T.P. Cooke took a breather, there was not much room in 1829 for opera as Cooke and *Black-Eyed Susan* swept all before them. Music for the latter was composed and arranged by the Surrey's expert Jonathan Blewitt, a copy of whose score, inscribed to Elliston with good wishes, resides appropriately in the National Maritime Museum.

On 11 February 1830 there was the first performance of a setting by Blewitt of Moncrieff's *Van Dieman's Land.* This was not entirely Blewitt's own work but a pasticcio taking material from at least ten other composers. The libretto had been written for the occasion: two of Elliston's children were emigrating to Tasmania, as Van Dieman's Land is now called. There were also revivals of *The Barber of Saville, Der Freischutz, The Slave,* Braham's *English Fleet in 1342* and Michael Kelly's *Forty Thieves.*

In 1831 were produced all of the following: Arnold's *Castle of Andalusia, The Beggar's Opera* yet again, Pocock's *Miller and his Men* with music by Bishop, *Robin Hood; or, Sherwood Forest* (a pasticcio by Shield and others), *The Slave* by Bishop, *The Siege of Belgrade* (a pasticcio by Storace and others). There were also *Fontainebleau; or, Our Way in France*, a pasticcio put together by Shield in 1784 and already seen by Surrey audiences in 1811 as *John Bull in France;* and *The Waterman* by Charles Dibdin. As well as its hit tune 'Then farewell, my trim-built Wherry' the latter included the song 'Let Fame sound the Trumpet' which had been heard a month earlier interposed in *The Barber of Seville.*

If there are doubts as to whether these musical patch-work quilts constitute operas, one might ask whether there are definitive versions of *Boris Godounov* or *Don Carlos?* Is not *Turandot* to some extent stitched? The process is still going on today, for example *The Deluded Bridegroom* from Mozartian fragments (1956) and *Christopher Columbus* from the lesser-known work of Offenbach (1976). Nobody seems to mind.

Other offerings in Elliston's time were *Midas* by Bishop with Mrs Alexander Gibbs as Apollo and, surprisingly, the clarinettist Tully as Mars; perhaps he worked up to the part from playing First Archer in *Robin Hood; or, Sherwood Forest.* Before her marriage Mrs Gibbs was the Miss Graddon who sang Agathe/Linda in the1827 *Freischutz.* Then followed *The Savoyarde,* an operatic vaudeville by J.M. Jolly, and finally *Ivanhoe* – probably a revival of Sanderson's burletta first produced at the Surrey in January 1820, rather than Parry's version premiered at Covent Garden in March 1820.

This flowering of opera at the Surrey, albeit still mainly ballad-opera, was blighted but not killed by the death of Robert Elliston in the summer of 1831. He was succeeded by his son, Charles Robert Elliston, who took over in the middle of the opera season. Alhough no doubt long prepared for by his father, Charles Robert takes nominal credit for *The Exile, The Siege of Belgrade, The Devil's Bridge, Der Freischutz, The Waterman, The Beggar's Opera, Fontainebleau* and *Midas* – which shows that operatic taste still favoured the home-grown product.

Two names of significance can be found in Elliston's orchestra. Erskine, principal violin, had been with the Surrey ten years earlier in Thomas Dibdin's time and was himself a composer, having provided the mood-music for such melodramas as *The Two Farmers* and *Trenk the Pandour* in 1823. Tully, the clarinettist who had played Mars in *Midas,* also made his name as a composer. Later, on 31 May 1847, the Surrey playbills announced that Mr J.H. Tully, conductor at the Theatre Royal, Drury Lane, would preside in the orchestra for the first night of a new

English ballad-opera entitled *The Forest Maiden and the Moorish Page,* composed by himself.

Osbaldiston did little to further the cause of opera at the Surrey in his short period of management (1832-34). One looks to Osbaldiston's successor Davidge with his second wife Frances to bring through-composed opera to the Obelisk. Not immediately, however: Davidge had the problem that there were few singers in his company able to tackle the continental style of singing. So from September 1834, in his first year at the Surrey it looks as if he picked up where Elliston left off, putting on *Rob Roy, Love in a Village, Lord of the Isles* (a world première), *The Shipwreck, Robin Hood and Little John, The Beggar's Opera, The Exile, The English Fleet in 1342, The Heart of Midlothian, The Waterman, My Spouse and I, The Slave, The Castle of Andalusia, Peg of the Petticoats,* and *The Haunted Head* (another world première for the Surrey).

In our days only *The Beggar's Opera* would be recognised by the opera-going public. It might be thought that the others were merely Surrey pot-boilers run up for the occasion, with little intrinsic merit and no claim on posterity. It is thus necessary to emphasise that of the fifteen named, six were premiered at Covent Garden, two at Drury Lane and two at the Haymarket. Two others were Surrey 'firsts'. We are in fact looking at a selection of the most popular operas of the time, which only goes to show how foreign, and particularly Italian, opera was to submerge the native product in a year or two. One can also get the first surprising hint that where opera was concerned, the Surrey might not be far behind Covent Garden and Drury Lane!

As for Elliston's earlier experiments in balladising imported works, Davidge recognised that this was not the right way forward even though the singers available, not having been trained in the bel canto tradition, were as yet unable to tackle continental opera's long-breathed line and coloratura. As *The Satirist* wrote in November 1835: 'Italian music may be instrumented in this country, but it cannot be sung. It is not composed for English throats. It is too liquid – nature formed us for something more substantial'.

Equally, Surrey audiences would not – and never would – stand for foreign languages. A series of agreements was put together by Davidge for translations into English by the top writers. He commissioned a new translation of Rossini's *La Cenerentola* by Rophino Lacy and of Auber's *Cheval du Bronze* by J.T. Haines, and in particular, of Donizetti's *L'Elisir d'Amore* which received its first performance in English on the Surrey stage; this was translated by T.H. Reynoldson who also sang the role of Sergeant Belcore.

Mozart's *Die Zauberflöte* had been heard earlier, for example in 1833 at Covent Garden, but a new translation was requested for the Surrey from W.T. Moncrieff. Davidge used this as a bargaining point with Alfred Bunn of Drury Lane (a good friend of his). As a result a further version of *The Magic Flute* by James Robinson Planché received its first performance at Drury Lane on 10 March 1838, with a Papageno sung by Michael Balfe (later composer of *The Bohemian Girl* and other operas, but then more concerned with his career as a baritone). In return, Bunn lent Balfe to the Surrey to sing Doctor Dulcamara in the English version of *L'Elisir d'Amore*. Edward Fitzball would have it differently. He wrote in his memoirs: 'Macfarren dramatised the Zauberflote for the Surrey and they brought it out with unusual splendour, but it did not succeed'. With hesitation I would say that Fitzball had misremembered. The agreement with Moncrieff (not Macfarren) is held at the Minet Library. Neither the British Library catalogue nor Allardyce Nicoll's hand-List shows any *Magic Flute* entry for Macfarren, and I can trace neither playbill nor advertisement for a *Magic Flute* at the Surrey. I say 'with hesitation' as I sympathise with Fitzball's other sentiments:

> It is a bad story, work it into whatever form you may. I have seen it since performed at the Theatre Royal Drury Lane... during Mr Bunn's management, got up accurately, as regards music and superb mounting; but I doubt if it ever paid its expenses. Formerly the literary merits of a libretto were thought of very little consequence, but a happy change has come over the spirit of the dreams of composers, and the first inquiry of a manager is also now whether it be 'a good book'. Our most popular operas are unquestionably excellent books, although Davison [the music critic of *The Times*] declares that Balfe could make an opera out of an act of parliament.

All this activity meant that Davidge had to build up an operatic company from very little. Edwin and Ransford could carry the male leads, and Davidge himself played and sang in two operatic pieces, Bailie Nicol Jarvie in *Rob Roy* and Justice Woodcock in *Love in a Village*. Some of the smaller female parts were filled by 'family': my great-great-grandmother Mrs Harriet Henrietta Pearce, who had taken small parts with Davidge at the New City Theatre in 1832, and her daughters – Frances, who as Miss Frances had similarly taken small parts with Osbaldiston at the Surrey in 1833 and who later would be Davidge's second wife, Emily my great-grandmother, and the twins, Louisa and Maria. Under Davidge at the Surrey they adopted the stage name of Parker. But they were no prima donnas. To fill this gap Davidge's first choice was Miss Somerville, who sang the leading roles in *The Exile, The Castle of Andalusia* and *The Forty Thieves* –and then left to marry Alfred Bunn. Davidge did well to obtain the services of Miss Emma Romer, who recruited a specifically operatic company for him. She had learned her trade at Covent Garden and had first set foot on a south bank stage at the Victoria (formerly Coburg) in 1833 during the disastrous management of Abbott and Egerton. Miss Romer was to lead opera at the Surrey for the next twenty years. Even though she became Mrs Charles Almond shortly after being taken on she kept her maiden name in the bills.

Davidge's next opera season ran for two months. The English ballad-operas were balanced with the well-known adaptations of *Der Freischutz* and *La Cenerentola,* and an 'entirely new German opera, entitled *Hate and Love; or, The Exile of Genoa,* founded on *Das Fischermadchen* by Theodore Korner'. Actually Korner only wrote the libretto; the music was by Johann Philipp Schmidt, who composed it in 1818. It received at least ten performances at the Surrey in 1836. Also new was an English version of Auber's *Cheval du Bronze.* It was reported thus in *The Times* on 13 January 1836:

> The second novelty was an adaptation of the Bronze Horse by Mr Haines who has been particularly successful at this and other theatres. The piece was preceded by the original overture and contained the most favourite melodies from the original score of Auber. The plot is somewhat varied from the opera of the same name at the patent theatres but is not the less dramatic from the alterations.... The experiment has, however, been completely successful....

The Satirist was more pointed in its comparisons with the patent theatres:

> We are in doubt whether this is not the best version yet produced; of a certainty, it is the easiest to sit out; it is more amusing than that at Covent Garden, and we are spared the misery of hearing Auber's fine music thrown away upon insipid nonsense, which we are forced to endure at Drury Lane.

The Age had other favourites:

> Miss Mary Atkinson has made her appearance at the Surrey in Weber's opera *Der Freischutz.* Her reception was of the most flattering description and her singing gave universal satisfaction. She will prove a valuable acquisition to this theatre.

The great years of opera at the Surrey Theatre were off to a good start.

For the 1839 season Alfred Bunn again lent Michael Balfe to the Surrey, to sing Count Rudolph in the English version of Bellini's *La Sonnambula.* He also sang his old role of Dulcamara in Donizetti's *Love Spell,* as the English version of *L'Elisir d'Amore* was called. But Balfe the baritone was also Balfe the composer. The Surrey produced his *Maid of Artois* on 20 May. Thereafter a third component joined the old ballad-operas and the continental imports in Surrey opera-seasons, namely the new operas of Balfe such as *The Bohemian Girl* and of Wallace such as *Maritana.* These still get a hearing today.

By the end of Mrs Davidge's management in 1848, the Surrey had added to its regular repertoire *Fra Diavolo* (Auber), *Lucia di Lammermoor* and *La Figlia del Reggimento* (Donizetti) and *Queen for a Day* (Adam). As far as one can tell they were performed as written, not balladised, and an opera season could go on for five months with hardly a ballad-opera to be heard. The change-over was complete.

Pantomime, at the start of this story in 1806, had its 'Dark Opening' as already described, then a short prelude of one or two scenes, often with a fairy tale or ballad as its basis. This led to the transformation scene, followed by the Harlequinade, largely without words, which comprised the bulk of the evening's entertainment. Harlequin was the main character; Clown was not essential and was often omitted, the humour being supplied by Punch or Pierrot. By 1856 the pattern was completely changed. I now summarise how this happened at the Surrey.

'Joey' Grimaldi set this change in motion with *Mother Goose* at Covent Garden in 1806. It has to be remembered that there was only one Grimaldi and there were many theatres. It was a long time before Clown displaced Harlequin in every pantomime in every theatre. It took nearly thirty years for the Surrey to adapt to the Grimaldi style. It took a further twenty years to make the adjustments to what would be recognisable as a modern pantomime.

Even after Grimaldi himself brought *Mother Goose* to the Surrey in 1822 the theatre was unable to engage a suitable clown for each pantomime. When Joey retired in 1824 his son, J.S. Grimaldi, tried to present himself as his father's true successor; but, firstly, he just did not have the skill, and secondly, he did not have the application and swiftly went downhill. He was engaged by the Surrey on three occasions in 1828 and 1829. He could not sustain a full pantomime and so appeared only in odd scenes taken from his father's best shows.

The Surrey's next attempt to find a regular clown was to accept two pantomimes written and produced by the idiosyncratic Dicky Usher, the cat-handler from Drury Lane. He would probably be prosecuted by the RSPCA these days. As given on the playbills for *Clown's Trip to the Moon* on 11 May 1829 he would make an 'Aquatic Excursion, in triumph, like Neptune in his car, (on the Thames) drawn by his four favourite Geese, then proceed... on the High Road from Waterloo Bridge, drawn by his Four Thorough-Bred Mousers...'. During the course of his show Usher would 'mount his vehicle and drive his favourite Cats, 4 in hand, several times round the stage'. No doubt this ensured full houses for the novelty of it all, but it is clear that his act could seldom be incorporated into any meaningful story line (what could the others in the cast do while he was so engaged?) and he was not invited back to the Surrey again.

In July 1832 the pantomime *The Elfie's Son; or, Harlequin and the Magic Horn* was staged with Clown played by Tom Matthews, looked on by many as Grimaldi's successor. To support this belief he used to sing Grimaldi's songs 'Tippitywitchet' and 'Hot Codlins'. About Matthews Sherson wrote:

> His speciality was the singing of 'Hot Codlins', always demanded and redemanded by the gallery. This was considered a very broad not to say shocking song, but it was only a very vulgar duet between the singer and the big drum which would come in at the end of a line with a bang to supply the place of what was thought to be a 'naughty' word! I append the words for the information of those curious in such matters; we are not so easily shocked now!

Sherson was writing in 1925. Sixty-odd years later the words hardly seem funny though, of course, so much would depend on the singer. I thus only quote one verse:

> A little old woman her living she got
> By selling codlins, hot, hot, hot;
> And this little old woman who codlins sold,
> Tho' her codlins were hot, she felt herself cold;
> So to keep herself warm, she thought it no sin
> To fetch for herself a quartern of... (Bang, Bang).

Although a Grimaldi pantomime had in many respects moved away from the pantomime of Rich, the founding father in the eighteenth century, in the 1830s they were still alike in being an entertainment aimed at an adult audience. Many a critic referred to these adults as 'children of larger growth'.

Tom Matthews had been but a guest artiste. Though he paid a visit to the Surrey in 1848 in *Harlequin Lord Lovell,* and again in 1849 with a revival of *Mother Goose,* the Surrey still had no regular clown. Indeed the Surrey was not keeping or engaging a regular pantomime team. There might be a new combination each year. Tricks with machinery were supplanting the split-second timing of the old practitioners.

A further change can be seen by 1836. Henceforth pantomime became a Christmas entertainment, and Easter, Whitsun and August pantomimes were seldom staged. By 1848 when the Surrey staged *Cinderella and the Fairy Queen; or, Harlequin and the Little Glass Slipper,* the Prince was played by Miss Daly. The day of the female 'Principal Boy' had arrived. The Surrey pantomime for Christmas 1856 was *Harlequin and the Summer Queen; or, King Winter and the Fairies of the Silver Willows.* This signalled another major change in the nature of the art, although the critic of *The Times* was too close to events to appreciate it. He describes the 'opening':

> It is magnificently put upon the stage, under the sole superintendence of Mr Shepherd. The introduction is from the pen of Mr Stocqueler, and founded upon Mr T. Oxenford's song 'The Genius of Spring'.... His frigid Majesty (Mr Vollaire), though in his dotage, is deeply in love with the Queen of the Summer (Miss Ellis) who is betrothed to Prince Snowdrop, the Genius of the Spring (Miss A. Biddles).... The scenes which perhaps surpassed all the rest in dazzling splendour were the reception room in the golden palace of King Sol (Mr Yarnold) in which Queen Blaza Flara (Mr Tappin) and her effulgent progeny disport themselves.
>
> Mr Buck as Clown, Mr Bradbury as Pantaloon, Madamoiselles Agnes and Marie as Columbines and Mr Glover as Harlequin continued by their spirited acting to keep the house in a roar and the curtain fell amid thunders of applause.

The first point to note is that the 'opening' is now completely detached from the Harlequinade, in that no-one in the first part has a place in the second, and vice versa. There is no transformation. The second point is that the 'opening' now has a pantomime dame, Mr Tappin, *and* a 'Principal Boy' in Adelaide Biddles. True, there had been pantomime dames ever since *Mother Goose* in 1806, and a Principal Boy since 1848, but this piece brought them together for the first time at the Surrey. All it now needs is for the Harlequinade to be dropped entirely, or its characters absorbed into the opening, perhaps as 'Broker's Men' – and one has a modern pantomime, and the connection with Rich and Grimaldi, Jemmy Barnes and Sophia Parker, is gone.

Dance of one form or another had of course always been a part of the Surrey fare, either by itself or as part of some other entertainment. For example the nautical dramas usually included a hornpipe, even a hornpipe in fetters, but one could hardly argue that that was ballet. Not even when the Surrey put on Edward Stirling's 'nautical burletta' *Blue Jackets! or, Her Majesty's Service* in March 1839, which featured twelve female Able Seamen who danced a 'hornpipe of 12 with Pike and Cutlass Exercise', could one say that it was in the nature of ballet; it sounds more like a tap-dancing chorus of twentieth-century musical comedy.

Reference books suggest that one source of ballet in this country was via pantomime. Certainly old prints of Grimaldi's usual Columbine, Mrs Sophia Parker, make her look just as we would expect a prima ballerina to look. Similarly, Harlequin has a balletic component in his appearances. Most managements employed a ballet master whose job was not merely to train those members of the regular company who were required to dance but also to create new works to be performed as interludes, perhaps while other members of the company changed costume between acts. Usually the ballet master also performed the leading role in these interludes, so he would be responsible for story line, choreography, casting *and* performance. Thus in May 1808 in Cross's time we see Giroux arranging the dances for *The Farmer's Boy; or, Harlequin Zodiack,* with one of his daughters taking the role of Columbine. Giroux leaves the Surrey for a while but is back in 1819 for Thomas Dibdin with *Heads and Blockheads,* and again in the 1827/28 season with a variety of pieces for Elliston such as *The Birth Day,* and *The Young Queen on her Travels.* It is difficult to assess the merit of these pieces or their impact on the audience in these early days. Firstly, they were seldom reviewed by the critics, who would concentrate on the play given at the full price; secondly, the song and dance items between the main events would suffer a degree of disruption with the entry of the half-price customers and the intrusion of pot-boys and fruit sellers.

As with Giroux, so with Ridgway in the 1820s – pantomime was the basis of his dance. He started by reworking Thomas Dibdin's *The Poet's*

Last Shilling in May 1821, playing Harlequin himself (and finding parts for his two sons), with Miss Adcock, described as Principal Dancer, as Columbine. He also 'composed and got up' several ballets (such as *Juan Fernandez; or, The Island Ape* and *The Old Commodore; or, Cross Purposes,* both in 1825) which, although independent of pantomime proper, had a large knock-about content. For a more stylish form of ballet Charles Dibdin the Younger employed 'Mons. Simon, from Paris' whose first effort at the Surrey did not go quite according to plan. This was *L'Amour En Corset; or, The Dandy in Distress* with Simon as the elderly gentleman and Miss Louisa Fairbrother as the young beauty – it is not difficult to guess the plot! It was first staged on 16 May 1825 and stayed in the bills for months. It had a new name on 18 July, *La Jambe de Bois; or, The Old Dandy in Distress.* Why the wooden leg? Mons. Simon had had to rework his ballet, the bills stating that he had 'dislocated his Ancle'. By October he was back on two feet (see p.45).

It was in Charles Dibdin's time that there is the first trace of a ballet 'company' at the Surrey, and then it is only Mrs Searle's company of juveniles. They were followed by Monsieur Hullin and his pupils with *Cendrillon; or, The Little Glass Slipper* 'as they Performed it at the Theatre Porte St Martin in Paris'. Hullin's company consisted of more than thirty juveniles. Cupid was played by 'Mademoiselle Angelina Worgman' and Cendrillon (Cinderella to British audiences) by 'Mademoiselle Mélanie Duval', supposedly aged five and six years respectively. Another ballet in the infant repertoire was D'Auberval's *La Fille Mal Gardée.*

There was not much ballet at the Surrey in Osbaldiston's time. However, the next manager, Davidge, had the idea of putting on a full-length ballet (or something like it) when he bought from John Dalrymple the rights in 'an Operatic & Fairy Ballet' entitled *Gian Ben Gian; or, The Loadstone of the Earth* which was staged on 27 March 1837. The cast is almost entirely composed of actors rather than dancers, so the piece may have been closer to pantomime than ballet.

The first Surrey production of a ballet standing by itself with adult performers, independent of play, opera or pantomime, was probably in April 1840 when *La Sylphide* was presented (seventy years before Fokine put together *Les Sylphides).* The persons named do not appear again and I think cannot be regarded as a resident company. Similarly, 'a Favourite Ballet' *Le Pont Neuf* was staged on 17 December 1840, again with outsiders. Another visiting company came in June 1842, 'Monsieur Lebarre and Madlle. Cromini of Her Majesty's Theatre', bringing excerpts from *Giselle* and other ballets to the Surrey under Honner.

During the remainder of Honner's management in the 1840s he was to present a number of further ballets. The three principal dancers from the ballets of February and April 1843 appeared again in December in excerpts from the ballet sequence of Auber's *La Bayadère* in which they were joined by two guest artistes, Signor Milano and his wife Thérèse Cushnie. These two had been trained by Mrs Conquest senior, a famous dancer in her day who also supplied the Surrey with dancers such as Herr Deulin and Dickie Flexmore: but more of them in due course. Also in December 1843 Harvey produced another full-length ballet, *Polichinel in Italy*. Polichinel was a 'Mr Punch' figure; his adventures had been featured in other pieces, though they were more like pantomime than ballet.

No other full-length ballet was presented until February 1845, when 'a new Ballet Divertisement Introducing the Entire Strength of the Pantomime Company' and called *The Gnome of the Red Rich Mountain* was announced. The playbills continue: 'The action of the Ballet arranged by Mr T. Ridgway; The Dances composed by Mr W.H. Harvey'. Both these gentlemen performed together with four other principals, probably for seven nights – one cannot always be certain that what the bills promise will actually happen. In the following week, another 'Ballet Divertisement', *La Fête de Terpsichore,* was offered to the customers. I cannot find any later trace of Harvey and his team. For a while in the later 1840s ballet at the Surrey was provided by visiting companies.

But this genre record gets me ahead of my chronology.

Chapter Nine

Osbaldiston as Playwright

In an earlier chapter we saw David Webster Osbaldiston as Elliston's leading actor and later he will appear as manager of the Surrey. There is another aspect of his talent which runs through both periods and, indeed, continues after he left the Surrey – Osbaldiston as playwright. He receives no mention in the first and second editions of Allardyce Nicoll's *History of Nineteenth-Century Drama,* but creeps into the Supplement to Volume 4 with four plays to his name. Giving them their full titles and putting them in date order of production these are: *The Brigand; or, La Compagna di Villa Rosa* at the Surrey on 14 September 1829; *Vive La Liberté; or, The French Revolution of 1830,* Surrey 14 August 1830; *Baron Trenck; or, The Fortress of Magdebourg,* Surrey 11 October 1830; and *Naomie; or, The Peasant Girl's Dream,* which was produced at one of his later ventures, the City of London Theatre, on 28 June 1838 with Miss Eliza Vincent taking the name part.

The British Library catalogue has only one entry for Osbaldiston: *Catherine of Russia; Or, The Child of the Storm,* published in 1850.

Three more can be traced from an announcement in the Surrey playbills for 31 December 1833 when Osbaldiston addressed managers of other theatres, inviting them to make bids for plays whose copyright he owned. Five of his own composition are included in a list of twelve. In addition to *The Brigand* and *Baron Trenck* identified by Nicoll, there are: *Montralto; or, The Mountain Pass,* produced at the Surrey on 8 August 1829; *The Felon of New York,* Surrey, 24 August 1833; and *Fra Diavolo,* based on Auber's opera, first produced at the Surrey on 4 March 1833 with the title *The Devil's Brother; or, The Inn at Terracina,* but changing its name to *Fra Diavolo* from the third performance onwards.

One can add another four by looking at the custom of playwrights not to identify themselves until they are sure that their new work is a success; so a first production will often be described as '*X*, by the Author of *Y* and *Z*'. So we have *The Twin Brothers; or, Pride and Patience* at the Surrey on 1 February 1830 'by the Author of *The Brigand, Montralto,* etc.' Then, in like fashion, *Valley of Wolves* on 20 September 1830 and *Bertram, The Pirate of the Isles,* based on the Rev. R.C. Maturin's play *Bertram; or, The Castle of St Aldrobrand.* Osbaldiston's version of *Bertram* had its second performance on 18 October 1830 but I cannot trace its first. Lastly in this group is *The Returned Pirate; or, The Farmer's Daughter of the Severn Side,* with music by Blewitt, on 12 August 1833.

I have not searched for Osbaldiston's work at the other theatres he managed after he left the Surrey, namely Covent Garden, Sadler's Wells, City of London and the Victoria, though there is a reference to his work in a biography of Frederick Fox Cooper, *Nothing Extenuate:* on 11 February 1839, *The Figaro* alleged that 'Mr Osbaldiston had pirated the title and plot of a piece mentioned in confidence to him' by Fox Cooper. This had been advertised at the City of London Theatre as *King Death,* 'a spectacle from the quill of the manager, Mr Osbaldiston'.

Allardyce Nicoll provides a degree of confirmation in the 'Unknown Authors' section of his work, recording that when *The Felon of New York* was given at Sadler's Wells in 1836 it was said to be by the author of *The Brigand, Baron Trenck, The Returned Pirate* and *The Twin Brothers.* There are thus ten plays of his at the Surrey over a four year period with another two at the City of London Theatre five years later, plus *Catherine the Great* published in 1850. I have a feeling that there are more to be found after he had left the Surrey. Quantity aside, what about quality?

Quality in the theatre is a subjective matter, but I have not found a single notice of any of these plays in the press. This should not be taken as adverse criticism in itself. At that time, plays at the Surrey were hardly ever reviewed by critics from over the river – pantomimes, yes, but not melodrama. One has to rely on the views of the man buying his ticket at the box office; so for 'quality' read 'box-office appeal'. There is a danger even in this approach. The obvious difficulty, when one sees that these plays are often coupled with a 'smash hit' such as *Jonathan Bradford,* is whether the theatregoer ever made a conscious decision about the merit of the Osbaldiston pieces.

There is a second problem. In most of these plays Osbaldiston played the lead part – or, in the case of *The Twin Brothers,* both leads. When he was managing the Surrey we have Osbaldiston the playwright writing star parts for Osbaldiston the actor, to be staged by Osbaldiston the manager. Was there ever any second opinion as to the worthiness of the piece?

We do not have this problem while Robert Elliston was still alive. As Fitzball said, he was an excellent judge of the drama. So the number of performances in Elliston's lifetime, about twenty for *The Brigand* and ten each for *Montralto, Vive La Liberté* and *Baron Trenck,* suggests that there was some merit in these pieces. At the other end of the scale, I can only trace one performance of *The Twin Brothers,* which may go to show that even Elliston was fallible. Osbaldiston himself did not bother to advertise the performing rights of *The Twin Brothers, Valley of Wolves* and *Bertram,* so he presumably accepted that they were not salable commodities. He did not advertise *Vive La Liberté* either, probably because it had lost its topicality; it had about a dozen performances in the three weeks when the French Revolution of 1830 was still news, but none thereafter.

Osbaldiston continued to stage *Montralto, The Brigand* and *Baron Trenck* during his own period of management and took them to his later theatres. Of the seven Osbaldiston pieces staged at the Surrey in Elliston's lifetime, therefore, three were continuing successes, with an ephemeral success for *Vive La Liberté,* and three were failures.

One can project a second managerial opinion of *The Returned Pirate.* Davidge, late manager of the Coburg and soon to take over the Surrey, appeared as guest star in the character role of Mr Twinkle, with a song, 'Fighting for the Breeches' – not only during its first week at the Surrey in 1833 but also a year later, when it was revived under the name *Broken Heart; or, The Returned Pirate.* I do not think that Davidge would appear twice in a flop, so let us credit Osbaldiston with another success.

Davidge also gave *The Brigand* his managerial blessing after he had taken over the Surrey from Osbaldiston, staging the play in April 1835. Looking for further evidence of the popularity of Osbaldiston's work, one can fall into the trap of claiming that Skelt's Toy Theatre sheets included *The Brigand.* However, by comparing the names of the characters given by Skelt with the corresponding playbills, one sees that they link with the play first produced as *The Brigand Chief,* also in 1829, by J.R. Planché, and not with *The Brigand* by Osbaldiston. With even hand, Davidge staged the Planché version, by now also billed as *The Brigand,* in November 1835.

If one concludes that Osbaldiston was some way from the top flight of contemporary playwrights, nevertheless, bearing in mind his acting and managerial efforts, one has to give him full marks for industry.

Mifs Vincent as Gofsamer.

Mr. Osbaldiston as Grindoff.

Chapter Ten

Osbaldiston as Manager (1831-34)

During nearly three years in command at the Surrey (26 December 1831 to mid-September 1834) Osbaldiston continued the mixture much as before: quasi-Shakespeare, drama, melodrama, farce and ballet but a lot less opera than in Elliston's time. The programme for 20 May 1833 gives a fair sample of the Surrey fare he provided. It was the final night of the engagement of Ira Aldridge, the first great American black actor, billed as the African Roscius. He played Zanga in scenes from the tragedy *Revenge* and Shylock in scenes from *The Merchant of Venice.* The company then took over with Osbaldiston's *Baron Trenck,* followed by *The Padlock* by Charles Dibdin senior which was described as a farce on the playbill, though there was enough music in it for it to be classed as a comic opera. There were three songs given to the African Roscius, though I doubt if the third one, 'Opossum up a Gum Tree', had much to do with Dibdin's plot. There was a song 'The Old Maid' sung by Eliza Vincent and a Pas de Deux by Miss Fairbrother and Miss Blanchet. The evening finished with the drama of *The Castle Spectre,* with Mrs Osbaldiston playing the name part. Not a bad evening's entertainment.

Edward Fitzball, who had written plays for Thomas Dibdin and for Watkins Burroughs when they had managed the Surrey, also wrote for Osbaldiston. Unfortunately his first contribution under the new management was a comparative failure, though he describes it as 'one of my most pains-taking productions'. This was *Andreas Hofer! The 'Tell' of the Tyrol,* staged on 9 July 1832. It had 'the fine acting of Mrs W. West, the comic drolleries of Sam Vale and clever little Rogers, and the most picturesque scenery by Tomkins'. Fitzball thought highly of its leading lady,

> Mrs West, in my mind, one of the best actresses of my time. Her voice was music; her deportment ladylike in the extreme. Mrs West was a striking example that it is possible for a gentlewoman to be upon the stage, in all conditioned theatres, and *remain* a gentlewoman. This melodrama succeeded, but was not attractive; it was too high an attempt for the Surrey; or the Surrey was out of tune, as theatres are sometimes.

As for the quasi-Shakespeare, *The New Monthly Magazine and Literary Journal* of March 1832 commented 'Shakspear has been seen and heard here lately in a style that might surprise some who are too exclusive to set their feet in any but patent establishments'. I assume this to be praise and encouragement, but *Figaro in London* a year later was scathing: 'Mr Osbaldiston is running an insane career at the Surrey and is overwhelming the bargemen, in the classic neighbourhood of St George, with the pathos of the hulks and the touching twaddle of the treadmill'. Justification for such comments is hard to see; there seems a singular lack of hulks and treadmills in the playbills of the time. Now, if this had been a criticism of Davidge a few years later, it might well have stuck....

Erroll Sherson claims another 'first' for the Surrey at this time: Madame Celeste spoke!

> For some years she spoke not a word of English, and when playing in English-speaking countries always took the part of a dumb character as for instance, Fenella, the dumb girl in *Masaniello*. She was very good in what were known as 'Breeches' parts.... It was at the old Surrey, some time in the forties of the nineteenth century, that she first spoke on the stage. The house was then under the direction of Osbaldiston, who never announced new pieces weeks beforehand, as is the custom nowadays, lest a rival manager should forestall him. His novelties were always given out on a Saturday, and, with Sunday intervening he was fairly safe.
>
> On one of these Saturdays he announced that Celeste would appear on the Monday in a speaking part for the first time. The house was crowded as he had expected. The moment came when in a pathetic scene she exclaimed, 'My shee-ild! My shee-ild!' That was all she had to say.

A good story again, but perhaps not very accurate. For her first appearance on the Surrey stage on Monday 16 July 1832, Osbaldiston announced in the bill for the previous Monday that 'Mademoiselle' Celeste would play in *The French Spy, The Wept of Wish-Ton-Wish* and *The Wizard Skiff*. She played three parts in *The French Spy* – Mathilde de Gramont, Pierre Graziot and Omir Almorid; in *The Wept of Wish-Ton-Wish* she played Hope Gough (disguised as a Cavalier and pretending to be dumb) and also Naramttah the wife of an Indian Chief; in *The Wizard Skiff* she played Alexa Mavrona (a Greek Lady), Alexis (Chief of the Wizard Skiff) and Agata (a Wild Zingaro Boy). If Sherson is to be believed, her words 'My shee-ild! My shee-ild!' were all that were required for all eight parts.

Anyway, should Sherson give the credit to Osbaldiston and the Surrey? On 21 December 1831, at the Coburg then under Davidge, we find Madame Celeste in all three parts in *The French Spy* and in both parts in *The Wept of Wish-Ton-Wish.* Could she have played these five parts with not even the 'My shee-ild! My shee-ild!' line, and in particular could she play the part of Hope Gough 'pretending to be dumb' without at some time speaking to demonstrate the pretence? Or does some other character come on saying 'Hope Gough has just been telling me...'? With regret, I think this story also must go into the Apocrypha.

'Wishtonwish' was recently used as an unusual word which had to be defined on the television game 'Call My Bluff'. It means 'a breed of Indian dog'. In the play, based on a novel by Fenimore Cooper, the name refers to a whole Red Indian tribe and not just their breed of hunting dog, which suggests that the dogs have survived but the tribe has not. The 'Wept' was the tribal leader.

Sir Walter Scott died on 21 September 1832. The Surrey, which had performed so many adaptations of his novels over the years, took the plunge and put on his play. The playbill of 22 October took liberties: 'Strange to say THE SECRET TRIBUNAL, gifted as was Sir Walter, with the most admirable descriptive and conversational powers, was the ONLY DRAMATIC WORK he ever attempted'. (Nicoll actually lists six.) In his *Life of Sir Walter Scott* Lockhart describes this as the re-working of a piece by a minor German dramatist. Scott sent it to Lewis in London, 'where, having been read and commended by the celebrated actress, Mrs Esten, it was taken up by Kemble, and I believe actually put in rehearsal for the stage. If so, the trial did not encourage further preparation, and the notion was abandoned'. The Surrey evidently agreed with Kemble's view that the play would not do as it stood, for the playbills continued: 'Some alterations and transpositions requisite for its production on the stage have been ventured upon, which the adapter confidently trusts, will not in any wise detract from the effect, intended by the Poet, to be produced'. One of the alterations was to change Sir Walter's title, *The House of Aspen,* to *The Secret Tribunal.* The 'boat-song of Clan-Alpin' mentioned by Lockhart, described in the playbills as the 'Song of Victory – The Battle and Scar', alas proved inappropriate:

> Joy to the victors, the sons of old Aspen,
> Joy to the race of the battle and scar!

As far as I can trace the play was performed only two or three times on this occasion, so despite the presence of Mrs W. West and Miss Vincent in the cast Kemble's judgment was vindicated. Although Osbaldiston makes a fuss about this production as if it were a world première, Elliston had in fact put it on, with Blewitt's music, in November 1829.

The homage to Scott continued with *The Fortunes of Nigel* and *Rob Roy,* and a cocktail of extracts billed as 'Tableaux Vivans! The Poet's Study, at Abbotsford. Sir Walter on his couch and... passing as in a dream before him', chunks of *Guy Mannering, The Lady of the Lake, The Bride of Lammermoor, The Heart of Midlothian, The Legend of Montrose, Rob Roy, Marmion,* and *Ivanhoe.* As most of these were already in the repertoire, it was an easy way of filling the bill.

The 1832 pantomime turned to Scandinavia with *The Valkyrae; or, Harlequin the Patriot Pole and the Maid of Muscovy,* the playbills asserting that the Valkyrae 'are supposed to be three sisters, employed to weave the web of Fate.' I thought those were the Norns, but the story seems to have changed coming via Poland and Russia. Nelson Lee was Harlequin, Wood was Pantaloon, Signor Grammani Clown and Miss Fairbrother Columbine.

The attractive Eliza Vincent had a 'Farewell Benefit' on 28 March 1833 on leaving for the Haymarket Theatre. Conditions on the other side of the river did not suit her, for on 4 May she was back at the Surrey.

Meanwhile Osbaldiston sought out Fitzball for another drama, though the author was somewhat reluctant to oblige bearing in mind the failure of *Andreas Hofer.* According to Fitzball, Osbaldiston took a more relaxed view.

> 'We cannot account for these things', was Osbaldiston's manly and spirited reply, 'notwithstanding the non-attraction of Hofer, which *ought* to have drawn considerably, I am quite willing to give you the same terms, (the best terms I apprehend ever given at the Surrey,) for another drama; and the sooner you can let us have it, the better; for we are sadly distressed.'
>
> 'And have you any subject?' I enquired nervously. 'No! write whatever you will; I'll produce it.'

Without any real thought they settled on the story of *Jonathan Bradford,* and Fitzball set about trying to make up for the earlier failure. What he gave Osbaldiston was a new concept of staging, the enactment of one scene being carried on in four separate rooms simultaneously. This ambitious project must have seemed untimely to Osbaldiston who was suffering from a prices-war with the Coburg under Davidge's management. At the end of 1832 Osbaldiston had had to halve the price of his seats in an attempt to maintain his share of the market. After six months he was feeling the pinch. An account of this famously-innovative production is best told in Edward Fitzball's own words.

Plate I The Surrey Theatre, St. George's Circus, 1812
(note the bill on the Obelisk advertising the elephant)

Plate II
(a)
Robert William Elliston (lessee and manager of the Surrey Theatre, 1809–14 and 1827–31)

Plate II
(b)
Samuel Thomas Russell (manager of the Surrey Theatre for Elliston, 1812–14)

Plate III Royal Circus (Surrey Theatre) with pantomime scene (Ackermann's *Microcosm of London*, 1808–11; see also end-papers)

Plate IV Frances Elizabeth Copeland (later Mrs Fitzwilliam), 1820 ('regular' Surrey actress and favourite ingénue in opera and comedy)

> Having written my drama of 'Jonathan Bradford', I took it myself to the manager, who resided at that time in Prospect Place.... The following morning, on calling in Prospect Place to learn the impression made by my new melodrame, I met Osbaldiston in the garden, the M.S. in his hand, a cloud upon his brow. Jonathan did not meet with his approbation. Still he would keep the M.S. for a future occasion, as he had ordered it, pay me the terms agreed on, and I must write another piece.

Fitzball was not to be put off, and persisted that *Jonathan Bradford* should at least be given a reading, despite the fact that the same story had been previously tried at Drury Lane when it proved a disaster.

> It was read in the green-room. Henry Wallack, who was to play Dan Macraisy, quitted the green-room before its conclusion: no great compliment to the author, but the fact was, he was frightened, and for me. When it came to the four-room scene, everyone stared at each other, asking mute questions with their eyes, like people who look over a game of chess, without comprehending a single move. When the reading came to a conclusion, some glided mysteriously one way, some another, as if afraid of being trapped into an opinion.

Mrs West, who was cast for Ann Bradford, made it clear that, although she could not understand how people could act in concert in four rooms at once, she nevertheless had faith in Fitzball and advised Osbaldiston to rely on him.

> Then came the comparing of parts; then the rehearsals. One part of my system was never to go near them till they had made some progress.... From 'Jonathan Bradford', however, there was no staying away. Every half hour I was sent for by a double express. They had got into a sad muddle... and a round robin was constituted to induce Osbaldiston to insist on my leaving out this perplexing, unexampled, undramatic, unactable four-roomed scene.

For a while Osbaldiston dithered but eventually came out in full support of Fitzball. The cast took longer to convince.

> Sad murmurings were heard, during the rehearsals in the four boxes... where the performers could neither see each other, nor hear each other's voices. As the night of

SURREY THEATRE.

PROPRIETOR, MR. OSBALDISTON.

The National Theatre of this side the water, for the Performance and Production of the REGULAR DRAMA, &c. established as such, by the late Mr. ELLISTON, and conducted on the same principles of Management, by the present Proprietor.

BOXES 2s. Half Price 1s. PIT 1s. NoHalf Price. GALLERY 6d. NoHalf Price.

FIRST NIGHT OF THE NEW ORIGINAL DRAMA.
Fifteenth, Sixteenth & Seventeenth Nights of the grand COMIC PANTOMIME!

Mr. SHERIDAN KNOWLES' New Play,

THE WIFE: A TALE OF MANTUA!

is in preparation, and will shortly be produced.

Colman's Play of **The IRON CHEST** will be performed as early as the forthcoming Novelties will permit.

WEDNESDAY, June 12th, 1833, THURSDAY, 13th, and FRIDAY, 14th,

Will be presented (NEVER ACTED) an entirely new original Domestic Drama, (written expressly for this Theatre, by the Author of *"The Red Rover," "Innkeeper of Abbeville," "Flying Dutchman," "Soldier's Widow," "The Pilot," &c. &c. &c.*) and to be called

JONATHAN BRADFORD!

Or, The Murder at the Road-Side Inn!

The Scenery, by MARSHALL. The Music, by JOLLY.

THIS ORIGINAL DRAMA

Is founded on REAL FACTS. Jonathan Bradford actually kept an Inn on the London road to Oxford, and bore an unexceptionable character. The extraordinary affair which led to the construction of this Drama, was the conversation of the whole county. The innocent and unfortunate Landlord, accused of a cruel murder, perpetrated under his very roof, and borne down by a long train of overwhelming circumstantial evidence, in vain pleaded not guilty: all conspired to condemn him: his assertions were of little avail: never was presumptive conviction more strong. There was little need of comment [illegible] the Judge in summing up the evidence, no room appeared for extenuation, and the Jury brought in the Prisoner GUILTY, even without going out of the B[illegible]!!!

Jonathan Bradford, (*Landlord of the Inn by the Roadside*) Mr. OSBALDISTON.
Dan Macraisy, (alias *Gentleman O'Connor*, alias *Ratcatching Jack*, alias &c. &c. &c.) Mr. H. WALLACK.
Caleb Scrummidge, {*an aspiring Watchmaker, of Seven Dials---aristocracy the mainspring of his ambition, apprenticed by himself to the trade of a gentleman.*} Mr. V[illegible]LE.

With a Parody on the popular Song of "The SEA, the SEA, the OPEN SEA."

Farmer Nelson, (*Father to Bradford's Wife*) Mr. RUMBALL.
Mr. Hayes, (*Merchant retiring from business*) Mr. DIBDIN PITT.
Jack Rackbottle, (*New Boots at the Inn, wishing to supply, in every respect, the place of Old Boots*) Mr. ROGERS.
Lawyer Dozey, (*a sleepy companion*) Mr. YOUNG, Surveyor Rodpole, (*a character of calculation*) Mr. BANNISTER.
Serjeant Sam, Mr. LEE, Corporal, Mr. BRUNTON, Gaoler, Mr. BRAND, *Soldiers, Peasants, Constables, &c.*
Ann, (*Wife to Bradford*) Mrs. W. WEST, Ann & Jane, (*her Children*) Misses BRUTON & ELLIS,
Sally Sighabout, (*Widow to the Old Boots, and Nursery Maid to Bradford's Children*) Miss VINCENT, with a New Song

"A KIND OLD MAN CAME WOOING TO ME!"

***Scenery, &c.---*EXTERIOR of the GEORGE INN, on the OXFORD ROAD.**
Another View of the Inn, showing also the Inner Apartment;
☞ In this peculiar Scene, an effort will be made so as to harmonize Four Actions, as to produce

ONE STRIKING EFFECT!

Never yet attempted on any Stage.

The MURDER of Mr. HAYES;--Arrival of the SOLDIERY;--APPREHENSION of BRADFORD.
THE STRONG ROOM;---ESCAPE THROUGH THE ROOF.
Interior of the Manor Vault, with Iviced Window and Broken Tomb
The Inn, and Road conducting to the newly-erected Gibbet on the Heath, intended for
THE EXECUTION OF JONATHAN BRADFORD!

Top part of bill for the first night of *Jonathan Bradford*, 12 June 1833.
(Reproduced by kind permission of London Borough of Lambeth Archives Department)

This present Evening, TUESDAY, December 3, 1833, will be performed the Drama, in Three Acts, called

Jonathan Bradford.

This Drama is founded upon the singular Trial of JONATHAN BRADFORD, who was Executed at Oxford, upon Presumptive Evidence, for the Murder of CHRISTOPHER HAYES, Esq.—The evidence given against him was to the following effect: Two gentlemen who had supped with Mr Hayes, and who retired at the same time to their respective chambers, being alarmed in the night, by a noise in his room, and hearing groans, as of a wounded man, they got up in order to discover the cause; and found their landlord, with a dark lantern, and a knife in his hand, in a state of astonishment and horror, standing close to his dying guest, who almost instantly expired. The facts attending this dreadful tragedy, were not fully brought to light, until the death of the confidential valet of the ill-fated Traveller, who then confessed, that, knowing his master had considerable property about him, he had committed the horrid act, and secured his treasure but a few moments before the landlord entered the Apartment of the expiring man.

Jonathan Bradford, Landlord of the George Inn, by Mr MONTAGUE STANLEY—Squire Hayes by Mr HUDSON,
Mr Dorry by Mr POWER—Surveyor Rodpole by Mr THOMAS—Farmer Nelson by Mr ROBERTS,
Dan Macraisey by Mr BARRETT—Sergeant by Mr PEDDIE—Corporal by Mr ELLIOT—Backbottle by Mr MURRAY,
Caleb Scrummidge, a runaway Apprentice, by Mr LLOYD, in which Character he will sing

THE SEA, THE SEA, THE HUGLY SEA.

Ann, Wife to Bradford, by Mrs BARRETT,
Sally Sighabout, Chambermaid at the George Inn, by Miss NEWTON, in which Character she will sing

NICE YOUNG BACHELORS.

PROGRAMME OF THE PRINCIPAL SCENERY AND INCIDENTS.

ACT I.—SCENE 1. THE EXTERIOR OF THE GEORGE INN.

ACT II.—Scene 1. APARTMENT IN THE INN.—Scene 2. EXTERIOR OF FARMER NELSON'S COTTAGE.

3. FRONT SECTION OF THE GEORGE INN, DIVIDED INTO FOUR APARTMENTS, ACCORDING TO THE FOLLOWING PLAN.

ACT III.—SCENE 1. STRONG ROOM IN THE VILLAGE—PAINTED BY MR G. GORDON.
Scene 2. THE EXTERIOR OF THE VILLAGE CHURCH—DESIGNED AND PAINTED BY MR JONES.

SCENE 3.—INTERIOR OF THE VAULT BELOW THE CHURCH—MR JONES.

SCENE 4. LANDSCAPE.—SCENE 5. VIEW of the EXTERIOR of the GEORGE INN.

The four-room scene as illustrated on playbills
(Reproduced by kind permission of the editors of *Theatre Notebook*)

> representation approached, more than one of the actors began to unravel, and to catch a glimpse of that singular effect, and to anticipate a favourable result....

The Surrey presented *Jonathan Bradford; or, The Murder at the Roadside Inn* on Wednesday 12 June 1833, with scenery by Marshall and music by Jolly. This 'Original Drama' was announced as founded on 'real facts': that Jonathan Bradford actually kept an inn on the London road to Oxford, and bore an unexceptional character. The unfortunate landlord was accused of murder, perpetrated under his own roof. Borne down by a train of circumstantial evidence it was in vain that he pleaded not guilty. His assertions were of no avail; never was presumptive conviction more strong. There was little need of comment from the judge in summing up the evidence. The jury brought in the prisoner guilty without going out of the box. He was hanged – but he was innocent, if Fitzball and the popular opinion of the time are to be believed. At this period the theatre had fallen into bad repute, according to Fitzball, and the house was not so crowded as had been anticipated. When it came to the four-roomed scene, the audience looked at each other exactly in the same way as the actors had done at the reading. Then like all English audiences they took the lenient side and gave a fair measure of applause on the fall of the curtain at the end of the first act.

> Up went the drop again. All the clamour hushed in an instant – you might have heard a pin fall; till it came to the scene in the church vault, where Jonathan turns the tables upon Dan Macraisy, and rescues poor Caleb from his rascally clutches. The house then became apparently electrified; Osbaldiston, who had a fine firm voice, and was an excellent declaimer, gave the speech its due –
>
> > Yes, monster; that Jonathan Bradford whom you would so wantonly have sacrificed: the husband of a devoted wife, the father of children, whom you would have plunged into irretrievable infamy. Heaven hath heard my prayers – heaven sent me hither seeking concealment, even in a tomb – to witness for myself – to avenge – to punish.

Jonathan Bradford ran for 264 consecutive nights and was said to have brought the manager £8,000. Fitzball gives some vivid pen-portraits of the manager and the cast.

> Osbaldiston was a man for whom I always considered it a great pleasure to write. He had none of that smooth double-facedness which managers in general consider it necessary to assume towards popular authors (so disgusting to rational minds); at the same time he did not wound the feelings of the unpopular by a haughty, tinsel-crowned arrogance, which I have seen some assume....

[Surely he cannot be referring to Elliston?]

> In Dan Macraisy, Henry Wallack made a most unlooked for impression. He suddenly, as the rehearsal proceeded, seemed to launch into the character, and to discover its opportunities by degrees, as a boy discovers a problem in mathematics.... The audience testified their appreciation of Wallack's performance by calling for him at the fall of the curtain night after night, which was a very unusual compliment in those days....

[Wallack, however, did not return the compliment:]

> On the twelfth night of *Jonathan Bradford,* H. Wallack left England, at very short notice, taking with him a M.S. of the piece, which he produced in America, with equal success. Wallack, leaving us somewhat abruptly, to my great regret, threw us all aground; what was to be done with a part which his fine acting had rendered his own?... I despairingly suggested the idea of installing Mr Dibdin Pitt in the vacated part of Dan Macraisy, dressing him exactly the same, and letting Wallack's name remain in the bill.... It was done; and so well and artiste like, did Pitt acquit himself, that at the end of the performance, he was unanimously called for, to receive the customary honours, just the same as those conferred on the original actor, which inflated me a little, with the idea that the piece might have had something to do with its own popularity, after all.
>
> Vale [in the part of Caleb Scrummidge] was the character itself.... His natural joy, in the vault where he is spared from signing his own death warrant, was acting not to be described. So racy – so tottering between tears and laughter.... Miss Vincent [as Sally Sighabout] was so truly pretty, and so young, then – and sang so sweetly, no marvel every one was pleased with her.

(Her manager more than anyone, as will transpire.) Eliza Vincent's song in this piece was 'A kind old man came wooing'; was this perhaps Rossini's

'Il vecchiotto cerca moglie' from *The Barber of Seville?* She also had songs in the two accompanying pieces on the same bill, 'Listen, dear Fanny' in *Is He Jealous?* and 'The magical circlet of gold' in *Ellen Wareham.* However, of the female cast it was Mrs West who made the greatest impression.

> Of Mrs West, as an actress, I have no need to repeat my sentiments; the devotion and affection which she threw into this drama, as a wife and a mother, had in them a feminine charm, as beautiful, as peculiarly her own. I do not believe any one, that witnessed her personation of Ann Bradford, would find it possible to forget her in one exclamation: 'Oh, my children! my children! What will become of them?' The expression, and her look of pale maternal despair, as she uttered the words, were a never-failing signal for universal tears; and how very often have I seen females, mothers perhaps, taken out in hysterics?

Although Fitzball does not mention Mrs West's husband, William West, he can be found in the Surrey playbills of this period, for example as Kilian the hermit in *Der Freischutz* and Dominie Sampson in *Guy Mannering.* He had also composed a song for young Master Burke on his previous visit.

Fitzball gives a pleasant picture of the celebration party, marking the hundredth performance of *Jonathan Bradford,* which seems to have been held on Sunday 12 October 1833:

> Mr Osbaldiston gave a sumptuous déjeuner on the stage, to his performers, on which occasion, to my utter surprise, I was presented with a costly silver cup, bearing a highly complimentary inscription. Mrs West, as the Melpomene of the theatre, was deputed to present the cup; and, would it be believed, so affected, and so nervous was the amiable lady... in presenting this tribute of... the general esteem of the company, with only two or three words to utter, that she would have fallen to the ground, had I not actually sustained her while she addressed me.

When *Jonathan Bradford* closed on 15 December 1833 Osbaldiston took the big decision to cash in on its success by carrying straight on to produce Fitzball's next play, *Walter Brand.* The author describes the first night's excitement:

> From the reputation of the last drama, they expected an impossible representation, and absolutely stormed the roof of the theatre – burst open the doors, and broke in at the sky-

> light; the manager was necessarily compelled to call in the police, to keep the people *out* of his theatre. In the interior, all was noise, confusion and turmoil. The drama went off in dumb show; for several evenings not a word was heard, and when it was heard, the story was too refined for them.

Although the play was not a smash hit like its predecessor Fitzball was scarcely fair to himself when he described it as 'a comparative failure'. His play was still running at the end of January. It was the pantomime, *One-Two! Come Buckle My Shoe! or, Harlequin and the Fairy Queen,* partnering *Walter Brand,* which was the flop, being withdrawn after a couple of weeks.

For a time Osbaldiston now shared management of the Surrey with Yates. As reported in *The Age* in March 1834 the manager of the Adelphi Theatre, with his wife 'and part of his troop,... take up their quarters at the Surrey, for a limited period'. Yates brought the Adelphi company to the Surrey as he had no summer licence for his own theatre. The joint company put on another of Fitzball's adaptations, this time *Esmeralda* based on *The Hunchback of Notre Dame.* It opened on 14 April. Fitzball wrote that it was 'beautifully produced. Scenery, costumes, perfect. Yates's peculiar genius fitted him for Quasemodo.... Of Mrs Yates, the charming interesting Mrs Yates, then all the rage, she was the veritable Esmeralda.... But the great part to be spoken of was Mrs Wm. West's Gudule [mother of Esmeralda].... I wish Victor Hugo could have seen her'.

The reviewer in *The Age* thought well of it too, but noticed that the current successes at the Surrey and at Astley's under Ducrow caused 'desertion' from the neighbouring Royal Victoria Theatre (so named since 1 July 1833). Abbott and Egerton had set out at the Victoria to present up-market entertainment, but they had ignored Aaron Hill's classic saying, 'It is not the business of managers to be wise to empty benches'. Their break came at the beginning of June 1834, when Egerton left the partnership. He was made bankrupt shortly afterwards. Abbott struggled on alone. He managed to keep the Victoria going until the middle of August, when he surrendered the lease to the younger Glossop who had inherited the theatre from his father.

At the Surrey the dog star 'Neptune' returned on 4 September 1834 with *Murder on the Cliff; or, The Smuggler's Dog,* which he had performed at Sadler's Wells in the previous March. The following week he was joined by 'Carlo' in *Red Indians; or, The Shipwrecked Mariner and his Dogs*. This piece by Hector Simpson had gone the rounds under various names. It was first seen at the Surrey in March 1824 as *The Red Indian; or, The Shipwrecked Mariner and his Dogs* and revived with 'Carlo' and

'Lion' in February 1827, now entitled *Cherokees; or, the Dogs of the Wreck.* It turned up again at the Coburg in February 1833 as *The Cherokee Chief; or, The Dogs of the Wreck.* Now here it was back at the Surrey in 1834. It would be interesting to know to what extent such plays were written for particular dogs, to accommodate their known talents, though in this case it would seem that 'Neptune' was trained (and auditioned?) for the part originally played by 'Lion'.

Osbaldiston had decided not to renew his lease of the Surrey Theatre, about to expire in September 1834. He had grandiose plans, no less than prising the lease of Covent Garden away from Alfred Bunn. He would then have one of the patent theatres, and be free of so many of the restrictions which afflicted the minor theatres. He succeeded – though I suspect that Bunn, who also had the lease of Drury Lane, was happy to see the Covent Garden lease pass into the hands of someone he did not fear as a competitor. The Surrey lease was then advertised to be let to the highest bidder, and Davidge won.

Osbaldiston was showing enterprise in other quarters as well. E.L. Blanchard, the future 'King of Pantomime Writers', comments in his *Reminiscences* that Osbaldiston's 'elopement with Miss Vincent made a great stir at the time'. In the course of a Surrey review the reporter of *The Age* commented on 20 July 1834, 'Miss Vincent has not yet returned to these boards – on dit, she is on the eve of producing something "very lively" for Osbaldiston'. As one can find all three (Osbaldiston, Mrs Osbaldiston and Eliza Vincent) in the farce *Is He Jealous?* at the end of 1833, in 1834 it must have become rather a public affair.

Although Osbaldiston's lease had expired it was not the end of performances by his Surrey company. 'On Monday 29 September 1834 and during the week' the Pavilion Theatre, Whitechapel, under the control of E. Yarnold, announced the 'Union of the Surrey & Pavilion Company'. Three pieces from the Surrey repertoire were staged – *Jonathan Bradford, The Lord Mayor's Fool* and *The Inchcape Bell,* with Dibdin Pitt, Heslop, Vale and Mrs W. West playing their well-known parts.

A postscript to Osbaldiston's time at the Surrey can be found in *The Satirist* for 7 August 1836. Two years after Osbaldiston took the lease of Covent Garden he let it to Willis Jones (later to be Davidge's partner at the Surrey) and took the lease of Sadler's Wells, which he ran much as he had run the Surrey and Covent Garden, with melodrama, ballad-opera and a bit of Shakespeare. A Mr Ewing then took legal action – *The Satirist* described them as 'a couple of dozen double actions' – against Osbaldiston for breach of the terms of his licence at Sadler's Wells, for in 1836 the patent theatres still had their monopoly. Osbaldiston as lessee of Covent Garden would hardly sue Osbaldiston as lessee of Sadler's Wells, but there was nothing to stop a virtuous citizen laying information against a sinner. The story behind the story was that Osbaldiston had swindled Ewing over some money which Ewing had invested in the Surrey Theatre. As *The Satirist* reported:

> When Ewing sought to establish his right to a partnership share in the Surrey, Osbaldiston's defence was that the entire transaction was illegal; that the performances at that theatre, under his own management, were contrary to law, (although he admitted having induced Mr Ewing to invest £1,000 for carrying on the theatre without giving him the slightest intimation that the performances were intended to be of an illegal character, until it answered his purpose to do so). This was Osbaldiston's defence, one more dishonourable could not have been set up. It however succeeded. As Ewing was defrauded of the money he advanced, with a share of the profits which were considerable, by the plea of the performances being illegal at the Surrey, he is perfectly justified in thus employing the illegal performances at Sadler's Wells as a means of repaying himself with ample interest.

Osbaldiston fled the country for a while. Irrepressible, he turns up on the Surrey-side again as manager of the Royal Victoria from 1841 until his death in 1850. His successor there? – Miss Eliza Vincent.

MRS. WEST AS ANN BRADFORD.

Chapter Eleven

'Dirt Cheap': Prices and Price-wars

In his book *The Old Vic Story* Peter Roberts comments on Davidge introducing the 'shilling order' system at the Coburg to bring in a 'large audience dirt cheap. And it brought in a dirty public. One commentator remarked that "dust-men, chimney-sweeps and greasy butchers are too much in evidence"'. Such a policy might well have affected the Surrey. It would be as well to set his comments in context and see what really happened.

From the beginning of the nineteenth century prices of admission had been remarkably constant: four shillings for a seat in one of the boxes, two shillings in the pit and one shilling in the gallery. These prices were halved at the interval, assuming there were still any unfilled seats. Such prices were much the same in all the minor theatres. Drury Lane and Covent Garden boxes were usually seven shillings, with varying prices in other parts of the house.

In his autobiography (published in 1827) Thomas Dibdin commented on the situation existing when he leased the Surrey in 1816:

> A custom had insensibly obtained, for which they give credit to the folly of a Surrey manager long before my time, of giving a certain number of orders to every house or shop where a playbill was conspicuously exhibited, and that very frequently.

He does not say how many free tickets he himself was issuing but says of his main rival:

> It is certain that at one period, when not in possession of the present managers, the Cobourg Theatre sent out six hundred large bills weekly to shops for which each shop received three double orders, admitting two persons each per week, making in total thirty-six hundred people admitted gratis weekly.

When this was written Davidge was in charge at the Coburg, so Dibdin absolves him from introducing the system and concedes that the Surrey was doing likewise. However Thomas's brother Charles Dibdin gives another version in his *Memoirs* written in 1830. Referring to his period of management at the Surrey from 1824 to 1826, he writes that it had preserved its standards 'by not adopting the custom, now so general, of admitting the Public to the Boxes for one shilling each, through the specious subterfuge of an Order, or free admission'. This change in custom probably goes hand-in-hand with the change from the equestrian lay-out to the stage-dominated theatre. For those exhibiting playbills, a free ticket to the circle became a reduced price entry to a box. Charles Dibdin tells us:

> This custom originated at Sadler's Wells, at the period that the Pony Races were exhibited in the extensive enclosed area connected with that Theatre; and it had this peculiarity attached to it... that the audience within could not see the race without; and every person who paid his money for admission to the Theatre, was supplied with a ticket of admission to the race ground also, without which he could not be admitted to the course. The Proprietors, therefore, as the Pony races increased their attraction made it a sine qua non that each person should pay one Shilling for seeing the Pony Races, the order admitting him into the auditory;... when the Ponies were withdrawn, so few of the Public were agreeable to pay full prices, to see the Stage Entertainments alone, that in their own defence, the Proprietors were obliged to continue the shilling orders; which habit has now acquired an inveteracy which I imagine will hardly be eradicated.

1827 was the last year of the pony races at Sadler's Wells. The continuation of the shilling orders north of the Thames seems to have affected the size of the audiences on the south side of the river, at the Coburg under Davidge, at the Surrey now under Elliston and at Astley's under Ducrow. Davidge reacted first, not by re-introducing that system but by cutting prices at the Coburg. The effect was felt immediately at the Surrey. The contest of words started mildly enough with an announcement by the Surrey box book-keeper, William Wardell, on 2 October 1828.

> In consequence of the numerous enquiries which have been made at the Box-Office for the purchase of Orders, I deem it necessary (by permission of the Proprietor) to announce, most respectfully, to the Public, that the system of SHILLING BOX ORDERS carried on at Sadler's Wells and the Coburg Theatres, has never been contemplated at this Theatre, and I am authorised to state that no such plans will, at any time, be ever contemplated.

Apart from this notice by a rival house there is no evidence that, at this time, the 'shilling box orders' were issued by Davidge at the Coburg, though he did issue free tickets to the Press and other privileged persons – much as happens today.

To the problems of the minor theatres at a time of financial depression was added another hazard which did not impinge equally upon them. In 1831 an epidemic of cholera swept London. The cholera pandemic had started in India in 1826 and reached Moscow in 1830. It passed through Germany and reached Britain in October 1831. No cure existed. Sufferers had a fifty-fifty chance of survival and sometimes only a few hours in which to contemplate their chances. There were over 6,000 deaths by the end of the year. Medical opinion was that the infection was air-borne. The truth that it was a result of contaminated water supplies had not yet dawned on most people. The older settlements south of the river, Lambeth, Kennington and Southwark, had been developed far beyond the capabilities of the Parish Vestries to provide clean water and sewage facilities and suffered heavily. Those people who could afford it – perhaps the same people who could afford the full price of a Box at the theatres – moved out to the developing suburbs of Battersea, Wandsworth, Tulse Hill and Norwood. The Coburg, the Surrey and Astley's were thus fighting for the custom of the impoverished remainder, the 'dustmen, chimney-sweeps and greasy butchers' referred to by Peter Roberts.

Edward Fitzball wrote that he was there when

> the cholera broke out in London; people were naturally terrified, or had no longer any desire to enter the doors of theatres. It was a truly awful calamity. One was almost afraid to enquire after one's friends, or acquaintance. Every face you encountered at home or in the street, wore a look of consternation and dismay; every heart seemed agitated with a dreadful apprehension. Under these melancholy circumstances, it is not to be wondered at, that theatricals were at a low ebb.

North of the Thames, the New River brought clean water to the doors of Sadler's Wells – even indoors during its Aquatic Spectacle period – and its clientele remained, by comparison, healthy.

Elliston died in the same year, 1831. Osbaldiston took over the Surrey at the end of that year but immediately found that his prices had been undercut by Davidge at the Coburg, just up the road. In October 1831 Davidge had announced

> the Necessity of Retrenchment and Economy... has determined Mr DAVIDGE to yield to the Current of Opinion, and by Reducing the Prices of Admission to the Royal Coburg Theatre, to suit the means of the real Lovers and Supporters of the Drama....

Feeling it 'necessary to make a few remarks' in vindication of this step, Davidge continues in a long broadside to criticise the practice of free orders, which obliges managers 'to exact a high Price of Admission from those who do pay, to remunerate them for providing an Entertainment for those who do not'. He makes a comparison with the publishing trade, where lower prices have brought increased sales, and offers 'this Principle of Reduction creating Multiplication' to the 'Supporters of the Theatres':

> He therefore begs to announce... that, in future, BOX ORDERS, which may be obtained at the Places enumerated at the Foot of this Bill, will be admitted at the Doors, on the Payment of ONE SHILLING and SIXPENCE each Person; and ORDERS for the PIT, on Payment of ONE SHILLING each Person,... the GALLERY affording comfortable Accommodation to 1800 Persons, the BOXES holding 1200 Visitors, with Ease; and the PIT Nightly containing 1100 Occupants....

Although not very clear, it seems that the system was to buy a one-shilling box or pit order from the ticket agencies and pay the further sum at the door; that is, a discount was given for advance booking. Thus a 'shilling box order' meant different things at different times at different theatres.

At the Surrey Theatre Osbaldiston held out against this attack for about six months but eventually capitulated and announced price reductions, 'in accordance with the general aspect of the times', to:

First Price	Boxes 3s.	Pit 1s.6d	Gallery 1s.
Second Price	Boxes 1s.6d	Pit 1s.	Gallery 6d.

This was on Easter Monday, 23 April 1832. The earlier admission prices had been four shillings, two shillings and one shilling for the full performance, and half those after the first interval. It was therefore the Surrey's boxes that Osbaldiston was trying to fill, there being no reduction for the gallery or the second-price pit. Davidge at the Coburg replied a week later, cancelling his advance booking scheme and bringing his prices to the same level as at the Surrey, saying 'Nor will any Pay Orders, or Admissions of the kind, be issued directly or indirectly'.

At that moment there was no outright quarrel. Indeed, in May Osbaldiston made a guest appearance at the Coburg Theatre, while Davidge released the Coburg's juvenile ballet company under Mrs Searle to appear at the Surrey for a benefit performance. By the summer of

1832 Osbaldiston was feeling the financial effects of his reductions and on 3 July had to put the Surrey's prices back to their old level. This annoyed him. He took further action on 15 September:

> TO THE PUBLIC. In nothing has the 'March of Intellect' been more palpably exemplified, than in the steady and progressive improvement which has, of late years, raised the character of the MINOR THEATRES of the Metropolis.... Amongst others, the SURREY THEATRE, commencing under the auspices of the late Mr ELLISTON, has attained an elevation, not only envied by its numerous rivals, but feared by the Patent Houses themselves. This elevation, the present PROPRIETOR has studied to confirm;... and he is proud to add, that an unlooked for success has been the result of his unwearied exertions: what then must be his mortification, as well as that of all well-wishers of the Drama, to see a structure, thus based and thus elevated, threatened with total destruction, if not timely prevented by some bold and decisive step. The PROPRIETOR of the SURREY THEATRE, without impugning the motives of others, is determined, though at some personal sacrifice, to attempt the annihilation of a system which, while it gradually draws destruction on itself, yet... spreads its baneful influence around. The SYSTEM alluded to, is the ruinous and extensive distribution of what are called PAY ORDERS, given by the COBURG and other THEATRES, without discrimination or without limit.
>
> To avert this overhanging calamity,... by employing the very means now used to extend it, the PROPRIETOR OF THE SURREY THEATRE begs to announce, that
>
> HENCEFORTH ALL ORDERS ISSUED BY THE COBURG AND OTHER MINOR THEATRES, WILL BE ADMITTED TO THE SURREY, AT ANY TIME OF THE EVENING, BY THOSE PARTIES PRESENTING THEM PAYING ONLY HALF-PRICE ADMISSION

Davidge's reply came two days later.

> Royal Coburg Theatre, Sept 17 1832. The Proprietor of the Surrey Theatre having distinctly mentioned the Coburg Theatre, by name in his Bills as having by the conduct of its management tended to depreciate the Dramatic Art, Mr Davidge feels it necessary to ask, Whether, instead of Pay Orders, the Boxes of the Surrey Theatre have not lately been filled with Orders, the Possessor of which paid NOTHING AT ALL: and, whether, even in its much higher condition, under

> the late Mr Elliston, those Boxes were not... filled, as far as they were filled, at FIVE PENCE per head? It is a notorious fact that Admissions for Six Persons are, and for a long time have been, constantly issued from the Surrey Theatre at the Price of 2s.6d. under the pretext of paying for the Bills, a thing unheard of in the annals of Minor Theatricals.

Davidge's long riposte continues with further criticisms. He lampoons Osbaldiston's literary style and grammar as well as the 'turpitude' of his business practice, and reproduces one of his rival's orders as evidence of hypocrisy. Finally Davidge airs a particular complaint about Osbaldiston which has all the appearance of a harboured grudge:

> If further confirmation were needed of the relative conduct of the two managements, the instance of the production of the TOWER OF NESLE at each House would be amply sufficient. At the Coburg, announced without puff, or any attempt at exciting a false popularity, it has been completely successful. Three weeks after its announcement here, the Manager of the Surrey boasts of his private understanding with the Proprietor of the Porte St Martin, in Paris, as affording him a copy of a Piece actually PRINTED IN MAY; and not content with this palpable abandonment of truth he sends a hired Author to the Coburg Theatre for the express purpose of exactly fitting the Drama to be produced at the Surrey to the part of Buridan, performed by the same Actor at each house. His assertion and his conduct need no further comment, the Part of Buridan at the Surrey, Mr Davidge fearlessly asserts, will be found word for word, the one acted at the Coburg.

Although one cannot always believe either of the contestants, it is likely that Davidge was right to say that Osbaldiston had cribbed the Coburg version. Davidge had gone to Paris himself to obtain the English rights to *The Tower of Nesle* and either had translated it himself or had arranged the translation.

Osbaldiston's reply of the next day,18 September, denied the selling of orders and descended to further personalities, accusing Davidge of 'much injury' and having 'DEBASED and DEGRADED the Cause of the Drama'. He did not respond to the charge of plagiarism, though. Davidge came back quickly, on 20 September, with further 'evidence' of Osbaldiston's malpractice and a justification of his own struggle to 'maintain and elevate the Drama'. This included reference to 'the Penalties... incurred at the suit of the Patent Theatres', whereby Davidge had twice been fined £50 for quasi-Shakespearean productions at the Coburg (in 1827 and again in 1828). After laying into Osbaldiston's character, Davidge submits somewhat belatedly that 'he is little inclined to court such an altercation, but as little is he disposed to pass over in silence... the vulgar and illiterate attacks of a rivalry which he thinks might be conducted in a manner more creditable to the Parties'.

Two days later, Osbaldiston announced that the Surrey would admit unlimited orders 'at whatever personal sacrifice;... thus earnestly hoping to destroy the end by the very means now used to extend it'. Davidge does not seem to have thought it necessary to comment on this. There is in fact nothing new therein. He also had other things on his mind, as shown by his playbill for Monday 15 October 1832:

> Last Six Nights of the Season, And positively the last Appearances, for some Months of several of the most established Favourites of this Theatre, in consequence of the approaching Opening (under the Management of Mr DAVIDGE) of the Royal Amphitheatre, Liverpool.

This was to be Davidge's third concurrent theatrical venture, as he was already running the New City Theatre in Milton Street, Cripplegate, as well as the Coburg. It could well be that he was over-stretching himself.

A month later, on 23 October 1832, Osbaldiston renewed the paper war.

> TO THE PUBLIC. THE PROPRIETOR of the SURREY had hoped never again to have come in contact with ANY Theatre, save in the spirit of good will and friendly feeling; but the low practice still persevered in by the COBURG, demands an exposition of a system, degrading alike to the Drama as to its professors. Is it to be believed, that the Manager of any LICENSED Theatre would open his doors GRATIS, to overflow ONE part of his house, in order to ensnare his victims to pay a paltry pittance to go into ANOTHER ? – Yet so it is; – The Pit of the Coburg capable of containing 1000 persons, is thus, every night, filled GRATUITOUSLY to an overflow, PURPOSELY and AVOWEDLY to extort money from those, who are by these means rendered uncomfortable, and consequently induced to give a few pence to obtain refuge in the Gallery and Boxes.... It is, therefore respectfully announced, that in future, there will be a limited distribution of SUBSCRIPTION TICKETS, ADMITTING TWO PERSONS, and on such terms as it is hoped will meet the general approval of the Public. The Subscription Tickets to be had of Mr Wardell, at the Box-Office of the Theatre, and at principal Music Shops.

Osbaldiston is thus copying Davidge's earlier plan of issuing discounted tickets in advance. As this flier appeared on the day that Davidge opened in Liverpool for a two-month season (while the Coburg was being refurbished), Osbaldiston was safe from any immediate riposte. Until 26 December, that is:

> Royal Coburg Theatre.... The old custom of Free Orders, unjust in its principle, as rendering the Manager's nearest friends his worst customers, will be entirely abolished.... The PRICES will themselves be Reduced to
>
> BOXES, 2s. PIT 1s. GAL. 6d.
>
> The Custom also of HALF PRICE, which has long been considered by Foreigners the stigma of the British stage, converting the Theatres into mere lounges... will thus be greatly curtailed, by being limited to the BOXES ONLY, where ONE SHILLING will be the Admission for the SECOND ACCOUNT.

Of course Osbaldiston had to follow suit, cutting the Surrey prices to the same level on the same day.

How fared Ducrow at Astley's in Westminster Bridge Road, while the Surrey and the Coburg were trying to cut each other's throats? As it happened it was unnecessary for him to get involved in the battle for the south bank audiences. He had finished his summer programme by introducing zebras to his display and by putting on what purported to be a bull-fight in which the 'bull' was generally thought to be a padded horse, possibly one trained in the time-honoured 'wounded horse' routine. As long planned, he closed Astley's after the performance on 6 October 1832 and took his company to Brighton to prepare for a Command Performance for King William IV on November 19, the riding school behind the Pavilion being turned into a circus ring for the occasion. Ducrow did not return to his London base until 8 April 1833. By this time Davidge had been overthrown at the Coburg. Its winter season had been announced as ending on 30 March 1833: it did – and Davidge never re-opened there. He had lost not only his lease of the Coburg but also all his working capital. The Coburg was taken by Messrs Frampton and Fenton who must hold the record for the maximum historical effect in the shortest managerial period. They only lasted three months but in that time renamed the Coburg the Royal Victoria Theatre. Frampton (who turns up at the Surrey a dozen years later as director of a ballet company) and

Fenton were succeeded at the Victoria in 1833 by Messrs Abbott and Egerton who lasted little over a year.

Osbaldiston had been saved from defeat by Davidge's bankruptcy, even though discharge from that bankruptcy came quickly. He gave Davidge several weeks' employment at the Surrey from 22 July 1833 in such melodramas as *The Returned Pirate.*

There was then a theatrical 'General Post'. Davidge had said farewell to the New City Theatre on 13 January 1834, and starting in July that year did a three-month spell at Astley's under Ducrow. Abbott and Egerton quit the Royal Victoria. The seven-year lease of the Surrey granted to Elliston in 1827 expired and Osbaldiston did not renew. Davidge left Ducrow and took the Surrey Theatre, opening on 6 October 1834. The Victoria passed from Abbott and Egerton to the younger Glossop, then at the end of 1836 was taken by Lawrence Levy.

Again there was conflict between the two theatres, recounted by Edward Stirling, in his *Old Drury Lane:* 'An action for breach of contract was brought by Levy, of the Victoria, against Yates [of the Adelphi] and tried before Lord Denman.... The cause of the action was as follows: Yates had bargained to take his company and Adelphi pieces to the Victoria in the summer'. As it had been Yates's habit since Osbaldiston's time to summer at the Surrey, it was no wonder, Stirling tells us, that 'Davidge of the Surrey, alarmed at this arrangement, offered Yates better terms. Unjustly he broke with Levy, under the plea that it would have been illegal to perform pieces licensed by the Lord Chamberlain in an unlicensed theatre'. Stirling was called as a witness as to the nature of pieces which could be performed in an unlicensed theatre. Levy lost.

It might well be asked how the Levy/Yates contract could be deemed invalid while the Davidge/Yates contract was unassailable. Surely the Surrey was just as much an unlicensed theatre as was the Victoria? True, but by a quirk of jurisdiction the writ of the Lord Chamberlain did not run in St George's Fields, where the Surrey was situated. Tough on Levy! Possibly it was all a device by Yates to get better terms out of Davidge, as Yates had a very close relationship with Davidge and thereafter continued to bring his Adelphi company to the Surrey. Indeed the whole idea of the Surrey and the Victoria relying on legal approbation as to what they could or could not stage is ridiculous. On 20 March 1836 *The Age* had written:

> The performances at the Coburg and Surrey, licensed by law to consist of dancing and music, burlettas and so forth, are broken forth from the limits of all law and play nightly the copyright pieces of the two patent theatres.

It was another six years before the patent theatres lost their monopoly, but as Bunn at Drury Lane was a personal friend of Davidge and as Osbaldiston, now at Covent Garden, had long pontificated against the monopoly while at the Surrey, threats were not expected from that direction.

Stirling does not date the Levy/Yates action, but it may have been caused by Yates's visit to the Surrey in May 1837. The Surrey playbills refer to the Adelphi Company and say that 'Mr and Mrs Yates, Mr John Reeve, Mr Buckstone, Mr O. Smith, and Mrs Fitzwilliam will re-appear in a new drama, embracing the talent of the two companies, written by Buckstone'. There is also newspaper comment in February 1839 on the legal ties hampering the Adelphi but not the Surrey: 'DAVIDGE – ever on the alert – ever vigilant in the cause of popular entertainment, has once more engaged the Adelphi company to play on those nights on which the law so ridiculously prohibits Mr YATES from opening his own theatre'.

Lawrence Levy's lease of the Victoria ran out in 1841 and he did not renew. Instead Osbaldiston relinquished Covent Garden and took the Victoria over from Levy. The battle for the south bank audiences was now no longer between Davidge of the Coburg and Osbaldiston of the Surrey. It was to be between Davidge of the Surrey and Osbaldiston of the (Coburg)/Victoria. Once again it was the Surrey which won.

From their public exchange of accusations and insults I get a picture of Osbaldiston as a shade pompous, if not pretentious; of Davidge as a sharper blade with a naughty sense of humour, though (despite his taunting of Osbaldiston) with no better a command of the English language. Yet I have the feeling that they were merely acting out on their playbills their favourite parts on the stage. Osbaldiston, in this period, played Macbeth, Andreas Hofer, the tribune Caius Gracchus, and Baron de Trenck – all the 'name' parts of the various plays, all high and mighty. In the same period Davidge played Mr Twinkle (with comic song) in *The Farmer's Daughter,* Griffon, a low gambler, in *Victorine* and Harry Hammer, an amorous auctioneer, in *The Golden Farmer* – not one 'name' part, but all suitable for a little comic business.

What about Peter Roberts's comments on Davidge 'bringing in a large audience dirt cheap. And it brought in a dirty public'? Well, there is a sort of truth in this. All one can ask is, with cholera on the streets, what other audience is there to have?

Chapter Twelve

Introducing Davidge

As already recorded, Davidge appeared at the Surrey as an actor, singer and even horseman at various times from 1816 onwards. It is ironic that he fought such doughty battles against the Surrey as a manager elsewhere when his main connection with the theatre was as its manager from 1834 until his death in 1842. I think his contribution to the development of the Surrey has been much undervalued. It is not easy to put a finger on its exact nature but the results are easily defined – success and prosperity. When so many of his predecessors started with ample funds at the Surrey and finished bankrupt, it is the measure of Davidge that he started when just out of bankruptcy and finished with a small fortune.

G.B. Davidge was born in Bristol in 1794. At the age of fourteen he was apprenticed to a printer. He did not serve out his time. According to Edwin Fagg in *The Old 'Old Vic'* he was so fascinated by the playbills he was required to set up that he decided to become an actor. He must have acquired many of the skills of the printing trade, as in the 1830s he had his own printing press and was turning out playbills for his theatrical managements at the New City Theatre and at the Royal Amphitheatre, Liverpool. He tried to cope with the print run for the Coburg in 1831 but it was too much for him and he eventually contracted it out. He never attempted to do so at the Surrey though he was able to handle the output required by his smaller ventures.

Before he was twenty he had acted with some of the greatest names on the English stage. Edward Stirling tells a story of a production of *Henry VIII* at the Theatre Royal, Bath, with Sarah Siddons playing Queen Katherine and John Kemble as Cardinal Wolsey:

> The power of Mrs Siddons's eyes is so well known, having been so often noticed by her biographers. On the occasion about to be related, their effect upon a young actor of the name of Davidge, acting the Surveyor to the Duke of Buckingham was remarkable. At the words 'The Duke shall govern England' in a speech accusing his master, Buckingham, of treason to the King, Mrs Siddons (Katherine) fixing her piercing gaze upon him; he,

> kneeling with his back to the audience, received the full force of her fiery, flashing glances.
>
> *Q. Kath.* ...Take good heed
> You charge not in your spleen a noble person
> And spoil your nobler soul; I say, take heed;
> Yes, heartily beseech you.
>
> *King.* Let him on.
> Go forward.
>
> Not he; he was dumb; such was the effect of Mrs Siddons' eyes. Powerless with fright, the Surveyor remained transfixed to the ground. After a long pause, Kemble urged him to go on; the prompter repeatedly gave the words, 'On my soul, I'll speak the truth'. Neither truth nor falsehood could he utter with those terrible orbs, enraged, centred upon his timid face. The curtain was rung down amidst confusion and threats heaped upon the head of the unfortunate Davidge, who ran wildly out of the theatre, leaving Buckingham to be found guilty without his evidence.

Stirling later recounts that Davidge 'always retained in memory his first escapade, and resolved to redeem it. He carried this out by taking the Old Theatre Royal for two seasons, acting several of his best characters, Sir Peter Teazle, Justice Woodcock, etc.'.

Another good story of his early life shows him much more at home in the theatre, to the point where he could indulge on stage his life-long enjoyment of a joke. The *Memoirs of Joseph Grimaldi* (edited by Charles Dickens) recount how Grimaldi 'first became acquainted with Mr Davidge, the late lessee of the Surrey Theatre. He was then the Harlequin at Bath and Bristol, and although he afterwards became a round and magisterial figure, was then a very light and active pantomimist'. Davidge as Harlequin and Grimaldi as Clown worked with a 'very indifferent' Pantaloon whom they dubbed 'Billy Coombes' (not his real name). Coombes's occasional intoxication and other offences caused Davidge to desire revenge:

> One evening, while the pantomime was in progress, and the two friends were exciting much mirth and applause, Davidge pointed to a chest which was used in the piece, and whispering that there was a lock on it with a key, remarked that Billy had to get into it, and asked whether it would not be a good joke to turn the key upon him. Grimaldi readily concurred, and no sooner was Billy Coombes beneath the lid of

> the chest, than he was locked in, amidst the plaudits of the audience, who thought it a capital trick. There were but two more scenes in the pantomime, which Davidge had to commence. Just as he was going on the stage, Grimaldi inquired whether he had let out the Pantaloon.
>
> 'No,' he replied hastily,'I have not, but I will directly I come off.' So saying, he danced upon the stage, followed by Grimaldi, who felt very tired when he had gone through his part, in consequence of his recent illness, went straight home, and was in bed a very short time after the curtain fell.

When Pantaloon was absent from the rehearsal call next morning, Grimaldi assumed it was because the actor had taken their 'conduct in high dudgeon', but Davidge was stricken.

> 'By G—,' said Davidge, 'I never let him out of the box!' They lost no time in inquiring after the chest, and it was at length discovered in a cellar below the stage. On raising the lid, the Pantaloon was discovered, and a truly pitiable object he looked, although they were both not a little relieved to find he was alive, for, not knowing that the chest was perforated in various places, they had entertained some serious fears that when he did turn up, he might be found suffocated. Every necessary assistance was afforded him, and he never suffered in the slightest degree from his temporary confinement. He said he had shouted as loud as he could, and had knocked and kicked against the sides of his prison, but that nobody had taken the least notice of him, which he attributed to the incessant noise and bustle behind the scenes. With a view of keeping the stage as clear as possible, everything used in a pantomime is put away at once; the chest was lowered by a trap into the cellar, notwithstanding the shouts of the Pantaloon, who, knowing that he would be released next day, went to sleep very quietly.

Dickens as editor commented that this was 'the version of the story given by the ingenious Mr Coombes, and in this version Grimaldi was an implicit believer', though he thought that 'Mr Coombes might have thrown an additional light upon the matter by explaining that he had got into the chest that morning to turn the tables upon his assailants, the more so, as he received various little presents in way of compensation for his imprisonment, with which he expressed himself perfectly satisfied'. Myself, I am rather disposed to think that Mr Davidge might have thrown an additional light upon the matter by explaining that he had set up the whole affair as a joke against Grimaldi!

An account of the next part of Davidge's career can be found in his *Times* obituary of 1 February 1842. '...After many efforts in the private theatres then abounding in Bath and Bristol, he visited London and was engaged as a compositor by Mr Glendinning of Rupert Street, Haymarket. He worked there by day but played at night at the Dominion of Fancy, a small theatre opened by John Bologna and situate between Burleigh Street and Southampton Street, Strand.' Amongst Glendinning's customers was Charles Dibdin the Younger for whom he printed summaries of productions at Sadler's Wells, giving the words of the songs and descriptions of the scenery. These were then sold at the theatre. Who knows, but some of these may have been set by Davidge.

On 2 January 1812 Davidge married Jane Rutherford at the church of St Mary, Marylebone. It seems likely that she was from a theatrical family, not only because she appeared many times on stage with her husband, but also because her sister, Mrs Laura Meyer, a witness at her wedding, can be found at theatres and in small parts, gained as far as one can tell without Davidge's influence. For example a Surrey playbill for 26 December 1817 shows 'Mrs Meyer, of the King's Theatre, her first Appearance' in *The Christmas Tale.*

While on family matters, perhaps it is now time to get Davidge's full name right! A.H.Saxon's book *The Life and Art of Andrew Ducrow* has many references to Davidge and the Surrey Theatre and will keep referring to 'William' Davidge who was someone quite different, an actor with little or nothing to do with the Surrey. This is a mistake shared by other American authors – see, for example, *A History of the Theatre* by George Freedley and John A. Reeves, published in New York, which also refers to 'William' Davidge of the Surrey. The reason seems to be that this other man,William Pleater Davidge, managed to die in Wyoming of all places, and risks being adopted by the U.S.A. as the prototype of all Davidges. 'George Bolwell Davidge' is the name for the record. Another recurring error is to call him George Bothwell Davidge. This can be traced back to an obituary in *The Dispatch* of 13 February 1842 in which the reporter describes his 'coffin, which was of polished oak, thickly studded with black nails, bearing the inscription, "George Bothwell Davidge"'. This has been much copied since, yet the evidence for his middle name being 'Bolwell' is overwhelming – in his Will at the Public Record Office, in his business contracts at the Minet Library, in the records of Nunhead Cemetery where he was buried, in the index of deaths at St Catherine's House and in the parish records of his two marriages.

In his early twenties George B. Davidge made his 'First Appearance' before the Surrey audience he was later to know so well: on 15 July 1816 in *Who's the Murderer; or, A True Tale of the Twelfth Century.* This bill is interesting for the number of names which turn up time and again in the Surrey story: John Kirby, a renowned clown (who, like William Pleater Davidge, went to America and died there); Miss Smythies, the dancer; T.P. Cooke, Davidge's eventual executor; Yarnold (but which one of that large family?); Edward Fitzwilliam, who married Miss Copeland – both Surrey regulars.

Davidge was also in the pantomime which opened at the Surrey on 26 August 1816, *Dog and Duck; or, Harlequin in the Obelisk.* Davidge played Punch, Bologna was Clown, Yarnold Harlequin, Miss Tree Columbine and Miss Worgman Columbinetta. It ran to the middle of October. Davidge filled out the rest of his engagement with a series of small parts in pieces now known only from the playbills – *False Friend, Love in Full Gallop* and *Man in the Moon.*

Davidge then did a stint at the Sans Pareil (later the Adelphi) and was at the Coburg (later the Victoria) on its opening night of 11 May 1818, playing the part of Albert in *Trial by Battle* written by William Barrymore. Albert gets murdered in the course of the play – Davidge seldom played the hero or the romantic lead. Even though only 24 he was happy playing 'character' parts. In the notes made in 1818 by Edmund Simpson, an American talent-scout chronicled by Philip Highfill in *Theatre Notebook XII,* he is roughly written off: 'Mr Davidge called, old men etc. – understand he is a mouthing actor, fit only for the situation he now holds'. Certainly he was no Shakespearean. In his *Thirty-Five Years of a Dramatic Author's Life* Fitzball described Davidge as

> a man that caught at any popular chance, no matter what, so long as it served the immediate purpose of his pecuniary interest. He was a good, dry actor: in old men of blunt feelings, requiring to be well stirred up, quite at home. His veteran of a hundred years has left no competitor.

This refers to one of Davidge's favourite parts, Philip Gaibois 'an Invalid Soldier, aged 102', in *102; or, The Veteran and his Progeny.* As well as acting the old man, the play required him to sing 'Tho' time its snows hath sprinkled across my silver brow'. He chose *102* as his opening piece at the New City Theatre in November 1831, and at the Surrey on 6 October 1834.

In his early years, like any actor he was taking what he could. This included a two-week engagement at the beginning of May 1822 at the Royalty in Goodman's Fields, one of the first theatres to be built in the East End. The play was yet another version of Tom Moncrieff's *Tom and*

Jerry. This one was called *Tom, Jerry and Logic* and Mrs Jane Davidge also had a part. At best one could call it knock-about farce, but the 'Tom and Jerry' plays always drew good houses at that time, just as the 'Tom and Jerry' engravings of the day sold well. As Victorian standards supplanted those of the Regency, so the doings of the drinking, gambling, swindling, wenching 'heroes' lost favour. A later attempt to revive their old theatrical popularity was heavily attacked by the critics.

Following a short run at the Coburg the young Davidges obtained a six-month engagement at the Surrey, then under Watkins Burroughs, starting in October 1822. The Surrey was in one of its equestrian moods, with Messrs. Adams and Woolford in charge of the horses. Jane Davidge appeared in Amherst's horse-opera *The Infernal Secret,* with such company as Paul Bedford, the comedian and singer, and Tom Blanchard, celebrated clown and father of E.L.Blanchard whose scripts from 1840 onwards earned him the title of 'Pantomime King'. Another star was the Beautiful and Sagacious Pie-bald Ass. There are ten scenes. Act One starts on the 'Superb Gardens and Terrace of the Marquis Antaldi, on the Banks of the Ebro' while Act Two ends in the 'Interior of Bandits' Cavern with Secret Pass. This Scene is so constructed as to represent the greatest Extent of Subterranean Rock Scenery ever exhibited on any Stage, and for which Purpose the Back of the Theatre has been enlarged.' As to plot, I see that the sagacious Pie-bald Ass releases his master at some point and escapes with him, but it is not clear whether this is before or after the 'Sudden Appearance of Banditti, when the whole of the beautiful STUD of HORSES will make their Entree; Destruction of Palazzo by Banditti... Defeat of Banditti – and EXPLOSION of CAVERN!!!' Davidge himself was in 'a new comic burletta, to be called *Next Door Neighbours; or, A Matrimonial Noose',* in the part of Gripe, husband to Amelia, in love with Clarissa; while Richard Lawrence, later to be Davidge's Treasurer at the Surrey, played Flint, husband to Clarissa, in love with Amelia. Mrs Jane Davidge was Clarissa, and John Kirby was Davy, Gripes' servant, employed to keep an eye on Clarissa. That gives as much about the plot as anyone is likely to need.

The Infernal Secret ran for many weeks, with varying pieces in support, such as *The Barber; or, The Mill of Bagdad,* taken by Fitzball from *The Arabian Nights,* with Davidge as Hacko the Barber and Jane Davidge as Zena, again with Bedford, Blanchard, Kirby and Lawrence in the cast. In between these two items, 'Mr Carnegy will exhibit his astonishing Polandric Evolutions, Surrounded by a brilliant Display of FIRE WORKS! also his wonderful Antipodean Feat of Standing on his Head on the Point of a Spear 8 Feet high! BLOWING A TRUMPET!' – a hard act to follow.

Another supporting piece was *The Tread Mill; or, Tom and Jerry at Brixton.* The Davidges played Mr and Mrs Pringle. The story-line may have been slanted by Edward Fitzball in their direction, since he appears as 'first man' and she as 'first lady', while Corinthian Tom, Jerry Hawthorne and Logic come in well down the cast list.

On 30 December 1822 the Surrey put on *Massaniello, the Fisherman of Naples.* This was the play, not one of the two operas of which Henry Bishop's version was mounted in 1825, while the one much better known by Auber had its première three years after that (with Davidge directing it for the stage – but this is to anticipate).

London had seen magnificent processions on stage since at least the time of Marlowe and Shakespeare, but here is a touch of Japanese style in *Massaniello's* 'Magnificent Procession of the Viceroy in his State Carriage, drawn by 6 Real Horses.... This splendid Procession will be brought in a novel and highly effective Manner over a Platform crossing the Spacious PIT of this Theatre, and forming a Line of March upwards of 200 Feet in Length, constituting one of the most splendid Spectacles ever seen in any Theatre'. It seems impossible that Davidge was aware of the kabuki hanamichi – yet there it is at the Surrey in 1822.

When Watkins Burroughs had to leave the Surrey in March 1823 Davidge had a spell at Astley's. He seems to have learned some tricks during his association with Adams and Woolford, the horse-masters, as he had a riding part as Corinthian Tom in yet another 'Tom and Jerry' saga. From his riding career to one as a vocalist: at a benefit for Bengough at the Coburg on 4 October 1824 it was announced that '500 copies of a Comic Song to be sung by Mr Davidge' would be available. He also sang a duet with Miss Tunstall, 'Polly Hopkins'. He was sufficiently successful to get a year's engagement at the Coburg in 1824. He appeared mainly in English ballad-operas such as *The Beggar's Opera* on 22 November (as Peachum, with Buckstone as Filch and Mrs Fitzwilliam as Lucy Lockit); *The Ethiopian* (actually Henry Bishop's opera *The Slave* adapted for the occasion) on 17 October 1825; and on 7 November *The School for Maids* (Thomas Arne's *Love in a Village,* again adapted) in which Davidge played Justice Woodcock, a part he would play on many later occasions, while Jane Davidge played Madge. Then on 14 November they both appeared in a 'Popular Operetta called *Sir Peter Pry* written by Holcroft.' Whatever the relationship, if any, between Sir Peter and the better-known theatrical nuisance, Paul Pry, played by Davidge on 10 April 1826, the latter part requires pantomimic agility to carry off such moments as the approach to the rear-end of a red-hot poker. Davidge's days as Harlequin no doubt assisted.

Surrey Theatre.

On MONDAY, 30th Dec. 1822, & following Nights

Will be presented a new and splendid Serio-Comic, Hippo-dramatic, [illegible] Melo-Drama and Neapolitan Spectacle, called

MASSANIELLC

The Fisherman of Naples,

AND

DELIVERER of his COUNTRY !!!

[illegible] Music composed by Mr. [illegible]. The Scenery by Mr. [illegible] [illegible] The Machinery by Mr. [illegible] The Properties by Mr. [illegible]. The Dresses by Mr. [illegible]. The [illegible] arranged by Mr. [illegible].

The Whole produced under the immediate Direction and Superintendance of Mr. DAVIDGE.

SPANIARDS.

The Duke of Arcos (*Viceroy for the King of Spain of the Kingdom of Naples*) Mr. LAWRENCE. Duke of Mataloni (*Grandee of Spain*) Mr. SMI

Don Pepe Carafa (*his Brother, Secretary of State*) Mr. GALE. Cardinal Filomarino (*Archbishop of Naples*) Mr. ADCOCK.

Ricardo (*Serjeant of the Spanish Guard*) Mr. J. KNIGHT. Valverdo (*Officer of the Spanish Guard*) Mr. SHAW.

NEAPOLITANS.

Tomaso Aniello (*commonly called Massaniello*) Mr. H. KEMBLE. Popoloni Aniello (*his Cousin*) Mr. DAVIDGE.

Dominico Perrone (*Captain of a Band of Outlaws*) Mr. AULD. Gregorio Perrone (*his Brother and Lieutenant*) Mr. WOOLFO

Zulio Genoino (*Regent, or Chief Magistrate of the City*) Mr. MORETON. Andreas Anaclerio (*Elect of the People*) Mr. BEDFORD.

Baptiste, Guiseppe, and Iachimo (Three Fishermen) Messrs. JERVIS, CLARKE, and BRUNTON.

And Giulo Genovino (*an outlawed Monk*) Mr. BENGOUGH.

Leona (*Wife of Massaniello*) Mrs. POPE. Teresa Aniello (*Wife of Popoloni*) Mrs. DAVIDGE. Giacinta, Miss JONAS.

Spanish Officers and Guards, Dignitaries of the Church, Outlaws, Neapolitan Citizens, &c. &c. by the Rest of the Company, aided by upwards of SIXTY SUPERNUMERARIES expressly engaged for the Occasion.

Julius Cæsar, by the PIE-BALD ASS. Pompey the Great, by Little BLACK BOB.

ACT II.——SCENE V.

The Court Yard of the Citadel, adjoining the Viceroy's Palace.

Magnificent Procession !

OF THE VICEROY IN HIS

STATE CARRIAGE, drawn by 6 REAL HORSES

Attended by all the Spanish Authorities in their Official Costume.——Cardinal Archbishop, attended by all the *Dignitaries and Grandeur of the Romish Church.* [illegible] Grandees of Spain, splendidly apparelled, MOUNTED ON HORSES ELEGANTLY CAPARISONED [illegible] and other Insignia of State. Powerful MILITARY BAND, engaged expressly for the Occasion. Massaniello mounted on a

BEAUTIFUL WAR HORSE, IN COMPLETE ARMOUR.

Attended by the Whole of the Patriotic Citizens of Naples, armed.

☞ This splendid Procession will be brought in a novel and highly effective Manner over a Platform crossing the SPACIOUS PIT of this Theatre, and forming a *Line of March upwards of 200 Feet in Length*, constituting one of the most splendid Spectacles ever seen in any Theatre.

Act III.——Scene 5.——Street in Naples.

Solemn FUNERAL PROCESSION of Massaniello !

His Corse borne on a splendid Funeral Car, drawn by Six Horses !

(Original curtailed at margins)

From all-round performer to manager: in 1826 Davidge took the lease of the Coburg and gave work to all the family. His opening piece, on Easter Monday 27 March 1826, was *The Manager's Vision* with 'Mr Davidge at his Fireside' reminiscing, and introducing his company (and family) to his patrons. Again, on the playbill for 26 December 1826 can be found not only Davidge and his wife, but also his brother-in-law Meyer (as Sir Christopher Hatton in *The Golden Days of Good Queen Bess)* and his nephew Master (George) Meyer as Hymen in a Cinderella ballet. The playbills for his benefit on 14 May 1827 show his private address as 5 Charlotte Terrace, on the New Cut, easy walking distance from his 'shop'. Six weeks later (25 June) Davidge put on his favourite piece *102,* playing, of course, the old veteran Philip Gaibois.

Next year comes the only letter written by Davidge that I have been able to find. It is held by the Garrick Club. Dated 15 June 1828, it is addressed to an unidentified theatrical agent.

> My Dear Sir, I have just seen Mr Larkin I wish to engage him for Monday next, but am without a Female singer can you send me one, the two [Patent] Theatres are about closing perhaps some lady may be selected and permission obtained for her leaving before the end of the season. Have you written to Miss Field? I am My Dear Sir Yours etc. G.B. Davidge

The playbills of Monday 23 June show which lady was selected, giving 'Advance Notice: New Operatic Drama in which Miss Hallands and Mr Larkin from Theatre Royal Covent Garden will make their First Appearance'. But they didn't. 'Monday June 30 1828 In consequence of a Domestic Calamity the appearance of Mr Larkin is postponed' – but only until Monday 21 July:

Wreck of the Leander Frigate

Falkland	Mr Larkin who will introduce the favourite Ballad of 'The Young Blooming Bride'
Ulah an Indian Girl	Miss Hallands
Ben Block	T.P. Cooke

A series of accounts by various writers now enable us to see something of Davidge's acting and character. Edwin Fagg describes the requirements of a part performed by Davidge in Douglas Jerrold's play *Descart, The French Buccaneer* (September 1828). As the timid traveller, Tramp, who supplies the comic relief, the manager.had to show 'his fear of the savages, who, rolling their eyes and licking their lips, are assessing him in terms of possible cutlets. While [he is] hiding up a tree, a blackamoor embarrasses his Betsy... whereupon the indignant Tramp fires, scores a bull's eye, and becomes a hero'. When he plays a contrasting role, Davidge gets the approval of *The Times* (21 April 1829) in a Coburg piece

> which attracted the particular attention of the audience, entitled *Peter Bell, the Waggoner.* The plot is sufficiently full of natural incident to touch the feelings, and is worked out with sufficient skill and effect to satisfy the judgment. The acting of Mr Davidge in the character of Peter Bell, while he is labouring under the mental anguish caused by a false accusation of murder, called forth that silent tribute which is the most decisive meed of approbation – the sympathy of his hearers.

Davidge shows up well in Charles Dickens's account of Joey's son in *The Memoirs of Grimaldi.* 'The great clown's son had fallen into bad company and into the lowest state of wretchedness and poverty. His dress had fallen into rags, his feet were thrust into two worn-out slippers, his face was pale with disease and squalid with dirt and want, and he was steeped in degradation... even his own parents could scarcely recognise him.' Hardly the material for the theatre; yet at Christmas 1829, Dickens continues, he obtained a situation at the Coburg through the kindness of Davidge and there he remained until Easter 1830.

There is also a record of Grimaldi junior appearing with Davidge in *Don Juan* at the New City Theatre in March 1832, playing Scaramouche, the part with which he had started his career at Sadler's Wells in 1815. Osbaldiston also gave young Grimaldi a chance on 7 May 1832 at the Surrey, in *Harlequin and Oberon,* with Ellar and Barnes (two of Joey Grimaldi's partners) no doubt doing their best to prop up his son. Unfortunately by this time young Grimaldi was past saving. The debtors' prison and an early death brought his sad story to an end. It cannot have been easy to follow such a famous father.

A further insight comes from Fitzball. Kemble and Fawcett, managing the Theatre Royal, Covent Garden, requested a new melodrama. On Fitzball asking of what kind it should be, he was told by Fawcett to 'Look into the papers, incidents enough invented there! The other day, a girl carried off by a savage fellow! Rock of Charbonnier'. Fitzball had to admit having dramatised the subject already for Davidge at the Coburg. 'Hem! you should have brought it here. Savage fellow, T.P. Cooke! Girl carried off, Mrs Vining!' The incident treated by Fitzball was a French cause-célèbre in which a girl had been abducted by a 'wild man' who had concealed her somewhere amongst the rocks of Charbonnier:

> This piece I had sold to the manager, Mr Davadge *[sic]* at the Cobourg and it was already in rehearsal. The following morning, during rehearsal at the Cobourg, I happened to tell Davadge what had transpired between myself, Mr C. Kemble, and Mr Faucett *[sic]*, respecting the story of the Charbonnier. Davadge, who was a blunt man, a little in the Faucett school, was nevertheless of a very good disposition, immediately took the M.S. from the prompter, and handing it over to me, observed, 'Your fortune is made; this is a capital piece, send it to Covent Garden, they will read, and bring it out in style, so far exceeding anything we could possibly do, that I have not the slightest doubt of its making a most tremendous hit, and you can write for us another drama, on any subject you think proper.' This was a very generous action, I forwarded my melodrama to Covent Garden; it was at once read and accepted.

In due course Fitzball returned the favour. During Davidge's first two months of managing at the Surrey Theatre he asked Fitzball if he could 'supply him with some novelty'. Fitzball provided his Scott-based 'operatic drama' *The Lord of the Isles*. This proved so successful that Davidge cleared £700. It 'set him so upon his legs, that it led to a train of good fortune, whereby he died worth, at least, £30,000', says Fitzball, giving details of this production:

> The singers engaged for this purpose were Wilson, Edwin, Morley, Miss Somerville and Miss Land. This was, according to my recollection, the first operatic attempt at the Surrey Theatre, and exceedingly well it answered the purpose. Rodwell's music pleased everybody. The 'Bridal Ring' and 'Flower of Ellerslie', especially, became quite popular airs. We have seen, since, how that audience has been taught to relish and appreciate the music, not only of our own Balfe and Wallace, but of Bellini, Meyerbeer, and Donizetti: while our first national singers have found a sanctuary on the boards of the Surrey Theatre, when the national doors were all closed against them.... *The Lord of the Isles* ran, I believe, eighty nights – most astonishing for an opera then on that side of the water.

Fawcett's advice to Fitzball to 'Look into the papers, incidents enough invented there!' seems to be an echo or condensation of advice given by Saint-Romain, the manager of the Théâtre Porte Saint Martin, in Paris. When one realises how many Surrey pieces came in translation from that theatre, it is not surprising that its manager's views should also be known: that aspiring playwrights should select themes dark and terrible by visiting criminal courts, the gallows, the morgue, the mad-house and the hospitals. Davidge had himself gone at least twice to the Porte St Martin theatre and brought back plays for translation. Fitzball did not approve of the English theatres borrowing foreign pieces (taking the bread out of his mouth?), but was prepared to accept that

> The drama of the present day seems nearly all composed of translations; the real merit, then – that is to say, the inventive merit – must be awarded to our French allies in particular. The drama of the last half century was more the coinage of English brains.

The Davidge story can be taken up again by Edwin Fagg:

> In 1832 Davidge became proprietor of the New City Theatre and the Coburg company played there and at the Coburg on the same night. The City Theatre was one of the many subscription theatres which had come into being with the object of evading penalties incurred by stage entertainment without patent authority; price of admission was paid in a neighbouring shop.

Erroll Sherson expands on this, explaining that in 1831 John Kemble Chapman had opened the New City Theatre in Milton Street, Cripplegate:

> This out-of-the-way little theatre aspired to be a sort of dramatic Academy for beginners. It is also probable that the Directors imagined by thus putting instruction in the forefront they might be able to 'drive a coach and horses' through that particular Act of Parliament which forbade any dramatic shows except at the Patent Theatres.... After a time, Chapman got tired of fighting the Patent Theatres and gave up the direction of the City Theatre to Davidge of the Coburg across the water, who made it a double of that house in the most ingenious manner. Coaches were employed to take the company from one house to the other, fitted up as dressing-rooms to save time.

The playbills suggest that Davidge had an interest in the New City Theatre as early as November 1831. He and Jane Davidge appeared in *Victorine* and *102;* and as he later chose *102* with which to open his term at the Surrey it looks as if he regarded this as his 'signature tune'. From January 1832 the playbills, though bearing no indication as to management, show at the foot: 'Davidge, Printer, Lambeth.' It does not look as if the same pieces were played at the Coburg and the City on the same evening, nor were players transferred wholesale. Davidge and his wife and one or two leading players may have used the travelling changing-rooms, but the supporting players at each place were different. When Mrs Chapman appeared at the Coburg she was specifically described as of the City Theatre. One finds the same ballad-operas at the two venues – *Beggar's Opera, Native Land* (Rossini's music, arranged by Bishop) and *Midas,* but well spaced out. Other Davidge stock pieces also appear at both places: *The Old Oak Chest,* in which he took three parts (the bold buccaneer Tinoco de Lasso, Father Philip and Dame Juggett), and *Broken Heart; or, The Farmer's Daughter of the Severn Side* in which as Mr Twinkle he 'will introduce the Popular Song of "Fighting for the Breeches"'. We note in passing that Richard Shepherd, later to become lessee of the Surrey, who had a small part in *Broken Heart* at the New City did not secure that part when the production was moved to the Coburg in April 1832.

Davidge's next, and concurrent, venture was announced on the Coburg playbills for 15 October 1832, namely the re-opening under his management of the Royal Amphitheatre, Liverpool. He took this from 22 October. How he thought he could run three widely-separated theatres simultaneously defies the imagination, unless he was influenced by the developing railway system. The last night of that Coburg season was 'in aid of the Fund for supporting the Cause of the National Drama against the pretensions of the monopolists' – that is, the patent theatres. With hindsight it would have been better for Davidge to have put the whole proceeds into his treasury.

On 22 November 1832 the Liverpool Amphitheatre staged *Dominique the Resolute* (which Davidge had put on at the Coburg in September 1831) under the 'immediate superintendence of Mr Davidge who had visited Paris expressly for the purpose of witnessing the performance'.

In an obituary of Davidge is a remark that 'by his first wife he had a daughter who, it is said, died of grief at his absence (he was at Liverpool at the time)'. I have been unable to verify this; presumably her death would have been in this period.

He was back at the Coburg for Boxing Day 1832. He appeared in *The Golden Farmer* with many of his old team, Eugene Macarthy, Robert Honner, Mrs Searle (who was Columbine in the pantomime), and Tom Blanchard as Pantaloon. Perhaps through bad communication, or too many things to think about when he was in Liverpool, he missed payment of the lease rent on the Coburg. Randle Jackson, who had a financial stake in the theatre, smartly put him into the bankruptcy court. In fact

Davidge was able to meet all his liabilities and was commended by the Commissioner of Bankruptcy for so doing, but it meant that he had forfeited his lease of the Coburg. It was also the end of his Liverpool adventure. He had to run his cash down to rock-bottom. When he died the obituary in *The Times* commented on the money he had put into the Coburg: 'This sum he lost and had no resource save an annuity of £200 per annum which in his prosperous days he had settled on Mrs Davidge'. His management of the Coburg finished at the end of March 1833.

This left him with just the New City Theatre, though he appeared as guest artist at the Surrey in July. Perhaps this was Osbaldiston's way of showing magnanimity to his opponent of the Battle of the Pay Orders. In August 1833 Davidge revived *102* at the New City, but he had another theatre in his sights – the New Globe Theatre, otherwise the Rotunda, in Blackfriars Road. This was a peculiar place. Originally a museum of curiosities and then a penny wax-works show run by a Mr Checketts (who had another wax-works at 67 Fleet Street), it then became a circus and juvenile theatre, one of the attractions being 'Pincushion Jenny with 7 legs shod, and stands on six feet'. On 29 January 1833 there had been an auction of 'the 7 legged mare' and furniture and fixtures 'under execution for Rent'. Davidge acquired the lease of this curiosity shop, thus vacated. The playbills of the New City Theatre of 4 November announced 'Entirely New Management. Mr Moncrieff... has taken the above theatre. Mr Davidge having been engaged for a limited period, previous to his opening the New Globe Theatre....' Davidge took his farewell of the New City Theatre on 13 January 1834 in *The Village Shark*. If he did open at the New Globe, his footsteps in the sands of time have been obliterated. A clue at the Greater London Record Office suggests that the Globe ceased to be a theatre in 1838.

Because of his somewhat unceremonious departure from the Coburg at the end of March 1833 there had not been the opportunity for Davidge to take the usual farewell benefit. As we know, he had been succeeded by Messrs Frampton and Fenton who lasted a mere three months (but changed the theatre's name to the Royal Victoria). They in turn were succeeded in July 1833 by Messrs. Abbott and Egerton, a pair of actors who had been together at Covent Garden. Davidge's version of his dispute with them over a benefit can be found in a public announcement, a copy of which is held by the Garrick Club:

> A few friends who took a kind interest in my behalf, applied to Messrs. Abbott and Egerton to ascertain whether the use of the Victoria Theatre could be obtained for one night, to afford themselves and the public an opportunity of evincing their

> opinion of my character and conduct. After several interviews, extending through a period of twelve days, Messrs. Abbott and Egerton declined letting the Theatre for a specific sum (on which terms any stranger might have obtained it) on the plea that the receipts on this night would be so very great, as materially to injure those of the nights to follow, and the only terms to which they would accede were to take one half of the entire receipts, a determination expressed in the following letter:
>
> Royal Victoria Theatre, Monday 10 February [1834]
>
> Dear Sir,
> I am desired by Mr Abbott and Mr Egerton to inform you that they will have great pleasure in giving you a Monday night, the receipts to be equally divided. The first open Monday will be the 3 March next.
>
> I am, dear sir, your obedient servant,
> Charles Broad
>
> To G. B. Davidge Esq.
>
> Considering the affair concluded on this basis, I immediately communicated the matter to my friends and proceeded to give to the approaching benefit every possible degree of publicity, in the course of which proceedings I disposed of near 1600 Box and Pit Tickets.

Then Abbott called on Davidge and told him that 'from certain orders, instructions or commands of the Proprietors, the Benefit could not take place', and on 24 February Abbott wrote to Davidge confirming this and proposing arbitration. Davidge then approached the proprietors, Francis and Joseph Glossop, to find out why his benefit was forbidden. Francis Glossop wrote on 27 February that he knew nothing of the matter, and 'I wish Mr Davidge may receive a beneficial engagement, so far as my interest in the Theatre I wish him to enjoy'.

Messrs Abbott and Egerton then moved their ground. They claimed that they were forbidden by Randle Jackson, 'The Executor of a Mortgagee on the Victoria Theatre, not in possession', and that they were unable to proceed with the arbitration fixed for 1 March on a plea that the arbitrator they had proposed was 'about to leave town'.

Davidge clearly doubted their story: 'Would any men in their senses accept a lease of a Theatre encumbered with clauses depriving them of the power of letting for such purposes and to their own advantage?' (Abbott and Egerton were to get half of the benefit proceeds, after all.)

So, with 1600 tickets sold and two days to go, Abbott and Egerton announced the 'postponement' of the benefit – though still, it would appear, hanging on to the whole of the proceeds. But as recounted the Abbott/Egerton management was falling to pieces in the face of the Surrey successes; the Victoria was 'literally deserted'. Egerton left and shortly after was bankrupt. By August 1834 Abbott had surrendered his lease to the younger Glossop. If we accept that Randle Jackson was at the root of this trouble (we know that he was the person quick to slap a court order on Davidge when he was away) we may well wonder, as did Davidge, how relations between them reached this state. He records that he had been paying £2,000 a year rent:

> This I paid for a period of between nine and ten years; and then, with four years of my lease unexpired, I am suddenly dispossessed, in a manner which I scruple not to say was disgraceful to the party who projected it.... He is the same, who now comes forward with this new act of oppression.... Whence should this spirit of persecution arise? Can this intermeddling party show that from any other hands the same amount of rent, for so long a period, could ever have been received?

Whatever the reason, there is no trace of Davidge ever having given his final benefit performance at the Coburg. Nor is there word of the tickets sold in advance, so the proceeds may have been swallowed up in Egerton's bankruptcy.

Osbaldiston decided not to renew his lease of the Surrey. It was announced at the end of June 1834 that the Surrey Theatre was to be let to the highest bidder. At the end of August, *The Age* disclosed that 'Davidge is the new lessee of the Surrey Theatre – he is to pay seventeen hundred pounds per annum rent for it. It is said little Wilkinson has joined him in the speculation'. James Pimbury Wilkinson of Prospect Place, Southwark, referred to in Davidge's will simply as 'my friend', was a member of the Adelphi company under Frederick Yates. He would be seen at the Surrey when Yates took his company there for the summer season. Mrs Wilkinson appeared more often at the Surrey, for example under Osbaldiston in July 1832, and later with Davidge.

Davidge appeared as a guest artist at Astley's between July and September 1834 but, as *The Age* reported on 7 September: 'Davidge is all activity,and intends opening the Surrey early in October. A new stage will be laid down, and the house will be re-imbellished and improved'. Glossop at the Victoria did not like this turn of events and planned to re-open his theatre on the same night as Davidge launched his Surrey venture. The battle for the Surrey-side audiences was in full swing again.

One feature of Davidge's forthcoming time at the Surrey is the way he adapted himself to Elliston's ideas of increasing the operatic content of the bills, and established his own policy of producing foreign operas translated into English. If these were his own ideas, one ought to be able to see some earlier pointers to coming events. His earliest experience of opera was his appearance in *The Young Hussar* at the Surrey in 1823, but when he took the management of the Coburg in 1826 the operatic content for his first two years was minimal. There were no more than three a year, and those the standard English ballad-operas favoured by all the minor theatres such as *The Beggar's Opera, The Slave, The Exile, Lodoiska,* and *Love in a Village*; the foreign-composed content was nil. In 1829 however a distinct change in policy appeared. Seven operas were staged, including 'the celebrated German Opera *Das Donauweibchen* by Kauer and Bierey arranged by T. Hughes and M. Corri'. As the effort runs a year or more behind Elliston at the Surrey, we may take it that Davidge saw how Elliston was drawing the crowds and set out to copy him. Part of the delay seems to have been due to inadequate resources of the resident company as at this time Davidge started engaging musical talent from elsewhere, in particular George Stansbury from the Theatre Royal, Covent Garden, 'who when he has not the honour of appearing on stage will preside at the Piano Forte'. Stansbury later moved with Davidge to the Surrey as his Musical Director and was remembered in his will.

None of Davidge's slight operatic manifestation at the Coburg seems to be more than a nervous twitch in response to Elliston's pioneering work at the Surrey. There was a gap of eighteen months between Davidge leaving the Coburg and taking the Surrey. Nothing in that period suggests that he was suddenly bitten by the opera bug. What motivated him? Could it have been because, at the Coburg/Victoria, Joseph Glossop's daughter had blossomed as a composer of opera, and her works were being announced for production there? Davidge may have been beaten by Elliston in the operatic field, but was he determined not to be beaten by Miss Glossop? If so, he need not have bothered. *The Satirist* of 8 February 1835 reported: 'The marriage of Mr à Beckett, the clever farce writer... with Miss M. Glossop, was, we hear, a stolen one. The parties had been three weeks in the happy state before it reached the ears of her father.' The operas of Mrs Gilbert Abbott à Beckett, née Glossop, now appeared at the St James's Theatre, no competitor of the Surrey.

G. B. Davidge as Tinoco de Lasso in *The Old Oak Chest*

Chapter Thirteen

Davidge's First Year at the Surrey (1834/35)

After Davidge took over the Surrey's management from Osbaldiston in September 1834 very few of the same names appear in the theatre's playbills. It looks as if virtually the whole of Osbaldiston's company chose to go off with him to his new venture at Covent Garden. Only five actors threw in their lot with Davidge, namely Maitland, Rumball, Dibdin Pitt, Edwin and C. Hill, though Carberry the box-office manager and J.M. Jolly, leader of the band, also remained.

Davidge must have faced great problems in building up a new company without losing his audience while he did it. His whole career shows him rising to such challenges as this and thriving on them. In his first two months he staged about fifteen melodramas, three operas (one, *The Lord of the Isles,* a première) and *Hamlet;* of all these, only one had been in Osbaldiston's repertoire.

Others of his New City company such as Eugene Macarthy joined him at the Surrey. He drew on the dramatic resources of Ducrow's company, for example casting Mrs Stickney, wife of one of Ducrow's riders, as Queen Gertrude in *Hamlet.* He also persuaded Miss Watson and the comedian William Smith to leave the Royal Victoria and come back to the Surrey. Within a short time Miss Macarthy followed, perhaps on her father's recommendation.

A staunch follower of Davidge was Thomas Eallett, property-man, who had been responsible for the 'Decorations and Embellishments' at the Coburg, and who considered himself Davidge's personal retainer rather than the employee of any particular theatre. He stayed with Davidge literally to the death. There was also a fine scenic artist, Phil Phillips, who served Davidge and the Surrey well for several years before taking a tavern with some land attached at Stangate, on the south side of Westminster Bridge. Here he built the Bower, a place of entertainment something like the Grecian in City Road. He drew on his old friends at the Surrey for his acts. William Smith went there from the Surrey in 1846 and at least two of his young hopefuls, James Fernandez and Adelaide Biddles (later Mrs Charles Calvert), went from the Bower to the Surrey in leading roles.

Robert Honner who had made his name at Sadler's Wells also joined Davidge as actor and stage manager. He was later to give rise to some public interest in his private life. *The Satirist* of 1 November 1835 came up with the story that 'Mr Honner, stage manager of the Surrey was last week united to Miss Macarthy of the same theatre'. Her father contradicted this story in the next issue. 'My attention has been directed to a paragraph in your paper of Sunday last announcing the marriage of Miss Macarthy to Mr Honner of the Surrey Theatre, and, as there is not the slightest foundation for such a report, I trust you will do me the honour to contradict it. Eugene Macarthy, Pownall Cottage, Kennington Rd.' Well, it is a wise father who knows his daughter's heart. The three of them continued appearing together at the Surrey, father and daughter for example playing Gratiano and Portia in *The Merchant of Venice* on 7 March 1836, and Honner and Miss Macarthy playing Roderigo and Desdemona in *Othello* on 22 March. And on 21 May they appeared at the church of St Mark, Kennington, where Maria Macarthy married Robert Honner. *The Satirist* had had the right idea all along but was just a little early with the news.

Maria was of star quality. She played Poll against T.P. Cooke in *My Poll and My Partner Joe* and Virginia against Elton of the Adelphi in *Virginius*. Just before her marriage, *The Times* reported on 5 April:

> Miss Macarthy... played with her usual good taste and feeling. This young lady is a most promising actress and will become – or we should rather say, has already become – a very valuable acquisition to the stage. Without any effort at imitation, her acting reminds us more of the simple and natural manner of Miss Kelly than of any other lady at present on the stage (Mrs Fitzwilliam and Mrs Yates excepted)....

This is somewhat qualified praise, but it puts her at number four in the theatrical hierarchy. Both she and her husband were loyal to the Davidge influence at the Surrey and appear time and again until that influence ended in 1848.

Davidge was thus laying good foundations for excellence at the Surrey. From the start of his management it forged ahead of his former theatre, once the Coburg, currently the Royal Victoria (the Old Vic as it was to become). On 5 October 1834, for example, *The Age* lambasted the Victoria for its 'Othello and Iago being misrepresented by Elton and H. Wallack. Glossop has relied on a sheet of glass; he had much better have procured a good company with the money he has expended on that bauble'. The manager, young Henry Glossop, evidently put too much faith in his looking-glass curtain as an attraction to the public.

When B.S. Fairbrother, who had been Osbaldiston's treasurer, temporarily withdrew from theatrical matters to devote himself to the management of the adjacent Equestrian Tavern and Coffee House, in his place Davidge appointed his old acting companion of the 1820s, Richard Lawrence. *The Age* of 19 October 1834 mentions two other acquisitions:

> Davidge is determined to rival the majors, and has engaged Butler to perform Shakspeare's characters; he has personated Hamlet, Shylock and King Lear and has made a wonderful impression on the good people of Surrey. Mrs Lovell has also become an established favourite on that side of the water. It is somewhat singular that the lady and gentleman possess talents of the first order, and have tried their luck at the patent theatres, and succeeded; why then are they compelled to cross the river for support? In the present dearth of talent, they are invaluable; and much praise is due to Davidge for engaging them.

The Satirist spoke well of the new venture. On 9 November 1834 readers were told that 'Davidge is doing well in his new speculation. *The Seven Clerks* are beneficial accessories to the treasury accounts. Davidge's own acting is enough to save the piece, were it otherwise unworthy'. Again, on 14 December and then 1 February 1835:

> We dropped in on Davidge on Monday evening, and found, what must have rejoiced the manager and all parties concerned, an uncommonly crowded house. It was a goodly sight to see boxes and pit crowded to overflowing; and the gallery, nearly the largest in any theatre, densely crammed with human beings in a high state of fun and perspiration....

> Davidge possesses a very excellent judgment in the selection of his company; each department is complete. W. Smith is gifted with a happy sense of humour; Honner's quick judgment and stage skill is of a very superior order; Edwin's singing is tasteful and delicate... and then there is the ever-pleasing, smiling, good-tempered Rumball.

As Osbaldiston had done in the previous year, Davidge offered the use of the Surrey to Frederick Yates of the Adelphi Theatre during the periods when Yates, who only had a winter licence, could not act in his own place. *The Age* of 12 April 1835 reported that 'Davidge has secured the assistance of the Adelphi stars for his Easter piece, which has been some time in preparation. It is written by [Benjamin] Webster of Drury

Lane, and the principal characters will be personated by Mrs Yates, Mrs Honey, Miss Vincent, Yates, Reeve and Buckstone'. A week later *The Satirist* added its comments:

> Davidge, we perceive, opens with a new piece, in which many of the Adelphi actors will perform. The junction of the two companies will enable him to make head against all competitors, should he have any, which just now he has not. A clear field is now open to him, and we trust he will reap all the advantage from it he deserves.

A popular acquisition for the Surrey was the writer John Thomas Haines whose plays pulled in the crowds, particularly *My Poll and My Partner Joe, Jack Sheppard* and *The Tower of London* . A criticism appears in various sources that Davidge was hard on his authors. He and Haines got on well together, though *The Satirist* obviously had heard rumours to the contrary and broadcast these on 22 November 1835:

> Davidge brings out a new nautical drama, entitled *Tom Tackle; or, Happy Go Lucky,* tomorrow evening. It will be played after *My Poll and My Partner Joe,* a drama which seems destined to rival the most long-lived of its predecessors. We have heard, by the way, of some particulars of the latter piece, from which it appears that the manager drove what may be termed a 'hard bargain' with the author, taking care at the same time to secure wholly to himself all the profits of its marvellous success. Davidge, in short, seems to have a thorough and scientific knowledge of the power of the 'screw', and in this instance, if we are informed aright, has turned his knowledge to good account – much to the dissatisfaction of the author, Mr Haines. It is common enough certainly for the poor author to come off but scurvily in these matters; still parsimony, on the part of a manager is neither just, nor, in the long run, profitable.

I have not traced the agreement regarding *My Poll and My Partner Joe,* presumably made in August 1835, but an agreement between Haines and Davidge made six months later is still held at the Minet Library in Lambeth. It was hand-written by Haines personally on 13 January 1836 (shortly after the comments by *The Satirist)* and shows no signs that he bore any resentment of the terms reached. It gives Davidge sole performing rights in London, but Davidge 'renounces all profit or remuneration that may be derived from... publication, or from the performances of the said drama in the provinces... to mean beyond ten miles from London'. A wide-ranging letter from Haines accompanying an agreement dated 9 May 1838 is also couched in friendly terms:

> I send the Agreement which I have had ready for some days in the expectation of seeing you – the piece I spoke of I am not yet ready with but have a pantomime Melodrama – with a part which Mrs Henry Vining would play very well indeed and a good one for my beloved William Smith. I see you are announced to act at Drury. Will the next Affiche be as Lessee?
>
> I am not very expert at drawing up Legal things – but I believe the enclosed is right – I draw them up as I would if they occurred in a Drama – good Logic but bad Law perhaps,
>
> With my very best respects, I am, Sir, Yours very truly,
>
> J.T. Haines
>
> P.S. Pray remember the bearer Mr Forbes if possible in the way of Engagement.

Davidge did remember Mr Forbes, in fact gave him a year's employment in such parts as Mr Sowerberry in *Oliver Twist,* Archbishop of Cologne in *The Rich Man of Frankfort* (in which Mrs Henry Vining and 'beloved William Smith' also appeared), the Notary in *La Sonnambula* and several other minor roles.

The view of Davidge being hard on his authors is repeated in the *Reminiscences* of E.L.Blanchard, later to become the 'King of Pantomime'. As he was only in his mid-teens in 1835 and did not reach the theatrical mainstream for another five years I suspect that the story had been 'improved' by the time it reached him. Thomas Egerton Wilks had written a two-act burletta, *Lord Darnley; or, the Keep of Castle Hill,* and Blanchard writes that

> Davidge of the Surrey proved sweet on the play. Finding this to be the case, Wilks, who usually was paid about a pound an act for his dramas, saw an opportunity to get a better price. 'I like your piece very much.' 'Glad to hear it.' 'What's the price?' said the parsimonious Surrey manager. 'Fifteen pounds.' Davidge started as from an electric shock. Wilks remained obdurate. 'Come', said Davidge, 'don't be hard. Look here', and drawing out a greasy canvas bag he jingled the pieces inside, and laid out one by one in a row before the fascinated eyes of Wilks, seven sovereigns and a half-sovereign. 'I closed with him', said the playwriter; 'it was the sight of the precious metal. No cheque, not a banknote, could have produced such an effect.'

Wilks's burletta reached the Surrey stage in the autumn of 1837. As he received over three times his normal rate, and as Blanchard himself had only £10 for one of his pantomimes from Shepherd at the Surrey fifteen years later, one wonder why 'parsimonious' was inserted into the story.

There is another story said to illustrate Davidge's tightness with his employees. As it appeared some forty years after his death, like Blanchard's story it may have been 'improved'. J.A. Cave, writing in *The Entr'acte Almanack* under the title 'Managerial Economy', imaginatively rcounts how an unheralded caller asked to see Davidge:

> The eccentric little manager went to the stage-door, and seeing the individual who had dared to request an interview, said – 'Well, sir and what is this important matter you want to speak to me about?'
>
> The answer was, 'I am a stranger in London, and am looking for an opening as scene-painter, and I thought perhaps –'
>
> Now, look here,' interrupted Davidge, 'you can see by the bill that I have my own scenic artist; then why do you waste your time and mine, by making an application of this kind?'
>
> 'Yes,' said the artist, 'I fully understand that; but what I wanted to propose to you, was to paint a scene for nothing, in order that I may give managers an opportunity of judging my work.'

Davidge pondered, consulted his scene-painter, and gave permission for the applicant 'to paint a snow scene'. Disappointed at this lack of scope, 'the rustic' suggested that 'he could make an effective picture by covering it with frost'. In those days frost effects were obtained by using powdered glass. Davidge objected not only on grounds of excessive cost but also because, as he is reported as saying,

> 'It is composed of a most deadly poison, and the scene-shifters would run the risk of cutting their hands in moving the flats. Who knows, perhaps some poor fellow would get some of this terrible stuff into his hands, would lose a limb, perhaps die, and his widow and family would look to me for compensation. Oh! I should never forgive myself for endangering the limbs and lives of anybody in my employ'.

The artist regretted Davidge's objections, 'for it is *very* effective, and it would have cost you nothing, for I happen to have a large quantity by me'.

> Davidge paused, rubbed his chin, looked upwards, and then said – 'Well, after all, I don't see why I should take such trouble

> about my scene-shifters; they wouldn't care what happened to me, so that they got their weekly money. You paint the scene, sir – use as much frost as you like; and if the carpenters and scene-shifters are so careless as to permit this stuff to poison their hands, why, they must put up with the consequences'.
>
> Thus Mr Davidge got a cheaply painted scene, and I never heard that any of the scene-shifters were frost-bitten.

There is not enough information to link this story firmly with a particular production or a particular scene-painter. There is no certainty that Davidge gave the applicant a permanent post: but it just so happens that when Phil Phillips, chief scenic artist, left to set up the Bower in early 1839 he was succeeded by Brunning, whose name had not previously appeared in the bills. One of Brunning's first scenes was 'A Winter Prospect'. This may just be coincidence. Perhaps Cave's anecdote should be looked on merely as a recognition that Davidge had his eye firmly on his budget. Madeleine Bingham's comments on Garrick's practice seventy or so years previously are illuminating in this respect:

> Garrick with good and careful management and the drawing power of his genius, had made a considerable fortune from Drury Lane. He had won an equally great reputation for parsimony. But running a theatre is like housekeeping, it has to be done with prudence. Small things make all the difference between profit and loss, and the small things had been attended to by Garrick. As a result, the profits went up under his management. In 1771, on an expenditure of £26,410 the income was £32,548, netting him a profit of over six thousand.

Garrick and Davidge were out of the same mould when it came to housekeeping.

T.P. Cooke, who had become a Surrey celebrity under Elliston, returned to serve Davidge, and 1835 was indeed his year. As well as *My Poll and My Partner Joe* and *Tom Tackle,* he appeared, amongst others, in *Black-Eyed Susan, Newton Foster, The Flying Dutchman, Red Rover, The Pilot, The Ocean of Life, The Illustrious Chief, Luke the Labourer* and *Ben Brace.*

My Poll and My Partner Joe was 'founded on a popular Song of the celebrated Naval Poet, C. DIBDIN', that is, the father of two previous managers of the Surrey, Tom and Charles the Younger. His song 'Tom Bowling' is still heard today and the Surrey was regularly putting on his ballad-operas *The Waterman* and *The Quaker*. Haines's *My Poll and My Partner Joe* had a large cast. T.P. Cooke played Harry Hallyard of Battersea with Robert Honner as his partner, Joe Tiller; Maria Macarthy (Mrs Honner) was Mary Maybud, otherwise Pretty Poll of Putney. The plot is fairly straightforward. Harry and his 'Poll' are to be married; 'an unexpected interruption' comes from the Press Gang, 'The King wants men', and it is Joe they first seize on. 'Harry's sacrifice' – off he goes off in Joe's place and joins H.M.S. *Polyphemus.* He escapes a court-martial by jumping overboard and gets picked up by a slaver, Black Brandon, but a report of his death by drowning gets back to Poll and partner Joe, who... well, the rest is predictable, including the tear-jerking finish when Harry returns.

Not all melodrama has to finish in tears. There is a well-known print of a scene from *The Pilot* where T.P. Cooke, returning disguised as an old woman in bonnet and cloak, rips off his borrowed clothes to disclose the avenging sailor, pistol in waist-band: just the thing for the gallery.

The Surrey is sometimes referred to as 'the home of nautical drama' and sometimes in disparagement, but this might well be another reason why the Surrey overwhelmed the Victoria at this time. It found the mood of the day and gave customers what they wanted. However, not to overstate the case, it is worth mentioning that 1835 was the only year in which nautical drama took up the major part of the programme. Other attractions included the two-month operatic season already mentioned.

Although 'nautical drama' and 'T.P. Cooke' became almost synonymous, it is clear that Davidge himself had mastered the genre. From 8 December 1834 he played Old Tom Beazley in *Jacob Faithful.* This ran until mid-January, being paired with the pantomime after Christmas. To compress the *Times* report of 9 December 1834: 'A new local drama... was last night produced at this house. It is called *Jacob Faithful; or, The Life of a Thames Waterman;...* acting of Davidge entitled to unqualified praise;... as a veteran sailor is unequalled by any player now on the stage;... house was crowded almost to suffocation in every part'. The Sunday paper *The Age* also thought highly of the acting, saying 'Davidge's personification of Old Tom Beazley ought to immortalize him, it is perfect and does him infinite credit'. There was a second review in *The Age* of 4 January 1835: 'At the Surrey *Jacob Faithful* is a great favourite and deservedly so – the acting of Davidge in this piece is alone sufficient to ensure it a long and successful run'.

The critic of *The Satirist* of 4 January 1835 was more interested in the pantomime, *Harlequin and Little King Pippin:*

> All the nooks and corners of this theatre have been crammed every evening in the week, to witness chiefly.... the new pantomime. Nor have these Christmas congregations had reason to be dissatisfied with the mirth and humour, tricks

> and oddities it contains. It is, in truth, cleverer than most of its brethren of the season, and, setting aside a dull commencement, its satirical shafts are directed with more successful aim....

'Dull commencement'? Had Davidge gone back to the earlier tradition of a 'dark opening' to pantomimes? *The Times* of 27 December 1834 had no such criticism: 'The house was literally crammed, not a space from which a view of the stage could be obtained was unoccupied.... Perfect good humour, however, seemed to prevail even in the pit, which in some parts exhibited the appearance of a waving field of corn'.

This was Davidge's first pantomime at the Surrey and the audience clearly enjoyed his contribution to the seasonal entertainments. Indeed, year after year, in newspaper after newspaper, the critics looked on the reaction of Surrey audiences on Boxing-night as an entertainment in itself, sometimes devoting as much column space to them as to the pantomimes.

Let us pause for a moment. In the past, under other managements, critics had made the point that the noise made by a Surrey audience during the pieces which preceded the pantomime turned them into nothing but 'dumb show'. Yet no-one said that Davidge, in *Jacob Faithful,* could not be heard. Had Davidge, in his first year, found how to dominate the rabble? This must be so, for when one looks at reviews of the 1841 pantomime (Davidge not acting in the preceding piece) one is back to the 'dumb show' situation.

The critic of *The Satirist* was obviously a Davidge fan. On 18 January 1835: 'The Surrey under Davidge has its full share of success, and he deserves it all, from the activity he has displayed'. On 1 February:

> Fortune is again favouring the indefatigable Davidge, and no manager ever deserved it more. On Monday last he produced three pieces, which though not all new ones in themselves, were at least so to a Surrey audience. *Wealth and Want* was formerly played at the Queen's under the title of *Barn Burners,* but many alterations have been made, which have rendered it far more effective. The acting of Davidge was exceedingly impressive.... [The audience] filled every part of the house.

The role that Davidge played in *Wealth and Want* was that of Robert Luttrell, a tenant farmer. Over the rest of his life he made this part his own.

Giving his address as '1, Great Surrey Street, Blackfriars Road, Next the Theatre' (that is, the Equestrian Tavern), Davidge took his first benefit on 24 March 1835. He announced a 'Splendid Display of OPERATIC TALENT' comprising Messrs. Edwin, Plumer, and Ransford with the

Misses Land, Martin and Somerville. The opera was *The Castle of Andalusia,* Samuel Arnold's old war-horse of 1782 which still had life in it. Also in the bill was *Wealth and Want* with Davidge of course playing Robert Luttrell. The last night of Davidge's first winter season on 11 April 1835 featured an adaptation of Scott's *Lady of the Lake* with another of Arnold's operas *(The Shipwreck),* a drama and a fairy-tale burletta.

The Satirist (3 May) early praised a summer-season offering:

> The indefatigable Davidge produced another drama on Monday, written by Leman Rede, called *The Skeleton Witness*.... Davidge's acting... is masterly; the hardened sailor, Watherly, who perpetrates the crime, could hardly be better portrayed. In parts of this description Davidge is always excellent. J. Vining and Miss Watson are also entitled to praise, while the comic acting of [William] Smith served to relieve the sombre character of the piece.

On 20 September *The Satirist* comments that

> Davidge has the Thespian field almost completely to himself, on the Surrey side.... We are told in the bills of 'extra seats in the pit' and the impossibility of keeping places because the theatre is filled, boxes, pit and gallery in about five minutes after the opening of the doors;... there is not much exaggeration. *My Poll and My Partner Joe* is still the great attraction, and T.P. Cooke's acting one of the chief reasons why it is attractive.

The celebrities of the day had no objection to appearing at 'the home of nautical drama'. Madame Vestris played in at least five different pieces. She is described in *The Concise Oxford Companion to the Theatre* as having preferred 'during her distinguished career on the London stage... to appear in light entertainment,... at her best in burlesque, or in the fashionable ladies of high comedy'. Tailor-made for the Surrey! *The Satirist* thought so too and forecast in its issue of 5 July 1835:

> Vestris is to make her first appearance on this [Surrey-] side of the water, on Tuesday, in *The Deep, Deep Sea,* which is to be got up, as at the Olympic [of which she was the lessee] for that special purpose. Davidge is very industrious in catering for the amusement of his friends, and... Vestris' engagement will probably fill his theatre and put money in his purse.

A week later the prediction was confirmed: 'Vestris made her first curtsey on this side of the Thames on Tuesday, and received a warm and boisterous welcome from a crowded audience. Madame is well – in truth she has not looked so charming for some time'. Then on 26 July, 'Vestris concluded a very successful engagement here on Friday, when the crowded appearance of the house must have fully satisfied her that her attractions, as an actress, are not on the wane.... Both the manager and Madame are, we hear, quite contented with the result of the speculation'.

The Times occasionally criticised the way the Surrey Theatre was managed. For example on 8 July 1835, after viewing Madame Vestris's performance, their man took a dim view of 'the numerous private boxes which remained unoccupied during the whole of the evening' while the rest of the house was overflowing. Davidge evidently did something about this, but there was no pleasing the *Times* writer (28 December):

> The house was crowded in every part, not excepting the private boxes into which we were sorry to perceive what used to be 'gallery company' were admitted and behaved even worse than they did in the gallery. We were told that this was done from a wish to accommodate those who could not find room in the pit or the gallery and who were anxious to get admission. We have no doubt it was done from a wish to oblige but surely after such scenes as were witnessed from some of the drunken occupants of the private boxes on Saturday night, respectable parties will not be in a hurry to take seats in them. It is, we should imagine, the proprietor's own interest that some places in the theatre should be kept select.

Nautical drama, opera, Madame Vestris – what else in Davidge's first year as Surrey manager? For 13 April 1835 a selection of sacred music from *The Messiah* and *The Creation* was announced to commemorate the anniversary of the death of Handel. (This enshrines one of those erroneous 'facts' which seem more acceptable than the real thing. Handel expressed the hope that he would die on Good Friday, 13 April 1759, but spoilt everything by lasting out till the Saturday!) The Surrey promised a 'band upwards of 70; chorus supported by 80 professional ladies and gentlemen. Leaders Mr Jolly and Mr Hughes. Conductor H. Rodwell'. Rodwell was a composer in his own right. It was his music in the opera *Lord of the Isles* which had been premiered six months earlier.

Summing up, I think that innovation and sheer hard work were the keys to Davidge's first-year success, but luck had a lot to do with it. His nearest competitor, the Victoria, was in the hands of a comparative amateur, the younger Glossop. On 8 February 1835 *The Satirist* commented on Glossop's management:

> No novelty yet – verily the manager is blessed with more philosophic contentment than the public at large.... We have noticed sundry pronouncements of novelty in the bills, but as yet we have seen little of substantial fulfilment. The box prices are, however, lowered – a step which had become absolutely necessary from the successful progress of the enterprising Davidge.

By 22 March 1835 *The Satirist* was writing that the Victoria, 'from present appearances, is doomed to terrible demolition. Glossop has decamped and left all his company, box-keepers, scene-shifters, tradesmen and friends in the lurch. An execution has been put into the house for rent [actually for mortgage interest] and all the properties are advertised for sale'. The same issue commented that Davidge's management at the Surrey 'has proved highly successful, and his good fortune, judging from the appearance of the theatre latterly, is likely to continue; few managers deserve it better'. The story was taken a step further by *The Age* of 12 April, referring to Davidge: 'We hear, moreover, that this fortunate manager purchased some of the best of the scenery used at the Victoria, which is now completely gutted'.

The Victoria remained shut for six months by order of the court, re-opening on 28 September again under Glossop who had cleared the worst of his debts. Davidge made the most of this hiatus. At the Surrey he provided a variety of entertainment quite unlike anything he had himself put on at the Coburg, or anything Osbaldiston had put on at the Surrey before him. Did Davidge think this out for himself, or was he prompted? He may have had some useful advice from 'little Wilkinson' or from his associates (and in-laws from 1837), the members of the Pearce/Parker family which had many years of operatic experience. Did they encourage Davidge to increase the musical content of his offerings?

Chapter Fourteen

From Strength to Strength (1835/36)

I have mentioned innovation as one of the foundations of Davidge's success. He continued to attract, and hold, faithful audiences at the Surrey by his knack of presenting novelties adroitly blended with old favourites.

During the last few months of 1835 Davidge was relying heavily on the tried and true drawing powers of T.P. Cooke in nautical drama. As he went into his second year at the Surrey *The Satirist* was, in the main, still batting for him. Their theatrical reporter wrote on 18 October 1835:

> Davidge continues to cater successfully for the amusement of his patrons, as is evidenced by the full houses which his theatrical bill of fare almost invariably attracts. In T.P. Cooke he has secured an actor who can always command the sympathies and applause of a Surrey audience, and with whom the best days of the theatre are in a manner associated. His last engagement has proved as profitable as the manager could wish, judging from the full attendance.

As well as the expected nautical roles in *My Poll and my Partner Joe* (which had been running since August), *Tom Tackle* and the like, T.P. Cooke also revived his 'Gothic horror' parts, such as Ruthven in *The Vampire* and the eponymous *Monster; or, The Fate of Frankenstein.*

The Satirist of 8 November 1835 reiterates the Surrey's supremacy:

> Davidge continues quietly his career of success, undisturbed by the troubles which affect managers in other quarters. The theatre is still well attended, notwithstanding the comparatively little variation in the performances. The great card, *My Poll and My Partner Joe* seems destined to rival *Jonathan Bradford* in longevity.

The critic probably had two other managers in mind as being in trouble: Glossop, who had re-opened the Victoria on 28 September, but with no better success; and Osbaldiston, who had left the Surrey to take Covent Garden which he tried to run as he had run the Surrey and had halved his prices to compete with Bunn at Drury Lane. *The Times* referred to an over-crowded gallery, noise, riot and confusion, with Bunn having the 'wine' of the talent while Osbaldiston had the 'lees', concluding 'we never heard the national anthem so untuneably sung'.

The Age of 22 November 1835 confirmed the drawing power of *My Poll and My Partner Joe* at the Surrey and continued: 'But we perceive another nautical piece is in preparation, entitled *Happy Go Lucky* [that is, *Tom Tackle*], in which T.P. Cooke will personate the hero. This gentleman has proved an excellent card for Davidge,... his theatre being regularly besieged every evening'.

Then for once *The Satirist* took a bite at Davidge in its issue of 20 December: 'Among the benefits announced, we perceive, is that of Davidge himself. We have always regarded managers' benefits as great humbug, and we confess that we see nothing in this to make it an exception'. When the whole of the profits were going to the manager anyway a benefit does seem a bit pointless. However, the rationale was that he would persuade his friends engaged by other managements to provide their services at his theatre for one night without a fee, thus without breaking their existing contracts. If they proved to be a good draw, a future contract was in the making. In any case he would provide his own services free, or release one of his own artists, when his friends in turn called on him for their own benefits. Despite such criticisms the system went on. For example in May 1838 Mrs Yates of the Adelphi had her benefit, when not only did Davidge release T.P. Cooke for the event but also appeared himself.

The pantomime at the close of 1835 was *Old Daddy Long Legs; or, Mary, Mary Quite Contrary*. The review in *The Times* gave it a mixed reception:

> As is usual on such occasions, the nursery rhyme does little more for the story of the piece than furnish its title and a personification of Old Daddy himself who strides about on enormously high stilts.... The mechanist had a hit or two at the New Poor Law Bill;... one was the sudden change of a barrel of table-beer into a tub of water-gruel. He is not so successful in his hit at the comet. It was a wretched failure and ought to be omitted.

This is a reminder that 1835 was a year for Halley's comet. Robert Honner played Harlequin, with Asbury as Pantaloon; Columbine was 'Miss Stanley from the Newcastle Theatre, her first appearance on London boards', while the clown was another newcomer, Paul Herring. Although it ran for a month the pantomime was a comparative failure. It only remained in the bills as a back-up to the operas which accompanied it.

Young Burke (he was 18 now) returned in February 1836 in *The March of Intellect,* in which he had first shown his six-part talents ten years earlier. He also repeated his portrayal of Young Norval in *Douglas,* but the surprise was his playing the Baron in *Cinderella,* which calls for a good deep singing voice to go with the comic business.

At this point Davidge suffered two blows in his private life. *The Age* of 28 February 1836 reported that 'On the 23 inst., Mrs Jane Davidge, wife of G.B.Davidge, Lessee of the Royal Surrey Theatre, departed this life after a long and painful illness, deeply lamented by a numerous circle of friends'. Although she had been shown as a member of the original company when Davidge took the Surrey, she does not appear in the subsequent bills, and I should think her illness went back before October 1834. Less than twelve months later came the death at his home of his mother, aged 77 according to *The Age* on 15 January 1837.

This seems a good place to introduce my great-grandfather, Joseph Kerschner. He was the son of a goldsmith and citizen of London, the descendent of a goldsmith of Hessian origin who had married the daughter of General Crossley; the combined Kerschner and Crossley coats of arms are on record with the College of Arms. Young Joseph showed no wish to be a goldsmith and obtained a job with Davidge as box-office keeper, being first mentioned on the playbills for 2 December 1835. Through this he met Emily Maria Dixon Pearce, whose stage name was Miss E. Parker, then appearing in Auber's *Bronze Horse.* She was sixteen years old. They were married by special licence on Christmas Day 1837 at the church of St George the Martyr, Southwark. Davidge was one of the witnesses, having by then married Emily's elder sister, Frances, as his second wife. Together with Joseph's elder brother, Joseph and Emily Kerschner then took the Equestrian Tavern next to the Surrey. It was there that my grandmother, Frances Davidge Kerschner, was born on 21 May 1839.

Returning to the Surrey Theatre, we find that there was little competition to check Davidge's forward march. The Victoria apparently decided it could not draw away the Surrey patrons so would see if Astley's audiences could be suborned. On 21 February 1836 *The Age* reported that 'An Equestrian Melo-drama, under the title of *Lochinvar; or, The Bridal of Netherby* has been brought out at this establishment [the Victoria]. A very good stud of horses are introduced, which appear to be the great attraction. The bipeds are but a secondary consideration with the frequenters of this theatre'. Across the river Osbaldiston at Covent Garden was also being trounced: 'The *Quasimodo* produced at this ill-fated theatre is no more than the *Esmeralda* produced some time since at the Surrey Theatre; and the few persons it has attracted have therefore been trepanned into the belief of an express novelty having been prepared for them worthy of such a theatre as Covent Garden' – a slur which

Osbaldiston might have regarded as unfair, as it had been he who commissioned *Esmeralda* for the Surrey in the first place.

A month later the Victoria had closed its doors. As *The Satirist* reported on 20 March 1836: 'Davidge has had a clear field of late, and has reaped a proportionate harvest.... His audiences have large theatrical appetites, and it is a matter of moment to supply them with plentiful, if not very delicate, fare, and this object has been successfully attained'.

T.P. Cooke returned with half-a-dozen of his best pieces for another run of three months starting in April 1836, to the eminent satisfaction of the Surrey patrons. They were not so impressed with the subsequent Shakespearean productions, as *The Satirist* of 24 July recorded:

> During the performance of *Macbeth* on Tuesday, Banquo's ghost did not make its appearance in the banquetting scene, an omission which was no sooner perceived by the acute critics in pit and gallery, than it was resented. The performance ceased, and Macbeth with tragic dignity, strided forward to offer an explanation; the audience might as well demand to see the apparition of the dagger as Banquo's ghost; that both were only imaginary appearances, and not needful to be visibly represented. The audience did not seem much edified by Mr Butler's reasons; all was not right without the ghost, whom, by the way, we detected amusing himself by drinking brandy and water at the side scenes.

A month later aspects of the season were summed up by *The Satirist* with a mock news-item headed 'A Den of Murderers', unmalicious if childish:

> A gang of ill-disposed persons have occupied for some time past a building near the obelisk, in St George's Fields, where they have maintained themselves by a system of plunder and imposition. One of their last exploits has been the... ill-treatment of a well-known and very popular individual named William Shakespeare, who falling into their hands not long since was barbarously assaulted.... They are in the habit of meeting every evening, together with their minor associates, at half past six o'clock, and they usually continue their unhallowed doings until long past midnight; and as they have carried on their proceedings for nearly two years, it is believed that the amount of plunder which they have accumulated is immense.

The satire identifies 'a tall, lanky fellow, an importation from Yorkshire, and formerly a "butler" by profession', and by its use of the pointed nicknames 'Lushy Dib, most commonly seen with Conkey Bill and Baker-kneed Bob' suggests peculiarities of Dibdin Pitt, William Smith, and Robert Honner. Richard Lawrence, the treasurer, is characterised as 'the fellow in whose hands the plunder is deposited', while Davidge is the 'captain of the gang' who

> ...once took up his quarters in Lambeth Marsh [the Coburg] where he carried on nearly the same game as at present, though not with the same success; he was, in truth, obliged ultimately to quit the neighbourhood. The inhabitants of the vicinity have long winked at the irregularities which have been going on, but the late barbarous assault and mutilation of so respected a character as Mr William Shakespeare has aroused a general feeling of disgust, and it is thought that something will be done to prevent the recurrence of such atrocities.

On a less trivial note Davidge and the Surrey scored a major 'first' when the black-faced minstrel show was introduced to English audiences. As recorded by Phyllis Hartnoll, an American named T.D. Rice appeared at the Surrey in 1836 'and started the enormous vogue of the minstrel show'. Rice came to the Surrey in July 1836 in his role of 'Jim Crow' with his signature tune:

> Wheel about and turn about
> And do just so;
> Ebry time I wheel about
> I jump Jim Crow.

The playbill for 19 December 1836 promised that 'Mr T.D. Rice will appear with his Yankee Debil in a scene from the opera of BONE SQUASH DIABLO and sing a New Version of his celebrated Song of JIM CROW'. This was not his only act at the Surrey. On 12 September 1836 he had played 'Cupid (God of Love – a Black-a-Moor)' in the musical extravaganza *Black God of Love*. The next day *The Times* reported:

> There is something inexpressibly comic in his deliniation of the Black God; and though his audience did not at first appear to understand his drift, it was not many minutes before he completely secured their attention and gained their applause.... The audience were however resolved to have a further treat and an unanimous call for 'Jim Crowe' succeeded. The curtain again rose, and Mr Rice in the character of Jim Crowe, immediately came forward and sang the song, which was encored four times!

Rice appeared regularly at the Surrey. *The Age* reported on 2 July 1837 that he had 'not only entered into an engagement for life, which he did on Wednesday last at St John's Westminster with Miss Gladstanes' but had also 'commenced an engagement with Davidge and made his appearance on Thursday in a new piece called *The Court Jester,* in which he jumped Jim Crow to the satisfaction of a crowded audience'.

We can date the first Black-faced Minstrel Show earlier than the 1830s if we define it as a show put on by white folk with burnt cork on their faces, imitating in song and dance with varying degrees of accuracy (and condescension) the culture of black plantation slaves in the New World. Once again the credit goes to the Surrey (but to Elliston in 1812 rather than Davidge in 1835) for putting on the 'Grand Jonkanoo Ball', with Jonkanoo, the Master of Ceremonies, played by Bristow, repeated by Watkins Burroughs in 1821 and Elliston again in 1831. For the record, Davidge's second wife Frances subsequently revived the piece on 17 March 1842 – that is, after her husband's death – with the part of Jonkanoo played by Wilson. Jonkanoo is the popular song and dance festival of the Bahamas – 'is' because, although very little Black-faced Minstrelsy is performed anywhere in the world today, Jonkanoo still happens every year, on Boxing Day and New Year's Day. One can even obtain tape cassettes containing such traditional and current gems as 'Bahamas, we born there', 'Abaco people' and – of course – 'Junka-junka-junkanoo'.

It is interesting that in those days the term, now so opprobrious, of 'Nigger Minstrel Show' was only applied in England to acts where white men played with blacked faces. Black performers might be referred to as 'sons of Africa'. Ira Aldridge's colour was seldom mentioned and then only indirectly. There were early descriptions of him as a 'native of Senegal' (not true except perhaps in spirit, as he came from the United States which would not accept him as an actor), or 'The African Roscius'. After that no descriptions of colour were needed. Similarly Joseph Hillier was with Ducrow as Master of the Horse and Ringmaster for fifteen years with little reference to his origin. It took a visiting American to slur him as 'a nigger'. At this time discrimination in England had little or nothing to do with colour. A Mr Cashel, giving Ira Aldridge a letter of introduction to a friend, wrote on 25 June 1839: 'He is received everywhere into the very best society, he is a perfect gentleman and his lady is highly connected in England'. The barrier to be overcome was not that he was black, but that he was an actor. No doubt prompted by Aldridge, it quickly dawned on the Surrey management that 'nigger' was an unacceptable term and within a year the minstrels became 'Ethiopian Serenaders'.

So if white Americans were singing 'Jim Along Josey' and 'Jim Crow' at the Surrey, what did black Americans provide there? On 8 January 1838 the American Black Band, comprising Messrs. F. Johnson, A. Connor, Roland and Apps, demonstrated their skills with a programme consisting of the overture to Bellini's opera *Il Pirata,* an air varié for the violin by De Bériot (husband of the great opera singer Malibran), an air on the clarinet from Boieldieu's opera *La Dame Blanche,* the 'Dolce Concerto' by F. Johnson on the 'Key Bugle', and finally an arrangement of 'God Save the Queen', 'Hail Columbia' and 'Yankee Doodle'. There is an interesting ambiguity in the reference to the American Black Band. Should it really be 'F. Johnson on the Key Bugle'? – or rather 'F. Johnson on the [uncapitalised] key bugle'? Blom's *Dictionary of Music* describes the key bugle as 'an instrument invented in the early 19th. century; a bugle with side holes covered with keys similar to those used on woodwind instruments'. However the Metropolitan Museum of Art, New York, has a Key bugle, a bugle (without keys) made in 1811 by the Englishman Thomas Key.... It does not help to know that Key himself performed musical solos at the Surrey on 11 November 1830, though on that occasion he played the 'clarionet'.

In his search for novelty Davidge picked many winners. On 12 September 1836 his playbills featured 'Jim Crow' together with

> Real Bedouin Arabs... from the Theatre Porte St Martin, Paris... whose inimitable Performances have been the theme of such universal wonder and admiration.... Evolutions, Dances, Exercises, &c. peculiar to the Arabs, which will be pourtrayed as an Arabian Festival! Introducing the Wonderful and Novel Feats of the Native Bedouins.

This was a success and ran for some months. Davidge was evidently keeping up his links with Paris and the Théâtre Porte St Martin, whence he had obtained *Tower of Nesle* some four or five years earlier.

Not all those engaged at the Surrey were satisfied. On 9 October 1836 Davidge was reported as having been brought before the Southwark Court of Requests by a Mr Percy who was appearing on behalf of Joseph Atkins, a Surrey chorister 'lately engaged... as an extra singer for the opera of *Paul Clifford'.* Mr Percy stated

> that his client performed in the above opera on each of the twelve nights that it was played, and had been paid for doing so. That in the course of these twelve days he had been requested to attend the rehearsals of another opera, *The Lord of the Isles,* and after attending seven of such rehearsals, Mr

> Davidge informed the performers that it was not his intention to produce the opera at all, in consequence of his inability to accede to the terms required by Mr Collins, who was to have played the principal character. On the twelfth night of the performance of *Paul Clifford* his client was informed that his services were not required, and no remuneration was allowed him for the loss of time in attending the rehearsals. It was for this remuneration that his client had been compelled to summon the defendant.

Davidge was defended by his solicitor Mr Lewis, who submitted 'that it was quite unusual for the proprietors of theatres to pay even their extra choristers for their attendance at rehearsals'. The point was debated and witnesses' opinions were taken. In the end, 'the commissioners decided that, although they regarded it as a very hard case, as far as Mr Atkins was concerned, they could not, as he could adduce no precedents in his favour, order Mr Davidge to pay the money sued for'.

As it happens Davidge did manage to sign up Mr J. Collins of the Haymarket Theatre just over a year later, on 26 October 1837. The fee was £14 for six nights, to sing the name part in *Paul Clifford* and Count Calmar in *The Exile*. It is not recorded whether Joseph Atkins was in the chorus.

During this period Davidge also engaged the so-called Monsieur Gouffé. He was basically an acrobat and dressed up as an ape for effect. *The Times* on 26 October approved the Bedouin Arabs but remarked that

> M. Gouffé performed the part of a monkey in a manner somewhat too natural to be entertaining. The manager would do well to restrain some of the liberties this gentleman occasionally takes with the audience or get rid of him altogether; the indecencies of a monkey may be copied too closely to be tolerated.

The Surrey audiences were not put off. As *The Times* itself recorded of the man-monkey's antics, 'They were received with loud plaudits by a house filled to overflow in every part' (27 December 1836), and 'Long before the time of commencing the performance of the evening, it was crammed with a somewhat uproarious but good-tempered audience, two-thirds of which, at least, consisted of persons under the age of 20' (16 May 1837).

The Surrey management was not embarrassed by the strictures of *The Times* and continued to employ Monsieur Gouffé, though he was steered away from impromptu cavortings towards acting within the bounds of a script. On 9 April 1840 he is in 'the Pantomimic Drama' of *Jocko, the Brazilian Ape*. Two years later he has progressed to *Perouse;*

or, the Monkey of the Desolate Island which actually had a plot, even though it was little more than a *Robinson Crusoe* look-alike with Gouffé in the Man Friday role.

He was the second of two Messieurs Gouffé. As we saw earlier, the first was John Hornshaw in the time of Charles Dibdin the Younger. The second one is identified by Edward Stirling in his *Old Drury Lane* as one Sam Todd, who, as a pot-boy,

> amused the customers of the house by climbing and running round ceilings, shelves and every available place in tap-rooms; and imitating in a most natural manner monkey tricks, utterances and habits. Davidge heard of him, and engaged him for the Surrey. Sam Todd, transformed into Monsieur Gouffé just arrived from South America, appeared in a new monkey piece at the Surrey, and made a real hit, for months drawing large sums to Manager Davidge's treasury.... Gouffé unfortunately found a lady who... spent his money, and when the poor monkey's attraction ceased, eloped and left him to die in a workhouse.

Sam Todd was probably too young to have seen and imitated the original but Davidge, who was acting at the Coburg at that time, may well have seen the previous Island Ape and decided that a revival or re-incarnation would fit his bill. Charles Dibdin claimed in his *Memoirs* to have invented the name 'Gouffé', which appeared in many variations. Its resonance brings to mind Disney's 'Goofy' a century later. By all accounts the cartoon dog's simian fore-runner was equally well-known and popular in his own day and deserves his own niche in history.

TO THE FREQUENTERS OF THE ROYAL

1832.

Surrey

Theatre

His Friends, and the Public in general,

B. S. FAIRBROTHER, Sole Proprietor

OF THE

EQUESTRIAN COFFEE-HOUSE, immediately adjoining THE THEATRE,

Licensed by the Magistrates pursuant to Act of Parliament,

Has the honor to announce that this commodious and extensive Establishment has been

ENTIRELY RE-PAINTED & EMBELLISHED

by several first-rate Artists, in the style of the most approved *Salles* in Paris, and is now

Open for the Season:

Engagements having been entered into with many

DISTINGUISHED FOREIGNERS,

for the supply of their choicest Champagne, Port, Sherry, Madeira, and other Wines, Brandies, Rums and Liqueurs; also with a celebrated Distillery and Brewhouses, employing

NATIONAL TALENT

in the production of Gins, Cordials, Compounds, Ales, Stout, &c. The Proprietor is enabled to offer to his Visitors a

Succession of Entertainments

highly conducive to the refreshment of the body, and exhilaration of the mind, supported by a

COMPANY,

which he can boldly assert is the most select and numerous of any similar house in the Metropolis.

Not to be too minute in detailing his bill of fare, the Proprietor will merely observe, that both

AMATEURS AND ACTORS

may here find that *Agreeable Surprise*, a *Cure for the Heart-Ache*—that those who may choose for a moment to unbend from the cares of *Married Life*, can here, without going further a-field, enjoy more than *Rural Felicity*.—

That every one may find himself perfectly *At Home*, those who may come

BEFORE BREAKFAST,

will find themselves legally attended to by the Master of the *Rolls*; the "*cups* that cheer but not inebriate," will not want their *toast*, but will furnish a pleasing

CHINESE DIVERTISEMENT

to commence the Entertainments, whilst any Gentleman who may be

Too Late for Dinner!

and may choose to solve that most interesting question,

WHERE SHALL I DINE?

by favoring B. S. F. with his company, may have any production that he may *bespeak* got up on the shortest notice, and in the best manner.

The *Dressings* of the various dishes after the most correct *Costume*, attended to by that distinguished artist, Mrs. COOK.

The Decorations by Messrs. JOHN and THOMAS, who will be in *waiting* on the occasion

The Properties by the Proprietor of the establishment, assisted by the Messrs. CRUETS.

If required, a *Little Pickle* will attend to enliven the whole

The Cloth laid precisely at the hour specified, and the Performances to commence immediately.

The *Battle of Hastings* will be occasionally brought forward in the *Pea* season, in conjunction with the *Flitch of Bacon*, and other works of *taste*.

Although a friend to harmony, the Proprietor is not one of those who insist upon

NO SONG, NO SUPPER!

Those who wish to finish the evening by taking in the *Natives*, will here find the most favourable opportunity.—The admirers of *Rice Fruit* will find that pleasant fellow, Pat Murphy, who has so often been *roasted*, as warm as ever in their service: attended by those congenial associates, Pale Dorset and Cambridge, both of the same *kidney*.—*Welsh Rabbits* will not be wanting; and every order for the piquant relish of a slice of *Hung Beef* will be properly executed.—Chops will always be ready to meet chops (that of "kissing comforts;") and the unbearable nuisance of having to wait for the Steak, will be sedulously avoided.—The admirers of *Mellow Drams*, after the more weighty performances, will find great care taken that the drops go regularly down.—The mirth-inspiring *Punch* will attend on the slightest notice.

THE PRICES WILL REMAIN AS HERETOFORE!

Notwithstanding the enormous outlay in the fitting up of the Equestrian Coffee-House, all the Entertainments will continue to be in every particular of the most genuine quality, but no addition will be made to the Prices. **PRIVATE BOXES** without any extra charge.

The Proprietor is aware it is the custom of some houses to issue a notice that ***No Orders will be admitted***; he begs on the contrary to say, that at his Establishment all Orders will be punctually and thankfully attended to, without any restriction as to time, whether before 7 or after 7.

The Doors open the first thing in the morning, and continue so till the finish of the Performances.

No Money returned. (VIVANT REX ET REGINA!) S. G. Fairbrother, Printer, Exeter Court, Strand.

Advertisement in playbill-style for Fairbrother's 'Equestrian Coffee-House'
(Reproduced by kind permission of the Guildhall Library, Corporation of London)

Chapter Fifteen

'The First Nautical Theatre in Europe' (1836-41)

In the mid-1830s there were indications that the Surrey was drawing on a much larger audience than the inhabitants of Southwark and Lambeth alone. Ten years earlier the playbills had announced that 'Mr MATSON's Coach calls Every Evening at HONEYMAN's Coffee House [that is, the Surrey Coal-Hole] to convey Passengers to Deptford and Greenwich'. By December 1836 the further information was that 'An Omnibus will call at this Theatre at a Quarter past 11 every Night for Fleet-st., Holborn-Hill, the Post Office and Islington'. Those who had fled the cholera to the new suburbs were thus being encouraged to find their way back to their old haunts, if only for the evening. Was Sadler's Wells Theatre also being put under pressure?

The 1836 pantomime was *Harlequin and the Lady's Bower; or, Cock-a-doodle-doo*. It had the same principals as the previous year – Honner, Asbury, Herring and Miss Stanley – but as it ran a respectable six weeks, presumably the mechanist had improved his tricks.

Davidge himself still appeared on stage at regular intervals. *The Age* reported on 12 February 1837 that he 'determined on shining himself; and has accordingly appeared in *The Three Generations*. His acting in this drama is well known – it is quite equal to anything the 'Cock Salmon' [a nickname for the elder Farren] has done, and must be seen to be appreciated'.

It is clear from the playbills of 13 February 1837 that some people never learn! One would think that after what happened in April 1824 the last thing the Cross family would do would be to lend the Surrey another camel. Yet there it was announced – *Forty Thieves* with 'The Camel of the Desert selected for its docility for the exclusive use of the favourite LADY OF THE HAREM (from Mr Cross of the Surrey Zoological Gardens)'. Announced, yes, but the animals which actually appeared were Nepaul Bulls – for one night only. (Had the word gone around?)

Davidge's search for novelty and his way of presenting unusual acts to the public is shown in the puff for the Chanteurs Styriens who came to the Surrey on 10 April 1837. They were two alpine singers who

> during the primitive Pastoral Occupations of their early life, through their ardent love of Music, their exquisite taste, and

> constant practice, in those wild and singular strains with which the deep Echoes of their native hills are so often awakened, [learnt] to cheer the many solitary hours passed in the pursuit of the Chamois....

If yodelling had seldom or never been heard at the Surrey before, perhaps the puff was necessary.

One person who disliked puffs in general was Charles Rice, a keen theatre-goer, who thought that the Surrey kept its enthusiasm within bounds. Writing on 9 June 1837 he criticised 'the absurd and fallacious system of puffing' practised by the managers of the patent theatres, Bunn and Osbaldiston, whose 'egregious falsehoods [caused] public estrangement'. He recommended 'a persevering silence in respect to theatrical success by both playbill and newspaper':

> ...As one proof, I will now instance the state of the Surrey. Scarce one production or appearance out of ten that occurs at this theatre is noticed by the papers; the bills merely announce the number of nights a piece has run, without any 'immense success', 'unprecedented attraction' or other humbug, and yet, go when you will, the house is full; Mr Davidge avoids all bickering with his performers, there is a conviviality among the members of the company.... Such conduct in a body of men is laudable, and deserves every success it meets with.

One 'appearance' which was noticed by the papers concerned one of the spectators who may have thought they were not getting enough knock-about farce, and determined to provide it single-handed. On 23 April 1837 *The Weekly Dispatch* reported a recent incident at the Surrey which led to 'John East, a well-dressed young man', being charged with creating a disturbance.

> During the progress of the play, and while Mr T.P. Cooke was performing the character of Bobstay in a nautical piece, the defendant occasioned a considerable degree of clamour in the theatre, by jumping from the pit over the orchestra on the stage. When he got there he stood with his back to the audience, and, throwing himself into various grotesque attitudes, in imitation of a sailor, he made a rush towards Mr T.P. Cooke, and giving a hitch to his own trousers, exclaimed 'Do you think that you are a sailor? I'll do the character as well myself if only the people will let me'. There was a general cry of 'Turn him off!' But Mr Cooke, perceiving that the intruder was under the influence of liquer, requested that he would go back

> again from whence he came; but the latter... continued on the stage, making himself appear very ridiculous....

At length East jumped into a nearby box containing 'a party of ladies' and harassed them with his antics. Refusing to leave at the request of the box-keeper,

> he caught firm hold of the rails in front, and held on while the officers were attempting to drag him out by the scruff of the neck. The defendant, however, still persevered in his efforts to keep possession; and before he was finally ejected from the box he tore down part of the railing, besides creating a disturbance in the house. When before the Magistrate, the defendant expressed his contrition for the noise and uproar he created in the theatre, and said that it was all owing to his having exceeded the 'bounds of moderation' after dinner.... The boxkeeper said that the proprietor was not anxious to proceed to extremities in the case, as the young man had evinced sorrow for the manner in which he had acted, and that, if he paid the amount of damage he had done, it would meet the justice of the case.

This was done and East was discharged. Later, another commotion in the audience was again reported by Charles Rice. This was during a performance of *The Quaker* at the Surrey on 12 August 1837. The piece began well but just as Solomon (William Smith) was declaring his love for Floretta (Mrs Fitzwilliam) the gods erupted,

> occasioned in the first instance by some boy amongst the Olympians, who render'd himself conspicuously disagreeable, being taken out by the officer, and a determination on the part of the gallery assembly that no performance should go on till the said boy should be reinstated and the officer expunged from the gallery.

After twenty minutes Honner, who 'was at the wing superintending', came before the audience but for nearly as long again was prevented from speaking by the uproar. At length he was heard:

> He said he had no doubt the officers used all necessary forbearance before they put the boy out, (hissing from the gallery) and if they would keep quiet the police should in no wise interfere; the gods responded with a hearty cheer, and *The Quaker* recommenced. But the officers being still at their posts in the gallery, the row was renewed, and the performance was again suspended for a few minutes, but Mr

> Honner waving his hand to the leader of the orchestral band, the quintette which concludes the first act was performed in dumb show, and the drop curtain fell.

When the curtain drew up for the second act, again 'hissing, yelling, and all the other sounds musical, appertaining to the human, demoniac, canine, and feline species, were put in full force', until Davidge appeared on the stage. As an 'old acquaintance' he was greeted with applause and 'partial quietude'. Informed by a gallery spokesman that 'your officers have took a boy out for nothing, and we want him back again', the manager gave a measured response:

> He was at any time averse to coercive measures; the audience must be aware that one individual in the gallery was enough to disturb a whole assembly; such an individual was the boy removed;... all the disturbance and clamour of the gallery company could not alter his determination; the boy should not be allowed to re-enter! He desired the audience to consider what an arduous duty is that of a manager; he was the caterer for their amusement, and he would be the guardian of their comforts; the officers had been acting under his direction;... if any disapprobation was due, it was to him, and not to the ladies and gentlemen in the farce, that it should be shown, and he therefore hoped they would allow the piece to proceed; he threw himself on the protection of the respectable portion of the audience; whilst he was proprietor of this or any establishment, he would be master, the boy should not be readmitted!
>
> This manly address was followed by great cheering, and waving of hats and handkerchiefs, and the farce concluded amidst great applause....

That report says a lot about Davidge's character: courage, loyalty to his staff and complete control of his audience. These qualities paid off. As *The Age* reported on 12 November 1837:

> Davidge is the luckiest manager in existence and must be making a rapid fortune – he has got the tide with him and every piece he produces is sure to succeed; even the old drama *The Exile* revived on Monday last filled the house to the ceiling. It was very well acted by Mrs Honner, W. Smith, Collins and Saville.

Davidge continued to contribute to the Surrey's successes as an actor as well as manager. One of his performances in a nautical piece was reported by *The Times* of 16 November 1837:

The name of the novelty is *Wapping Old Stairs,* a name with which most persons are familiar. The drama is founded, as the bills announce, on the old popular ballad of the same name. Some incidents are introduced to render the effect dramatic, and an opportunity is afforded for some effective acting of Mr Davidge, in the character of Poor Jack of which he fully availed himself and secured success to the piece which in itself is not without merit. Mrs R. Honner as Molly, was also extremely effective. The scenery is very good; Wapping Old Stairs by moonlight will revive many almost obliterated memories of some of the old water-side visitors of this house....

Surrey audiences were familiar with the ballad on which the drama was based. Miss Tunstall had sung it there the previous December. It featured Molly, betrothed to Tom (E.F. Saville) who has an eye for the girls. Surely this extract from the ballad tells it all:

Your Molly has never been false, she declares
Since the last time we parted at Wapping Old Stairs;
When I said that I still would continue the same
And gave you the 'bacco box marked with my name.
When I passed a whole fortnight between decks with you
Did I e'er give a kiss, Tom, to one of your crew?
To be useful and kind, with my Thomas I staid,
For his trowsers I'll wash, and your grog too I made.
Though you promised last Sunday to walk in the mall,
With Susan from Deptford and likewise with Sall....

The Age also thought well of the piece, reporting on 26 November: 'Davidge's re-appearance in the nautical drama *Wapping Old Stairs* has caused this theatre to be filled to the ceiling every evening'. And a fortnight later: 'At the Surrey, Davidge has put forth a tremendous power of attraction, by aid of which, we suppose, he means to compress all the good people of Surrey into squeezable commodities'.

Two members of the cast of *Wapping Old Stairs,* William Smith and John Dale, were about to achieve another kind of fame though still inside the profession. In the following year they were the Surrey representatives of the General Theatrical Fund Association, set up to avert 'the combined evils of age and poverty among the great body of actors'. This society, now the Royal Theatrical Fund, still performs its task today.

The Christmas pantomime of 1837 was *Harlequin and Old Dame Trot,* with Thomas Ellar as Harlequin, Morelli as Pantaloon, Southby as Clown and Miss Sharp as Columbine. This is a complete change from the previous year, as Robert Honner – then the Harlequin – had left the

Surrey, carrying some of the regulars with him, to take over the management of Sadler's Wells. (The parting was entirely amicable; after Davidge's death, his widow invited Honner back to the Surrey as manager.) Though a change, the 1837 pantomimists were not exactly a 'new' team. Ellar had been at the Surrey in 1809 under Elliston. His 'signature' was a tribute to Rich, the original Harlequin; that is, to show, during the opening scenes, a hint of the spangles under his first costume to indicate the transformation to come. Southby was no newcomer either. He had worked for Charles Dibdin the Younger in 1822; his 'signature' would be to introduce fireworks into his act. There was a Morelli working as prompter for Charles Dibdin in 1803; as Pantaloon is typically old and decrepit, it would not be impossible for it to be the same man.

The Age was having trouble in finding new ways of reporting the Surrey's popularity. On 25 February 1838, reviewing London's entertainments generally, the reporter found 'nothing remarkable, except that on one night at the Surrey only a hundred and four people were turned away from the doors for want of room. Mr Davidge must really look into this'.

It may have been the money brought in by the 'nautical dramas' which Davidge used to re-decorate the auditorium in appropriate style. The playbills for April 1838 described the Surrey as

> The most chaste and elegant Theatre in London, [its ceiling decorated with] Emblematical Nautical Designs of Nymphs and Naiads bearing Shields and Trophies... commemorative of the most brilliant Victories... of Nelson! Howe! Duncan! & Hood!.... The Fronts of the Boxes are divided into beautiful Marine Vignettes, giving an accurate description of Dibdin's Popular Song of 'The Pride of the Ocean':
>
> THE LAUNCH
> In contempt of all danger, from quicksands and rocks
> 'The Pride of the Ocean' is launched from the stocks.
>
> THE CHASE
> Now the signal is flying, and fleet in her course,
> She chases a sail far superior her force.
>
> THE ACTION
> Next yard-arm and yard-arm entangled they lie,
> The tars loudly swearing to conquer or die.
>
> THE CONVOY
> The prize is sent home, and alert in a trice
> Then make gaskets and points, and they knot and they splice.

THE SHIP BECALMED
Till all of a sudden a calm, then a scud,
A tempest brings on the face of a flood.

THE STORM
The thunder and lightning and wind so deform,
'The Pride of the Ocean' scarce lives out the storm.

THE SHIP HOMEWARD BOUND
While knowing Jack Tars of their gallantry talk,
Tell who served well Boscawen, and Anson and Hawke.

THE SHIP IN DOCK
Her timbers all crazy, all open her seams,
Torn and wounded her planks, and quite rotten her beams.

THE SHEER HULK
No trace of her rate, but her ports and her bulk,
'The Pride of the Ocean' cut down a sheer hulk.

As well as the pictures, the theatre also boasted 'New Magnificent Glass Lustres, constructed by Stevens and Son, St George's Circus, Decorative Paper Hangings by Messrs Townsend and Parker, Goswell Street' and other embellishments to make the Surrey 'the First Nautical Theatre in Europe'.

During the run of *The Field of the Cloth of Gold* in 1838, Davidge tried on his Surrey audience for the first – and only – time a French play and an Italian opera in the original languages. 'For One Night Only', 27 July, he presented a French Vaudeville company under Monsieur Bernard in *Zoë; ou, L'Amant Prêté*. An English version of this had previously been staged under the title of *The Loan of a Lover,* so the plot would have been known to some of the audience. This was followed by excerpts from Italian operas (where would one hear Donizetti's Barcarole from *Marino Faliero* these days?), a piece by 'the celebrated Spanish Guitarist, M. Huerta', and, finally, Rossini's *Il Barbiere di Siviglia* (though condensed into one act). The experiment seems to have been a failure. It was twenty years before Shepherd tried the same thing, with equal lack of success. Surrey-siders wanted roast beef, not continental cuisine.

Yet still the reviews are favourable. *The Age* of 12 August 1838 wrote of Davidge that 'we believe he is the only manager at present in London who is in possession of a profitable theatre'. A wry note could still creep in, however, as in the patronising irony of 26 August: 'At the Surrey, we are happy to hear that this elegant and fashionable establishment is now so well conducted, as to allow the proprietors to dispense with the heretofore customary services of the police. This is truly gratifying; not less so is the agreeable fact, that nothing under gin and ginger-beer is allowed to be drunk in the dress-circles'.

By now, praise for Surrey pantomimes, nautical dramas, Bedouin Arabs and the man-monkey must seem to come naturally, but Shakespeare? Bearing in mind the harsh criticisms made by *The Satirist* two years earlier, we recognise that Davidge must have tightened up his Shakespearean productions, for thus spoke *The Age* on 28 October 1838: 'Cooper, Butler and Mrs Allison have been starring it during the week at the Surrey. *Romeo and Juliet, Macbeth* and *Othello* have been the plays in which they have appeared and the house has been crowded every night to excess. Really, Mr Davidge, you are a most fortunate man and must be envied by your brother managers'.

After the Shakespearean season, *The Rich Man of Frankfort* was revived, followed by *Oliver Twist* with Cooper playing Mr Brownlow. (This production is given a later chapter of its own.) On 16 December 1838 *The Age* commented: 'John Cooper continues at the Surrey and will not leave it as long as Davidge can afford to pay him twenty pounds per week. Sober John says that Davidge is worth a hundred Bunns'.

One might think that Bunn would resent such a comparison, but he must have taken it in good part. When Miss Romer was in charge of the 1839 opera season which commenced on 6 May, Bunn willingly released Michael Balfe from Drury Lane, where he had been singing, to enable him to appear at the Surrey. There Balfe appeared as Count Rudolph in the English version of *La Sonnambula,* as the Marquis of Chateau Vieux in the première of *Maid of Artois* and as Dulcamara in *Love Spell,* the English version of *L'Elisir d'Amore.* As reported by *The Times* on 30 May 1839:

> Much pains had evidently been bestowed on the production of this work; new and beautiful scenery had been painted, the chorusses went off with effect, and the singers did their best, particularly Miss Romer and Mr Balfe; who played with a great deal of humour and point, the latter being a far better representative of the quack doctor than either of his Italian predecessors. The audience was extremely attentive throughout and listened to every air with marked pleasure, nearly every piece of importance being encored without dissent. Although the opera be not a work of the highest character, yet the success of such a work at all, the interest taken by the population of a new region for an Italian comic opera when well and completely got up, augers favourably for the growing musical taste of the country.... At the fall of the

> curtain, pit, boxes and gallery, burst forth into a clamour of applause, which continued for some minutes, and Templeton, Balfe and Miss Romer appeared before the curtain in answer to the numerous calls of the audience.

Davidge's next hit was *Jack Sheppard* which opened on 21 October 1839. It had been adapted by J.T. Haines from W. Harrison Ainsworth's novel. The playbills stressed that it had been 'produced under the immediate inspection of the Author'. Indeed, they went so far as to reproduce a letter from Ainsworth to the effect that he had 'no hesitation in giving [his] entire sanction to the performance'. A bonus was that Davidge had acquired the services of the great cartoonist, George Cruikshank, to superintend the painting of the whole of the scenery. As there were thirty-nine scenes he must have been well paid. The play ran until Christmas. No doubt Davidge did quite well out of it. Many a theatre put it on subsequently, either under its original name or as *Jonathan Wild, the Thief-taker.* Erroll Sherson tells that a burlesque version was mounted at the Gaiety in 1885, with Harriet Coveney in the cast – a Surrey trouper still going strong.

The 1839 pantomime, *Queen Bee; or, Harlequin and Little Goody Two-shoes,* was reviewed by *The Times* thus: 'The proprietor seemed to have spared no expense in giving it full effect, by equally splendid and tasteful dresses and decorations.... The whole of this performance was loudly applauded by an audience overflowing to inconvenience in every part of the house'.

Up the road, the Victoria was getting a rap over the knuckles from *The Times*. 'Fully an hour and a quarter elapsed between the conclusion of the second piece and the commencement of the pantomime;... the delay is much too long for the patience of ordinary mortals, and could not be endured at any other time than Christmas.' Clearly the Surrey had the measure of its old rival when it came to staging pantomime.

J.T. Haines came up with two more hits for Davidge, first *Jane of the Hatchet* – with one hundred female warriors! – which notched up sixty performances on its first run commencing in July 1840, and then *The Wreck of the Royal George* which immediately followed *Jane* and ran until Christmas. Nautical drama – but not with T.P. Cooke. Perhaps he did not fancy dying in a crowd:

> A thousand hearts were beating there,
> Close by their native shore;
> One moment, and tho' skies were fair,
> Those bold hearts beat no more.

There was another successful collaboration between Harrison Ainsworth, J.T. Haines and George Cruikshank which led to the production of *The Tower of London.* This opened in January 1841 and ran for over thirty performances. The story was of Lady Jane Grey, the 'Nine Day Queen', and Mary Tudor. There were eighteen scenes in and about the Tower of London, finishing with the scaffold as the place of Lady Jane's execution.

With one exception the 1841 opera season was much as before. *La Sonnambula* took pride of place, supported by a bevy of English ballad-operas. The exception was a new realisation of *Macbeth* which merits a chapter of its own. So also does the visit of Ducrow's company. These two events are mentioned here only to set the chronology in place.

The critic of *The Times* attending the 1841 pantomime gives a word-picture of a Surrey audience and its reaction to any piece preceding the main entertainment of the evening. After trying to describe the plot of the first piece he goes on: 'Thus much we were able to collect from the bills and an occasional word from the performers, but beyond these all was dumb show. The noisy impatience of the "gods" and "goddesses" rendered any attempt to follow the performance in all its parts absolutely unavailing'. He considered *Harlequin Jack Frost and King Thaw* a very splendid affair:

> Comparing it with what we remember of pantomimes of 'by-gone days', we should say that whether regarding the dresses and decorations, the scenery, machinery, tricks and transformations, we don't remember a more happy combination of all, or a more lucky hit since the days of *Mother Goose.*

High praise indeed!

Chapter Sixteen

'Artifical Light and Real Water' (Stagecraft 1837-49)

During the 1830s theatres were generally lit either by Argand lamps (paraffin lamps, more or less) or by gas. Theatres were all too often destroyed by fire. Indeed, Thomas Dibdin had complained that 'since the fires at Covent Garden, Drury-Lane, the Circus, Astley's and other play-houses', the insurance companies which 'had become uncommonly cautious respecting theatres, (many would not insure me at all) charged me at rates amounting to three hundred and sixty pounds per annum'. Dibdin had to pay this to insure the building for £9,000 and the contents for £3,000.

However a new method of illumination had been invented in 1825 by Thomas Drummond, then a lieutenant in the Royal Engineers. The 'Drummond Light' was used first in surveying and mapping. It is recorded that its light was visible between two mountains nearly sixty-seven miles apart. Basically, two gas jets, of oxygen and hydrogen, burnt on a revolving cylinder of lime. The application of this system to stage lighting was inevitable. In *Theatre Lighting in the Age of Gas* Terence Rees infers from confusing data that its first use under the cumbersome trade name of Phoselioulamproteron *[sic]* was by Macready at Covent Garden for the pantomime of Boxing Day 1837. Davidge's enterprise and the Surrey's achievements have been overlooked. He got in first as a playbill for 13 November 1837 testifies: 'The Stage will be lit by a new light!' The event illuminated was of the 'living statues' type, quite popular then, when actors posed in representation of various works of art. These

> will be exhibited by the Phoselionlamproteron *[sic]*, a Light of the most extraordinary brilliancy, its intensity being such as to produce distinct shadows in the brightest sunshine, and EQUALLING THE POWER of 264 ARGAND LAMPS!!! It will also illumine objects 10 miles off, and has been seen at a distance of 120 miles by means of a Parabolic Reflector. One of the greatest advantages of this Light in its application to the Arts is the peculiar property of exhibiting all shades of color with a faithfulness unattainable by ordinary Artificial Light; many colors, as is well known, being either changed or destroyed after Sunset – a circumstance universally regretted by all Artists.

Thus did limelight come to London and a new word enter theatrical vocabulary.

Royal Surrey Theatre.

Under the Exclusive Management of Mr DAVIDGE.

First Night of a New **NAUTICAL DRAMA** *of intense interest,*

By the successful Author of NEWTON FOSTER, BEN BRACE, MILLER'S MAID, &c.

This Theatre being highly popular for the production of so many successful Nautical Dramas founded on favorite Ballads, induced the Author, in the present instance, to venture upon the subject of perhaps one of the most beautiful of the kind, dramatized, feeling confident, from the manner in which it has been treated, that its success will equal any of its predecessors.

RE-APPEARANCE OF Mr. DAVIDGE.

In order to keep pace with the liberal encouragement bestowed on his efforts, the Manager has great pleasure in announcing, that he has entered into an Engagement for a limited period, with those celebrated Artistes,

M.M. FLEURY, ROSIZET FEMILLE, &c.

WHO WILL APPEAR EVERY EVENING THIS WEEK.

MONDAY, NOVEMBER 13th, 1837, and DURING THE WEEK,

Will be produced, an entirely New Nautical Drama, (with New Scenery by Messrs TELBIN, MORELLI, &c.—Music by Mr. JOLLY—Dresses, &c.) founded on the popular Ballad of

WAPPING OLD STAIRS!

Lieutenant Willoughby, Mr. GREEN, Squire Craverly, Mr. DIBDIN PITT,
George Craverly, *(his Nephew)* Mr. ELVIN, Tom, Mr. E. F. SAVILLE,
Old Adams,........Mr. DALE,
Robson, Mr. DILLON, Clarke, Mr. CULLEN, Sam Shallow, Mr. W. SMITH,
Poor Jack,..................Mr. DAVIDGE,
Molly,..........*(Daughter to Adams, & Betrothed to Tom)*..........Mrs. R. HONNER,
Sally, ...*(alias Vegetable Sarah)*....Miss MARTIN.

INTERIOR of OLD ADAMS' HOUSE ON THE BANKS OF THE RIVER.

[illegible]

STREET IN WAPPING!

[illegible]

WAPPING OLD STAIRS, (Moonlight) OUTSIDE OF THE ADMIRAL'S HEAD,

[illegible]

Your Molly has never been false she declares,
Since the last time we parted at Wapping Old Stairs;
When I said that I still would continue the same,
And gave you the 'bacco box marked with my name.

When I passed a whole fortnight between decks with you
Did I e'er give a kiss, Tom, to one of your crew?
To be useful and kind, with my Thomas I staid,
For his trowsers I washed, and his grog too I made.

VIEW NEAR THE ISLE OF DOGS.

[illegible]

MAIN DECK OF AN INDIAMAN.

[illegible]

Though you promised last Sunday to walk in the mall,
With Susan from Deptford and likewise with Sall,
In silence I stood your unkindness to hear
And only upbraided my Tom with a tear,

Why should Sall, or should Susan, than me be more prized?
For the heart that is true, Tom, should ne'er be despised.
Then be constant and kind, nor your Molly forsake,
Still your trowsers I'll wash, and your grog too I'll make.

[illegible]

TERRIFIC LEAP FROM THE MAST HEAD

She's Saved, She's Saved.

ACT SECOND.

OLD ADAMS' HOUSE!

[illegible]

A VIEW IN WAPPING.—MORE OF THE YARN!

[illegible]

STRONG ROOM IN CRAVERLY'S HOUSE.

[illegible]

Between Decks of an Indiaman.

[illegible]

THE BERTHS BETWEEN DECKS, WITH HAMMOCKS SLUNG!

Good Night and Safe Repose.....The Shadow.....The Robbery.....The Attack.....[illegible]

ACT THIRD.

STRONG ROOM AT CRAVERLY'S.

INTERIOR OF OLD ADAMS' HOUSE.

BETWEEN DECKS OF AN INDIAMAN!

INTERIOR OF ADAM'S HOUSE.

WAPPING OLD STAIRS, Moonlight.

HAPPY DENOUEMENT!

THE STAGE WILL BE LIT BY A NEW LIGHT!

SCULPTOR'S WORKSHOP!

IN WHICH SOME OF THE MOST CELEBRATED PIECES OF

Ancient and Modern Sculpture!

Will be represented by Male and Female Living Artists.

The whole being arranged in such a manner as to give to the Spectators a perfect idea of the Original Works in Marble; the Living Figures at the same time imparting a truth and elegance to the Groups, which must be witnessed to be understood and appreciated. *The Subjects selected for MONDAY, and the Present Week, are the following:—*

HERCULES AND CACUS,	CANOVA'S VENUS,
INFANT APOLLO,	RAPE OF THE SABINES,
MARS AND VENUS,	GLADIATORS,
FIGHTING GLADIATORS,	MURDER of the INNOCENTS.

PHOSELIONLAMPROTERON

A light of the most extraordinary brilliancy, its intensity being such as to produce distinct shadows in the brightest sunshine, and **EQUALLING THE POWER of 264 ARGAND LAMPS!!!** [illegible]

BOURBONS AND BUONAPARTISTS!

Adolphe Amien, — (*Ex-Prefect of Lyons*) — Mr. E. F. SAVILLE,
Fitchette, — (*a Rogue, in the assumed disguise of Captain Bamboozl*) — Mr. R. HONNER,
Jean Fice, — (*a Cy-devant Buonapartiste, but now a Bourboniste*) — Mr. DIBDIN PITT,
Jaques Hilliare, and Antoine, — (*his Creatures*) — Messrs. ASBURY and PHILLIPS,
Monsieur Dubot, — (*a Rich Merchant*) — Mr. DALE,
Eugene, — — — — (*his supposed Son*) — — — Mrs. R. HONNER,
Madame Potel, — (*Hostess of the "Three Olive Trees"*) — Miss MARTIN,
Jules Janesse, { *Foster-Brother of Eugene, & Foreman of Mons. Dubot, with most sweet and intoxicating reasons for being in love with Madame Potel,* } Mr. W. SMITH,
Varpeur, (*a notorious House Breaker*) Mr. CULLEN, Pierre and Robert, (*his Associates*) Messrs. GREEN and R. GREEN,
Madame Liebet, Mrs. LOWE, Annette, (*an Orphan, betrothed to Eugene*) Miss GRANT.

To conclude with on *Thursday, Friday and Saturday*, [illegible]

DE MONVAL!

OR, THE GYPSIES OF LANGUEDOC!

Sir William Alford.........(*an English gentleman, residing at Languedoc*).........Mr. GOLDSMITH,
Henry.....(*his Son—secretly united to Justine*).....Mr. DIXON,
Benjamin Goosequill.....(*Serving Man to Sir William—marvellously given to the Muses*).....Mr. W. SMITH,
Larry O'Bull.....(*an Irish Emigrant, Rat-catcher, Heated Shoemaker, and Cow Doctor*).....Mr. DIBDIN PITT,
Espinoit and Andre.........(*Two Gypsey Chiefs*).........Messrs. CULLEN & ELVIN,
Rollo and Peitre.....(*Two of the Tribe*).....Messrs. BARNES & DIXIE,
Henri.........(*a Dumb Boy, under the protection of the Gypsey Tribe*).........Mrs. R. HONNER,
Clopero.....(*a Provincial Magistrate*).....Mr. YOUNG, Barquette.....(*a Drunken Gaoler*).....Mr. BORELLI,
De Monval.........(*an Exiled Nobleman*).........Mr. DILLON,
First Officer.........Mr. GREEN, Second Officer.........Mr. DIXIE,
Mrs. O'Gigol...Miss MARTIN, Justine...Miss GRANT.

[illegible]

The oxygen and hydrogen required for this lighting had to be produced on the premises, unlike coal gas which was eventually piped in (to illuminate the auditorium, for example). The Surrey set up its 'Gas Department' and eventually its operator earned a special mention on the playbills.

The Surrey had also been experimenting with another element – water. On 7 June 1835 it advertised *The Water Queen; or, The Spirits of Donau and the Goblin Page* in which 'a Fountain of Real Water will be introduced'. It looks as if the first attempts were not very successful, as it was six years before 'Real Water' and the Surrey became firmly associated in the public consciousness.

Davidge also set about trying to improve the diorama, a panoramic scenic device brought to the Surrey by Elliston. The name of this had been pirated from Louis Daguerre's scenic 'Diorama', a stationary exhibition in a show-room which opened at Regent's Park in September 1823. The theatrical diorama, first engineered by Clarkson Stansfield for Elliston's Drury Lane pantomime of Boxing Night 1823, was a vast sheet of painted canvas drawn across the stage as a back-cloth, originally as a display in its own right, then to provide instant scene-changes, and later to give the impression of movement through space of the actors appearing before it. The impression it thus sought to create was that now achieved in film and television epics by back-projection. An early Davidge experiment staged in December 1835 was *The Wreck of the Royal George* with a 'Magnificent descriptive Scenic Pictorial Dioramic induction, Painted solely by Mr Brunning – consisting of a Series of Picturesque Local Scenery, seen during a supposed Cruise Round the Coast'. Eliminating the redundancies in the description, it means that the ship on stage stays where it is – subject no doubt to a little up-and-down motion – while the coast goes past behind it.

Another example can be found in October 1839 for *Jack Sheppard,* showing the 'Procession from the Old Bailey to Tyburn'. Jack is put on a cart outside Newgate, but the diorama pauses on Holborn Hill, outside St Andrew's Church, for a scene where the mob attempts to rescue him. The cart 'moves' on to the Crown Inn, where, during another pause, 'according to Ancient Custom, the criminal Drank his Last Refreshment on Earth'. Finally, the cart 'moves' on to Tyburn Tree for the final scene. No doubt the cart had a hidden stage-hand to turn its wheels at the appropriate moments to add to the illusion.

The Satirist of 2 January 1842 remarked on an interlude in the pantomime when

> Mr Brunning's 'magnificent annual panorama' lulled the audience for a while into admiration. It commences with new London Bridge, and represents all the scenes and objects down the river to Greenwich, Woolwich (including the launch of the warship*Trafalgar*), Gravesend, Harbour at Margate, crosses the Channel, terminating at Boulogne; and delighting the audience by the fidelity with which every object is pourtrayed.

This, of course, was merely travelogue; but anything which could capture the attention of the Surrey-siders during a break in the pantomime must have been good!

Brunning was still producing dioramas for Mrs Frances Davidge after her husband's death: the 1842 pantomime *Harlequin Puck; or, The Elfin Changling and the Enchanted Statue of the Crystal Fountain* was brought to a close with a dioramic trip round the Isle of Wight. Starting at the Royal Yacht Club-house, West Cowes, the journey proceeded via Newport, Carisbrook Castle, Tolland's Bay, The Needles and so on to Ryde Bay and Pier, 'passing to a General View of Portsmouth Harbour'. I am sorry I cannot explain what Oberon and Titania were doing at the end of Ryde Pier. (Perhaps waiting for the ferry?)

These two examples may not seem of much import to modern eyes, but to the average Surrey-sider before the days of cheap transport Boulogne and the Isle of Wight could have been on another planet.

Davidge made other attempts to impose a distinctive style on his productions. In the Surrey's nautical days many a set depicted ships' decks, above and below, to accommodate courts-martial, mutinies or battle-stations. *The Satirist* of 12 June 1836, reviewing *Ben Brace*, found 'the last scene superbly terrific – it represents the main and quarter-decks of a man-of-war at the time of an engagement, and all that fire and smoke, swearing and noise could effect, was here given in all its glory; the audience, we need not say, applauded most convulsively'.

With Davidge in the fore-front, one aspect of the productions in theatres of the day which strikes the modern play-goer is not just the complexity of some of the sets but also the sheer number of them. *The Law of the Land* in August 1837 had fourteen settings ranging from an ante-chamber in St. James's Palace to the condemned cell in Newgate Prison. Three months later *Wapping Old Stairs* had the same number, including the main deck of an Indiaman and Wapping Old Stairs by moonlight. But these are nothing compared with *Jack Sheppard* which had thirty-eight! The efforts of scene painters and scene shifters alike seem superhuman.

Davidge also achieved a scene of 'over-powering magnificence' by buying up some of the 'costly fittings-up' from Westminster Abbey after Queen Victoria's coronation there on 28 June 1838. The Surrey had celebrated the day suitably. As the playbills announced,

> On Thursday, the 28th instant, the Day of Her Most Gracious Majesty's Coronation, the Performances will comprise the National Anthem 'God save the Queen' To which will be added, the New Historical Comedy of *The Puritan's Plot!* To conclude with, Last Night But Two, the Splendid Romance of *Crichton!* On this occasion BY ROYAL COMMAND the Public will be admitted Free. In order to avoid any confusion that might arise, no person will be allowed to pass without a Ticket, and a sufficient number will be circulated to fill the Theatre comfortably and conveniently; the Tickets will be given away at the Box Office, between the hours of Twelve and One on the day of the Ceremony.

Not content with merely celebrating the coronation, however, Davidge clearly saw how it was, in theatrical terms, 'staged' – and set about buying up the scenery. *The Field of the Cloth of Gold* was mounted on 23 July as a 'Grand Regal Festival':

> The Proprietors having purchased the Costly Fittings-up of the western aisle in Westminster Abbey, they will be exhibited in all their richness of blazonry and overpowering magnificence as the last scene in the *Cloth of Gold.* The last scene formed by the Gothic screen, richly carved gold balustrades etc. erected facing Her Majesty's throne: a scene rivalling the wildest conception of Eastern splendour.

It seems to have attracted the crowds. *The Age* reported that the piece had 'provided a hit for Davidge the fortunate, who is filling his coffers with the coin of Victoria the First. We believe he is the only manager at present in London who is in possession of a profitable theatre'.

At this time the pantomimes always relied on elaborate stage-craft, though it is not easy to work out how some of the tricks were achieved. There was a striking 'special effect' in the 1840 pantomime *Harlequin and My Lady Lee; or, Goosey Gander and the Spell-bound Goslings,* written by Moncrieff. The opening is simple enough, featuring a false

Lady Lee, with the rightful Lady Lee disguised as a goose-girl; this part of the story is told in four scenes while the Harlequinade takes up fourteen. As well as Harlequin (M. Huline), Columbine (Miss Sharp), Pantaloon (M. Lehman) and Clown (Southby), there are Hobbynob and Jack o' Both Sides to add to the chaos. According to *The Satirist* of 3 January 1841,

> the scene which caused the greater sensation was the 'Great Fitzwhistle Railway Station' in which an explosion is got up which covered the stage with legs and arms &c. The audience roared with delight at this 'accident' and still more when the disjectae membra being collected, their owners were fitted with the wrong limbs and members, and obliged to make the best of them into the bargain.... It is moreover worth while to see the audience enjoy it so heartily, closely packed as they are, each increasing the merriment of each other by the force of example and good humour. This is evidently the theatre for the 'masses', as the appearance of pit and gallery sufficiently showed.

One scene seems to have caused a minor diplomatic row with a 'Futile attempt of the French Cock to crow over the English Bull Dog'. The Parisian papers were said to have objected to a duet in which the victories of Agincourt, the Nile, Trafalgar and Waterloo are flaunted One verse goes:

French Cock: Vat's Vellington, fortune de guerre,
'Twas fate, not he dat beat him.
Ve'll eat him – boot, cock-hat and all,
Next time dat ve sall meet him.
Ah! vait a bit, ve'll cut your corn,
Your head and all your clovere,
Dat is, ve do intend to do all dis,
If we get overe.

Bull Dog: Bow, wow, wow,
Do you remember Waterloo?
Bow, wow, wow.

On 5 May 1841 the Surrey employed its best scenic resources in putting on *The Cedar Chest,* a piece written by George Almar for Sadler's Wells in 1834 when Robert Honner had starred as the King of the Burning Mountain. The story – at Sadler's Wells – was in two parts. The first was 'The Lord Mayor's Daughter' set in the time of Henry VIII, with the painter Hans Holbein as a principal character. The second part was called 'The Silver Palace or the Golden Poppy', a masque or water pageant. This was an allegory of 'Fire versus Water'. Volcano, the Fire King, challenges Coral Crown, the Water King, with the words:

> Vengeance, I pant for thee! For thee I pine!
> Wilt try thy element in fight 'gainst mine?

Volcano forces his way into the Silver Palace and captures My Lady Lumina, gloating:

> Then perish in a cataract of fire!
> Where art thou, Water-King, her heart to cheer?

Re-enter Coral Crown, who delivers the final blow:

> True to his pledge, the Water-King is here.
> Gush, streams and water-spouts,
> At this my potent spell.
> And strike thee, demon, to thy native hell!

In 1834 Sadler's Wells had still been in its aquatic phase, with a large tank of water (fed from the New River) under a retractable stage. It could put on naval battles, rescues from drowning and tidal waves as the script required. The Surrey in 1841 could do nearly as well with mountain torrents and limpid pools. Volcanos were no problem to the back-stage staff, but tidal waves and water-spouts were a bit beyond them. So, if the theatre could not deal with the play as written – change the play! The masque was largely omitted, though it kept an echo of its aquatic origin in 'its Brilliant Pageant of Real Water' with 'Fountains in Full Play' and 'Splendid Conjunction of the Fiery and Watery Elements'. There was also a link with its original star, in that Robert Honner was the stage-manager while his wife played the Lord Mayor's Daughter.

The Satirist of 7 June 1846 reviewed 'the production on Monday night of a new oriental spectacle, entitled *The Dark Falcon; or, The Prince Diver and the Shah's Goblet* in which piece cascades and cataracts of real water are employed'. The term 'real water' became something of a catch-phrase, the former trade-mark of Sadler's Wells now being taken over by the Surrey. It was recognised by other theatres, for example in a play first put on at the Adelphi in 1847, *How to Settle Accounts with your Laundress*. The laundress in question is trying to lure her customer into marriage and fakes her suicide by putting a dummy head-first into his washing-tub. The young man is wondering how not only the press but the playwrights will sensationalise his case, and says 'They'll make three shocking acts out of one fatal act at the Victoria, and they'll have the real water and water butt at the Surrey'. It became quite common thereafter for newspaper critics to work the phrase 'real water' into their comments on Surrey productions.

Luckily, 'real fire' was not produced during a staging of *The Two Locksmiths* in December 1841. *The New Satirist* wrote that

> during its progress some persons in the gallery raised a cry of 'Fire! fire!' and the whole house was in commotion. The pit was cleared in a few seconds; the boxes were empty in almost as short a space of time; and the rush to the gallery doors was terrific. All the actors came forward to the front of the stage, calling out, 'Keep your places, there is no cause for alarm'. The door-keepers also assured the flying audience that it was a false alarm, and prevailed on the greater part of them to return and await the conclusion of the piece. It is, however, exceedingly probable that some person in the gallery may have perceived a light in the painting-room over the theatre, where preparations are going on for the pantomime, and not knowing that there was a work-room in that situation, may have imagined that the ceiling was on fire. The alarm spread outside with great rapidity, and in less than five minutes an engine was at the door, which, however, drove away when the firemen had ascertained how matters really stood....

When the theatre did burn down twenty-three years later, it was a real fire in the paint shop over the auditorium that caused the mischief.

Electricity reached the Surrey with the 1849 pantomime, *The Moon Queen and King Knight; or, Harlequin Twilight,* when *The Times* reported that a 'fairy bower and celestial hemisphere, in which the electric light was skilfully introduced, may be especially mentioned as scenes of unsurpassed brilliancy on the Surrey side of the water'. These lights were accumulator-powered, and mains electricity does not appear in my story.

G. B. Davidge as King Artaxaminous in *Bombastes Furioso.*

Chapter Seventeen

Oliver Twist (1838 ff.*)*

Among its dramatic successes the Surrey had one 'smash hit' running almost consecutively to about ninety performances – *Oliver Twist.*

Charles Dickens published his second novel *Oliver Twist* in monthly instalments from February 1837 to October 1838. From the outset it attracted such public interest and acclaim that the first 'play of the book' to reach the stage was clearly set to be a sell-out. Since his work was not protected from adaptation by the existing copyright laws, Dickens recognized that he could only cash in on its success by getting his own version on the boards first. He proposed therefore to dramatise it, or to superintend its dramatisation, for Frederick Yates, the actor-manager of the Adelphi Theatre. He discussed this proposition in a letter (undated, but on internal evidence written before October 1838) quoted by the actor's son, Edmund Yates:

> Supposing we arrange preliminaries to our mutual satisfaction, I propose to dramatise Oliver Twist for the first night of next season. I have never seen Mrs Honner, to the best of my recollection, but, from the mere circumstance of her being a Mrs, I should say at once that she was 'a many sizes too large' for Oliver Twist. If it is to be played by a female it should be a very sharp girl of thirteen or fourteen, not more, or the character would be an absurdity. I don't see the possibility of any other house doing it before your next opening night. If they do, it must be done in a very extraordinary manner, as the story, unlike that of Pickwick, is an involved and complicated one. I am quite certain that no one can have heard what I mean to do with the different characters in the end, inasmuch as, at present, I don't quite know myself: so we are tolerably safe on that head. I am quite sure that your name as the Jew, and mine as the author, would knock any other attempts quite out of the field.

Dickens also discussed a possible dramatisation with Macready, the leading dramatic actor of the day, but this came to nothing. Macready's diary for 10 November 1838 reads: 'Forster and Dickens called; and told them of the utter impracticability of Oliver Twist for any dramatic purpose'.

While Dickens was canvassing these ideas shrewd impresarios were already far advanced in their plans to steal a march on him.

The Pavilion Theatre in the Mile End Road staged a version of *Oliver Twist,* written by C.Z. Barnett, as early as 21 May 1838 when the serial publication of the novel still had five months to run. As the plot was a closely-guarded secret the dramatist had to make up his own ending. Dickens could rightly discount this as a threat to his own work. What Dickens seems not to have taken into account was that Frederick Yates, besides being the manager of the Adelphi, was also lessee of the Pavilion where Barnett's unauthorised version was being presented.

Davidge in the meantime was also making plans to put a dramatised *Oliver Twist* on the Surrey stage as quickly as possible. He signed a contract on 2 June 1838 with George Almar who agreed to write 'a certain drama called Oliver Twist. And I do hereby agree that the same shall not be performed at any other theatre without the express permission in writing of the said G.B. Davidge'.

On 12 November Davidge launched his bombshell with the announcement that the Surrey would present *Oliver Twist* on the following Monday. The cast of 31 was to include a boy, Master Owen, as Oliver; Heslop as Fagin; John Cooper as Mr Brownlow; another boy, Master Young, as Noah Claypole; E.F. Saville as Bill Sikes; Miss Martin as Nancy; Miss France as 'Little Dick, a pauper child'; Ira Aldridge as 'Mr Fang, the Sitting Magistrate of the Metropolitan Police Office' – nobody seems to have thought it out of the way to cast a black actor in the role; and the adapter, George Almar, as Toby Crackit. Davidge must have been preparing, casting and rehearsing in secret ever since the agreement of 2 June with George Almar who must in turn have dramatised each monthly part as it appeared, the cast then being fed their scripts in instalments. For most of them it did not matter that even Dickens was not quite sure how the story would end; the episodic nature of the story might well write their characters out of the plot long before the end of the story.

The critic of *The Times* gave the performance a rave review on 21 November 1838, in fact preferring the play to the book:

> A new drama of more than ordinary merit has been produced at this theatre. It is an adaptation to the stage of the novel of Oliver Twist and bears the name of the original production of 'Boz'. Of the merit of the novel it would be idle to speak; it has become a favourite, and as the majority of the public are content to follow the judgment of a very slender minority, somewhat on the principle that one fool

> makes many, it has reached a degree of popularity which is frequently withheld from works of ten times its worth. The drama, however, may be spoken of with almost unqualified praise, both as regards the incidents selected for scenic effect, and the manner in which they are rendered effective in the representation. The tedious portions of the novel are necessarily left out, the monotonous descriptions are avoided and the repetition of endless vulgarisms removed. In a word, the play is the essence of the book. The spirit of the jokes, incidents and peculiarities is preserved, and the worthless residuum not thrust upon the spectator as it is on the reader. The play however is rather too long. Some of the scenes might be left out altogether, as they encumber the action and retard the plot....

The reviewer identifies the cast, giving due praise, and ends: 'The audience, which was one of the most numerous ever crowded within the walls of a theatre, testified their approbation by a deafening uproar'.

Dickens could not be expected to share the enthusiasm. After all, he was not making a penny from the exploitation of his novel. His biographer, John Forster, reports that in the middle of the first scene of the Surrey production Dickens laid himself down on the floor in the corner of the box he was occupying and never rose from it till the act-drop fell. This may have reflected anguish at seeing a travesty of his own brain-child, as his son Charles Dickens junior later implied, but it seems more likely to me that he was shattered because in those first few minutes he recognised a winner – and it was not his! He had been beaten on every count – adaptation, timing, casting and all.

It is quite clear that Dickens had no idea what Davidge had been up to, but I would guess that Davidge was fully informed of Dickens's hopes and plans. There had been close collaboration between Davidge and Yates, not only during the annual visits of the Adelphi company to the Surrey but also when they jointly purchased a play, *The Death Poker,* from Thomas Egerton Wilks on 24 May 1837. I do not think it can be coincidence that on the same night that Davidge premiered *Oliver Twist* at the Surrey, Frederick Yates premiered *Nicholas Nickleby* at the Adelphi. To make the message clearer, when the Surrey playbills on 15 February 1839 announced the next 'Union of the Surrey and Adelphi Companies', Davidge and Yates put on *Oliver Twist* and *Nicholas Nickleby* on the same evening. Until the end of the season, Yates with his wife and company performed at the Surrey. With Yates and Davidge acting in concert, Dickens never stood a chance.

Oliver Twist continued to pack the audiences in. When the Christmas pantomime was added to the bill not even the seat of a critic was safe, as *The Times* reported on 27 December 1838.

> The bill of fare consisted of *Oliver Twist; or, The Parish Boy's Progress* and a new grand comic Christmas pantomime.... Of the performance we regret we cannot speak as we should wish to have done, having through the petulance of a subordinate box-keeper been unfortunately deprived of our seat, and the pressure without the range of boxes being such as to prevent us seeing or hearing much of what transpired....

He was able to say however that 'as early as 4 o'clock the doors of this theatre were besieged by crowds, eager to obtain admission and participate in the fun and frolic so plentifully provided by the enterprising proprietor and spirited corps of this favourite place of public amusement'.

As the run continued, Davidge was able to advertise in the *Weekly Dispatch* of 20 January 1839 the Surrey's 'Nightly overflows still beyond conception – Continuation of the unexampled popularity of *Oliver Twist* – witnessed already by upwards of 170,000 persons'.

A month later the critic of *The Satirist* was clearly getting bored with having to review the play yet again:

> One fault we must find with Davidge – it is, that he will give us no opportunity to speak of his establishment as we should wish to do; for, while *Oliver Twist*, the pantomime and other pieces, to which we have repeatedly adverted, are kept so long a period in the bills, it is not our fault. Let a change take place, and we shall be most happy to report progress.

Well, if one has to write yet another criticism of a long, successful run, that is one way to go about it.

The Almar version had a further run at the Surrey from 26 October 1840, the playbill boasting of the 'Celebrated Tableaux Vivans Designed by Cruikshank for that popular Work, which were witnessed by upwards of 300,000 persons during the extraordinary run it had when first produced at this Establishment'. There were a number of cast changes. Oliver was now played by a girl, Miss Chartley, who had played Susan in the first run; Susan was now played by Mrs Davidge's sister, Maria; Aldridge had given way to Edwards as Fang, the magistrate, while the adapter had been displaced by J.T. Johnson in the part of Toby Crackit.

In the face of such enthusiastic public demand other theatres could not be expected to leave the Surrey's presentation of *Oliver Twist* unchallenged. Various adaptations were made, including one staged by

Yates with Dickens's approval in February 1839 at the Adelphi. The Almar version which gave Davidge his hit can be identified with that printed in Dick's *Standard Plays;* it matches the details on the playbills as regards description of scenes and number of characters. To my mind it also has a good Dickensian atmosphere, as mentioned in the *Times* review. Act one scene one starts in Mrs Corney's parlour:

> *Mrs C.* *(Shuddering)* What a bleak, dark and piercing night! A night for the well-housed and fed to draw round the bright fire, and thank God that they are at home – now then to solace myself with a cup of tea... Oh, come in!
> *(Enter Mr Bumble)*

There is another version of *Oliver Twist* in an early French's acting edition. It is by an unnamed author and it is awful, enough to get all pirated versions a bad name. Charles Dickens junior did not of course see the Surrey production (he was one year old at the time) but I would guess that he had read French's version and was confusing it with the Almar dramatisation when he wrote:

> If one may judge fairly of a piece by reading it, this drama, which was first played at the Pavilion Theatre in May 1838 and afterwards at the Surrey in the following November was a very bad play indeed – so bad, in fact, that even the very long list of bad adaptations of popular stories can hardly contain anything worse. The play itself is too wretched for quotation or analysis....

Charles Dickens junior had some doubts himself as to whether he had correctly identified the play his father had seen. In a footnote to the comments quoted above, he added: 'It is clear that the play which was produced at the Pavilion could not have been identical with that which Charles Dickens saw at the Surrey. The latter piece concluded with the murder of Nancy and the death of Sikes, of which scenes, seeing that these incidents were not given to the public until October 1838, the dramatist of May 1838 could have had no knowledge'. Quite so.

So what is French's version? It is probably not the play staged at the Pavilion, as French includes Nancy's murder and Sikes's death. It certainly is not the Surrey production seen by Dickens, but there is an indirect link between the Surrey Theatre and a dramatised version by T.L. Greenwood for Sadler's Wells. Robert Honner left the Surrey for a couple of years in 1838 to manage Sadler's Wells. While there he commissioned Greenwood to produce his own *Oliver Twist* epic, as he could not use Almar's work which was exclusive to the Surrey. His show opened on 3 December 1838, with Honner playing Fagin and his wife playing Oliver. Altogether there were twenty-four people in the cast as against thirty-one in the Surrey version. On 1 August 1842 Honner signed an agreement with Mrs Frances Davidge to manage the Surrey for her. Once installed he took a benefit night on Monday 12 December 1842. There were half-a-dozen short entertainments given by visiting friends; for instance T.P. Cooke obliged from *Black-Eyed Susan* with Mrs Honner as Susan. The evening was 'to conclude with, First Time here, Boz's Oliver Twist', with Honner as Fagin and his wife as Oliver just as at Sadler's Wells. The only record I have seen of this entertainment is a leaflet, not a full playbill, and only nine characters are shown as against nineteen in French's printed version. As with French's version, the leaflet does not name the adapter.

If 'First Time here' is to be believed, then the author was not George Almar. Could it have been Greenwood? I am supported in this idea by a Surrey playbill of 22 May 1848 when Joseph Kerschner invited the Honners (who had moved on) back as guest artists for a short season. In one programme was *Oliver Twist* described as 'by permission of T.L. Greenwood'. As at Sadler's Wells and at the 1842 benefit, Oliver was played by Mrs Honner and Fagin by Honner. In my opinion this is the play which Charles Dickens junior read. Regretfully I must admit that it was played twice at the Surrey, as Honner's contribution to the confusion. But if Greenwood's version at Sadler's Wells had twenty-four characters, as against nineteen in French's printed edition, the identification is dubious and this confusion remains.

Another confusion concerns location. At the Surrey Theatre Bill Sikes was played by E.F. Saville. In Erroll Sherson's book *London's Lost Theatres* there is a passage which seems to transfer the action a couple of hundred yards north to the Victoria – I expect 'without the express permission in writing of... G.B. Davidge'. Sherson writes: 'At the Vic, the representative of Bill Sikes was one E.F. Saville, a brother of Helen Faucit (Lady Martin)'. He continues by quoting John Hollingshead's description of Sikes's business in the scene where he murders Nancy, which was the big moment, 'the clou of the play':

> Nancy was always dragged round the stage by her hair, and after this effort, Sykes always looked up defiantly at the gallery, as he was doubtless told to do in the marked prompt-book. He was always answered by one loud and fearful curse, yelled by the whole mass like a Handel Festival Chorus. The curse was answered by Sykes dragging Nancy twice round the stage, and then like Ajax, defying the lightning.

> The simultaneous yell then became louder and more blasphemous. Finally, when Sykes, working up to a well-rehearsed climax, smeared Nancy with red ochre, and taking her by the hair (a most powerful wig) seemed to dash her brains out on the stage, no explosion of dynamite invented by the modern anarchist, no language ever dreamed of in Bedlam, could equal the outburst. A thousand enraged voices which sounded like ten thousand with the roar of a dozen escaped menageries, filled the theatre and deafened the audience, and when the smiling ruffian came forward and bowed, their voices in thorough plain English expressed a fierce determination to tear his sanguinary entrails from his sanguinary body.

My first thoughts at reading this were simply that Hollingshead (and Sherson) had mixed up the two theatres. The difficulty with such a view is that there was a production of *Oliver Twist* at the Victoria on 20 October 1845 with the same E.F. Saville as Bill Sikes. This may have been the piece that Hollingshead saw. There is not enough on the Victoria playbill to indicate which version was to be performed. It seems unlikely, though, to have been Almar's version, as on that very same night the Surrey was performing Almar's version in a revival, with N.T. Hicks as Bill Sikes. So my guess is that Manager Osbaldiston at the Victoria put on the Greenwood version commissioned by Honner. It did not do him much good – it did not run. But Hollingshead uses the word 'always' which (unless it refers to standard business performed in every production) does suggest a long run of this particular presentation. I am persuaded, after all, to the conclusion that Hollingshead's vivid description may well relate, not to the Victoria, but to the Surrey – or to both!

DAVIDGE'S ROYAL

SURREY THEATRE.

FOR THE BENEFIT OF

Mr. R. HONNER,

(MANAGER)

On which occasion he has the satisfaction of announcing that

Mr. T. P. COOKE

has most kindly given the aid of his gratuitous services.

On MONDAY, December 12th, 1842,

The Performances will commence with (First Time here) a New Drama, entitled

TEMPTATION!

Or, The Progress of Crime.

Principal Characters by Messrs. H. HUGHES, N. T. HICKS, R. HONNER,
W. SMITH, WALTON, HESLOP, &c.
Mrs. R. HONNER, Miss E. TERREY, and Mrs W. DALY.

Miss E. HONNER will sing the highly popular Ballad of '**Happy Land,**'
Originally sung by her, together with
Made. VESTRIS' Ballad of "**I'll be no Submissive Wife.**"
Mr. COLLINS will, for this Night only, sing his highly popular Song of
"**Hurrah for the Road.**"
Mr. J HERBERT will give his celebrated Version of the '**Statty Fair.**'
In the course of the Evening.
The Cracovienne, (in Character) by **Miss SMYTHIES.**

After which, the Nautical Drama of

BLACK-EYED SUSAN.

William, — — Mr. T. P. COOKE,
Black-Eyed Susan, — Mrs. R. HONNER.

The whole to conclude with, First Time here, "**BOZ's**"

OLIVER TWIST!

Oliver Twist, — (First Time here) — Mrs. R. HONNER,
Fagin, (First Time here) Mr. R. HONNER, Bill Sykes.....Mr. N. T. HICKS,
John Dawkins, (commonly called the Artful Dodger) Mr. J.W. COLLIER,
Mr. Bumble, Mr. W. SMITH, Mr. Brownlow, Mr. NEVILLE,
Nancy, — — (on this occasion) — — Mrs. H. VINING.

BOXES, 2s. PIT, 1s. GALLERY, 6d.

Tickets & Places to be had at the Box-Office of the Theatre; and of Mr. R. HONNER,
at his Private Residence, 19, Homer Street, Pentonville.

S. G. FAIRBROTHER, Printer, 31, Bow Street, Covent Garden.

Chapter Eighteen

Macbeth (1841 ff.)

The first thing a contemporary must take on board is that after Shakespeare's day until at least the mid-nineteenth century *Macbeth* was all but a 'musical', if that is not putting it too boldly. To Pepys (as quoted by G.C.D. Odell) it was even 'in the nature of an opera'.

One can still see musical traces in the original play as currently printed: in act three scene five – 'song within, Come away, come away'; in act four scene one – 'Music and a song, Black Spirits', and later in the scene, 'Music. The Witches dance and vanish'. Needless to say Shakespeare does not provide a score; indeed, he did not even provide the words, which were in all probability taken from Thomas Middleton's *The Witch*. The composer of the original witch music was Robert Johnson, a friend of Shakespeare. His music survives for the first witch song, 'Come away, come away', as do his settings of the songs in *The Tempest*.

When theatre was released from puritanical restrictions at the Restoration in 1660 Sir William Davenant added another 'musical witch' scene to his *Macbeth* (published in 1674). This was in act two, just after the discovery of Duncan's murder and the flight of Malcolm and Macduff. It is the treatment of this long-enduring scene at the Surrey, in various productions starting with the one that opened on 12 July 1841, which is at the heart of this chapter. It is first worth looking to see how it had been treated at other times and places.

In Davenant's version (so-called, though it seems to have gathered accretions from another hand at some point), Hecate, chief of the witches, sings with four other soloists, backed by a large chorus of other witches. There were fifty-eight in one production at Drury Lane in late 1818. The Surrey only ever managed half that number, though led by Mrs Emily Kerschner (my great-grand-mother). We are thus looking at a scene, not just with an occasional song as might have been suggested in First Folio stage-directions, but with forces one would expect in grand opera.

The music for Davenant's additional scene was written by Matthew Locke. It was so popular that the tags 'the whole of Locke's celebrated music' or 'The Famous Music' became major selling points in the advertising of *Macbeth* for some forty years. There was a change for a 1702 production at Drury Lane, when *The Daily Courant* announced the 'Vocal and Instrumental Musick, all new Composed by Mr Leveridge and performed by him and others'. Richard Leveridge not only composed the music; he sang the bass role of Hecate, and continued to do so for fifteen years. While he did so he was given credit as composer, but after his death the tag about 'Locke's celebrated music' crept back into the playbills. In his article 'The Music to *Macbeth'* Robert E. Moore was convinced that the music used for productions at the end of the eighteenth century was by Leveridge, whatever the playbills might say. His reasoning holds equally well for productions at the beginning of the nineteenth century. So when one finds a Covent Garden playbill for 12 September 1808 announcing the 'Overture and Symphonies by Mr Ware; Vocal Musick by Matthew Locke', or an advertisement for *Macbeth* at the Surrey Theatre in *The Morning Chronicle* of 16 September 1809 stating that 'a greater part of the composition of Matthew Locke will be preserved. The new overture and other music by Dr. Busby', it is a fair bet that the music in fact owes nothing to Matthew Locke. Leveridge, possibly, but not Locke. When one comes to the Surrey productions in the 1840s, one still finds them advertised as being with 'Locke's Famous Music'. Though Locke can immediately be rejected as the composer it is not so easy to press the merits of Leveridge. His work was over a century old. Tastes were changing. Surrey audiences were getting to know the Italian and German composers and finding they preferred them to the home-grown product.

The fact that something new and special had hit the Surrey Theatre in 1841 can be appreciated by comparing numbers of performances. Usually *Macbeth* played two or three times in a longer Shakespearean season, no matter at which theatre. In London, there might be ten or twelve performances in any year, counting all the theatres, though Macready did notch up eight *Macbeths* in his 1846 season. But at the Surrey in 1841 there were 21 performances in a space of 25 days, and even then the run ended on 5 August for extraneous reasons. In June Astley's Royal Amphitheatre (just up the road) had burnt down and Davidge wanted to help his old friend, Ducrow, to get going again. He announced that as from Monday 9 August Ducrow's company would perform at the Surrey. So it was that the customers had *Mazeppa* rather than *Macbeth.*

Early in 1842 the Surrey lost its sense of direction for a while, with the death of Davidge and temporary occupation by another horse-master, Batty, while Mrs Frances Davidge was picking up the reins. When she took charge in June 1842 *Macbeth* was revived, with six performances in a fortnight. There were further revivals of this production in June and December 1847 with equal success. New music is most likely to have been the reason. Could an interesting double concerning Siward and a witch also have suggested to some minds a clever twist to the plot, achieved without altering a single word of Shakespeare?

Robert Moore comments on the Witch scene that had been introduced by Davenant into act two, saying that four witches are listed in Davenant's text, and that 'the scene continues with alternate singing by Hecate and the chorus of witches'. There, it seems, Moore is making an assumption that Davenant's 'First Witch' in this scene is Hecate, though the actual name is not given in the speech-headings according to the transcription in Christopher Spencer's *Five Restoration Adaptations of Shakespeare.*

This is where the Surrey production that opened in 1841 differs from all other versions, there being five or six witches in this scene, and Hecate not among them. As to the 'five or six' witches, there are six soloists in this scene and five of them are definitely witches. A playbill of 1842 shows in heavy type: 'Singing Witches; Miss Romer, Mr W. Harrison, Mr J. Webster, Mrs Searle, Miss E. Terrey'. But what of the sixth singer? In the 1841-42 production the pieces 'Speak, sister, speak', 'Many more murders', 'He shall spill much more blood', 'When cattle die' and 'When wind and waves' are sung by Dennis Lawler, who is shown in the cast list as Siward, Earl of Northumberland, the English general. Of course, according to the received text Siward does not appear on stage until act five scene four, though he is referred to in act four scene three and act five scene two. So if Lawler happened to have a good singing voice there is no practical reason why he should not double as Davenant's 'First Witch' in act two – this being an important personage, too, judging by the way he orders the other witches about and the amount of music he is given; yet he is not Hecate who is sung in the other witch scenes by Adam Leffler from the Theatre Royal, Covent Garden. Thus the Surrey's 'First Witch' is not one of Middleton's witches and not simply one of Davenant's either, because Lawler has taken over much of the part given by Davenant to Hecate. Was it thought that Leffler's part was too burdensome and the music split between the two singers? Unlikely, in view of Leffler's reputation.

There is certainly some merit in removing Davenant's Hecate from act two; otherwise the angry remarks by 'Shakespeare's' Hecate in act three to the other witches ('How did you dare to trade and traffic with Macbeth... and I, the mistress of your charms... was never called to bear my part') seem pointless, or at best somewhat belated. If one now looks at the playbills for the production opening on 7 June 1847 at the Surrey under Joseph Kerschner, one sees that the second-act pieces detailed above were sung by a 'Mr Somers' (corrected to Summers by the end of June). Neither his name nor the part of Siward are mentioned in the cast list, though in the Surrey's production of December 1847 under Alfred Bunn the part of Siward is played by 'Mr Summers', who in later playbills is better identified as Oliver Summers, a bass, capable of singing in grand operas such as *Robert the Devil* and *The Jewess*. So why did Bunn cast an opera singer as Siward, unless he is required to sing? Summers also takes the part of Siward in February 1848 after Bunn had left and Mrs Frances Davidge had resumed command, but as the singers are more or less the same as in Bunn's cast it might be stretching things to call this a new production.

Nevertheless, the playbills seem to give us the remarkable situation that the sixth singing witch in act two in four separate productions over seven years is Siward, the English general, alone and deep inside Scottish territory! Attractive and far-reaching conspiracy theories can be woven from this fantasy. Unfortunately we have to presume that the doubled roles were so far differentiated as to avoid confusion. At least that may have been the intention. In *The Doubling of Parts in Shakespeare's Plays* Arthur Colby Sprague tells us:

> The ease with which a particular double could be concealed had much to do with its popularity. Duncan often became Hecate, and a good deal less often was one of the Weird Sisters. There was a longer time in which to prepare for Hecate but the transitions to and from a Witch would not have been difficult.... Other characters besides Duncan have become Witches....

Such 'concealment' no doubt required the suspension of disbelief. A frisson could remain, however, as in the case of the singer-actress Mrs Howard Paul who in 1869 played what Sprague calls the 'sinister double' of Lady Macbeth and Hecate. Who knows what frissons quivered in spectators' minds at the Surrey when a chief witch turned up as General Siward?

The announcement in *The Times* of this *Macbeth* production was on Monday 12 July 1841, the day of its first performance, describing it just as Shakespeare's *Macbeth*. On the Tuesday this was expanded to include 'Locke's Music in *Macbeth* with magnificent effects'. On the Wednesday, despite the pressure on space through the reporting of the General Election results, the paper fitted in the following report from its drama critic, under the heading 'Surrey Theatre':

> The performances at this theatre have assumed a degree of excellence and the performers engaged in them are of a class

> of eminence, which entitles them to the patronage of the public. In addition to many good comic and melodramatic actors, old favourites of the Surrey side of the town, there are now the united talents of Messrs. Leffler and Wilson and of Miss Romer, in the operatic department and an excellent band of instrumental performers under the direction of Mr George Stansbury....

After praising Stansbury the review mentions the provincial reputation of the leading tragic actor, Mr Graham, 'who will soon be well known in London'. It gives a considered analysis of his performance which is of unusual interest for recognising and encouraging a more thoughtful trend in acting that was just beginning to make its mark:

> This gentleman has, this week, made his first appearance at the Surrey Theatre in the character of Macbeth and has succeeded even beyond the expectations of those who knew him in the country. The tragedy has been well got up at this house. The choruses of the witches are particularly good. The dresses and decorations, the scenery, etc. have been produced for the occasion and no expense has been spared to put this celebrated play well upon the stage. Mr Graham's reading of the part is perfectly natural and correct and his performance an equable piece of acting throughout. He does not play detached bits of the part and merely drawl through the remainder but he makes the whole tell and identifies himself with the imaginary being he represents.
>
> Of course the more emphatic portions of the character he makes more prominent by a judicious employment of emphasis and a more vigorous elocution. His voice is clear and calculated to impress; the enunciation is unembarrassed and his tones free from monotony. His gestures and attitudes are very good; he is exempt from the stage conventions which cripple the natural gait, and substitute an unmeaning strut in the place of natural motion.
>
> In the last act of the tragedy he was peculiarly effective and gave the speech commencing 'Tomorrow and tomorrow' with great felicity of manner. The performance was received throughout with applause, and at the falling of the curtain an unanimous thunder of approbation proclaimed his triumph over the difficulties of a very arduous undertaking. The house was crowded with auditors; there was, in fact, scarcely standing room in the space behind the boxes.

Such a review is remarkable when one considers that at this time one would recall Kean or look to Macready for a 'great' Macbeth – but who remembers Graham? Yet he sustained the role for 21 performances in a space of 25 days, a feat which Kean and Macready did not (would not? could not?) equal. But did the *Times* review reflect a consensus of opinion? *The Satirist*, for one, disagreed as to Graham's abilities. Perhaps it was looking for a less subtle style than *The Times,* more good old blood-and-thunder, in saying that

> the deficiencies of his performance chiefly regarded intellectual power, energy and intensity. Failing to grasp the mental attributes of the character, he failed also in portraying the varied emotions and feelings by which it is marked. His was a tame, a milk-and-water Macbeth – an outline which required to be filled up by the hand of an artist. One thing was attractively given – viz. the music of Locke, by the vocal stars engaged here, who, as far as manner could be relied on, were evidently the most important persons in the tragedy. They one and all, chorus and principals, did their spiriting well, and with the fervent approbation of the audience.

The Satirist reviewed the piece a second time a fortnight later: 'At the Surrey, they continue doing *Macbeth,* which is got up very creditably – excellently, as regards the music'. When the Surrey revived the production a year later the name part was played by Henry Hughes, again with success. This seems to confirm that the initial success was not due to Graham, *pace* the *Times* review, so it seems that either the production itself, or the music, or both would be the secret of its unprecedented run.

Although I am fond of my fancy concerning the Witch/Siward double, I cannot see it as the sort of thing to bring out the 'Standing Room Only' notices. Nor can I see anything in the stagecraft to account for the run – the actors and the back-stage staff were all Surrey regulars. So it must be the music, and new music at that, even if it masquerades as the 'Famous Music by Matthew Locke'. Of the composers with contemporaneous Surrey links, only Michael Balfe is really well known, with, for example, his *Bohemian Girl* of 1843, but his work is well-researched and no *Macbeth* music is attributed to him. Two other composers, E.J. Loder and J.H. Tully, had close Surrey links but again do not seem to have left any *Macbeth* music. So we appear to be left with George Stansbury, the conductor, and Miss Emma Romer, the principal soprano and operatic director, to be considered as the source of the musical inspiration, if such it be. Stansbury's surviving work consists of short pieces – nothing to suggest he could set whole scenes for seven principals plus large chorus. So far as the record goes Emma Romer has written nothing, but she had a brother to whom is attributed one single opera or burletta, *Fridolin,* produced in 1840. I cannot prove that he wrote the Surrey's *Macbeth* music, but I do know that he has not been the subject of much research. He does not even earn an entry in *New Grove*. In any case, none of these people seem to be of the calibre to write music which would have attracted so much attention. It was the sort of response which Verdi might have had if he had written his operatic *Macbeth* six years earlier and premiered it in London instead of Florence. So who did write the new music for the Surrey *Macbeth?* I am afraid I do not know. Nor, for the record, do archivists at the Shakespeare Birthplace Trust, the Shakespeare Library at Birmingham, or the University of Victoria, British Columbia, where a new Shakespeare Music Catalogue is being assembled.

However, if fantasy still hovers, what about Beethoven? Ridiculous? Yet if we look in *The New Everyman Dictionary of Music* by Eric Blom, 1988 edition, under Beethoven's 'Ghost Trio' we see that 'sketches for the work appear on the same sheet as sketches for a projected opera on Macbeth'.

Surrey Theatre,

Under the Management of

Messrs. DAVIDGE & WILLIS JONES.

DUCROW'S

STUD OF

HORSES

AND COMPANY.

Monday, Sept. 6, and during the Week

LAST SIX NIGHTS OF

LORD BYRON'S

MAZEPPA!

AND

WILD HORSE!

SCENES IN THE

CIRCLE!

DICK TURPIN's

Ride to York!

S. G Fairbrother, Printer, 31, Bow Street, Covent Garden.

Chapter Nineteen

Sharing with Ducrow (1841-42)

I have already mentioned A.H. Saxon's *Life and Art of Andrew Ducrow*. It is impossible to write about Davidge and the Surrey Theatre without treading on Saxon's ground. Again, one cannot mention Ducrow without bringing in Astley's Royal Amphitheatre at the other end of Westminster Bridge Road from the Surrey, which, like the Surrey, had been founded on a programme of equestrian feats and animal acts much admired at the time. Whereas the Surrey had for the most part shed its Circus image, the Royal Amphitheatre extended horsemanship into a fine art. Originally under Philip Astley then William Davis and later Ducrow, the management sought plays which would include, say, a cavalry charge or mounted combat as an integral part of the drama. Indeed, Davidge was a part of Astley's history, for on 9 June 1823 he had played the lead part of Corinthian Tom in an equestrian version of Moncrieff's *Tom and Jerry* under the direction of William Davis.

Ducrow and Davidge knew each other from at least 1833. In the period between leaving the Coburg and leasing the Surrey, Davidge appeared at Astley's in such forgettable masterpieces as *The Charmed Charger; or, Nipkins and the Spectre Steed* (Davidge as Tom Nipkins) for three weeks from 21 July 1834, and in *The Waggoner and the Murderer* (Davidge as the Waggoner) in August. It is likely that Davidge had some influence on the choice of programme during these weeks. Ducrow put on *The Old Oak Chest* in which Davidge played Tinoco, a part he had established for himself on a number of conventional stages; for that matter, he had played in another version of *Tom and Jerry* at the Royalty Theatre in Goodman's Fields in 1822: so it is not impossible that Ducrow built his productions round Davidge's established talents. Davidge's last appearance at Astley's (also his benefit night) was on 13 September 1834 as Richard Heartly in *Darnley, the Knight of Burgundy*.

By then Davidge's negotiations for the lease of the Surrey Theatre, to run from Michaelmas, had been successful. He opened there on 6 September. Although now a competitor for the custom of the South Bank audiences, he remained a lifelong friend of Ducrow. When Ducrow threw a banquet on 31 July 1836, on the guest list can be found Davidge and these other members of the Surrey company: T.D. Rice (Jim Crow), Paul Bedford the comedian, George Stansbury the musical director, Mrs W.

Daly and Mrs Fitzwilliam, both regular actresses on the Surrey stage. Also present was Mrs Stickney in the triple capacity of Surrey actress, widow of John Ducrow and wife of one of Andrew Ducrow's riders.

Saxon records that an 'American making his London debut at Astley's' in 1838 'was the lion tamer Isaac Van Amburgh...'. He had originally been a menagerie keeper. He took to the stage, complete with animals, in dramas which required him to be 'thrown to the lions' or discovered in a forest surrounded by wild animals. After his engagement with Ducrow he was taken up by Alfred Bunn at Drury Lane, where he caught the eye and imagination of the young Queen Victoria who paid half a dozen visits to see his show. On Monday 29 June 1840 Van Amburgh came to the Surrey with his play, *Mungo Parke,* based on the life of the Scottish explorer, 'with Lions, Leopards and Tigers' for a four-week season. He did not have the exclusive use of the theatre; there were other plays in the evening's entertainment, such as *Jane of the Hatchet* and *Factory Boy*.

Then for a while the Surrey reverted to its usual bill of fare: dramas, melodramas and pantomime. The *Times* critic wrote on 26 December 1840:

> The Surrey Theatre having had the good fortune, more than once, to produce 'the best pantomime' in the judgment of the 'noisy gods' whose numbers and power of lungs make them irresistible here, it was not surprising to find that at an early hour an 'overflowing house' had been drawn to witness the performance of the evening which commenced with 'a domestic drama of the most powerful interest' entitled *Martha Willis, the Maid Servant* a piece not altogether a stranger, we believe, to the public....

This review runs to about eight column inches all told, so the Surrey was getting as much attention from *The Times* as were the major houses.

By the beginning of 1841, at Astley's Royal Amphitheatre Ducrow's asthma was restricting his personal appearances. His already low spirits were further depressed when on 8 June his theatre and his adjoining home were burnt to the ground. As was customary, other theatres offered their services. Within a month of the fire Ducrow was mounting purely equestrian performances at Drury Lane, Sadler's Wells and Vauxhall Gardens. To place his establishment on a more permanent footing he arranged with Davidge (by now in partnership with Thomas Willis Jones, as his own health was none too good) to take over the Surrey, which was to be returned to its Royal Circus and Equestrian format. Davidge had two long-planned productions to clear first: his opera season, which had commenced on Whit Monday 31 May with *La Sonnambula,* and his new version of *Macbeth* discussed in the previous chapter. Of the opera season, *The Times* wrote on 15 June 1841:

> The spirit of music has crossed the water and the inhabitants of Surrey have given shelter to our English artistes whose rightful territory the Italian and German invaders have usurped. We need not inform our readers that Miss Romer, Mr Wilson and Mr Leffler have for some weeks past been delighting the Surrey audiences. Last night, M. Adolphe Adam's Opera *La Reine d'un Jour* was produced at this theatre under the title of *A Queen for a Day*. The adaptation is the work of Mr J.T. Haines who has acquitted himself of the task with all desirable success.

According to Eric Walter White in his book *A Register of First Performances of English Operas,* the opera *The Queen of a Day* (librettist unknown) was premiered at Her Majesty's Theatre on 13 August 1851. The corresponding playbill says that 'The Overture & the Whole of the Music composed by Edward Fitzwilliam'. The period, the setting, the synopsis of the plot, all seem to match Adam's. This is not meant as a criticism – otherwise I would be criticising Rossini for resetting *The Barber of Seville* or Puccini for a third go at the Manon story. I merely ask: could it be that White's 'librettist unknown' is none other than J.T. Haines of the Surrey?

Concerning the Surrey in the summer of 1841, Saxon writes:

> Following a final performance by the theatre's regular company on Friday, 6 August, a gang of machinists and carpenters immediately set to work, taking up the pit floor and reconstructing what was termed in the bills the largest circle in the world. Notwithstanding this sizeable addition, the pit was somehow enlarged to accommodate an additional 350 persons. By an ingenious mechanism, the front of the stage, together with the footlights and orchestra pit, could now advance and recede to cover or uncover a portion of the ring, depending on whether a stage spectacle or the scenes in the circle were being given at the moment. All this work was achieved in less than three days' time for the opening on 9 August.

This story must appear somewhere between 'slightly improbable' and 'miraculous', depending on one's views as to the willingness and capacity of the British working class. Saxon gives as his authority a *Times* report of 10 August 1841 which just goes to show that we should not believe everything we read in the newspapers, not even in *The Times*. What the reporter seems to have done is to run together two different examples of

Davidge/Ducrow co-operation, separated by nearly seven years. If one looks at the first playbill issued by Davidge on taking over the Surrey, regarding his opening on 6 October 1834, one reads that

> An important feature of the arrangements will be an entirely NEW MOVEABLE STAGE on a novel principle, invented and prepared by Mr KENDALL, the Mechanist of the establishment, together with Newly constructed Scenery and Machinery, by Mr MACKINTOSH, of the Royal Amphitheatre and Madame Vestris' Theatre, the immediate construction of which has been rendered necessary by the sale and removal of the whole of the old stock of the Theatre, the difficulty of hastily replacing which has been materially lightened by the kindness of Messrs. DUCROW and WEST, in permitting the progress of the new Scenery in the Royal Amphitheatre....

In 1834, in short, while Osbaldiston was getting rid of anything at the Surrey which might be useful to his rival, with Ducrow's assistance Davidge (the rival) was building new stock at Astley's.

It would seem, therefore, that the transformation of the Surrey over the week-end in August 1841 consisted of the ripping-out of the benches in the pit and putting up barriers round the newly-formed ring, the movable stage being already installed – a much more likely feat in the time available.

The 1841 bills show that what was now offered to the patrons was a mix of Davidge and Ducrow. The latter put on *Mazeppa* – that old war-horse of his – but the Poles and Tartars appearing therein included such names as Heslop, J.T. Johnson, J.G. Neville, N.T. Hicks, W. Smith and Morrison from Davidge's company, while 'Mrs Parker' (my great-great-grandmother) and the Misses M. Parker, Yates and Young appeared as shepherdesses. *The Satirist* of 12 September wrote:

> *Mazeppa* continues with some fifty-horse power to draw the public to this theatre. The pit presents nightly a sea of heads, and the gallery a mountain of ditto, all turned anxiously towards the stage, their owners gazing with all their might on the wonders unfolded by the 'double company' of 'horse and foot' in the circle or on the boards.

Supporting pieces included *Ben the Boatswain* and *The Old Oak Chest* cast entirely from Davidge's company. Ducrow did not himself appear. He had suffered a nervous break-down, attempted suicide, and was confined in a private nursing home. His wife Louisa and his company kept the show going until mid-September 1841. Ducrow was still not sufficiently recovered to attend to business matters for another month. One important question for his company was whether the spell at the Surrey Theatre would continue until Astley's could be rebuilt or whether new winter quarters would have to be found. Decisions regarding the Surrey were difficult because Davidge could feel his own end approaching and made his will on 1 September. He bequeathed two weeks' salary 'to each of my performers and all persons in my employ at the Royal Surrey Theatre'. There was an addendum: 'this bequest not to include Mr Ducrow's company'.

There was a further complication when William Batty, a very experienced Circus proprietor, summed up the situation accurately and moved into the National Baths on the south side of Westminster Bridge Road, half-way between Astley's and the Surrey. He called his venture the Olympic Circus at first and Batty's Equestrian Arena later. He relied on feats of strength, clowns and tight-rope walkers to back up his riders rather than integrating them into one dramatic piece as Ducrow would have done, though his 'juvenile company' starring Miss Isabel and Master Polaski did perform versions of *Cinderella* and *Masaniello* on horse-back! With both Davidge and Ducrow stricken, Batty was clearly the natural successor to the equestrian tradition on the South Bank. Ducrow's company moved out of the Surrey at the beginning of November 1841 and went on tour, opening at Leicester on 22 November and then at Liverpool for a Christmas show. Ducrow never rejoined his company. He made over to Batty the right to rebuild Astley's and died on 27 January 1842. Davidge died four days later.

There is just a hint that Davidge and Willis Jones might have had it in mind to forestall Batty by putting on a Ducrow-style season before the rebuilding of Astley's could be completed. Back in May 1841 the Surrey – according to *The Times* – had put on a new drama,

> *Claude Duval,...* from the pen of J.T. Haines. This piece cannot be strictly said to have a plot, but consists in the various incidents & exploits of this accomplished highwayman, interwoven with a story which, we have no doubt, is very well known to the author, though he has failed to impart this knowledge to his audience. On the Surrey side of the water however people are not generally particular as to whether a piece be intelligible or not, as long as the interest is sustained by a due succession of mortal combats, timely rescues etc. and the ears are regaled with an uninterrupted discharge of fire-arms....

This production was before the conversion of the theatre to accommodate Ducrow's company. On 20 November, that is after the theatre had been converted to stage 'horse-dramas' and after Ducrow's company had moved out, an agreement was signed with J.T. Haines for the drama *Claude Du Val; or, The Ladies' Highwayman.* Stemming from a new contract, this must be different from the production of six months earlier and implies a re-write on the Ducrow model, using the ring as well as the stage. This has to remain conjecture as I cannot trace that it was ever staged in this form. Its non-appearance could be due to Davidge's death.

In early 1842 Batty was on the move:

> The Public is respectfully informed, that owing to Mr Batty's intended sale of his National Menagerie on Thursday next, January 27th, his extraordinary Performing LIONS can only appear for three Nights Longer; and in order to give additional éclat to the remaining representations, he has arranged for the introduction of his Wonderful Colossal Performing Elephant....

In January-February 1842 the Surrey ran those pieces already in production, such as the Christmas pantomime, *Harlequin and Ice Queen,* and *Mrs Norma,* a skit on Bellini's opera with Norma and Adelgisa played by 'Signor Neville-i' and 'Signor Walton-i'. When Davidge's will was proved on 23 February 1842 by his widow, Frances Davidge, and by another named executor, Thomas Potter Cooke (not immediately recognisable out of sailor's garb), it was then legally possible to direct the Surrey's course. The first contract was with the only man who now mattered on the South Bank, William Batty.

Consequently at the end of March a playbill was issued for 'Davidge's Royal Surrey Theatre' announcing:

> Great and Glorious SUCCESS has attended the production of the New Grand Oriental EQUESTRIAN SPECTACLE, and the UNITED WONDERS, Matchless Feats of Horsemanship, and Gorgeous Pageants of Astley's and Ducrow's! By BATTY's Unrivalled and Unequalled Company of Foreign and English Artistes, and the FINEST STUD OF HORSES IN THE WORLD!... Commencing Every Evening, with HAINES'S Grand Equestrian Spectacle, entitled The PEARL OF THE HAREM.

Surely this cannot be *Claude Du Val; or, the Ladies' Highwayman* in a different setting again? Hardly, but the *Times* critic would presumably not have been surprised if it were. His comments included, 'To give anything like a connected detail of the story or plot of this drama, amidst the uproarious din of an Easter Monday jubilee would be impossible'. The audience did not mind. 'Notwithstanding the fine weather, and the countless attractions of Greenwich fair, the house was crowded in every part' – quite possibly to see the 'Wonderful Colossal Performing Elephant' which had somehow missed being sold by Batty on 27 January.

A sidelight on the animal-acts comes from Saxon. He records from a 'manuscript in the Ducrow Album, signed E.K.', that one observer of Van Amburgh's production had written 'a poetic missive... calling for a return to the traditional entertainments' –

> Let lions & Leopards to the Desert go,
> Give us thy riders, & thy stud, Ducrow!
> Nor let a scene, once famed for graceful Men,
> Be longer turned into a Lion's Den!

Saxon does not speculate on the identity of 'E.K.' – but I would suggest Emily Kerschner, Mrs Davidge's sister (and my great-grandmother), as the writer and Van Amburgh's appearance at the Surrey as the inspiration. Emily's husband Joseph would have been in the box office throughout Van Amburgh's engagement, while her mother and her sister Maria were appearing in *The Factory Boy*. Sharing dressing rooms, so to speak, with elephants – no problem ever since the 1811 pantomime; with horses – but of course: lions and leopards, however – never again!

For Whitsun 1842 at the Surrey Batty put on *Murat,* a drama 'freely Translated from the French... and adapted to the English stage by Mr J.T. HAINES'. The evening finished with *Sprig of Nobility,* a comic drama played by the old faithfuls of Davidge's company, Neville, Heslop, W. Smith and Mrs N.T. Hicks. The regular staff were also in attendance. Properties were by Eallett and music by Jolly, Fairbrother was in the Treasury, Kerschner at the box office, 'little' Wilkinson was Acting Manager: all Davidge's men and loyal to Mrs Davidge. Batty's season finished on 18 June 1842 and Mrs Davidge's first taste of independent production began – with opera.

Before we trace Frances Davidge's fortunes, though, let us take a closer look at her husband's last days.

Davidge's Royal

SURREY THEATRE,

Boxes 2s.—Second Price 1s. Pit 1s. Gallery 6d.

Doors open at half-past 5—Commence at a quarter-past 6—Half-price at half-past 8.

The Performances will terminate at a Quarter past Eleven, or, as near that as possible.

MONDAY, April 11, 1842,

AND DURING THE WEEK.

Amazing Increase of Attraction!

FIRST APPEARANCE here these THREE YEARS of the Astonishing

MONS. GOUFFE, THE MAN MONKEY

Whose Surprising FEATS have been the theme of Wonder throughout England, Ireland, Scotland, and America.

The Extraordinary Performances of the Sagacious Colossal

ELEPHANT

will also be added to the Scenes in the Circle, and all the

UNITED WONDERS

Of ASTLEY'S, DUCROW'S, & BATTY'S,

Realized by First-rate English and Foreign Artistes, and the

TRULY MATCHLESS STUD!

Acknowledged to be the most beautiful—the most highly-trained—and the most numerous in the World—under the Superintendence of

The Celebrated Mr. BATTY,

(the talented Successor of the late eminent Professor, Mr. DUCROW.)

ANOTHER WEEK OF

GREAT & GLORIOUS SUCCESS

having attended the spirited enterprise of the Lessee of this Establishment, he is determined to spare neither pains nor expence in catering for the amusement of the Public, and will continually offer for their approval, Attractions of surpassing Splendour, defying competition, which can now be seen to much greater advantage than heretofore, the newly-constructed and most

COMMODIOUS AND SPACIOUS PIT IN EUROPE

commanding a perfect view of the Stage and Arena.

Chapter Twenty

Davidge's Last Days (to 1842)

Fitzball relates that just as Davidge 'realised a good fortune, although accomplished in a very few years, he was attacked by a frightful malady, which hurried him prematurely to the grave, leaving him scarcely time to enjoy even a few golden days of his affluent prosperity'.

Fitzball does not put a date to his comments, but Davidge was aware of his condition at the beginning of 1839. The last time he acted was on 26 April 1839, in *The Curse of Mammon,* though he took a benefit on 1 April 1840 and appeared on stage on 11 April, at the end of the winter season, to address the audience. A biographical note on John Garside Neville in *The Theatrical Times* of 27 January 1849 says that after that actor was thrown out of a job by the failure of Montague Penley at the Lyceum, 'our hero was fortunate in engaging with Mr Davidge, at the Surrey, who gave up all his characters to him, and never played afterwards. He made his first appearance on Whit-Monday 1839 as Chrystal Baxter, in Haines' drama of *Alice Grey* and at once stamped himself a favourite with the Surrey audiences...'.

Remembering his early days and his debt to the people of Bath, Davidge took the lease of the Theatre Royal there from 14 November 1840 and installed the playwright Edward Stirling as acting- and stage-manager, with J.F. Loder as leader and conductor of music. In the main he used local talent for his company there though Eugene Macarthy and Monsieur Gouffee (thus spelt), old Surrey favourites, entertained the people of Bath in their particular ways, the first in *Irish Tutor* and the second in *Island Ape.* Stirling wrote a couple of pieces for the occasion, *Guido Fawkes* and a burletta *Horatio Sparkins.* Stirling himself played in several pieces. *The Satirist* of 17 January 1841 reported:

> The Bath Theatre, under the lesseeship of Davidge, and, this year, under the management of Mr Stirling, the husband of the interesting actress now playing at the Haymarket Theatre, is doing much better business than last season – in fact is doing well, in spite of the efforts of the saints to suppress everything like rational amusement in that city. A succession of novelties is the order of the day, and though not, perhaps, of a strictly legitimate character, yet appear to be

> duly appreciated by the Bath audiences.... We trust Davidge will, by the judicious management of this season, recover some portion of the losses experienced by him during the last year.

The high-light of the Bath venture was the four-week engagement of Charles Kean, son of the great Edmund Kean, who though not as fine a tragic actor as his father could nevertheless shine as Claude Melnotte in *The Lady of Lyons* or as the eponymous *Stranger*. No doubt risking unfavourable comparisons, he also acted Hamlet, Macbeth, Richard III and Romeo. One cannot honestly say that this gives the lie to the critic of *The Satirist* regarding pieces of 'not strictly legitimate character', as Shakespeare was flanked by two of Haines's pieces, *Jack Sheppard* and *Jane of the Hatchet* and by Jerrold's *Martha Willis, the Servant Maid; or, Service in London,* all popular Surrey melodramas. As for the 'efforts of the saints', these were attacks from the city's pulpits on theatrical performances generally. In her book *The Royal General Theatrical Fund* Wendy Trewin recounts a story told at one of its annual meetings by the M.P. for Bath, the Hon. F.H. Berkeley, that 'Mr Davidge, who had run the Bath Theatre, responded to more than ordinarily abusive sermons by staging *The Hypocrite* by Isaac Bickerstaff on the following Monday', something Davidge described as 'holding the mirror up to nature'. I have not actually found the playbill confirming this, but the story fits with Davidge's mischievous sense of humour.

Davidge – or Stirling – also tried on the people of Bath the favourite Surrey operas, *L'Elisir d'Amore, Der Freischutz* and *La Sonnambula.* They did not seem to have the same impact as at the Obelisk and the venture came to an end on 20 March 1841: 'Mr Davidge (having arrived) will make his first and only appearance this season and Deliver a Farewell Address'. It was indeed a farewell to his friends; he was dead within the year.

At this time Davidge was also directing his energy, such as remained, and the proceeds of his 'affluent prosperity' into building works, namely Davidge Terrace, comprising his own residence and six others, and Bolwell Terrace (after his middle name), comprising thirteen houses. These had a good mix of professional, theatrical and commercial occupiers, with government and railway officials as well as a Yeoman of the Guard. The middle house of Bolwell Terrace was occupied by two 'professors of music' at the 1841 Census, both employed at the Surrey: not a lot emerges regarding Lloyd Shepherd – unless he was the stage manager for the 1846 opera season – but Thomas Sullivan makes the reference books, not so much as clarinettist at one guinea a week, but as father of Arthur Sullivan, who was born there. The family moved away in 1845 when

Thomas Sullivan returned to the Royal Military College as bandmaster.

Bolwell Terrace, later Bolwell Street, a turning south-east from Lambeth Walk, disappeared under a block of council flats after the 1939-45 war, but Davidge Terrace is still to be seen as part of Kennington Road. Davidge's house is the one at the southern end with a portico, now numbered 160. His brother-in-law, Joseph Kerschner, my great-grandfather, had the house next door. At the time of the 1841 Census Davidge lived with his wife Frances, her mother Harriet Pearce, and his two sisters-in-law, the twins Maria and Louisa Pearce. There were also three female servants living in, two in their twenties and a 'tweenie' aged eleven.

Davidge also acquired two properties in Palace New Road, Lambeth, and another in Crozier Street, Lambeth. His investments in bricks and mortar proved a great deal more profitable than, say, Government stocks would have done.

Three snippets in *The Satirist* touch on the state of Davidge's health in 1841. The first on 4 April merely says about the Surrey that the 'management, for a brief period, passes at Easter from the hands of Davidge to Messrs. Wilkinson and Willis Jones, who will have no reason to complain if they can "manage" to ensure, comparatively, as large a measure of success as their predecessor'. This break did not, indeed could not, effect a cure; surgical techniques were not yet sufficiently developed. Davidge knew this and made his will on 1 September but still maintained an optimistic front. On 12 September *The Satirist* reported: 'The papers, by-the-way, have been killing the respectable manager of this establishment; Davidge, however, has contradicted the report on the best possible authority – his own; declaring that, though "he has been dangerously ill, he is now, thank God! better". We are glad to hear it, and trust he will live a "prosperous" gentleman a long time yet'. His affliction recurred. The report of 7 November was: 'We are gratified to hear that Mr Davidge, the active and intelligent manager of the Surrey Theatre, is, after a long and severe illness, convalescent, and is again able to resume the toils of management'. There is, in fact, no evidence that he did so.

Davidge died on 31 January 1842 'at 10 mins. past 5 o'clock in the presence of his wife', according to *The Times*. Douglas Jerrold, the writer who had deserted Davidge for Elliston, feigned surprise that he had died 'before the half-price comes in'. His age at death is given as 48 on the death certificate, though several newspaper reports make him up to two years older. The cause of death is shown as 'Fistula'. Fistulas are additional ducts or passages which form in the wrong place.

Some may be awkward, rather than fatal, such as an extra tear duct, but the one that killed Davidge was probably the one that by-passes the anus; nasty indeed.

The playbills for Monday 7 February announced that 'Tomorrow, the theatre will be closed on account of the funeral of Mr Davidge'. *The Dispatch* of 13 February 1842 gives this account of his funeral:

> On Tuesday the remains of this well-known manager and actor were removed from his late residence in Davidge's Terrace, Walcot-place, Lambeth, and conveyed to their final resting-place, at the South London Cemetery, Norwood, and deposited in a vault which had been constructed some time since by direction of the deceased gentleman. The funeral was not intended to be what is termed public, yet, notwithstanding the very unfavourable weather, long before half-past one o'clock... both sides of the road contiguous to the house were lined with spectators, amongst whom were a considerable number of theatrical gentlemen. About a quarter before two o'clock the cavalcade departed, the hearse preceded by a plume of feathers, and followed by four mourning coaches, the first containing Mr T.P. Cooke and Mr Wilkinson (the executors), Mr Willis Jones (the partner), and Mr R. Lawrence (the treasurer), and in the others were Mr Nash, Mr P. Bedford, Mr G. Stansbury, Mr Honner, Mr Bunn, Mr Stamp, Doctors Marsden and Bolton, and several other gentlemen, friends and relatives.... Many gentlemen of the theatrical profession proceeded to the cemetery for the purpose of witnessing the obsequies. On reaching the cemetery the crowd which had assembled round the gates had the effect of impeding for some minutes the conveyance of the body to the chapel.... The funeral service was performed by the officiating Minister, after which Handel's magnificent funeral anthem of 'When the ear heard her' was beautifully given by Messrs. G. Stansbury, P. Bedford, Green, Crouch, Perring, Lloyd, Miss Jackson, &c. The body was then lowered into the vaults beneath, whence it was conveyed by an ingenious mechanical contrivance to the tomb.... Any attempt to give a description of the disposal of the deceased gentleman's property would be premature, but it can be confidently stated that each lady and gentleman now engaged at the Surrey Theatre has been left a fortnight's salary.

This last is an understatement. The will was a beneficent one. There were many specific bequests to individual artists and others connected with the theatre, as well as to personal friends and charities, thus:

To each of my following friends as a mark of my esteem:

John Nash of Hercules Building [who was present at death, and who had acted as male nurse]	£200
T P Cooke [executor]	£ 25
J P Wilkinson [executor]	£200
William Tyler of the Adelphi [not the Theatre but the Surrey Zoological Gardens]	£150
Thomas Willis Jones of the Surrey Theatre [his partner]	£ 50
William Marsden, Surgeon	£ 50
my solicitors T C & G C H Lewis	£ 50
Robert Gardner, Baker	5 guineas
Richard Lawrence [his Treasurer]	£100
George Stansbury [of his musical staff]	5 guineas
Paul Bedford of the Adelphi Theatre	5 guineas
John Mowatt, Spirit Merchant	5 guineas
James Jones of Spitalfields	5 guineas
Samuel Russell of Bolwell Terrace	5 guineas
Edward Ratcliffe, picture dealer	5 guineas
John Woodward of Davidge Terrace, Builder	5 guineas
Mrs Vining, wife of Henry Vining, the sum of being a most obliging and talented actress.	10 guineas
Thomas Cobham, late of the Pavilion Theatre	£19 : 19s
to each of my performers and all persons in my employ at the Royal Surrey Theatre	two weeks salary
to William Simpson who has been my dresser at the said theatre and other places for 26 years	£19 : 19s
Thomas Eallett my property man and who has also been my faithful servant more than 20 years	£19 : 19s
to William Craddock my servant for 20 years	£19 : 19s
to Jolly, my musical director	£19 : 19s
to Mrs Lewis of the Surrey Theatre for upwards of 20 years	£19 : 19s
Mrs Sharp[e] [dancer]	£19 : 19s
John Thomas Haines [playwright]	£19 : 19s
William Smith [actor]	£19 : 19s
Benjamin Smith Fairbrother [former treasurer]	5 guineas
Goldsmith [actor]	£19 : 19s
Henry Hughes [actor]	5 guineas
William Goathman	5 guineas
Drury Lane Theatrical Fund	£105

Covent Garden Theatrical Fund	£105
to each of the following institutions	£52 : 10s

Guys Hospital
St Thomas Hospital
St Bartholomew's Hospital, Smithfield
Middlesex Hospital
St George's Hospital
St Luke's Hospital, Greville Street
Charing Cross Hospital
The Magdalen, Blackfriars Road
The Orphan Asylum, Lambeth
The Deaf and Dumb Asylum, New Kent Road
The Jews Synagogue
The Fever Hospital
The South London General Dispensary

to Jews Orphan Asylum in Leman Street	£ 25
Jews Charity for the Blind	£ 25
Smallpox Hospital	£ 25
to the Chief Clerk for the time being of the following police courts, to be placed in the poor box:	£ 10

Marylebone Union, Marlborough street, Hatton Garden, Queen Square, Bow Street, Lambeth Street, Thames Police, Worship Street.

There were also family legacies to various aunts and cousins, and also to 'Harriet Pearce, the mother of my wife' – that is, Mrs Parker on the stage; to 'Emily the wife of Joseph Kerschner, my wife's sister' – that is, Miss E. Parker; and to the other two Pearce/Parker girls. The residue went to Mrs Frances Davidge. It was estimated at between thirty and forty thousand pounds – say, a couple of million at today's values. When one recalls that ten years earlier, Davidge had been bankrupt, the success of his management is obvious.

Readers will see that the majority of individual legacies outside the family are to theatrical friends and employees. T.P. Cooke, friend, actor of sailor-characters *par excellence* and of the two executors the honorary one, was not in need of funds; his £25 was the appropriate 'token' bequest, to buy a jewel or other momento at today's equivalent of up to £1,000. Neighbours and friends receiving a welcome five guineas would not begrudge the nineteen guineas given to long-standing, loyal and valued members of his staff, a generous sum indeed to men and women some of whose salaries might not have been much more than £1–£2 per week. As for the institutional legacies, Davidge shows the breadth of his sympathies with public-spirited bequests totalling over £1,000 to hospitals and to charities for children, the disabled and the poor, including neighbouring Jewish charities amongst the twenty-six. One hundred guineas to each of the two main theatrical charities is more than matched by £837-10s for the care of the sick and deprived.

I leave the last word on Davidge to *The Satirist* of 6 February 1842:

> Mr Davidge, whose name has been associated with the metropolitan stage for many years, and who, as lessee of the Surrey Theatre established a reputation for management that left him without a competitor, departed this life on Monday evening after a very protracted and painful illness. It is but due to the memory of an excellent man to say his death has produced unmingled feelings of regret throughout the theatrical profession, for no man stood higher in the esteem of his dramatic brethren, and as a caterer of amusement for the public, by his tact and ability, he stood alone. Mr Davidge will be missed among those 'poor players' who have ceased 'to strut their hour upon the stage' for he had 'a hand open as day to melting charity' and in few, very few, instances was appealed to in vain to relieve the distress of an indigent brother.
>
> As an actor in a particular line of business, he was without an equal, and had he devoted his genius – for he had genius – solely to acting and not to management, there is no doubt but he would have acquired a reputation as an artiste that would have sunk into contempt the pretentions of many a modern actor, and would have secured for him name and fame superior to what could be earned in the mere drudgery of management. Mr Davidge died without issue, leaving an ample fortune acquired in the service of the public, and no servant was ever more deserving of the favours heaped upon him than was Mr Davidge, whose grave will be wetted by the tears of many friends who know how to estimate worth, and to cherish the memory of one who had too kind a heart to leave an enemy behind.

This Gentleman came from the Bath Theatre and for many years has been an actor of much merit at nearly all the minor Establishments in London. In a piece called "One Hundred and Two", he acted the part of "Philip Ga[i]bois" as well as ever Munden or Farren played <u>any</u> part.
"Natur, father, natur."

Inscription written by hand below a print of the portrait of G.B. Davidge in the possession of the Garrick Club.

Plate V George Bolwell Davidge
(lessee and manager of the Surrey Theatre, 1834–42)

Plate VI David Webster Osbaldiston, 1836
(lessee and manager of the Surrey Theatre, 1831–34)

Plate VII Mrs William West, 1819
('regular' Surrey actress and admired leading lady)

W. T. Page

MISS ROMER,

as

AMINA IN LA SONNAMBULA

Plate VIII Emma Romer (Mrs Charles Almond), c. 1839
(star and director of opera at the Surrey Theatre for twenty years)

Chapter Twenty-One

'The Only Operatic Theatre in the Metropolis' (1842-45)

For two or three years after Davidge's death the Surrey Theatre pursued a somewhat uneven course. Mrs Frances Davidge seems to have felt a bit uncertain about the dramatic (and melodramatic) aspects of management, but perfectly at home organising the operatic content of the bill. *The Times* approved of these efforts, recording on 25 June 1842:

> The operatic company which has during the week been playing at this theatre, has attracted very full houses. Miss Romer, Messrs. Harrison and Leffler are amongst the best vocal performers, & Mr G. Stansbury acts as conductor. The opera of Bellini, the *Sonnambula,* has been selected as the piece first to be brought out upon this stage and the result has proved the good judgment of the management. A very efficient chorus has been engaged, and the whole has been put upon the boards in a manner highly to the credit of the proprietress. No expense has been spared to make the representation of this fine opera effective, and to afford to the inhabitants of the Surrey side of the Thames a musical treat of the highest class.... Nothing was left to be desired in any department, and the whole was properly appreciated by one of the most crowded audiences we remember to have seen for a long time within the walls of a theatre.

Nevertheless, Frances Davidge cannot have had an easy time of it. For one thing, she took some while to secure the confidence of the company and demonstrate that she had inherited the managerial touch which had been her late husband's strong point. For another, she suffered from the enmity of Osbaldiston, who made it clear that his quarrel with Davidge continued beyond the grave and was now with her. Never one to let old grievances die, he signed on well-established Surrey performers at the Royal Victoria and trumpeted his success thus: '20 June 1842 First Night of Miss Martin who, so long a Favourite at the Surrey, and having seceded from that Establishment, has been engaged by the VICTORIA Management'. Miss Martin had played Nancy in the long-running *Oliver Twist* so there was a real loss to the Surrey. Osbaldiston played the same poaching game again two years later, but did not come out of it nearly so well, as will be seen.

When Robert Honner's spell at Sadler's Wells was coming to an end Mrs Davidge invited him back to the Surrey as manager. Their agreement, dated 1 August 1842, specifies a salary of £9 a week, plus 'two half clear benefits' a year, plus an eighth of the annual profit. Women's position was subservient in those days. In addition to Honner's own services as stage manager he was 'to grant and give... the services of his Wife as an Actress at the said Theatre it being thereby understood that the Wife of the said Robert Honnor *[sic]* shall divide (if necessary) what is termed first Business with any Lady that now or hereafter may be in the employ of the said Frances Davidge and that she shall in all respects conform herself to the Rules and Regulations of the Theatre as observed by the other Ladies of the Company' – and for no extra salary! Although stage manager, Honner had no power to 'hire and fire', but he could write free admission tickets. My personal method of interpreting old prices and wages is to think of them in terms of gold sovereigns and ask what it would cost me today to buy that number of sovereigns. At the time of writing, that puts their joint salary at about £600 a week, plus share of profits, so Mrs Frances Davidge was quite generous in her dealings. There is other evidence of her generosity, or at least her conformity with theatrical custom, as illustrated by a report in *The Times* of 28 July 1843. This followed the death of Elton (a well-established actor who occasionally came to the Surrey) in the wreck of the *Pegasus:*

> The company of the Surrey Theatre had a general meeting on the stage yesterday morning, when Mrs Davidge most liberally offered the free use of the theatre, and one and all connected with the establishment, including the opera company, resolved to give their gratuitous services for the benefit of the orphan children of the lamented Mr Elton. The Benefit will take place on Thursday next, the 3rd. of August, when the strongest attraction will be put forth.

As for the wreck of the *Pegasus,* this was a steamer on a regular run from Leith to Hull which struck a reef near Fern Island about one o'clock in the morning of 20 July 1843. Although probably not remembered by name, Fern (or Farne) Island is imbedded in the national subconsciousness, or at least in that of anyone who remembers the pictures of Grace Darling pulling on an oar with her father, heading for the wreck of the *Forfarshire* on the same reef a few years earlier.

Perhaps as a try-out Mrs Davidge let Honner produce an 'entirely new fairy opera, *Little Red Riding Hood* by Mrs G. à Beckett' (Miss Glossop, that was). *The Times* (of 9 August 1842) was not impressed:

> A dramatic piece much like this in plot and incident was brought out on the French stage and called *Le Chaperon Rouge.* The present drama has however some difference from the French one and is at least sufficiently original to be the vehicle of music. The music is of the Donizetti school; it is light, agreeable, not very difficult, and not very new.

However, the audience liked it:

> It was received by a very crowded house with unanimous approbation and given out for continued repetition amidst the plaudits of all the auditors. Great credit is due to Mr G. Stansbury, the conductor who kept the whole in order and compressed into concert the occasional vagaries of those over whom he presided.

It was on the playbills for *Little Red Riding Hood* on the day before this review, that is on Monday 8 August 1842, that the Surrey announced itself as the 'Only Operatic Theatre in the Metropolis' – a claim which was slightly cheeky and definitely premature. At the beginning of July there were three theatres in London producing opera. Covent Garden ended its season with *Les Huguenots* and *Robert the Devil* on 1 and 2 July. Her Majesty's, where M. Perrot was running a subscription series which included *Don Giovanni, Anna Bolena, Il Matrimonio Segreto, I Puritani* and *Lucia di Lammermoor,* finished with *Roberto Devereux* on 29 July when Michael Costa took the theatre for a week to put on *L'Elisir d'Amore* and *Cosi fan Tutte.* Only after that was the Surrey apparently left as the 'Only Operatic Theatre in the Metropolis' with its English versions of *La Sonnambula, Fra Diavolo* and *L'Elisir d'Amore* (under the title of *The Love Spell),* together with *Guy Mannering* and *The Quaker* as a reminder that 'opera' was once written in English. Unfortunately for the Surrey's proud boast, Her Majesty's was used in the following week for Rossini's *Otello* as a benefit night for Signor Rubini and there were two 'Extra Nights' in the week after that, finishing on Saturday 20 August with a mixed bag of operatic extracts which one can include in or exclude from the calculations as taste decides. Nevertheless, from 22 August for two weeks the Surrey really was the 'Only Operatic Theatre in the Metropolis'.

In trying to substantiate this claim it would be easy to overlook the enterprise of Tom Rouse at the Grecian Saloon in City Road, a tavern which provided music and ballet as well as the more usual forms of refreshment. Like the Surrey, the Grecian put on opera in English. In the time that Herbert Campbell was managing the Grecian for Rouse it was only on one night a week and not necessarily every week at that. I can trace only one performance of opera in the summer of 1842 – on Friday 22 July, when yet another *L'Elisir d'Amore* was put on with the lead parts of Adina and Nemorino sung by Miss Forde and Frazer, both of whom had learnt their art at Drury Lane. So the Surrey boast still stands. The Surrey opera season finished on 3 September 1842, the day that Covent Garden reopened with *Norma.* Apart from the suspension of disbelief that the Surrey was holding its own against Covent Garden and the rest of the West End, it is difficult to appreciate how much opera was available to the public at that time. These days, opera in high summer means Glyndebourne, not London. Was there ever an occasion in any season when London had as much opera to offer as in that summer of 1842?

The impression is given that over the period from the summer of 1842 to that of 1845 during which Honner was employed as manager, the opera content, overseen by Mrs Davidge, went from strength to strength, while the dramatic element under Honner stagnated. The old favourites were still produced but there seems to be no imagination at work, no reaching out for new experiences. From 3 September 1842 when the Surrey opera season finished, and until Christmas, the playbills look as if they come out of the previous decade. *Black-Eyed Susan* and *My Poll and My Partner Joe,* with T.P. Cooke and Mrs Honner, and *Wealth and Want,* with Neville in Davidge's old part, make up the bulk of the programme. Even the new items have an old-fashioned look to them. *Temptation; or, The Progress of Crime* was one; others *Black Law of Martinique; or, Zamba, the Runaway Slave* and *Richard Savage; or, The Disowned.*

It may have been Honner's bad luck that the Surrey's star writer, J.T. Haines, was drifting away in more senses than one. He wrote more for the Victoria towards the end of his life and died at Stockwell on 18 May 1843. The Surrey put on a benefit for his widow on 4 October 1843. Honner apparently thought this a good enough reason to put on *Wizard of the Wave* the following week, a piece Haines had written for Levy and premiered at the Victoria on 2 September 1840. I should not have thought that Levy's rights evaporated with Haines's death. As the Surrey repeated the play on other occasions let us put aside thoughts of piracy and assume that the Surrey paid for the privilege. Honner does not immediately seem to have found anyone to replace Haines. He fell back on the old favourites for the rest of his programme.

Mrs Davidge must have decided to spend some of her inherited capital on refurbishing the theatre, which closed for two months in early 1843. The playbills in April announced the re-opening of 'the most Superb Theatre in Europe' with an informative description that is worth quoting in full:

> The Extensive New and Magnificent Decorations of this Theatre have called forth the warmest encomiums of approbation and delight from all who have hitherto viewed them, and are unanimously pronounced by the Press and Public generally to be the very NE PLUS ULTRA of Taste and Elegance combined. In addition to which the comfort and convenience of the Audience have been studied in every Particular. Neither pains, trouble nor expense have been spared to render it not only the most costly but at the same time the most COMMODIOUS Establishment in the Metropolis. During the temporary Vacation every exertion has been used to effect a perfect Transformation in the Appearance of the Theatre. The CEILING Elaborately Decorated and forming a beautiful Dome in the LOUIS QUATORZE Style designed by Mr Brunning and executed by himself, Mr Cuthbert, Mr Turner, Mr Roberts and Mr Hawthorne; the PROSCENIUM supported by four handsome Columns, richly invested with Magnificent Gold Scroll Ornaments, surmounted by a Massive Carved Royal Coat of Arms, and the whole of the Superb Burnished Gold Devices that adorn the Fronts of the Boxes in the Area of the Theatre, designed and executed by Mr T. Eallett. The chaste and beautiful Crimson Flock and Gold Paper, furnished by Mr G. Ten of the Lowther Arcade and Clayton Place, Kennington. The Paddings of the Boxes lined and covered with expensive Crimson Tabaret. The Private Boxes fitted up in the most exquisite manner and hung with rich Geranium and White Damask Curtains by Mr Loader, Upholsterer, Finsbury Pavement, assisted by Mr Banham. The whole lit by an elegant and unique set of ORMOLU CHANDELIERS with ground glass vases, bearing bouquets of the most choice flowers and a Grand Central Lustre manufactured by Mr Hinkley of Great Duke Street, Westminster Road. A new Green Curtain has also been added, and to support the general Unity, an entirely NEW ACT DROP representing the Port of Ancona, on the Adriatic and Ruins of an Ancient Temple. Designed and Painted by Mr Brunning.

Brunning and Eallett were the heads of the scenery and property departments respectively. Any discount the theatre may have received for the 'commercials' it gave to its outside suppliers is not recorded, though Mr Hinckley later obtains a salaried post at the theatre in charge of the 'Gas Department'.

In 1843 for the first time the Surrey acquired its own corps de ballet, as distinct from companies hired for the occasion. On 20 February W.H. Harvey produced *Soldier's Dream,* danced by himself, Mrs Sharpe and Miss M.R. Fairbrother. As it included a Quadrille of Sixteen and finished with a Galope Finale by the 'whole Corps de Ballet', the Surrey could clearly now mount ballet as well as opera from its own resources. After the refurbishment, a 'Ballet Divertisement, *Une Nuit de Bal* composed by W.H. Harvey' was danced by him on 24 April, again with Mrs Sharpe and Miss Fairbrother as principals, together with three other named dancers and ten others in the corps de ballet. In the same way that opera started at the Surrey, as pasticcio, so did *Une Nuit de Bal* include chunks of the work of other composers. This may possibly have been to acclimatise Surrey audiences to the new genre by giving them familiar tunes here and there. They had already met Harvey and Miss M.R. Fairbrother a few months earlier at the Christmas pantomime – as Harlequin and Columbine – so management seems to have put a bit of thought into the introduction of pure dance to its customers.

The Times seems not to have thought much of Honner's early offerings at the Surrey, for none of his productions earned a review in nearly a year. When the opera company came back in July 1843, however, the *Times* critic wrote that the company 'seem to have taken a firm hold of the Surrey people and opera after opera is produced with wonderful steadiness'. Again under the direction of Miss Romer and George Stansbury, the season was not quite as grand as in the previous year but they still managed to mount their English versions of *La Sonnambula, Cenerentola* and *Fra Diavolo,* with *Lord of the Isles* as a representative of English opera.

As mentioned, Honner had the right to give out free tickets to his friends, and it is possible that he overdid this on one occasion. *The Times* of 18 September 1843 recorded:

> Serious disturbance at the Surrey Theatre. This generally well-conducted establishment was the scene of a most alarming disturbance on Thursday evening. It appears that the entertainments were for the benefit of Mr George Stansbury, musical director, and [as] several performers from the Princess's Theatre were advertised to appear, the 'bill of fare' was unusually attractive. The house was densely crowded immediately after the doors opened, and as numbers

> of persons kept pouring in, a scene of confusion ensued even before the rising of the curtain. The shrieks of the women in the pit and gallery were terrific, and several were carried out in an insensible state, with their clothes torn off their backs. The overture to *Fra Diavolo* was performed during the greatest tumult, and the rising of the curtain was the signal for an universal yell which continued until Mr Honner, the stage manager, came forward, and then cries of 'Return our money, we are being crushed to death', rose from every part of the theatre. Mr Honner stated that those who were uncomfortable might retire, and take a check for another evening. This arrangement, however satisfied no one, and an evident impression existed among a large number of the audience that more tickets had been sold than the theatre would hold.

Stansbury himself now came forward but still the demands were for money to be repaid rather than tokens for another night. At length,

> the malcontents became exasperated and threatened the check-takers with violence. Upon this, the money-takers made a precipitous retreat, and at the earnest solicitations of his friends Mr Stansbury made his appearance in the front of the house, and returned the entrance-money to all who thought proper to retire. This relieved the house of about 400 persons and the performance proceeded without further interruption, and concluded about 2 o'clock.

It may be argued that the overcrowding had nothing to do with Honner writing too many free tickets, as it was the custom to insert on the playbills for benefit nights words such as 'No Orders can possibly be admitted. The Free list suspended (the public press excepted)'. However, it is a fact that such words did not appear on the bills for Stansbury's benefit.

On 5 February 1844, a few weeks after it had appeared in print, with *A Christmas Carol* the Surrey put on another adaptation of one of Dickens's works. Edward Stirling, who provided the stage play, records that

> Dickens attended several rehearsals, furnishing valuable suggestions. Thinking to make Tiny Tim (a pretty child) more effective, I ordered a set of irons and bandages for his supposed weak leg. When Dickens saw this tried on the child, he took me aside; 'No, Stirling, no; this won't do! remember how painful it would be to many of the audience having crippled children'.

According to the playbills, the 'pretty child' was a Master Brady.

Stirling was one of the new team of writers recruited to fill the vacancy left by Haines. Another was Fitzball, who had earlier given Osbaldiston (when at the Surrey) the advantage over Davidge, then at the Coburg. With this sort of rivalry for the best playwrights and actors, it was not surprising that there was another public disputation between the Surrey and the Victoria in August 1844.

There was no indication of the forthcoming row on 24 June when the Surrey put on 'First Time in England, a new Drama, *The Carpenter of Rouen* with J. Hudson Kirby in the part of Marteau. As performed by him in New York, upwards of One hundred & Fifty Nights'. He was the son of John Kirby, clown at the Surrey thirty years earlier who had gone to America and died there. His son may well have thought he was 'coming home' when he took this engagement. He also took the name part in Richard III, about which *The Times* had this to say:

> Mr.Hudson Kirby, the American tragedian, took his benefit at this theatre last evening, and appeared in the character of Richard III. The principal merit of this gentleman is, that he is an original actor, and neither copies the celebrated favourites of past days nor the successful players of the present time. He was in some parts of the play extremely effective, and throughout what is technically called his 'reading' of the character was correct. If he were ineffective in any place, it was towards the conclusion of the play. He was rewarded with the applause of the house.... [The evening] concluded with a species of melodrama, *The Carpenter of Rouen,* which, allowing for the poetic or unpoetic license with which such productions abound, was full of excitement and well adapted to create terror if not horror, by the incidents and circumstances. Mr H. Kirby sustained the chief part, and made the piece effective.

Despite the not very enthusiastic review, Kirby's engagement filled the three weeks before the start of the opera season on 15 July. The Surrey's playbills then announced:

> J. Hudson Kirby, The American Tragedian. A further engagement has been entered into with this Gentleman, whose Appearance in London has created so Great a Sensation, and at the Termination of the Opera Season, he will RE-APPEAR, by which time he will have completed his Provincial Engagement.

The playbills for 5 August 1844 stated that 'Mr J. Hudson Kirby... will re-appear on Monday, Aug. 26 in a NEW CHARACTER' – but he did not. Something had gone wrong, as (according to one report) Kirby denied he had an engagement with Mrs Davidge. The matter was to have gone to the courts on 26 August. The villain in the matter seems to have been Osbaldiston at the Victoria whose playbills of 22 August recounted recent events, finishing with relish thus: 'Once more, and to conclude, Mr J.H. Kirby, three weeks ago, entered into a written engagement with Mr Osbaldiston, and will appear at the VICTORIA THEATRE ONLY'. He rubbed the message in on his bills for 26 August, when he re-opened after a short break: 'On Monday Next, Sept. 2, *Hamlet;* Mr J. Hudson Kirby who is engaged and can perform only at this theatre'. As it happened, *Hamlet* had to be postponed for a few days, and 'The Young American Tragedian' played Sir Giles Overreach in *A New Way to Pay Old Debts* instead. Kirby was then billed to play Othello on 19, 20, and 21 September. (To show how little colour mattered in those days, Ira Aldridge was to play the Duke of Venice.)

Again something went wrong. The tale unfolds in successive reviews and fliers. *The Times* of 21 September (copying from *The Globe)* reported:

> Scene in a Theatre. On Thursday evening, during the performance of the play of *Othello* at the Victoria Theatre, the audience were much excited by an announcement from the management. Towards the close of the play, and just before the last act was to be represented, Mr Osbaldiston came forward and addressed the audience as follows: 'Ladies and gentlemen, I am placed in a most painful position. I know not what to say. (Sensation) Mr Kirby, who has been drunk tonight, has insulted the whole company, and without saying a word to me has left the house.' (Cries of 'It's a lie, Mr Kirby is not drunk'.) Mr Osbaldiston proceeded – 'If it's your wish, I will send after him, and try to get him on'. (Great confusion.) Several gentlemen in the pit here rose and essayed to speak. One gentleman, after the confusion had subsided said 'Ladies and gentlemen, it is untrue to say that Mr Kirby is drunk; I have just seen him, and he is as sober as any person in the house this moment. The fact is, Mr Osbaldiston has grossly insulted Mr Kirby by telling Miss Vincent, in the presence of the whole company, not to speak the speeches, but to come to cues, and not be humbugged by the damned Yankey. (Great sensation) Mr Kirby has just attempted to enter the theatre and explain to you the nature of the great insult offered him, but Mr Osbaldiston has ordered the door-keepers not to admit him'. Great confusion followed this gentleman's remarks, and a noise at the box entrance added not a little to the uproar, and upon enquiry it was found that Mr Osbaldiston and Mr

> Kirby were at the door, the latter gentleman having paid for a box ticket, and the former refusing him admittance. The house thinned after the above affair, and the other pieces went off very tamely.

Osbaldiston's response to this bad publicity, demonstrating that there are always three sides to a dispute, was to add a note from Desdemona's viewpoint to the Victoria playbills for 23 September:

> MISS VINCENT'S STATEMENT OF MR. KIRBY'S CONDUCT Throughout the play of OTHELLO, on Thursday Night last, and on his leaving the Theatre without finishing his Character; the greatest insult ever offered to a British Audience. As Mr KIRBY, in his grossly false statements has thought proper to assert that he was insulted before me during his performance of Othello, I here declare, in justice to myself as well as to Mr OSBALDISTON, that such assertion is utterly false. Mr KIRBY received not insults from any one, but met with the greatest kindness from all the Ladies and Gentlemen connected with him in his most imperfect representation of Othello. From the commencement of the Play, I endeavoured to hide his deficiencies in the text; and by speaking many portions of his speeches with my own, contrived to keep together, as much as possible, the subject of the Author, not only for his sake, but on account of the vast trouble and expense that had been gone to by the Management in the 'getting up' of the Tragedy; but in the 3rd & 4th Acts I found myself placed in such unpleasant dilemmas, that I could no longer suppress my feelings at the annoyances I was subjected to, which, Mr OSBALDISTON perceiving, desired I would bring the Play to as speedily a conclusion as I could.... It is my opinion, that Mr Kirby, finding himself so unequal to the task, did not intend to finish the Part, as he frequently said to me during the night, 'What shall I do? I do not know one line of the 5th. Act', and this, too, after stating a week ago, that Othello was his favourite part, and he hoped, in playing it, to retrieve his many faults in Hamlet. I am sorry he has had recourse to such base untruths to screen his unparalleled conduct; and I am still more sorry that some of our Public Journals have given such an erroneous statement of the case, so insulting to the Management – so insulting to the Ladies & Gentlemen of the Theatre – so insulting to the Public – and so insulting to myself –
>
> Sept. 21, 1844. ELIZA VINCENT

So the charge moves from drunkenness to incompetence, though this is a two-edged weapon. What was Osbaldiston doing hiring an actor who did not know the part? In view of the earlier gossip that Miss Vincent was having Osbaldiston's baby, perhaps we might think that she was not necessarily the author of the words attributed to her. Certainly Kirby thought not.

Round four. Kirby had a notice as big as a playbill printed and presumably fly-posted all over Southwark and Lambeth:

> Mr HUDSON KIRBY's REPLY TO 'MISS VINCENT'S STATEMENT'; TO THE BRITISH PUBLIC – It was my intention not to have intruded further upon public notice with regards to Mr OSBALDISTON's CONDUCT towards me; but the statement made by the Management, in the playbills of the VICTORIA THEATRE, through a third party, who, out of gallantry, it could have been wished that Mr OSBALDISTON had spared, so far as not to make her the Champion and Leader in his cause, renders it incumbent upon me to reply to the foolish assertions therein contained, though I consider myself still engaged at this Theatre.
>
> The Management states that I was not insulted during the performance of OTHELLO on Thursday evening last. I will define what I deem those insults to be. In the first place, then, I conceive that to be an insult which the Management acknowledges was uttered... viz. that Miss Vincent was desired to bring the Play to as speedy a conclusion as she could. What! was I to insult the Auditors by appearing before them with a Lady, instructed by the Manager himself, to disgust the public with the performance by uttering only a word here and there? certainly not! I calmly deliberated. I sent to Mr OSBALDISTON to know if he purposed to insult the audience thus, and his reply was that he desired no words with me....
>
> If he desired to have me fail in my performance, he should have adopted some better-devised plan of operation. When a kind and generous audience had been receiving me through four Acts with a degree of approbation, of which I am proud, how durst he come forward with a 'grossly false' and unjustifiable statement, and with a careful concealment of the true course of my absence? I... will allude to the statement, that I was so imperfect during the Third and Fourth Acts that my speeches were delivered by Desdemona! Preposterous! Desdemona has little dialogue in these Acts with Othello, and it is my humble opinion that there is not... one Desdemona who could speak Othello's words and her own....
>
> Monday Morning, September 23, 1844. J. HUDSON KIRBY

What a pity that Osbaldistone did not let the unfinished performance continue. The sight of Desdemona strangling herself would have been a novelty worthy of the Victoria at its most egregious. In *Othello* at the Surrey a less contentious performance was provided by Madame Vestris and her husband Charles Mathews.

Perhaps not surprisingly, we shortly find Kirby appearing at the Surrey: *The Carpenter of Rouen* was revived on 4 November. He was one of a long line of American actors – quite apart from the minstrels – who found a place on the Surrey stage. Of other Americans, I have already mentioned Ira Aldridge. On 29 April 1844 the Surrey staged *Octavia Bragaldi,* 'written and played by Charlotte BARNES and acted by her upwards of Sixty Nights at the principal Theatres throughout the United States'. In April 1845 'Mr Marble, the Celebrated American Comedian' appeared in *Game Cock of the Wilderness* and *Vermont Wool Dealer,* and on 16 June of that year it was announced that 'Mr Henry Smith, from America, will appear, and sing the popular songs of "The Ship on Fire" and "The Maniac" while accompanying himself on the grand piano-forte'.

Another of the new authors joining the Surrey was John Fred. Smith, BA, who on his contracts described himself as 'Member of the D.A.S'. (the Dramatic Authors' Society). His first contract is dated 21 September 1844 for a drama entitled *The Protector.* This actually opened on 16 September, so perhaps Mrs Davidge wanted to see what her audiences thought of the new man before she laid out her money. (This was not the first time she played safe; *Union Jack,* with T.P. Cooke, was staged on 7 November 1842, but not bought until 3 December.) They must have liked it as she took Smith's next play as well.

Yet another piece obtained from the Théâtre Porte St Martin of Paris was *Don Caesar de Bazan,* staged on 20 October 1844. As a play it has not earned a place in the dramatic repertoire, but from it Fitzball constructed a libretto for Vincent Wallace and it still lives as the opera *Maritana.*

The connection with the Théâtre Porte St Martin is worth noting. For some thirty-odd years many a Surrey play was a translation of something which first appeared there in Paris. Writing of T.P. Cooke, Erroll Sherson mentions his role of the Vampire seen at the Surrey in July 1834, 'which he also acted in French at the Porte St Martin'. A Surrey playbill for 21 November 1842 'for this and every evening during the present week' advertises *The Monster! or, The Fate of Frankenstein!* 'in which Mr T.P. Cooke created so Great a Sensation in PARIS, when it was repeated upwards of 100 CONSECUTIVE NIGHTS'. It is odd to us, thinking of T.P. Cooke as the archetypal sailor, to realise that the French would see him as a second Dracula. It must be another's task to check the records to see what else he did at the Théâtre Porte St Martin, and whether any other Surrey dramatic horror walked their boards.

On 30 January 1845 *The Times* reviewed a new play brought out at the Surrey,

> *Wolsey; or, The Secret Witness*... with all the appliances of scenery, dresses &c. and... most favourably received. Though no expense has been spared to put this play upon the stage, it has intrinsic merits, in the plot, the language, and the dramatic incidents, which are of themselves sufficient to render it deservedly successful. It is the production of Mr J. Smith. The play is founded on an imaginary episode in the eventful life of the 'great Lord Cardinal'.... The part of Wolsey was played by H. Hughes with good effect, and Mrs Honner as the heroine was entitled to high praise. The whole is one of the best things which has been produced at this theatre for several seasons, and is likely to prove a lasting favourite.

Another conflict between the Surrey and the Victoria is apparent in two reviews in *The Times* of 25 March 1845 appearing on the same page:

> The performances at the Surrey Theatre last night gave indisputable proof that the spirited management of this establishment has employed much care and industry in catering for the public amusement during the Easter holydays. The bill of fare was exceedingly attractive, and the natural consequence was that the house was filled to overflowing. The first piece was a drama founded on the work recently published (written by Mr Cobbold) bearing the title *Margaret Catchpole, the Heroine of Suffolk; or, The Vicissitudes of a Real Life*. The piece was dramatised expressly for this theatre by Mr E. Stirling.

Then follows a long narration of 'the facts upon which this exceedingly interesting and attractive drama is founded': a young woman who steals a horse is convicted and transported to Australia, receives a free pardon and marries a wealthy settler. The report continues: 'The character of Margaret Catchpole was admirably sustained by Mrs Honner, who received, as she deserved, the repeated applause of her audience'.

And what was going on up the road at the Victoria? –

> It would be a difficult, and somewhat painful task, to enter upon a detailed criticism of 'the highly powerful and romantic' scenes of the new piece brought out here last night. It is sufficient, perhaps, to say, that it seemed to please those

> whom it was intended to please. The new drama is named *Margaret Catchpole! The Female Horse Stealer; or, The Life and Adventures of a Suffolk Girl....*

Then follows a long narration of a young woman who – etc. There is a new twist:

> There she appears as a convict servant to the proprietress of Dunmow-farm at a period when the Red Indians of the Wolf tribe are making a descent upon it to destroy it and murder the residents. Its incidents are made up of 'guns and drums and wounds', desperate conflicts brought about nobody knows how, and nobody cares to enquire, so long as it is a fight, for that seems to be 'the delicate touch' which is calculated to win the audience. Then we have red Indians in Australia, where red Indians never trod, in panthers' skins (no matter how or where obtained) and otherwise decked out, after the approved fashion of the North American Indians... with feathers and other gaudy habiliments. To be sure geographical knowledge is not very important in these matters, and we don't see why (in the play) we should not have Choctaws in Australia. To complete 'the highly powerful and romantic interest', we have the rest of the Indian tribe – the Black Wolf tribe (for it is only the chieftains that were ornamented with ruddle and tall feathers) – dressed as Roman citizens, as they last appeared in *Coriolanus,* only each had got a tiara of gold, or something like it, on his head. We suspect these must represent the inhabitants of that part of Australia Felix beyond the River Darling which has not yet been explored. However there was plenty of fighting, with numerous energetic scenes, prompted by hidden motives, of young officers seizing quaint and scampish vendors of needles and pins by the throat, giving rise to such impromptus as -
>
> Ven you collars,
> I hollers.

There must have been much chortling at the Surrey that morning. Yet the Surrey's Margaret, merely saving the wealthy settler from drowning in a flash flood, did not do half so much to win a free pardon as the Victoria's heroine of battles and siege.

The 1844 opera season was the last under the baton of George Stansbury, who received his benefit on 13 December 'previous to his retirement from his present appointment'. Miss Emma Romer also disappears from the Surrey bills at this time, not coming back for several years. Instead a new team was assembled under the direction of E.J.

Loder, an established composer of English opera. He obtained the services of Madame Eugenia Garcia as prima donna, so the Surrey was now on the international circuit. The supporting singers were in the main borrowed from Alfred Bunn at Drury Lane – Donald King, Miss Collett and Messrs. Weiss and Barker. The programme was, however, much as before, plus a revival of the Surrey's English version of *Lucia di Lammermoor*.

Robert Honner's management came to an end on 20 September 1845 after a three-week spell of guest appearances. These included Madame Vestris and Charles Mathews, who currently had no theatre of their own; two of the Drury Lane singers, Miss Collett and Donald King (who also played the Beast to Madame Vestris's Beauty in a little extravaganza); Mrs Fitzwilliam; and T.P. Cooke, who, with Mr and Mrs Honner, once again starred in *My Poll and My Partner Joe*.

DAVIDGE'S ROYAL SURREY THEATRE

Under the Management of Mrs. [illegible] DAVIDGE, Sole Lessee, [illegible] Surrey.

☞ ENORMOUS SUCCESS.

And great Sensation created by the Performances of the Eminent Tragedian,

Mr. MACREADY

☞ NO ALTERATION IN THE PRICES.

On Mr. MACREADY's Nights of Performing, not an Order will be admitted, & the Free List suspended, the Public Press excepted.

Monday, Wednesday, Thursday and Friday,

September 28th & 30th, October 1st and 2nd, 1846,

Will be presented Shakspeare's Tragedy of

MACBETH.

Duncan, — Mr HESLOP
Malcolm, Mr J. T. JOHNSON Donalbain, Miss BRADY
Macbeth, Mr MACREADY,
Macduff, — Mr COOPER
Banquo, Mr LEIGH MURRAY Lenox, Mr TYNDALL
Rosse, Mr T. FREDERICKS Fleance, Miss RUSSELL
Siward, Mr CLEMENTS Seyton, Mr PELHAM
Physician, Mr LEWIS Bleeding Captain, Mr HAWKINS
Murderers, Messrs CONWAY and COOKE,
Hecate, Mr NEVILLE First Officer, Mr POTTER
First Witch, Mr E. F. SAVILLE,
Second Witch, Mr H. WEBB Third Witch, Mrs W. DALY
Lady Macbeth, — Mrs TERNAN,
Gentlewoman, Mrs LEWIS,

SINGING WITCHES:

Mesdames KERSCHNER, E. TERREY, JACKSON, E. JACKSON, MAYNARD, VAUGHAN, WILSON, HAWKINS, M. TERREY, JONES, BRIGHT, DONALDSON, TETT.
Messrs MORGAN, CLEMENTS, JONES, DOBSON, BARNARD, DREW, DREWELL, THOMPSON, EDWARDS. GOUGH, JEFFS, E. JEFFS, J. TOLKEIN, &c.

On Tuesday, Sept. 29th, and Saturday, Oct. 3rd,

Will be presented a Play of great interest, in Four Acts, entitled The

VICTIM of ST. VINCENT

Baron St. Val, - Mr. COOPER.
Count de Clarville, Mr NEVILLE, Mayor of the Village, Mr TYNDALL
Curate, Mr CONWAY, Jerome, Mr HESLOP, Thomas, Mr POTTER
Christopher, (an Humor in the Service of St. Val) Mr J. T. JOHNSON,
Loupy, (a Beggar) Mr HENRY WEBB, Chambord, Mr LEWIS,
Brigadier, Mr PHELPS, Perrigotte, Mr CLEMENTS,
Roquet, Mr PELHAM, Notary, Mr HAWKINS, Germain, Mr COOKE,
Felix, - Mrs. CHARLES GILL,
Madame Thomas, Mrs W. DALY, Josephine, Miss E. TERREY,
Amelia - Mrs. TERNAN,
Borale, - Mrs MAYNARD, Perrietta, - Miss BRADY.

To conclude with on Monday, Tuesday, and Wednesday, the Drama of The

LAW OF THE LAND.

Sir Peregrine Platitude, Mr NEVILLE, Primmer, Mr TYNDALL,
Abel Dodsworth - Mr. COOPER.
Robson, Mr T. FREDERICKS, Nym Nabs, Mr J. T. JOHNSON,
Sam Scrag, Mr LEWIS, Snail, Mr H. WEBB, Fielding, Mr PELHAM,
Charlton, Mr POTTER, Aaron Woolf, Mr HAWKINS, Sharpe, Mr JONES,
Officer, Mr PHELPS, Gambler, Mr CLEMENTS,
Lucy Primmer - Mrs CHARLES GILL.
Amelia Platitude, Mrs E. F. SAVILLE, Queen Charlotte, Mrs W. DALY,
Flounce, — Miss E. TERREY, with a Duet and a Song,
Hebe Hobbs, Miss VAUGHAN, Olivia, Mrs. MAYNARD.

To conclude with on Thursday, Friday, and Saturday, the interesting Melo-Drama of

Jonathan Bradford:

Or, THE MURDER at THE ROAD-SIDE INN.

Jonathan Bradford, — Mr. E. F. SAVILLE,
Dan Macraisy, - Mr. NEVILLE, Farmer Nelson, - Mr. HESLOP,
Mr. Hayes, Mr. TYNDALL, Caleb Scrimmage, Mr. H. WEBB,
Jack Rackbottle, Mr. LEWIS, Lawyer Dosey, Mr. PELHAM,
Surveyor Rodpole, Mr. HAWKINS, Serjeant Sam, Mr. POTTER,
Corporal, Mr. PHELPS, Jailer, Mr. CLEMENTS,
Ann Bradford, Mrs. E. F. SAVILLE, Sally Sighabout, Miss E. TERREY,
Ann and Jane, (Bradford's Children) Misses MAYNARD and HAWKINS.

Stage Manager, .. Mr E. STIRLING
Acting Manager, Mr F. KERSCHNER. Treasurer, Mr J. T. HYDE

BOXES 2s. PIT 1s. GALLERY 6d. Doors open at 6, to commence at half-past 6.
All Applications for Seats and Private Boxes to be made at the Box-Office from 11 till 4.
☞ The Performances will be so arranged as to terminate as near as possible to half-past Eleven o'Clock.

[illegible] [S. G. Fairbrother, Printer, [illegible], Bow Street, Covent Garden

Chapter Twenty-Two

After Honner (1845-47)

From October 1845, when Honner's contract ceased, Mrs Frances Davidge seems to have operated successfully by arranging (usually for a year at a time) for people experienced in one aspect of the theatre to work at some quite different task. That done, she seems not to have intervened in the running of the theatre (though she continued to sign contracts which were usually witnessed by her Treasurer, B.S. Fairbrother, or by her brother-in-law, Joseph Kerschner). As examples, Kerschner was originally the box-office keeper but he became acting manager in 1846, writer of additional comic scenes for the pantomime of Christmas 1846 and full manager in 1847; the treasurer B.S. Fairbrother was the principal writer of the 1846 pantomime, while both he and Kerschner had in turn been licensees of the Equestrian Tavern, where much of the Surrey's business was transacted. One of Mrs Davidge's regular actors, Henry Hughes, has a spell in 1846 as acting manager, while the equestrian and actor Richard Shepherd gets a taste of the action as stage manager before he succeeds Mrs Davidge as lessee in 1848. Just as the writer J.T. Haines had a spell as stage manager for her husband, so did three of Mrs Davidge's writers get similar active experience. T.H. Webb, who adapted Shakespeare with *Seven Ages of Man* (December 1844) and Scott's *Fair Maid of Perth* for production in May 1845, becomes the Inventor and Director of Pantomime by September, while Edward Stirling, prolific playwright, is stage manager for most of the two seasons 1845 to 1847. Fox Cooper, whose *Old Fleete Prison* was produced in May 1845, is speaking from the stage and writing to the papers on behalf of the management at the end of 1846. This policy seems to have worked very well. There is a freshness that was lacking during Honner's spell of command.

The renewed attraction of the Surrey can be gauged by the report in *The Satirist* of 4 January 1846:

> If the lessee of this transpontine house could manage during the Christmas festivities to double the size of it, we are convinced she could find more than enough Surreyites to fill it, while at the same time it would be conferring a benefit on those who are not composed of such squeezable stuff as is,

> apparently, required for a visit to that theatre at this season. During the last week the house has been overflowing, and a tide of success seems to have set in....

In fact the Surrey pantomime of Christmas 1845, *Harlequin and the Old Witch of Teddington,* managed to go one better than Grimaldi, whose exploits had included building effigies out of vegetables (a mannikin, a wheel-barrow, etc) – the Surrey built a steam-engine! Another surprise was the appearance as Columbine of 'Miss Smythies', the name of the player of Columbine in the pantomime of 1816.

The Satirist of 22 February 1846 made a comment in its review of *The Sea-King's Vow* which one does not associate with the supposed primness of the Victorian era:

> The principal novelty of the piece consists in the appearance of an army of female warriors, numbering upwards of seventy young girls being apparently the picked beauties of the Lambeth peasantry. Miss Mary Glover made a successful debut as the chieftess of an Amazon army. She acted with grace, looked charmingly in the short tunic, displaying a delightful pair of legs.

Whatever next! But it was only as the era advanced that even the garments worn over legs became 'unmentionables'.

Despite the great rivalry between the Surrey and the Victoria, it seems that during Richard Shepherd's turn as stage manager he put out a hand of reconciliation to Osbaldiston when the Victoria had to close temporarily on 17 June 1846. The Surrey playbills for 29 June announced that

> Mr Shepherd has also the greatest satisfaction in announcing that he has entered into agreements, whereby he has been enabled to secure the UNITED SERVICES of Mr OSBALDISTON and Miss VINCENT With a Double Company of the acknowledged Favourites of the Surrey Side [of] the Water – thus forming AN UNAPPROACHABLE PHALANX OF TALENT! Never before equalled at this Establishment, even in its PALMIEST DAYS.

The joint venture ran until the first week in August 1846. The Victoria re-opened on 10 August.

We might think it was 'a hand of reconciliation' but during his short spell at the Surrey Osbaldiston was sharing and competing with Madame Albertazzi, the celebrated prima donna of the Italian Opera, and principal singers from Drury Lane who had commenced their opera season a week ahead of Osbaldiston. We can hardly see him getting the star dressing room. He certainly did not get star billing. The pieces in which Osbaldiston and Miss Vincent appeared do not sound particularly noteworthy. *Black Domino, Isabel Bertrand, The Stranger* and *Lucy Lisle* seem to have sunk without notice by the critics. Only *Susan Hopley* received any attention, perhaps because it contained, as Sherson reports, 'a scene in which the mouldering remains of a corpse fell out of a cupboard'; or perhaps because it was adapted by Dibdin Pitt, who wrote the 'Red Indians in Australia' version of *Margaret Catchpole* which caused such red faces at the Victoria; or because of the lively verse:

Memory of Susan Hopley!
Party treated most improp'ly;
Then the Vic enjoyed monop'ly –
Of such works, it had the pick.

The Satirist saw not a hand of reconciliation but a conspiracy. In the issue of 13 September 1846 the critic reported that

> at the commencement of the summer, the fair lessee thought proper to accept an offer to take the management off her hands for six weeks at the least, at a fair remunerating rental. But the manageress soon discovered that she had been trepanned into letting the theatre to a bitter rival, by a ruse that had been practised on her by one of her own company, who had thus surreptitiously introduced the old Victoria company into the citadel previously so well guarded.

As to Osbaldiston's productions, *The Satirist* called them 'melodramatic trash' and said that as regards his 'cheap domestic drama, its days are gone'.

Conspiracy or not, some good-will must have come out of the visit as Shepherd and Eliza Vincent teamed up to take the lease of the Surrey when Frances Davidge retired.

Did Osbaldiston feel slighted in any way, having to take second place to a mere singer? And then possibly ejected unceremoniously, if we are to believe in conspiracies? If he was looking for revenge, an opportunity would offer itself in a few months, As the Italians have it: 'Revenge is a dish best eaten cold'.

Despite her foreign name and her billing as of 'the Italian Opera', Madame Albertazzi was born Emma Howson, in London. She was a contralto and a pupil of Sir Michael Costa. She had indeed sung at La Scala, and in France and Spain. She died the year following her appearances at the Surrey. Fitzball, for one, greatly regretted her passing, remarking on the 'charms of the bewitching Albertazzi'.

I have remarked several times on the introduction of incongruous but popular additions to operas and musical plays. One such was in the production of *The Barber of Seville* in the 1844 opera season, when Miss Betts, as Rosina, sang, so the playbills say, 'Lo! here, the Gentle Lark'. In this instance, there was a perfectly respectable and long-standing tradition for Rosina to insert one or more 'show-off' pieces in the Lesson Scene; indeed, Rossini marked his libretto: 'Rosina sings an air, ad libitum, for the occasion'. However, in this 1846 season Miss Betts also sang 'Lo! here, the Gentle Lark' in a production of Shield's *Rosina.* Confusing to us, perhaps; but to Surrey audiences, in what opera they were to hear the gentle lark was neither here nor there.

According to *The Satirist*, writing of the Surrey on 6 September 1846:

> Mr Macready is announced to appear at this theatre on Monday. Mr Kerschner has undertaken the management during Mr Stirling's absence in the country, but we understand that Mrs Davidge has expressed herself so well satisfied with the 'new manager' that she wishes to retain him in the position he has temporarily filled.

As so she should, for my great-grandfather Kerschner had secured the services of the foremost tragedian of the age.

The Times thought highly of William Macready's season at the Surrey, saying on 9 November:

> On Saturday night this eminent tragedian terminated his engagement at the Surrey Theatre with the tragedy of *Virginius.* During the weeks of his stay on the other side of the water, he went through a regular series of Shakesperian characters, and succeeded in drawing crowded houses to witness them all. On Saturday the house was filled to suffocation, and a seat in the orchestra was a thing not lightly to be rejected. This engagement of Mr Macready will doubtless make a lasting impression among playgoers on the south side of the Thames, and aid in spreading that taste for the legitimate English drama which is now becoming so prominent a feature among the less aristocratic classes. By the care bestowed in getting up the various pieces in which Mr Macready has appeared, Mrs Davidge has done all in her power to increase the favourable impression and to elevate the character of her house....

This 'favourable impression' of the Surrey has been obscured over the years. Compare those contemporaneous reports with modern writing. For example, in a book on Macready by Alan S. Downer, we find:

> After a summer provincial tour, he came back to London to appear at another minor theatre, this time the Surrey. This was a genuine descent into the minors for the Surrey had long been the home of melodrama, of Newgate and nautical pieces, and its audiences were the roughest in London.
>
> Edward Stirling, the manager, had determined to try to duplicate the success of Phelp's Shakespeare revivals at the equally 'illegitimate' Sadler's Wells, and had led off with Macready. Perhaps to everyone's surprise, the Surrey audience took to him at once. On the opening day, they began assembling at two o'clock in the afternoon and on the closing night, the entrance doors were broken down by the rush of spectators.

So, no reference to the annual opera seasons; no reference to the ballet company; no reference to the fact that the Surrey was putting on Shakespeare long before Phelps took Sadler's Wells; no reference to the fact that ten years before Macready played Virginius there, the Surrey audiences had seen it played by Elton, he who was lost in the wreck of the *Pegasus;* no accuracy in having Stirling engage Macready, indeed having him determine anything, seeing that his main function was to write melodramas for the Surrey: it is all part of the misconception which now distorts current views of the theatre at that time.

Macready's season was followed up by more Shakespeare from the Cushman sisters, Charlotte and Susan. They were Americans who had not done too well at home and had come to England in the previous year to try their luck. Charlotte reputedly had a deep contralto voice but lacked feminine beauty and as a consequence chose male rather than female roles. Hence her repertoire included Romeo (with sister Susan as Juliet), Hamlet and Cardinal Wolsey. The *Illustrated London News* reported

> the engagement of the Misses Cushman, who made their appearance on Monday evening, in *Romeo and Juliet,* and performed in *Ion* on Tuesday: on both occasions to very excellent houses. We have more than once noticed the acting of the talented sisters in these plays, when they were at the Haymarket. The effect they produced upon the audiences at the Surrey was not one whit inferior to that they had made upon those in the more legitimate spheres. It has been a great mistake to imagine that the transpontine play-goers would not go to see anything but ultra melo-dramatic performances. They will support everything that is really good, and crowd to patronise it; but it must be first-rate

> whatever its nature. Macready and the Cushmans in tragedy; and Harrison, Miss Romer, and Leffler, in opera, have always drawn good houses here, which other artistes ever so slightly inferior have completely failed in doing.
>
> Miss Cushman and her sister are moderately well supported by the members of the stock Surrey company, one or two of whom, however, might become more perfect in their business with advantage.

This criticism may have been directed at Edward Stirling, who took upon himself the role of Mercutio.

The management's offering immediately after Macready and the Cushman sisters is commented on by Charles Dickens in a letter of 2 December 1846: 'Do you remember a mysterious man in a straw hat low-crowned, and a Petersham coat, who was a sort of manager or amateur man-servant at Miss Kelly's? Mr Baynton Bolt, sir, came out, the other night, as Macbeth, at the Royal Surrey Theatre'. Nearly right! The man's name was Bayntun Rolt. *The Satirist* of 22 November said that

> Mr Bayntun Rolt afforded us one of the richest evening's amusements on Thursday at the Surrey that it has been our lot to witness for some time. Mr Rolt is a tall and not bad stage figure; but his tread of the boards is like the measured stride of a Colossus at a funeral, while he throws his head so considerably backwards as to favour the idea that he was about to throw a summersault... and frequently, when conducting Lady Macbeth off the scene, stepped on the train of her robe, impeding the progress of both. In his encounter with Macduff, he displayed a physical force that led us to fear he was going to 'correct' Shakspere by making Macduff the victim, instead of being killed himself. It was a Surrey fight all over; Macduff had one sword shattered and the battle endured a respectable time. Indeed, Macbeth's dying scene was the best joke of the whole. After a wonderful struggle he fell – then bobbed up his head to see if all was right, and finally died, as hard as hardest Scot could desire. To sum up – Mr Rolt tried to imitate Macready at times – then to be original – and above all, dignified, the consequence was that *Macbeth* was metamorphised into a pantomime extravaganza. The audience seemed to enjoy the fun heartily.

It is just possible that Rolt meant this to be a skit on Macready's acting. He repeated his Macbeth at the Olympic Theatre a few months later when *The Satirist* reported on 7 February 1847 that he gave the

> most palpable imitations of the worst points of Mr Macready (studiously leaving out any of the best). He fights and dies as though he had been a pupil of the 'impetuous Surrey' all his life.

Now for an exercise in disinformation. *The Sun* of 22 December 1846 published a report of an 'Extraordinary Scene' at the Surrey, which was picked up and republished by *The Times* the following day, thus:

> It appears that Monday night was announced to be a 'grand supplemental night' being the only day before the Christmas holydays, for the benefit of one of the principal performers: and, as an additional attraction, numerous additions from most of the principal theatres of London, were to be made for that occasion only. The house at the usual hour being filled some very considerable delay occurred before the rising of the curtain; and at length the stage manager came forward to apologise for the absence of the principal performer of the first piece, a Mr Hudson Kirby, who had promised to attend at the requisite hour.

The audience chose to wait rather than submit to a substitute, says the report, and 'after a lapse of some time' the actor appeared, apologised, and performed the lead in *Damon and Pythias*. After the second and third pieces were given without interruption, 'a delay of nearly an hour occurred':

> At half past 12... the stage-manager again made his appearance (amid numerous cries of 'More apologies'; 'What next?' &c.) and spoke as follows: Ladies and gentlemen, what am I to do? It is now long past the hour of 12 and up to this moment I have not been able to learn the cause of absence of Mr John Douglass, who was to sustain the principal character in the play of *The Sailor's Home.*

He tells the audience that he has just received notice of an accident that befell Douglass that morning in the Marylebone Theatre, when he had a fall of forty feet and 'sustained some most frightful injuries'. Would the audience now wish a substitute actor to play Douglass's part? 'Cries of "Yes, yes", "go on", etc.'. Then –

> a minute had scarcely elapsed before the manager again addressed them in the following terms: Ladies and gentlemen, I have yet further to ask your indulgence. Mr Cowle, who was to have enacted the second principal character is also absent; but with your permission, a gentleman who has never appeared on any stage whatever, previous to this evening, will

> sustain that part, and endeavour to entertain you to the utmost of his power. Again repeating my heartfelt thanks for your kind indulgence, will you accept our best endeavours, or shall we discontinue for today, for it is now morning? A general cry in favour of proceeding with the announced play having been made, it was commenced, and was concluded a little before 2 this morning.

The Sun of 23 December then published the Surrey version in this letter from Fox Cooper, the stage manager:

> I make no comment upon the grossly exaggerated statement which appeared in your paper of last evening relative to the Surrey Theatre, but I feel it my duty to point out the palpable falsehoods which your critic has put forth, and I do this that you may see what reliance you can place upon his veracity in the future.

After setting out the previous day's allegations, the letter goes on:

> Now, Sir, there is not one syllable of truth in this scandalous statement. No apology was made or thought of for… Mr Hudson Kirby, that gentleman was at the theatre to the minute of his promise, and so satisfactorily performed his part throughout as to receive at its termination one of the loudest calls ever heard within the walls of the theatre. Lie upon lie follows in quick succession. Your critic, correspondent or whatever the person may be, evidently was not in the house at all. The stage manager did not go on the stage at half-past twelve o'clock as stated in your paper, for it was only eleven o'clock when I received intelligence of the accident which had befallen Mr Douglass, and I immediately felt it my duty to communicate it in person to the audience….

Fox Cooper denies the charge of going on into the small hours:

> The theatre was cleared a little after twelve o'clock, and the entire performance (with the exception of the change in the parts occasioned by the accident to Mr Douglass) gave every satisfaction to a brilliant and crowded audience. Every lady and gentleman who had promised to perform did so, and it is with peculiar pride and gratitude I embrace this public opportunity of thanking them for their friendly aid. As regards your correspondent, I hand him over to yourself, confident that you will never allow your columns to be prostituted to the purposes of falsehood and malice, for

> whatever may be the merits or demerits of the night in question, I alone am responsible for them.
> 17, Walcot place, Lambeth, Dec 22, 1846. Fox Cooper

The Editor added 'The account alluded to was furnished by an occasional reporter, who has been frequently in the habit of supplying us with information. We will cause enquiry to be instituted as to his authority for the statements made'.

In the next issue of *The Sun,* that for Thursday evening 24 December, another letter was printed, this time from Hudson Kirby:

> Having perceived, in your paper of yesterday, a paragraph headed 'Extraordinary scene' and which is calculated to do me most serious injury, I beg leave most respectfully to state, that in reference to so much of the article as refers to myself, that I was in the Surrey Theatre at a quarter before five, P.M. on the evening named, and was also dressed and prepared to go upon the stage three-quarters of an hour before I was required; and consequently was 'at my post' (as others can testify); giving a flat contradiction to the uncalled-for assertion that I was compelled to make an apology for my absence.

Hudson Kirby declares himself at a loss to know who or what was behind this 'utterly untrue' attack and ends:

> Under these circumstances, I trust to your well-known advocacy of justice and impartiality to insert these few lines, having already suffered so much from misrepresentation and garbled statements that I cannot but feel keenly the injustice of this most alarming falsehood. J. Hudson Kirby

The Editor added: 'We refer Mr Hudson Kirby to our note to Mr Fox Cooper's letter, assuring him that we never will suffer the same person to deceive us again'.

In view of this specific refutation, the question arises as to whom the original false report might be attributed. Do we know of anyone who might have had a grudge against the Surrey Theatre in general, and against J. Hudson Kirby in particular? Need we look further than Osbaldiston?

While quoting from *The Sun* and with the Surrey/Victoria rivalry in mind, I include the following reports of the respective pantomimes in the issue of 28 December 1846. For the Surrey, there is a summary of the plot of Stirling's *Hand of Cards* and of the pantomime up to the Transformation Scene, and then:

> The real fun of the evening then commenced, and no expense has been spared to render the tricks amusing. Most of the situations and tricks were entirely new, and there was little or none of the advertising system which has of late been introduced into pantomime.... It is but justice to observe that a more orderly Boxing night has rarely been witnessed at this theatre, every word of the performances being clearly heard, and nothing disturbing the harmony of the evening except interjectional remarks of doubtful propriety from the pit, with reference to hats in front. The curtain fell amidst loudest applause.

At the Victoria:

> The Christmas merrymakers assembled at this house on boxing-night in overwhelming numbers and long before the curtain rose, the theatre presented a condensed living, though hardly breathing, mass of human beings, abounding in unmistakeable specimens of the facetious low life of London, amongst whom Boz and his imitators so much delight to revel. Every available nook or corner, which afforded a seat or a sight, was eagerly contested, and those who could not secure a full view of the stage, were content to peer through holes and crevices, or strain their necks over the heads and shoulders of their more fortunate neighbours. A French translation called *The Black Doctor* was the first piece on the list, but, it would seem, the audience considered it undeserving of the least attention, and four acts were hurriedly performed in mere dumb show. The elevated portion of the auditory, however, amused themselves during its representation with cracking jokes on each other, and now and then the tedium was relieved by some caustic witticism giving rise to a slight ebullition of pugilistic feeling, which invariably ended with an appeal to a police officer, and a noisy request to 'Pitch him over'....

These contemporary reports speak for themselves.

Here is a little comment from *The Satirist* to show what my great-grandfather had been doing in his spare time beforehand.

> 29 November 1846. A grand attraction is to be provided here for the Christmas pantomime in the fair forms of the most showy corps de ballet, amounting altogether to about forty. On dit that Mr Kerschner, the tasteful treasurer of the theatre, is deputed to conduct the delicate investigation and to select the ladies out of about three hundred applicants! That

> gentleman's experience in such matters has, it is said, led to his appointment, as the most competent party to undertake so onerous, yet pleasing, a duty.

The writer later thought that great-grandfather had done a good job, as on 31 January 1847 he wrote:

> in personal stature, shape and poetry of motion, the coryphées, sylphides and elves will bear comparison, without marked disadvantage, with any house in London.

Edward Stirling put on another of his own plays, but *The Times* of 27 January 1847 gave it a two-edged review: 'A new piece of the thorough-going melodramatic school has been produced with great success, under the title of *Raby Rattler; or, the Scamp's Progress...*'. It contains 'a combat of three, fought with a vigour of which the degenerate race north of the Thames have not a notion. The piece, put on the stage in a liberal style, is a decided success'. I sense the unwritten qualification 'for those who like that sort of thing'. I think it must have been the same critic who wrote for *The Times* of 10 March 1847:

> *Lilly Dawson,* a new novel by the authoress of *Susan Hopley,* has been made the subject of melodrama at this theatre, which with its series of murders and domestic calamities, ending, of course, in the triumph of oppressed innocence, has the kind of interest usually possessed by pieces of the sort, and is relieved by the pleasantries of a pair of comic lovers, whose jokes are of the fashion approved for a long course of years.... The piece has been received with a true Surrey enthusiasm....

And again, on 1 April:

> The Arabs who are to perform on Easter Monday had a rehearsal yesterday. The vigour and agility which they display in their various feats, and the singular and apparently perilous combinations which they form, will doubtless render them highly attractive to all who take interest in exhibitions of this kind.

That is, 'for those who like that sort of thing'.

On 30 May 1847 *The Satirist* reported that:

> Mrs Davidge commenced the operatic season here on Monday last, and the inhabitants of Surrey seemed fully to appreciate the liberality with which the management has engaged 'the first living English artistes' to render the season a delightful one for the lovers of song.

After commenting on the productions, the critic

> noticed that the pit was crowded with a class of person of much higher respectability than ordinarily are attracted by the extremely moderate charge for admission, but we were sorry to see persons of respectability incommoded by vulgar pot-boy beer vendors in blue shirts and braces. Surely they might in propriety adopt a waiter's jacket.

It would appear that the middle-class patron was emerging, and that the Surrey would have to adapt.

The 1847 season, with the old favourites such as *La Sonnambula, L'Elisir d'Amore, Fra Diavolo* and *Barber of Seville,* was enlivened by the world première of Tully's opera, *The Forest Maiden and the Moorish Page.* Tully had been clarinettist in the Surrey orchestra but had risen to be conductor at Drury Lane. *The Times* of 3 June 1847 reported:

> Now that Drury Lane has closed its doors to the public, English opera has been compelled to seek refuge on the other side of the water. It is as well, however, that there is some spot where it can find a home, and that spot no barrener or less hospitable than the Surrey Theatre. A new three act opera has been produced here with complete success, the music of which is from the pen of one of the most deservedly popular of our vocal writers, Mr Tully. The libretto... is the off-spring of Mr Fitzball's seemingly exhaustless fancy.... Mr Tully's music has very considerable merit. He has modestly entitled his work a ballad-opera, but it contains, notwithstanding, some duets, choruses, and morceaux d'ensemble, which are written with a rare amount of musical feeling....

Giving further praise to Tully's music and conducting, the review comments on the effective singing of Harrison and Leffler, of Miss Rainforth ('graceful, unaffected, and pleasing as usual') and Miss Isaacs (who 'has greatly improved' but should learn to treat ordinary dialogue less emphatically). The encores were well deserved. The 'scenery and appointments are highly creditable'. Drawing good houses, the opera 'is likely to benefit the treasury'.

The production of Wallace's *Maritana* was reviewed in *The Times* of 30 June 1847, with this sequel:

> In addition to the operatic attractions, the Surrey management has produced an English version of *Le Chiffonier,* a melodrama, which has gained great vogue at the Porte St Martin, in Paris.... The translation is by Mr Stirling and bears the name

> of *The Ragpicker of Paris.* The piece is one of those amusing rhodomontades for which French drama is famous, or infamous, whichever term fits. Scarcely one of the incidents is probable, not to say possible; the situations are striking, but artificial and unnatural; the sentiment is exaggerated and morbid; the characters are violently contrasted; and the general effect of the whole may be likened to a phantasmagoric delusion, or to the distorted phantoms which delirium paints upon darkness.... The piece is a great hit....

A long run is forecast for *The Ragpicker of Paris,* its 'absurdities' notwithstanding. The actor Webb is described as an admirable 'expositor of the peculiar school of drama which obtains on the other side of the Thames'. There is the patronising note again. Despite the strength of the criticism, I find it interesting that the connection with the Théâtre Porte St Martin is as strong as ever.

Competing with Jenny Lind across the Thames was not something to over-awe the Surrey. At the end of August 1847 an 'Operatic Bagatelle' called *Jenny Lind or the Swedish Nightingale* was staged. The principal character was named Jenny Leatherlungs and played by Mrs Keeley. Unfortunately, I have been unable to find a review of the piece. A word about Mary Anne Keeley may be in place. Born in 1806 (née Goward), starring from the age of 16 and playing Rosina at the Lyceum as early as 1825, she married her fellow-player Robert Keeley in 1829 and sustained a commanding position in the theatre through most of the nineteenth century. Together with luminaries who, unlike her, are still household names today, she was profiled in volume two of *The Strand Magazine* in 1891 (in good company with the first-ever Sherlock Holmes stories), when her face was 'as merry and her eyes as bright as in the days of her youth'. She died in 1899.

When the opera season finished on 10 July 1847 it was Joseph Kerschner's turn to manage. *The Satirist* again, on 25 July:

> Mr J. Kerschner, who for so long a time has ably performed the duties of 'Acting Manager' has now entered on a new and enlarged sphere, in taking upon himself, for a season, the whole hazards and responsibilities of the house. Mr Kerschner sacrifices at the shrine of Shakspeare; and most opportune is the attempt to revive towards England's great dramatist a feeling for enthusiastic admiration.... If there be yet 'any true friend of Caesar' – or rather Shakspeare – let him to the Surrey, and he will be highly gratified.

It would appear that *The Satirist* was becoming a fan of my great-grandfather. On 15 August:

> The manager, Mr Kerschner, by his exertions has lately deserved well of the Surrey population; and if thousands were to cross the bridges to reward him, they would themselves receive their reward in five or six hours of spirit-stirring amusement and delightful merriment.... Novelty and spirit have been the characteristics of the present brief management, and the results promise to be every way satisfactory.

And again, a fortnight later:

> It is frequently said that 'theatricals are at a low ebb' but by the talent of Mr Kerschner in selecting successional performers and, consequently, change of performances, it has been proved here that the tide will turn and flow most prosperously. The successional system has been here carried out. To opera succeeded tragedy – to tragedy lighter drama and farces – wherein those sparkling geniuses, Mr and Mrs Keeley now hold possession of the boards....
>
> Mr Kerschner follows up his successional system by having engaged that general favourite, the nautical sentimentalist, T.P. Cooke.... We find the house crowded – night after night – private boxes not to be had after the performances have commenced; and many West-end admirers of genuine theatricals have had to wend their way homewards disappointed, in default of timely application.

Although there is uncertainty about the date of some of the incidents recorded by Edward Stirling, the following one seems to fit here. He tells a light-hearted story concerning Frances Davidge which he calls 'Surrey Theatre en fête', part of which describes 'a droll circumstance',

> connected with a garden ball which took place in a long space enclosed by walls. This the theatrical employés speedily converted into a ball-room superbly decorated with flowers, painting, chandeliers, and with a roof of canvas stretched on rafters from wall to wall. A numerous company were assembled; the orchestra included Balfe and Vincent Wallace. All were very jolly and festive; everything went happily and joyously as wedding-bells, when suddenly ensued consternation, fright, faintings, and tableau of horror! The roof fell in, with the chandeliers and floral offerings, and a page from next door dropped upon the

> affrighted guests. Buttons had inquisitively climbed on to the roof to peep at their 'goings on', was the cook's explanation.

This is undated but I would suggest September 1847, as both Wallace's *Maritana* and Balfe's *The Bondsman* were in production. It also looks as if the event were held directly behind the theatre, so that 'next door' would be the Equestrian Tavern which would have been capable of providing a cook and a Buttons as well as food for the guests.

ROYAL

SURREY THEATRE

Lessee, Mrs. F. DAVIDGE, No. 1, Davidge Terrace, Kennington Road, Surrey.

MR. BUNN

Has the honor of announcing to the public at large, that, in consequence

OF THE TWO NATIONAL THEATRES,

DRURY LANE AND COVENT GARDEN,

Of which he has for many years, jointly and severally, had the management, having both passed into the hands of Foreigners, he has entered into an arrangement with the Lessee of this Theatre, whereby he has become

ITS SOLE MANAGER,

and with the view of submitting to their approbation every variety of attraction, especially all the popular productions of his recent management, he begs leave to submit the names of many of the eminent performers who will have the honor of appearing before them.

The Artistes, whose talents have so long contributed to the public entertainment, (at Drury Lane Theatre especially) have, at the sacrifice of every consideration, consented to devote their services to the furtherance of Mr. BUNN's views, and the list will altogether comprise a phalanx of names never before attempted to be brought together in such an undertaking.

While the chief aim of the direction will be devoted to the advancement of

ENGLISH OPERA

BY NATIVE TALENT!

the performances will be interspersed with every other class of entertainment, and while it may appear almost incredible to bring together such an array of talent, with comparatively confined means,

THERE WILL BE NO ADVANCE OF PRICES,

but the Free List will be altogether done away with, (*the Public Press excepted.*)

THE THEATRE WILL OPEN
This Evening, Monday, Sept. 27, 1847,

ON WHICH OCCASION

Miss ROMER,

Miss REBECCA ISAACS,

Mr. W. HARRISON,

Mr. BORRANI,

Mr. RAFTER

AND

Mr. H. HORNCASTLE,

(*All from the Theatre Royal, Drury Lane.*)

Will have the honor of making their appearance.

Chapter Twenty-Three

Bunn (1847-48)

Much has been written about Alfred Bunn, especially by Alfred Bunn. A representative abstract of his career describes him as joint manager of Drury Lane and Covent Garden in 1833:

> He had difficulties first with his company, then with the Lord Chamberlain, and had a long-standing quarrel with Macready, which resulted in the tragedian assaulting the manager. In 1840, Bunn was declared a bankrupt but he continued to manage Drury Lane until 1847. Artistically, his control of the two chief English theatres was highly successful. He made a courageous attempt to establish English opera, producing the principal works of Balfe. He had some gift for writing and most of the libretti of these operas were translated by himself.

On his first playbill for the Surrey Theatre, on Monday 27 September 1847, Bunn announced his arrival as manager 'in consequence of the two national theatres...of which he has for many years, jointly and severally, had the management, having both passed into the hands of Foreigners'. He promises to bring his popular West-end productions as well as many of the Drury Lane artistes who have 'at the sacrifice of every consideration, consented to devote their services to the furtherance of Mr BUNN's views'. He finishes:

> While the chief aim of the direction will be devoted to the advancement of ENGLISH OPERA BY NATIVE TALENT! the performances will be interspersed with every other class of entertainment and while it may appear almost incredible to bring together such an array of talent, with comparatively confined means, THERE WILL BE NO ADVANCE OF PRICES, but the Free List will be altogether done away with, (the Public Press excepted).

He then goes on to list the artistes who will be appearing, including such Surrey favourites as Miss Romer, Miss Rebecca Isaacs and Mr W. Harrison. The full flavour of the announcement must be conveyed across where Bunn's name is in type four times larger than that of anyone else. The opening production was *The Bohemian Girl* –

'libretto by Mr BUNN, the music by M.W. Balfe', the second piece being ' Mr BUNN's farce *My Neighbour's Wife'*.

Before we look at his season, a look at his reason. As indicated earlier, there were three houses north of the river at which opera was usually mounted – Covent Garden, Drury Lane and Her Majesty's. Bunn had lost his lease of Covent Garden to Guiseppi Persiani in 1846. Persiani had made various alterations there and brought leading singers to it from Her Majesty's such as Giulia Grisi, Fanny Essler and Signor Tamburini plus its conductor, Michael Costa. It re-opened as the Royal Italian Opera House. Her Majesty's kept going for a while, thanks to securing the services of Jenny Lind 'the Swedish Nightingale' in the summer of 1847. She should have gone to Bunn, as the following jingle from a tailor's advertisement puts it:

> Bunn versus Lind
> The trial is over of 'Bunn versus Lind'
> And by means of the papers, the facts have got wind.
> Mr Bunn had his lawyers, and so had poor Jenny
> Who now, it appears, has to pay a rare penny.
> Two thousand Five hundred, besides all expences
> Is enough to make Jenny bereft of her senses.
> This minstrel, whose music has made us so fond
> Has to pay this amount, having broken her bond.
> Yes, in spite of the speeches of counsel vehement
> Jenny Lind is declared to have broken agreement....

Its patrons defected to Covent Garden when she left Her Majesty's and in 1848 it ceased to present opera. Bunn kept going at Drury Lane with, for example, *The Crusaders* (text by A. Bunn, music by Benedict; February 1846); *Loretta* (text by A. Bunn, music by Lavenu; November 1846); *The Bondman* (text by A. Bunn, music by Balfe; December 1846); *Matilda of Hungary* (text by A. Bunn, music by Wallace; February 1847). He was unable to renew when his lease ran out. So it was that, a few months later, he received the hospitality of Mrs Davidge at the Surrey, bringing with him his principal singers, the chorus and orchestra, his ballet company, even his stage hands. His place at Drury Lane was for a short while occupied by Monsieur Jullien, who started by giving 'celebrity concerts' and then tried a season of opera with Berlioz as conductor. It did not work, despite the first staged performances of *The Damnation of Faust,* and Jullien was bankrupted.

In the 1840s the world of the arts was badly riven. On one side were those, like Macready, Dickens and the editorial board of *Punch* –

Thackeray, Douglas Jerrold and Mark Lemon – who thought of art as a flowering of the soul, while on the other were Ducrow, Davidge, Yates and Bunn, who thought of art as sweat and hard graft. The feelings were quite vicious. In his diary entry for 6 February 1842 Macready wrote 'Rejoiced in my absence from Mr Ducrow's funeral', while Dickens, in a letter of 3 January 1844 to Macready, wrote 'My opinion is that our respected and valued friend Mr Bunn will stagger through another season, if he don't rot first'. Actually Bunn managed to stagger through quite a few more seasons without rotting. As for *Punch,* whose writers would refer to Hot Cross Bunn or Signor Bombastes Bunnerini, it was silenced when Bunn brought out a spoof issue in November 1847 and revealed some nasty skeletons in its writers' cupboards.

To Bunn's opening at the Surrey *The Times* gave much praise:

> Since the time when Elliston was the director [that is, fifteen years earlier] there has never been such an overflowing audience at the Surrey Theatre as that which last night celebrated the coup d'essai of Mr Bunn, the present sole manager of the establishment. Every part of the house was crammed, and standing room, or even a sight of the stage, was out of the question a short time subsequent to the doors being opened.

The piece given was *The Bohemian Girl,* with singers 'in excellent vein' as were the settings and the musicians under Tully, producing an audience 'in proportionate good humour – as they might well be to have so good an entertainment at so cheap a rate'. When Bunn was called on stage after the singers had taken their bows he made a short speech of thanks to 'his friends [who] had rallied round him on this new occasion'. He received 'renewed acclamations' from the audience and good wishes for success from the critic:

> Mr Bunn has begun his new undertaking under good auspices, and if he use the experience and tact which he has acquired in so many years of theatrical management with discretion, there can be little doubt of a prosperous issue, which, for the sake of his company, combining so many old favourites of the public in its ranks, no less than of himself, is to be earnestly desired. Improvements in the theatre are already in progress; among other things, a new gas apparatus, which will tend greatly to improve the lighting, a special entrance to the private boxes, and a thorough cleansing and re-imbellishment of the house – all of which desiderata have been long in request....

With such a notice, it is difficult to appreciate that Bunn and the Surrey were basically incompatible. Bunn liked long runs; the Surrey liked variety. Bunn repeated his first night's programme throughout the week – and the next week – and the next – and the next. The Surrey audiences occasionally took to long runs, for example *Black-Eyed Susan* and *Oliver Twist,* even *Macbeth,* but the supporting pieces were changed regularly so there was always something new to see before the 'half price' point. Bunn was not really interested in the Surrey clientele. His eyes were across the water, for his was a direct challenge to Persiani and Costa at Covent Garden: English Opera versus Italian Opera. It was the Covent Garden customers he hoped would come his way. They did not.

Bunn kept up the challenge for three more weeks, substituting *The Enchantress* (libretto by Bunn of course, music by Balfe) for *The Bohemian Girl* but that did not work either. By his twelfth week the penny dropped. Bunn put on only one of his own works, *The Bondman,* interspersed with other well-known English operas, *The Quaker, Maritana* and *The Beggar's Opera,* together with the English versions of *Lucia di Lammermoor* and *La Sonnambula,* plus the Surrey *Macbeth.* And all in the same week! That is what the Surrey audiences wanted. That is what brought in the local 'dustmen, chimney-sweeps and greasy butchers' to the opera.

Some of these operas are just names to most people these days, but their best songs get an airing occasionally. Balfe's *Bohemian Girl* might be remembered through 'I dreamt that I dwelt in marble halls' and Wallace's *Maritana* through 'Scenes that are brightest' or 'Yes, let me like a soldier fall'.

Frances Davidge's company was not without work during Bunn's season. Under the direction of her brother-in-law, Joseph Kerschner, it had been taken for a short and apparently disastrous spell to the Royal Pavilion Theatre in Whitechapel High Street. There was a dispute with the lessee, Mrs Yarnold. A court case threatened. The Surrey company found this announcement on the Pavilion notice-board:

> The Ladies and Gentlemen of the late Company are requested to attend To-morrow at 11 o'clock to hear a proposition that might tend to the re-opening of the Theatre on Monday. Mr Fairbrother has made a proposal to Mr Kerschner to release him from his liabilities of Rent, Taxes, Gas, &c. – and the Members of the Establishment to join in a Commonwealth and take their share in proportion to their salaries after the said liabilities are satisfied. It being further understood that any arrangement that may be concluded shall not in any way prejudice the legal proceedings that are now pending between Mrs Yarnold and Mr Kerschner.

Fairbrother had been temporarily displaced as the Surrey treasurer by Bunn's man. In the event the Surrey folk were saved by the calendar, as it was now pantomime time. This was not a matter in which Bunn would wish to be involved, though *Battledore and Shuttlecock; or, Harlequin Trap, Bat and Ball* appeared in the same bill as an English translation of *La Figlia del Reggimento* under Bunn's direction. The 1847 pantomime was written, as was the 1844 one, by Nelson Lee, the Surrey's Harlequin in 1832.

The Times of 22 December 1847 reported:

> An English version of Donizetti's *Figlia del Reggimento,* from the pen of Mr Fitzball, was produced at this theatre last night with great success. The major part of the pretty sparkling music was preserved, and... exceedingly well performed, under the valuable superintendence of Mr Tully. Miss Poole undertook the part of Maria.... Her singing was correct and brilliant... and her acting full of vivacity. Miss Poole was honoured deservedly with no less than three encores, those to the popular rataplan and the difficult finale air being enthusiastic....

(For those unfamiliar with the opera, the rataplan is a marching song to the beat – rataplan – of a side drum.) The reviewer told how the piece played to a crowded house; it was thought well put on and likely to run. Then:

> Mrs D.W. King, wife of the tenor, late of Drury-lane Theatre, has made considerable sensation here lately, in a version of *Lucia di Lammermoor*.... Her execution of the pathetic music of Lucia proves her to possess no small amount of feeling....

Alfred Bunn's connection with the Surrey ceased at the beginning of February 1848: 'Mrs Davidge (Lessee) has the honor of announcing that her engagement with Mr Bunn having terminated, she has resumed the Management of this Theatre'.

It is difficult to discern her touch in the next three months. Again the bills seem ten years out of date. Mr and Mrs Honner are back, with Ira Aldridge and E.F. Saville. The pieces are decidedly vintage: *Pizarro, The Waterman, The Whistler* (a version of Scott's *Heart of Midlothian), The Padlock* and *My Poll and My Partner Joe* are all long in the tooth. The reason may have been to give Joseph Kerschner more experience in pieces not likely to cause any production difficulties, supported by actors who knew their parts backwards; George Pearce, for example, took nine different roles in this period.

Another likely reason for not mounting new pieces is that Mrs Davidge failed to renew her lease of the Surrey, due to expire that autumn. She was preparing to say goodbye after fourteen years. By May 1848 she had moved to Riverside Cottage in Hampton, Middlesex. This was not exactly unknown territory as her brother-in-law Kerschner had lived there before coming to work at the Surrey. James Tully, her musical director, now seventy years of age, would also retire there shortly.

There may have been yet another reason for not splashing out on new productions in early 1848. One could not guarantee an audience when Westminster Bridge was cordoned off, with artillery commanding Waterloo and Blackfriars Bridges and public statements 'that rockets and other munitions of war will be issued to this arm of the service'. The Chartists were holding their convention on Kennington Common and were planning a march on Parliament on 10 April to present a petition, which Parliament interpreted as a prelude to bloody revolution.

The season finished on 15 April 1848 and re-opened on Easter Monday, 24 April, under 'ENTIRELY NEW MANAGEMENT'. As the playbills have it:

> The Public is respectfully informed that this Elegant Place of Amusement will commence the New Season Under The Direction of MR. KERSCHNER who encouraged by the Great Success his Management met with during a portion of last Summer has again become a candidate for the Patronage of the Lovers of the Drama. During the Short Recess, the Interior will be Re-Embellished and Renovated, And every attention will be paid for the convenience of the Public. The LIGHTING of the THEATRE Will undergo various improvements; the GRAND Central CHANDELIER Will be considerably ENLARGED, and rendered more Beautiful and Glittering by the Addition of several Thousand New Drops! Designed and completed by Mr J. HINKLEY, Gas Fitter, Duke Street, Westminster Rd. THE ENGAGEMENTS Have been so formed as to include ALL the ORIGINAL FAVORITES And many others of equal celebrity, rendering this UNRIVALLED COMPANY The most powerful – most effective – and without exception THE BEST IN LONDON.

The list of his company starts off with Mr and Mrs Honner, Mr and Mrs E.F. Saville and Mr and Mrs N.T. Hicks, so on the acting side it is the mixture as before. There are changes elsewhere. Harroway becomes musical director and G. Maskell is ballet master. This time ballet takes precedence over opera with an influx of Mrs Conquest's old pupils – the clown Dickie Flexmore and his wife 'Madlle. Auriol', and three of the Deulin family. Indeed, there was no opera season in 1848. If we want to find J.H. Tully (musical director), Miss Rebecca Isaacs, Adam Leffler, Horncastle, Oliver Summers and the rest of the old Surrey opera company, together with the English versions of *La Sonnambula, Barber of Seville, Daughter of the Regiment* and other time-honoured Surrey productions, we have to look to the Strand Theatre from 5 April or the Theatre Royal at Brighton between 22 July and 16 September 1848. It appears that an opera season had been planned, as the Surrey playbills announced in mid-February 'In Active Rehearsal – *Haidee or The Secret* (from Paris)' – whereas this opera, by Auber, did not appear at the Surrey but was Tully's first offering at the Strand.

There seems to be a number of links between the newcomers and the Grecian Saloon theatre in City Road. Harroway had been musical director there in 1840. He set as an operetta a story by E.L. Blanchard entitled *Arcadia; or, the Shepherd and Shepherdess* which had its première there in 1841. Indeed it was written for the place, as the Grecian had previously been known as the Shepherd and Shepherdess Tea Gardens. He also wrote and produced there a ballet pantomime in 1840, *Le Polichinel Chinois Vampire,* and one of the Deulin family was in that. Both Deulin and Flexmore were in the 1843 pantomime at the Grecian, and Deulin supervised the ballet there at Easter 1844. As for Maskell the ballet master, he had appeared at the Surrey five years earlier as Master G. Maskell in the ballet pantomime *The Soldier's Dream* under W.H. Harvey.

The Sun of 25 April 1848 reviewed the Surrey's opening programme of the season:

> This house, as a matter of course, was crammed from the floor to the ceiling with a somewhat noisy but upon the whole good-humoured audience; and the new season, under the direction and management of Mr Kerschner, has commenced with every prospect of success. During the short recess, various improvements have been made.... The performances commenced with a drama, acted some five years ago, entitled *The Bohemians; or, the Mysteries of Crime* which served for a re-introduction of several old favourites; including Messrs. E.F. Saville, N.T. Hicks, Dale, Lewis, R. Honner, Mrs Honner & Miss Eliza Terrey....

We learn that after those players had taken the bow for which they were recalled, the next piece, the comedietta *Ladies Beware*, 'was not well received, the audience being impatient for the commencement of the pantomime'. After a management appeal it was allowed to conclude. The 'great attraction of the evening' then took the stage, *Cinderella and the Fairy Queen; or, Harlequin and the Little Glass Slipper,* to be 'received with unusual approbation'. Miss Terrey played Cinderella, Miss Daly the Prince, Mrs Hicks the Queen of the Fairies and the Misses Marshall and Fairbrother the two Ugly Sisters. In the harlequinade Mlle Theodore and G. Maskell were Columbine and Harlequin, while 'Mr T. Barry as Clown, and Mr Morelli as Pantaloon, kept the house in a roar with their clever and amusing tricks...'.

The new ballet company was much in evidence in the summer season with two full-length pieces, *The Contrabandists* at the end of May 1848 and *Conscriptions de Basil* in July. T.P. Cooke turned up in an unusual role, the Count of Monte Cristo in *Chateau d'If,* as well as in his old favourite pieces. One addition to the company's repertoire is worth a special mention, the production of *Flowers of the Forest* in August. This was remembered until recently on the sign of the public house next door to the theatre, or rather the gap where the theatre once stood – but I fear that 'The Flowers of the Forest' will soon be another gap, pending redevelopment. The pub was originally called the 'Surrey Coal-Hole'. From 1845 to 1848 the licence was held by Richard Shepherd but he let it go when he obtained the lease of the Surrey theatre. Joseph Kerschner gave up his interest in the Equestrian Tavern on the southern side of the Surrey and took the Coal-Hole on its northern side, changing its name first to 'Creswick's Head' (in honour of the actor who had become the joint lessee of the Surrey) and then to 'The Flowers of the Forest'. (The link is not with the Scottish lament of that name as the play concerns a band of gypsies, not a beaten Scottish army.)

On 11 September 1848 there was an 'Union of Sadler's Wells and Surrey Companies... the extensive alterations of Sadler's Wells not being completed...'. For six nights Samuel Phelps and his team showed Surrey-siders how it was done on the northern heights.

The last two weeks of the lease were, as usual, given over to benefits, though *The Times* was in its condescending mood about one of them: 'There is nothing like the popularity of a low comedian on the Surrey side of the water. Mr H. Webb took a benefit last night, and played Mawworm in *The Hypocrite,* and the principal facetious gentlemen in two other long pieces; the house was crammed to suffocation'. When Fairbrother took his benefit on the next and final evening, 28 September, another old-timer showed up. This was none other than Watkins Burroughs, the old Belfastman who had taken the lease of the Surrey some twenty-six years earlier. During this space of time, and indeed subsequently, he worked the out-of-town theatres. *The Belfast Commercial Chronicle* was to laud him thus: 'People speak of Burroughs, and recollect the gentleman, the scholar, the artist, the man of genius:

know dignity in its elegance, scholarship in its refinement, oratory without a flaw, and versatility of personation having no competitor'. For Fairbrother's benefit at the Surrey Burroughs played the Don in *Don Caesar de Bazan,* with Mrs Honner as Maritana. The evening was rounded off with an operatic spoof by Oxberry on *Lucy of Lammermoor.*

The Times of 9 October 1848 carried the following advertisement in its 'Sales by Auction' section:

> Three Day Sale. Surrey Theatre. To the Theatrical Profession and others. Mr Priest has received instructions to SELL by AUCTION the whole of the superior FITTINGS, Scenery, Stage Property, Wardrobes &c. upon the Premises, as above, in Blackfriars Rd. on Wednesday Oct. 11 and two following days, at 12 each day, comprising the large chandelier, 13 suspending six-light chandeliers, 100 pieces of scenery, with braces complete, 400 lots of ladies' and gentlemen's wardrobe, several dozen chairs, noble chimney-glasses, 6 octave pianoforte, eight-day dial, the excellent fittings of the dressing rooms, large stock of useful stage property, a quantity of timber, sundry wheels, old iron, and numerous effects. May be viewed the day prior and morning of the sale. Catalogues to be had....

The actual sale was reported thus in *The Globe*:

> The Surrey Theatre, that once popular establishment, is doomed to feel the force of the 'tide of events', the scenery, costumes, properties, decorations, &c., having been during the week brought to the hammer. The attendance of the members of the corps dramatique and of theatrical managers, as might have been expected, was numerous, more particularly as many members of the sock and buskin wished to possess themselves of some relic of the once-famed 'Circus of St George's-in-the-Fields', which gave to the profession and the world a number of the most eminent dramatic, pantomimic, and equestrian artistes.

This obituary was somewhat premature. It is true that Mrs Frances Davidge did not return to the theatrical scene, though she soon tired of Hampton. She returned to Kennington to live with her unmarried sisters and her mother, Harriet Pearce, who died on 7 October 1851 aged 62. Frances lived until 20 July 1892, dying at 3 Brixton Hill, aged 82, with the fortune left to her by her husband, George Bolwell Davidge, largely intact.

Three months after the sale of 11-13 October 1848 the Surrey was up and running again.

ROYAL SURREY THEATRE

ENTIRELY NEW MANAGEMENT!

The Public is respectfully informed, that this Elegant Place of Amusement will commence a New Season

Under the Direction of Mr KERSCHNER

Who, encouraged by the Great Success his Management met with during a portion of last Summer, has again become a Candidate for the Patronage of the Lovers of the Drama.

During the Short Recess, the Interior will be

Re-Embellished and Renovated,

And every attention will be paid for the convenience of the Public. The

LIGHTING of the THEATRE

Will undergo various improvements; the

GRAND Central CHANDELIER

Will be considerably ENLARGED, and rendered more Beautiful and Glittering by the

Addition of several Thousand New Drops!

Designed and completed by Mr J. HINKLEY, Gas Fitter, Duke Street, Westminster Rd.

THE ENGAGEMENTS

Have been so formed as to include

ALL the ORIGINAL FAVORITES

And many others of equal celebrity, rendering this

UNRIVALLED COMPANY

The most powerful—most effective—and without exception

THE BEST IN LONDON.

THE SUMMER SEASON

WILL COMMENCE ON

EASTER-MONDAY, April 24, 1848.

The following Members are already included in the LIST OF THE COMPANY:—

Mr. N. T. HICKS	Mrs. R. HONNER
Mr. E. F. SAVILLE	Mrs. E. F. SAVILLE
Mr. R. HONNER	Mrs. N. T. HICKS
Mr. DALE	Mrs. DALE
Mr. JOHN HERBERT	Miss ELIZA TERREY
Mr. HESLOP	Miss M. TERREY
Mr. DRESSER JONES	Miss M. DALY
Mr. H. LEWIS	Miss FAIRBROTHER
Mr. G. MASKELL	Miss WOOD
Mr. H. BUTLER	Miss FYNE
Mr. KINGSTON	Miss GRAHAM
Mr. MORELLI	Miss HART
Mr. E. CONWAY	Miss FORSTER
Mr. CARRATT	Miss WATKINS
Mr. PHELPS	Miss PARTRIDGE
Mr. MOORE, &c. &c.	Miss MAY, &c. &c.

Mr. T. BARRY, THE CELEBRATED CLOWN,

Is also Engaged, and will appear in an ENTIRELY NEW GRAND FAIRY

COMIC PANTOMIME!

THE BAND will be Efficient and Complete.

Composer and Musical Director, Mr HARROWAY, R.A. Leader, Mr J. COOKE.

The Box-Office will be opened on SATURDAY, the 22nd inst.

Box-Book Keeper, Mr. NOTTER, of the Theatre Royal, Covent Garden,

Of whom Private Boxes and Seats may be obtained from Eleven o'Clock until Four.

Manager and Treasurer, — Mr. R. S. FAIRBROTHER.

Stage Director, Mr. CONWAY Ballet Master, Mr. G. MASKELL

Property Maker and Decorator, Mr. KALLETT Machinist, Mr. WILDING

Full Particulars will be announced in a Few Days.

Chapter Twenty-Four

Shepherd and Creswick (1848-56)

The Surrey re-opened on 26 December 1848, the lessees being Richard Shepherd of Clapham and Eliza Vincent of West Brixton. Both of them have already appeared in this story.

Very few of the previous company or back-stage staff joined the new management. Shepherd's biggest catch was to retain the services of Thomas Eallett who had been property man for G.B. Davidge since the early 1820s and knew the business inside-out. Joseph Kerschner was also still around and re-enacted his career with Davidge by working for Shepherd, first in the box office and then as Director. As for the acting company, *The Theatrical Times* of 27 January 1849 remarked on John Neville 'as being the only actor of the Davidge dynasty employed by the new management'.

One of Shepherd's friends from his days with Ducrow, Henry Widdicomb, joined him at the Surrey and provided the comic relief for over ten years. He was the son of John Widdicomb, the celebrated ringmaster at Astley's ('Widdicomb the cool… no emotion stirs him') where young Henry had kept the crowd in a roar with his antics.

They all managed to get off to a good start with a contribution from the 'Pantomime King', E.L. Blanchard, *Harlequin Lord Lovell; or, Lady Nancy Bell and the Fairies of the Silver Oak,* with a return visit by Tom Matthews, the clown billed as Grimaldi's 'legitimate successor'.

The ballad on which the pantomime was based is rather gloomy:

> The Baron beheld with a father's pride
> His beautiful child, young Lovel's bride
> While she with her bright eyes seemed to be
> The star of that goodly company.
> 'I'm weary of dancing now', she cried
> 'Here tarry a moment, I'll hide, I'll hide;
> And, Lovel, be sure thou're the first to trace
> The clue to my secret hiding place.'
> Away she ran, and her friends began
> Each tower to search, and each nook to scan;
> In the highest – the lowest – the loneliest spot
> Young Lovel sought wildly, but found her not.

With Tom Matthews were Herr Deulin as Harlequin and Mlle. Theodore as Columbine, both having appeared before at the Surrey, and a newcomer, J.B. Johnstone, as Pantaloon – he was also the regular prompter. But how did Blanchard make the change from the sombre opening, with the 'Haunted Chamber at the Top of the Tower', and the 'old oak chest that had long lain hid' (containing the body of Lady Nancy), to the knockabout fun of the Harlequinade? Well, in modern parlance, he fudged it, with the magical appearance of the Fairies of the Silver Oak going straight into the 'Transformation Scene'. Nobody compained. In pantomime of those days one expected a 'dark opening' to the fun and games.

The Surrey publicised itself in a 'ballad' more acceptable in polite society than 'Hot Codlins' and more cheerful than that of Lord Lovel and his vanished bride:

> Come over the water, and after your tea
> Pop into a box at the Surrey;
> The best of all pantomimes there you may see,
> If you want a good laugh in a hurry.

One unexpected name on the staff was George Osbaldiston, employed in the Treasury. He was the son of the Davidges' old adversary at the Victoria, so it looks as if the breach between the two managements was now being healed. As it happened, Eliza Vincent stayed a mere three months. She disappears from view for a while but when D.W. Osbaldiston died, she took over the fag-end of the Victoria lease. Like Frances Davidge, Eliza Vincent was unable or unwilling to renew but accepted the post of 'Directress' under the new lessee, Joseph Johnson Towers. One good thing seems to have come out of the Victoria's association with the Surrey and with Shepherd – there were no more public slanging matches between the two theatres.

For Easter Monday, 9 April 1849, Shepherd had a number of guest artists with a variety of talents. There was Mrs Stirling (wife of the playwright) in an 'Entirely New and Original Historical and Romantic Drama, in three Acts, written expressly for this Theatre by E. Fitzball, Esq.' called *Alhamar the Moor*. This was followed by another Minstrel show, this time led by G.W. Pell, notable for being the original 'Mr Bones', a character adopted into virtually every minstrel show since. The programme ended with a pantomime, *Mother Goose; or, Harlequin and the Golden Egg,* with Tom Matthews in a revised version of the show which had brought Grimaldi his fame in 1808. Very little in it was changed. We still have Squire Bugle, Colin and Colinette, though transformed into Clown (Matthews), Harlequin (Cormack) and Columbine (Miss Smithers). Avaro has been anglicised to Gaffer Greedy, who still gets the worst of it as Pantaloon (J.B. Johnstone).

It seems almost as if Shepherd then gave trial runs to potential partners to fill Eliza Vincent's place. On 30 April 1849 there was a two weeks' spell for James Anderson, 'the Great Tragic Artiste from the Theatres Royal, Covent Garden and Drury Lane' in such parts as Claude Melnotte in *The Lady of Lyons,* Beverley in *The Gamester* and Macbeth (the production being in the traditional pattern, with no opera singer in the part of Siward). William Creswick of the Theatre Royal, Haymarket, then had a four-week spell starting on 4 June, for example playing Master Walter in Sheridan Knowles's *Hunchback*. Shepherd made up his mind. When the dramatic season recommenced on 19 September, Creswick was his partner. Anderson had to wait nearly fourteen years for his turn! The preference may have come from the fact that Shepherd and Creswick had both started in 'horse-opera', Shepherd with Ducrow and Creswick with Amhurst.

Shepherd (now living at Apsley Lodge, Clapham) had seen how well an opera season went down with Surrey audiences. He invited Miss Emma Romer to direct and E.J. Loder to conduct the 1849 season. The favourite artists, Adam Leffler, Mr and Mrs Weiss and Miss Elizabeth Poole, sang the Surrey's favourite operas, *La Sonnambula* and *The Daughter of the Regiment*. Shepherd also brought in three new productions in his first year: translations of Donizetti's operas *Lucrezia Borgia* (another piece tailor-made for the Surrey clientele, we may assume) and *La Favorita,* and of Meyerbeer's *Les Huguenots* which ran for twenty-seven consecutive nights. These were supported by established English favourites, *Macbeth, The Bohemian Girl, The Waterman* and *Midas*. Loder also brought in his comparatively new 'Fairy Ballad Opera, *Robin Goodfellow*' (which had been first performed the previous year at the Princess's Theatre), with Mrs Weiss, Miss Poole and Miss Kenworthy singing the same parts,Titania, Robin and Oberon respectively, as at the première. A new tenor billed as 'Mr Travers' turns out to be another Romer, cousin of Emma.

The Times of 24 October 1849 commented:

> For some time past Mr Shepherd, the lessee of this house, has been zealously labouring to elevate its character. Sir E.B. Lytton's *Richelieu,* with Mr Creswick as the principal personage, proved a most successful production, and now we have a new domestic play, far above the ordinary 'run' of Surrey pieces, written by two established authors, Mr Bayle

> Bernard and Mr Westland Marston. It is called *Trevanion, or the False Position....* The drama is very well written, and has some strong situations, especially that in which the father is offended by his daughter's coolness. Mr Creswick, Mr Emery and Madame Ponisi by their acting did all they could for the piece, which was completely successful.

One can notice a gradual change in how *The Times* reports theatrical events, and not only at the Surrey. Far more space is given to an exposition of the plot – the Surrey had well over a full column on one occasion – but often only a line or two, as above, on the abilities of the actors and the detailed merits of the production. This is presumably what its readers wanted. As for the plays, no-one remembers Bernard or Marston these days, but as well as his place in national history Bulwer Lytton has a place in the Surrey chronicle with his plays *The Lady of Lyons* and *Richelieu,* and his novel *Paul Clifford* which formed the basis of the opera of that name.

Within a year or two, much of the good work done by Mrs Davidge had already been forgotten. *The Times* reported on 20 February 1850:

> This house, so long the stronghold of nautical melodrama, has of late been making strenuous efforts to join the ranks of the 'young legitimates'. A few relapses have indeed taken place in the course of the struggle, but still the lessee, Mr Shepherd, has shown a will to take the path towards elevation, if possible, and Mr Creswick, his chief actor, has, since he joined the Surrey corps, been gaining a firm hold on the Surrey audiences.

The writer calls the theatre's acceptance of *Old Love and New Fortune*, a five-act play in blank verse by H.F. Chorley, a 'new indication of an attempt to elevate the amusements of a populous neighbourhood, hitherto for the most part dieted with coarser food', despite the piece's poor construction as 'not so much a drama as a dramatic poem'. The Surrey's acting tradition is then made part of the same blanket insult as its audience: 'The manner in which the work is acted shows the existence of a great deal of histrionic talent, little known on this side of the Thames'. There is praise for players and staging:

> Mr Creswick, who plays the Templar, and forcibly represents a passionate interior, veiled by a show of reckless sarcasm, is, indeed, familiar to Westminster audiences. Not so are Madame Ponisi, who feelingly depicts the contrition of the haughty lady; Mr Mead, an excellent reader and careful

> representative of the chilly father; and Mr Fitzroy, who plays a veteran servant, and is a most able actor of 'old men' – all these performers work well together, and we may see in them the nucleus of a good practical company. The scenery and costumes, which illustrate the end of the seventeenth century, show that Mr Shepherd is emulous of the fame of his more northern competitors in the art of decoration.

It wold appear that five acts of a dramatic poem were enough, or too much, for the *Times* critic, as he does not mention that the bill also included 'the Gorgeous Comic Christmas Pantomime... *Moon Queen and King Night; or, Harlequin Twilight!* from the Pen and Pencil of Alfred Crowquill'. This was the pseudonym of A.H. Forrester, who apparently only wrote two pantomimes; the other was produced at the Surrey in 1853. His sketches for the costumes are held by the Minet Library. King Night and his soldiers display candle-snuffers as crown or helmets and spear points, to indicate their aversion to light, while Baron Blazenoff, later Pantaloon, would pass for Falstaff any day. Forrester also published in this year a booklet in comic-strip style, *Pantomime As It Is, Was and Will Be,* and he illustrated an edition of *Pickwick Papers.* One of the characters in *Harlequin Twilight* was 'Electric Light',described as 'a sort of Nobodyknowsanythingabouthim... it is supposed that he will eventually do away with Night altogether'. The part was played by 'Mons. J. Lupino, the renowned Contortionist'.

On 20 May 1850 there was another visit of G.W. Pell and his Ethiopian Serenaders. To add variety, the following week *The Beggar's Opera* was put on with an interesting mix of the dramatic and operatic regulars. Henry Widdicomb (the resident comic) played Filch, Jane Coveney played Lucy, and three of the junior singers, George Tedder, Elizabeth Poole and Delavanti, sang Macheath, Polly and Matt of the Mint respectively. Then back to the classical when Creswick returned 'from his provincial engagements' to play Lucius Junius Brutus in Howard Payne's play, *Brutus.* If this were too heavy for some people, there would be Widdicomb in one of his farcical roles. There was always something for everyone at the Surrey.

The 1850 opera season proper opened on 1 July and ran for three months. There was a new man in charge, Herr Wilhelm Meyer Lutz from the Munich Royal Opera House. More immediately he was organist at St George's Cathedral (Westminster Bridge Road), five minutes' walk from the Surrey Theatre. A new prima donna was Mlle Maria Dolores Nau from the Grand Opera, Paris. The Surrey was still on the international circuit. The programme included four new productions:

Rossini's *Othello,* Bellini's *I Puritani* and *Norma,* and Auber's *Masaniello.* Surrey audiences had known the play of that name for decades, which is probably why the alternative name of the opera, by which it is better known these days – *The Dumb Girl of Portici* – was not used.

This opera is credited with having brought Belgium into existence. There was an operatic tradition, taken up by many a composer, for tenor and baritone to sing an heroic duet, on the theme of friendship or patriotism. There was a similar leaning at that time for composers of countries under foreign rule to put into their operas veiled references to their oppressors. Verdi did so in *Nabucco* for Italy under Austrian domination and Erkel did so in *Bank Ban* for Hungary under the same domination. Belgium, then part of a Dutch kingdom, had to make do with a French composer, Auber, and an opera about Naples, which happened to contain the patriotic duet for tenor and baritone 'Amour sacré de la patrie'. This was sung in a production in Brussels on 25 August 1830 with such vigour that the audience went roaring out of the Opera and much to everyone's surprise overthrew the administration and declared independence. My difficulty in accepting this story is that the patriotic duet comes in act two of a five-act opera. There ought to be a Belgian equivalent of the American sick joke: 'Yes, Mrs Lincoln, but how did the rest of the show go?'

About another of the Surrey's operas at this time, *I Puritani,* one gets the impression that there was trouble in staging it. Originally billed for 10 July 1850, it was put off to 15 July and played seven nights. It was due to come on again on 14 August, but never did; *Lucia di Lammermoor* was substituted. As the opera does not have any difficult effects or staging problems I presume there was trouble with the singers. It was perhaps asking rather a lot of Mlle. Nau to sing in what were to her five new productions in one month, but of course there could have been other reasons. As well as the new productions, there were revivals of *Les Huguenots, Lucia di Lammermoor, Maritana, La Sonnambula, The Bohemian Girl* and *Macbeth* – quite a feast!

As usual, a farce or burlesque was added to the operatic programme. These generally sank without trace. One, however, kept going for some years thanks to the Surrey's funny man, Henry Widdicomb, who played the part of Wellington Figgs in *Sophia's Supper.* It can still be found in the bills many years later but now as *Wellington Figgs,* which shows how Widdicomb dominated the piece.

The 1850 pantomime – did theatre managers have a competition for the longest name? – was *The Merry Wives of Windsor; or, Harlequin and Sir John Falstaff and the Demon Hunter of the Enchanted Oak,* with

Forrester's costume-sketches for *Moon Queen and King Night*
(Reproduced by kind permission of London Borough of Lambeth Archives Department)

another member of the Lupino family as Harlequin, this time Monsieur G. Lupino. Somehow the Surrey was not keeping or engaging a regular pantomime team, and there seems to be a new combination each year. It looks as if tricks with machinery were supplanting the split-second timing of the old practitioners. Ten years later the *Times* critic commented generally on the new approach:

> Managers have a trying time of it at this season of the year. The production of a pantomime is a labour of months, and one attended with no little inconvenience and expense. If it does not stand the test of Boxing-night, the failure is complete. Once put upon the stage, it cannot materially be altered. There may be, and there usually is, retrenchment after the first performance; but the transformations and tableaux must remain pretty much the same, the same requires that the pantomime shall have its 'run' of six weeks or two months, whatever may have been the verdict pronounced on it by patrons and unprofessional critics.

When one looks back to the 1830s and sees Tom Matthews engaged in a pantomime planned to run for a single week, it is clear that stage management had become more important than the star.

The 1851 opera season, with a two-week break for dramatic works, ran for nearly six months from Whit Monday, 9 June, to 20 December. Three new productions were mounted: Mozart's *Don Giovanni,* Verdi's *Ernani,* and Donizetti's *Linda di Chamounix.* There were also revivals of just about every opera ever produced at the Surrey, twenty altogether in the period. What opera house can offer that choice today? – yet these were not poor quality productions. Thomas German Reed from the Haymarket was the conductor for the first half of the season and, for the remainder, Meyer Lutz who had conducted the previous year's season. The singers included many well-known in this theatre – Emma Romer, Elizabeth Poole, H. Corri, Travers and Borrani. The Romer family was further represented by Annie and Charles. There is one playbill announcement which I find puzzling; 'The Management are also in treaty with Signora Fenelle, (Prima Donna of the San Carlos, Milan)'. I cannot trace this lady in my books of reference, nor a San Carlos Opera House in Milan. San Carlo, Naples, or La Scala, Milan, yes, but not as shown. It might have been a reference to Claire Hennelle, but it probably does not matter as the lady does not seem to have made an appearance at the Surrey. Mlle. Deville of the Grand Opera, Geneva, appears instead, performing for example in *Norma.* Another catch from the international circuit was Mlle. Adèle Alphonse, 'the favourite pupil of the Celebrated

Donizetti (From the Opera Comique, Paris) who will make her First Appearance in England... in *Lucia di Lammermoor*'.

As the Ugly Sisters *Cinderella* had the talented Coveney girls: Jane, who had first appeared on the Surrey stage in the juvenile opera company in 1828, and Harriet, who had come to the Surrey soon afterwards. They kept going for another thirty years. In 1851 they also appeared in the operas *Midas, Mountain Sylph* and *The Beggar's Opera,* and in dramas such as *Roland the Rider; or, Second Love,* and *Madeline.* Another 'old-timer' back in 1851 was the leader of the band, J.M. Jolly, who had served Davidge and Osbaldiston before him.

For all these new and old favourites the 1851 prices were exactly the same as they had been since 1834: boxes two shillings; pit one shilling; gallery sixpence.

The Christmas pantomime, again written by that master of the art, E.L. Blanchard, was – (deep breath) – *Harlequin Bluecap and the King of the Golden Waters; or, the Three Kingdoms, Animal, Vegetable and Mineral.* In his diary for 27 September 1851 Blanchard noted that he sold the piece to Shepherd for £10, getting half down, and the balance presumably when it was staged. His diary entries are brief to the extreme, but the following give some idea of events.

1851	24 December Go to Surrey rehearsal at night. Not in bed till three. 26 December Evening – to Surrey – private box. All goes off gloriously. 30 December Write extra half flat (china shop) for Shepherd
1852	15 June Off to Kennington Gate; dine with Mr and Mrs Shepherd; magnificently entertained.

On the playbills the credits include Thomas Eallett, still going strong, for 'Decorations and Changes', and a newcomer, George Augustus Sala, to whom attribution was made in 'Comical Characters from Sketches by G.A. Sala'. The link with this talented but erratic family came at a lucky moment. George Augustus Sala's brother, Charles Kerrison Sala, the actor whose stage name was Wynn, had just had a row with the management of the Princess's Theatre and had resigned. At that time the Princess's was rehearsing a new play being adapted from the French of *Les Frères Corses* by Dion Boucicault, the theatre's resident writer. 'Mr Wynn' had had a small part in this play, and had little difficulty in persuading his brother to help him out. George Augustus Sala records:

> I took what I thought to be a very legitimate revenge by writing on my own account another version of *Les Frères Corses.* Without compunction – so comically are one's notions of ethics influenced by circumstances – I proceeded to purchase a copy of the French drama and turn it into English....

He worked all night, finishing the adaptation by ten the next morning:

> My brother took the drama to which we had given the title of *The Corsicans,* over to the Surrey Theatre, which was then under the management of my old friend Mr Creswick, the tragedian, and Mr Richard Shepherd, a transpontine actor of considerable ability. My brother returned at three in the afternoon; he had lunched with Creswick and Shepherd; those worthy managers at once accepted *The Corsicans;* and, moreover, they had offered my brother a twelvemonth's engagement at a handsome salary. *The Corsicans* was within seven days produced at the Surrey, and ran for more than a hundred nights.

So on 15 March 1852 the Surrey put on the play 'adapted by the Brothers Sala', though George goes on:

> I had associated my brother's name with my own as joint-author; but he had nothing to do with turning the French dramatist's prose into English. Our remuneration was not splendid; but it was sufficient. We received twenty-five shillings a night: a sum considered in those days to be prodigious for authors' rights at a minor theatre.

Creswick played the part(s) of the twin brothers but I cannot find 'Mr Wynn' in the cast, though he does show up elsewhere in various minor roles such as Merlin in *The Three Perils of Man* on 12 April 1852 and Titus in *Virginius* on 3 May.

It was in May 1852 that a noted Shakespearean actress, Isabella Glyn, appeared at the Surrey for a three-week season, first as the Duchess of Malfi. *The Times* of 11 May is worth quoting:

> Miss Glyn, who commenced a series of twelve performances last night, signalised the occasion by introducing to our Surrey neighbours old Webster's terrible tragedy of *The Duchess of Malfi*, to which, after it had slumbered for a long while on the shelves, and after Mr Horne had adapted it to modern exigencies, she first gave a visible form at Sadler's Wells. Even to the southern spectators, who are more used to murders and passionate excesses than the colder inhabitants

> of the northern bank, the scene of the strangulation, with all its precedent horrors, seemed a marvellously awful affair. Miss Glyn, who, from the first revival of the play, moulded the character of the Duchess completely after her own conception, played it last night in a manner worthy of herself. Her great principle is to make the personage in the earlier portion of the play a sort of grande coquette, and thus to bring out, by the strongest contrast, the horrible anguish which arises at last, when the greatness of the suffering appears to sanctify the erring woman. The air with which she encountered death was solemn, dignified and calmly desperate. Mr Creswick, as Ferdinand, the chief of the atrocious brothers, showed at first somewhat too great a predilection for that constant loudness which is so acceptable to the Transpontines, but his subsequent scenes proved that he had entered into the pathos of Webster, and the celebrated line – 'Cover her face, mine eyes dazzle; she died young' – could not have been more effectively delivered.

The writer also praises the acting of the difficult role neatly summed up as that of 'the reflective, scrupulous villain, Bosola'. This was played by 'Mr T. Mead,... a sensible, inobtrusive performer, who never exaggerates, but speaks what he has to say judiciously and distinctly'.

Can we put in a word about 'Mr T. Mead', commended here and noted earlier for his 'excellent chilly father' in the Surrey's *Old Love and New Fortune* of 1850? As the century wears on he becames 'dear old Tom Mead' in actors' reminiscences galore. His later career was spent playing secondary or lesser parts for Henry Irving, by which time his hold on a role was weaker than it was in the Surrey's *Duchess of Malfi*. A letter of 1885 quoted in Laurence Irving's *Henry Irving* writes of him as understudy when Irving was ill: 'Tonight, old Mead – the man with the big voice who plays the Ghost in *Hamlet* – is the Shylock, and as his memory is proverbially eccentric, we expect some entertainment'. One story must suffice. As a witch in Irving's *Macbeth* Mead had to say 'Cool it with a baboon's blood', a line that infallibly came out as 'Cool it with a dragoon's blood'. After the strongest remonstrance that Irving could give his old friend, Tom swore to get it right; but at the next performance the audience was regaled with 'Cool it with a dragoon's blood – I mean baboon's – s'help me, Guv'nor, I've said it again!' However, Tom Mead deserves a better memorial than this. Already described as an 'old veteran' at Sunderland in 1856 when Irving at eighteen joined the company, Mead befriended and coached the struggling young actor. Mead's 'good offices' then resulted in Irving being invited to join the Edinburgh company as juvenile lead in

1857. Irving's career took off from that point. Later he engaged Tom Mead at the Lyceum, thus fulfilling, says Laurence Irving, 'a promise made seventeen years ago at... Sunderland; the stammering, tongue-tied boy had risen and not forgotten'.

At the Surrey Theatre Isabella Glyn continued to make her mark. *The Times* reported on 25 May 1852:

> Last night Miss Glyn took her benefit at this house, and performed the two arduous characters of Julia in *The Hunchback* and Beatrice in *Much Ado about Nothing.* The latter of these parts is chiefly remarkable for the genial vivacity with which Miss Glyn, departing from her tragic atmosphere, allows herself to embody the most petulant and mirthful of Shakespeare's heroines. Julia, on the other hand, is signalised by a bold departure from all previous interpretations. Every actress who has undertaken the part has made the third act... an occasion for tragic display, but Miss Glyn keeps within the limits of comedy, and where her predecessors have exhibited the extreme of mental torture, she has been content to exhibit the effects of a pique.... By her peculiar reading Miss Glyn sacrifices many rounds of applause at well known 'points' but she has the satisfaction of working out a character according to her own conception, which she matures to a high degree of finish.

The crowded house gave Miss Glyn 'the honour of diverse calls'.

On Whit-Monday, 31 May 1852, the opera season opened 'under Sole Direction of Miss Romer'. It ran for three and a half months, with a dozen operas, and included the world première of Balfe's *The Devil's in It* on 26 July. This ran right through until the end of the season on 13 September. There was one other addition to the Surrey repertoire, Flotow's *Leoline.*

After a fortnight's break the dramatic season opened and soon had another hit, a dramatisation of Mrs Harriet Beecher Stowe's newly-published anti-slavery novel *Uncle Tom's Cabin.* This was still pulling them in at pantomime-time, so one could see this together with Blanchard's *Harlequin and the Land of Flowers; or, The Fairy of the Rose and the Sprite of the Silver Star,* with Milano as Harlequin and Annie Cushnie as Columbine. A new clown appears, W. Buck, who after one or two breaks manages to establish himself. Before long, he is being referred to as 'The Surrey Buck'.

There had been a charity performance before Christmas on behalf of the Engineers' Emigration Fund, referring to 'the late struggle between masters and men' which had been disastrous for the members of the Amalgamated Society. The playbills appealed for the support of fellow workmen to assist those thrown out of work to 'emigrate to the fertile land of Australia'. One hears a lot about convicts colonising Australia but less about the emigrant unemployed.

The 1853 opera season commenced, as usual, on Whit-Monday under the direction of Emma Romer and the baton of Meyer Lutz. There were two new productions: Meyerbeer's *Robert the Devil* and Balfe's *Siege of Rochelle*. (This was revived in 1987 by the John Lewis Partnership Music Society, which unfortunately saw fit to update it to the 1914-18 War; somehow Balfe's music does not sit well in the trenches.) Twelve of the established operas were also revived, with the home-grown product slightly predominating. Nominally the season ended on 24 September, but as the dramatic season was taken up firstly with a revival of *Macbeth*, then the pantomime, and then *Macbeth* again, there was not room for a lot of other drama before the 1854 opera season started. One interesting experiment came from guest appearances by Samuel Phelps of Sadler's Wells, who exchanged roles with Creswick in alternating Othello and Iago, Brutus and Cassius, Lear and Edgar.

The 1853 pantomime was again by 'Alfred Crowquill', as a change from Blanchard. This was called *King Muffin; or, Harlequin Heartcake and the Fairies of the Glow-worm Glade*. It re-introduced a character, Harlequina, who, like Sprite, never quite found a permanent place in the harlequinade; she was played by the elder of the Guniss sisters, the younger playing Columbine.

One would think that the long-established enthusiasm for opera at the Surrey – for twenty years if one looks only at the foreign element, and fifty years altogether if counting the home-grown variety – was something completely unknown , or if known misbelieved. Otherwise, the critic of *The Times* of 28 August 1854 would not have written:

> The operatic performances at this theatre, under the direction of Miss Romer, are drawing great audiences. Halevy's opera of *La Juive* – although one would have thought that the music was hardly ad captandum enough to come within the capacity of the transpontine amateurs – had a long run, and filled the treasury. Much of this must have been owing to the melodramatic interest of M. Scribe's libretto, translated with ability by Mr Henri Drayton, who himself sustained the character of Eleazar, the Jew – the music being transposed and altered from tenor to base....

> The spectacle, too, which was gorgeous and complete, had doubtless a great deal to do with the success.

(Transpontine amateurs, indeed! Ah yes, in the sense of loving connoisseurs.) The reviewer recalls that 'Many years ago *The Jewess* was produced, with great pomp and splendour, at Drury-lane Theatre, the whole of the music being omitted!' Compared with the music-less *Jewess* at Drury Lane, any 'short-comings of the Surrey version, were scarcely worth taking into consideration'. The success of a 'new essay... neither more nor less than the *Prophète* of Meyerbeer' is then noted:

> Miss Romer has succeeded in providing so attractive an entertainment for her patrons, that they seem never tired of coming, and their approval is testified by applause as frequent as it is enthusiastic. The scenery is remarkably striking, and the dresses, if not all historically correct, are, at least, new and costly. The coronation and its accompanying processions, the skating scene, and the burning of Jean of Leyden's palace at the end of the opera, are managed with great effect. Miss Romer, who plays Fides, sings the music extremely well, and seems to have lost little or none of that dramatic energy and feeling for which she was honourably distinguished at Drury-lane Theatre, during the long reign of Mr Bunn.

Further singers are praised, including Rebecca Isaacs who is 'more than respectable' as Bertha, and Augustus Braham who is clearly no actor yet 'gives much pleasure by his singing, when he refrains from over-exerting himself'; as his father's son 'he must study assiduously to do credit to the name he bears'. The report concludes:

> Altogether, for the mixed crowds that are in the habit of attending the Surrey Theatre, *The Prophet* is represented in a manner which leaves little to desire, and this should not be overlooked in criticising the performance. It must be remembered that the passage of the river Thames makes a vast difference in the character, tastes, and appreciation of all theatrical audiences, and of operatic audiences especially.

The hit of the autumn dramatic season in 1854 was *Brothers in Arms.* Its alternative title, to which it changed after the first few performances, *The Battle of the Alma,* is a reminder that the Crimean War was in progress. The Surrey was giving the equivalent of live television coverage. Also, on 14 December, there was a 'Free Benefit in aid of the Patriotic Fund' with 'The Entire Receipts Without any Deduction whatsoever... to give the Soldiers' Wives and Widows a Benefit Indeed'.

As for the new pantomime on Boxing Night, it seems almost as if the *Times* readers north of the river wanted the Surrey-siders to conform to a preconceived pattern of uncouth, uncultured proletarians. If so, *The Times* of 27 December 1854 gave them what they fancied:

> A visitor to the Surrey on Boxing-night has the advantage of a duplicate interest – in those who come to see, and those who come to be seen. It would be delusive to suppose that the actors are heard, and as delusive to imagine that the three or four thousand people, wedged together in the densest possible masses, are only seen. The management, therefore, with a true appreciation of the prevailing taste, usually serves up some stock piece (concerning which the most infinitesimal curiosity is never exhibited), to induce an evaporation of the more noisy excitement, and to prepare with comparative decorum for the grand attraction of the evening, the Christmas pantomime. A custom so convenient was duly observed last night, when, as the bills declare, the favourite drama of *The Foundling of the Forest* was presented; but... though several gentlemen, dressed indiscriminately as Hamlet, a Chasseur Britannique, an assassin, a nondescript officer, a full-plumed villain, and Polonius, were most vehement in action and energetic in speech, the tones of a sweltering pit, not yet shaken into tranquillity, were far too vehement and energetic to permit of many consecutive sentences reaching any of the audience.

The satire continues with a brief glance at the play's stock characters and plot, then describes the activities of the interval:

> Gentlemen in the pit resumed their waistcoats and coats, and betook themselves to the replenishing of flat bottles and the reckless purchasing of oranges for their fair and warm companions. Knots of oppressed individuals made a gasp for relief by standing on the benches, and here and there, constantly recurring, yet never seeming to lead to any disagreeable consequences, were pugilistic matches, worthy, in scientific display, of the warmest admirers of Saville-house. Ladies disencumbered themselves of their bonnets, and screamed lustily when stout men were passed over their heads or thrown unreservedly upon them. The demands for 'porter' and 'order', were about equal, though the former only was laudably attended to by a persevering potboy of compressible qualities.

At last 'a complete change, as if by magic,...came over the spectators. They sat themselves in regular layers, instead of confused heaps, and positively observed a modified silence'. This 'quiet, well-behaved audience' was rewarded 'by a most gorgeous and patriotic pantomime, under the title of *Harlequin and Little-One-Eye, Little-Two-Eyes, and Little-Three-Eyes; or, Beasts and Beauties'* in which Shepherd had transformed the Grimm folk-tale 'into an excruciatingly funny representation of the person and fate of the Czar'. There follows a summary of the plot, then the review concludes:

> The mechanism by which descents of fairies are accomplished, and coryphées turned out of silver cigar-boxes, is alone worth studying, without reverting either to the gorgeousness of the scenery or the patriotism of the plot. It is scarcely necessary to add that there was a dazzling denoument at last, and, if it came late, still seemed to come too soon for many of the delighted and vociferous spectators.

The poor reception of *The Foundling of the Forest* probably led to its being replaced by *The Seven Poor Travellers,* a dramatised version of one of Charles Dickens's Christmas stories. Another new dramatic production was *King Richard III,* with 'New and Extensive Scenery, Magnificent Dresses, Real Armour, Splendid Appointments, and Numerous Auxiliary Aid'. It does sound rather splendid, with Creswick as Richard, Shepherd as Henry Earl of Richmond and Mrs Ternan as Elizabeth (queen of Edward IV). Until this production, one could hardly call Shepherd a Shakespearean actor, but from now on one finds him in this field, graduating to major roles in a short space of time.

Another play which is revived to this day saw an early performance at the Surrey – Dion Boucicault's *London Assurance* on 12 March 1855 – so presumably he was not too upset at being forestalled over *The Corsicans.* One scene in *London Assurance* requires a fire engine to come on stage; with the Surrey's 'real water' tradition, I should think a good time was had by one and all.

The playbill for 23 April 1855 showed that:

> In consequence of the Great Success which, last season, attended the Engagement of MR. PHELPS (of the Theatre Royal, Sadler's Wells) The Management have much Pleasure in announcing that they have again succeeded in making an arrangement with that Gentleman For A Limited Number Of Nights, during which he will appear with MR. CRESWICK in a Round of Shakespearian Plays, commencing on Monday next, April 30th.

Phelps actually appeared several weeks before this announcement, in *Seven Poor Travellers* for example, and with Creswick in *The Iron Mask.* The Shakespeare plays staged were *Othello* and *Julius Caesar* as earlier, but *King John* instead of *King Lear,* with Phelps in the name part.

The 1855 opera season, the last under Emma Romer, showed other organisational changes. Edward Stirling was back as acting and stage manager, Dickie Flexmore was ballet master, and an important new functionary gets similar billing – Mr Hinckley, the 'Gas Superintendent', producing the gases needed for the lime-light. Another introduction was of 'PIT STALLS (to which Ladies are admitted without the Inconvenience of removing their Bonnets)' but as the price was three shillings, as against two shillings for the boxes, the idea was soon scrapped.

The season included the world première of *Mephistopheles; or, Faust and Marguerite* by Meyer Lutz, to a libretto by Henri Drayton who had translated *La Juive* the previous year and now sang the title role in the new work. It was unfortunate for Herr Lutz that, four years later, Gounod's *Faust* was produced, consigning his work to an oblivion even more profound than that which engulfs Paisiello's *Barber of Seville.* Nevertheless it is worth comparing the two works. Both set only Part 1 of Goethe's masterpiece, unlike Boito's *Mefistofele* of 1868 which sets both parts. The sequence of scenes in Lutz's opera is followed exactly by Gounod: Faust's study; the Baccanal with the students; Marguerite's garden; the ballet sequence (danced at the Surrey by Flexmore and his wife, Madame Auriol) and finally the Cathedral. Of course one cannot say that Gounod 'copied' Lutz, any more than Rossini 'copied' Paisiello. At most, the later composer can see where his predecessor succeeded and where he failed, and act accordingly.

The other operas produced were *La Sonnambula, Lucia di Lammermoor* and *Norma,* with a return visit of the prima donna, Mlle. Nau, supported by many of the company of previous years: Henri Drayton and his new wife (formerly Miss Lowe), Oliver Summers (the singer who doubled 'witch/ Siward' in the two 1847 productions of *Macbeth),* and St Albyn. There were also revivals of *Robert the Devil* and *The Bohemian Girl.*

On 22 September 1855 *The Times* reported the start of the London dramatic season, in which Drury Lane and Covent Garden were given over to foreign imports:

> While we ramble about in the most various directions to watch the progress of the national poetical drama in its state of exile, now sauntering along the rural banks of the New River to Mr Phelps's Temple of Melpomene, now penetrating the mysterious recesses of Marylebone in search of Mr W.

> Wallack, now hurrying down the unfashionable high road of Shoreditch, not to travel by the Eastern Counties Railway, but to visit the National Standard, which is placed opposite to the station, we ought not to overlook the exertions of nearer neighbours. We allude to Messrs. Shepherd and Creswick, the managers of the Surrey Theatre who are certainly doing great things in the cause of suburban legitimacy.

Shakespeare at the Surrey is said to be 'handsomely dressed and ornamented' and the house 'spick-and-span' after renovation. *Henry IV Part 1,* the opening play, was

> put upon the stage in a most praiseworthy style. Time-honoured characters are clothed in sparkling costumes; real armour clatters on the shoulders of doughty retainers; the scenes glow brightly from the canvas; the martial groups are so disposed that the modern Briton, reminded of the warlike disposition of his ancestors, is spirited into applause and associates Shrewsbury with the Crimea.

So the reviewer finds the production 'a real, good, stirring spectacle'. The performers are equally esteemed:

> Great pains, too, have been taken with the acting.... We dare say an overwhelming majority of our readers have never in their lives seen the name of Mr Vollaire,... but we can assure the play-going world that this Mr Vollaire... is an actor who can play Falstaff with force and unction, maintaining through his jollity an humourous gravity which many well-known actors miss altogether, and requiring little in the way of polish beyond a delicate suggestion that he should be somewhat more sparing of his lungs.... Mr H. Widdicombe has been stock 'funny man' at the Surrey for several years, in the broad sort of melodrama, but he plays the drawer Francis like a refined comic artist. The changes that come over his voice and countenance, when he grows less obedient to the summons of Poins, and the tempting offers of the Prince, cause him to infuse a tone of impatience into his perpetual 'Anon – anon, Sir', and are genuine touches of nature, given in the best style.

Managers Shepherd and Creswick are also praised for their acting, the first as 'the madcap Prince', the other 'fuming and fretting' as Hotspur. Then the 'grandiloquent Glendower... for the first time within the memory of man is conjured from the bookshelves and allowed to tread the stage as he ought'. When the curtain had 'fallen on the maiden victory of the future hero of Agincourt', the afterpiece, *Sam Patch,* was performed by 'Mr J. M'Vicker, a very racy American comedian, who has just come from the other side of the Atlantic'. He made the audience laugh, despite the play's tedium and absurdity, 'and therefore great in his triumph'.

The reference to Agincourt reminds me that, although everyone knows that the battle was won by the English archers, no-one can put a name to a single one of them. Generally speaking one cannot put names to the back-stage staff of a theatre, but at pantomime-time nearly everyone gets a mention: the machinery by Mr Rough, the scenery by Mr Dalby, assisted by Messrs. H. Sanders, [Charles] Brew, Cracknell, Burry, and Poole; the dresses by Mr and Mrs Vokes, the fairy devices by Mr Hall, the gas devices by Mr Pitt, the dances by Miss Frampton, the comic scenes by William Dorrington. It is perhaps not surprising to find Mr Cracknell, the scenery assistant, turning up in Shepherd's Czarist pantomime as one of the Russian villains, Snortem Growlemoff, though one does not expect another assistant, Mr H. Sanders, to be transformed into Harlequin! Then for the rest of the year most of these disappear into the shadow of the stars.

Mr J.H. McVicker was not the only American billed for that evening. The playbills announced that 'The Celebrated American Tragedian, Mr CHARLES BARRY will make his First Appearance in England as Hotspur', but this seems to have eluded the *Times* critic. If Creswick played Hotspur (as seems most likely, for he played the part again in 1859) then *Henry IV Part 1* also eluded Barry.

The Crimea still provided inspiration to the dramatists. J.E. Carpenter gave the Surrey *Love and Honour* – 'Act III Before Sebastopol' – which opened on 5 November 1855 and ran until displaced by the Christmas pantomime. The playbills were headed:

> Read what 'The Times' says of the Surrey Pantomime. 'Great as Mr Shepherd notoriously is in the production of Pantomime, he has undoubtedly outdone all his former efforts this year. As a spectacle, *A Prince of Pearls; or, Harlequin and Jane Shore,* may vie in magnificence and scenic effects with the most celebrated of the Lyceum burlesques, while the fun and humour of the comic business would alone insure the success of half-a-dozen pantomimes. Clearly the Management has been deaf to all promptings of economy in putting their Christmas piece on the stage – for beauty and splendour it is a triumph of mechanical effects and gorgeous decoration.'

I wonder whether the fulsomeness of this notice had anything to do with the fact that one of the scenes was set in the *Times* Newspaper Office; presumably the comic business was not too malicious. The notice is followed by a long puff by the management, full of excruciating puns; one has to know that there had just been an election in Southwark to appreciate the statement that the scene-painter had 'waited until the whole of the Borough was Canvassed, to Buy it all up'. No local knowledge is required for the warning that 'the Public are requested not to come in Ready-Made Clothes, as the frequent calls for Bursts of Laughter will be such that the Stitches Won't Stand It'. Another gag was to make the Duke of Gloucester a 'double Gloucester' (cheese) played by both Buck and George Yarnold. The new art of photography is mocked as 'the Foe to graphic art – Harlequin becomes a customer – Animated likeness – Pantaloon gets a striking likeness – Clown and Pantaloon get framed likenesses'. One can picture the 'business' that filled out these promises.

This pantomime ran nearly to Easter 1856. On Easter Monday a new piece was launched, *How We Live in the World of London,* based on Henry Mayhew's classic study of *London Labour and the London Poor.* There were fourteen scenes, including the exterior of Whitechapel workhouse, the dark arches under the Adelphi and the parlour of Mother Midnight's Dolly Shop. The adaptation was by J.B. Johnstone who, eight years earlier, was prompter and Pantaloon; he wrote in parts for his daughters to play two children in the new piece. I wonder whether Johnstone had any anguished self-criticism in considering one of Mayhew's scenes which describes the behaviour of a Surrey-type audience:

> At each step up the well-staircase the warmth and stench increase, until by the time one reaches the gallery door-way, a furnace-heat rushes out through the entrance that seems to force you backwards, whilst the odour positively prevents respiration. The mob on the landing, standing on tiptoe and closely wedged together, resists any civil attempt at gaining a glimpse of the stage, and yet a coster lad will rush up, elbow his way into the crowd, then jump up on to the shoulders of those before him, and suddenly disappear into the body of the gallery....

No, this is not at the Surrey, but at the Victoria. But should one dramatise the low behaviour at the place up the road? Hardly kind. Anyway, why give them free publicity? So he left it out.

A short season brought Mr and Mrs Keeley back to the Surrey with revivals of *Jack Sheppard* and *Martin Chuzzlewit* amongst others. Then it was time for the 1856 opera season, starting not at Whitsun as usual but a month later, on 9 June. This calls for a new chapter.

Chapter Twenty-Five

'A Big Mistake' (1856-60)

In 1856 Shepherd and Creswick caught a bad dose of Bunn's Disease, we might say, which was characterised by delusions of grandeur. They thought that they could pull the opera buffs from north of the Thames by putting on opera in Italian without losing the support of their faithful local audience despite doubling the prices. They soon found they could not. They had to cut their losses and end the season after only three weeks, followed by an unprecedented ten-week gap which must have added to their financial embarrassment.

They started off in high hopes, announcing:

> In attempting the introduction of Italian Operas at the above Theatre, the Directors desire respectfully to state, that they have spared no Expense in their endeavours to reflect credit upon the Establishment, and to satisfy the requirements of Musical Art. Every effort has been made to ensure the perfection of the Entertainments, and the Comfort and Convenience of the Audience.

They were to start with *Norma* on 9 June 1856. The British Library has an interesting draft playbill presumably never posted. It gives the Norma as Madame Caradori. In fact the role was sung by Madame Lorini, while Caradori sang the title role in *Lucrezia Borgia*. The Flavio in *Norma* is given as Signor N.N., the associate of that famous English cricketer, A.N. Other. The role was eventually taken by Signor Monte.

The Times of 11 June thought well of the venture:

> An attempt to introduce Italian opera on the Surrey side of the Thames is now being made, for the first time, under the auspices of Mr Willert Beale, and seems likely to prove successful. The opera of *Norma,* selected to start with, in consequence no doubt of its very extended popularity, was given last night for a second time, and for the most part in a highly efficient manner. Madame Lorini (from New York) who assumes the part of Norma, has a voice of powerful tone and good quality, sings with great energy, and looks the Druid Princess to the life. As an actress, too, the lady is evidently no novice. She treads the boards with ease, her gestures are graceful, and she is thoroughly familiar with the business of the stage....

Others commended are the Oroveso (Fortini), the Adalgisa (Mlle Sedlatzek) and the Pollio (Lorini, though he has 'a certain want of refinement'). The singers

> derive valuable support from a band of about 35, under the direction of Mr Alfred Mellon, and a chorus, which, though not numerous, is composed, like the band, of experienced performers. The mise en scene is complete and appropriate; and, indeed, everything has been done to propitiate and deserve the favour of the public. Madame Lorini seems to be in especial favour and from the opening cavatina 'Casta Diva' to the end of the opera is overwhelmed with applause.

Lucrezia Borgia was staged for the last three days of the first week and *Il Barbiere di Siviglia* was added to the programme in the second week, but by the end of June the season had fizzled out. Clearly the opera-goers north of the Thames were not being attracted in sufficient numbers and the Surrey-siders did not take to opera in a foreign language. Indeed they would not have it at any price, as Shepherd and Creswick found when they brought the prices down to the long-established two shillings, one shilling and, for the gallery, sixpence. The lost customers stayed away.

This box-office disaster signalled the end of operas sung in foreign languages at the Surrey, though there were plenty of later stagings of foreign operas translated into English. It also, much more regrettably, marked the end of an in-house opera company. With the retirement of Emma Romer and the hiring of outside companies, the 'permanent' or 'resident' team had evaporated and there was no longer a base on which an in-house season could be mounted. Perhaps it even suited the temperaments of Shepherd and Creswick, as they were dramatic actors with little or no reason to go out of their way to keep a competing art form alive. A big mistake though the introduction of opera in Italian proved to have been, the management survived.

There was no trace of a pre-planned programme until the dramatic season opened on 6 September 1856. The theatre was not completely dark during the preceding ten weeks. There was a benefit performance on 21 July for Tom Parry, the author, and a return visit on 4 August of 'Professor' Anderson, the Wizard of the North, with his programme of 'Magic and Mystery'. Also, from the autobiography of Mrs Calvert (Adelaide Biddles that was, of whom more later), it appears that a 'few weeks' before their marriage on 31 August 1856 she played Julia in *The Hunchback* at a benefit arranged for Charles Calvert. I have been unable

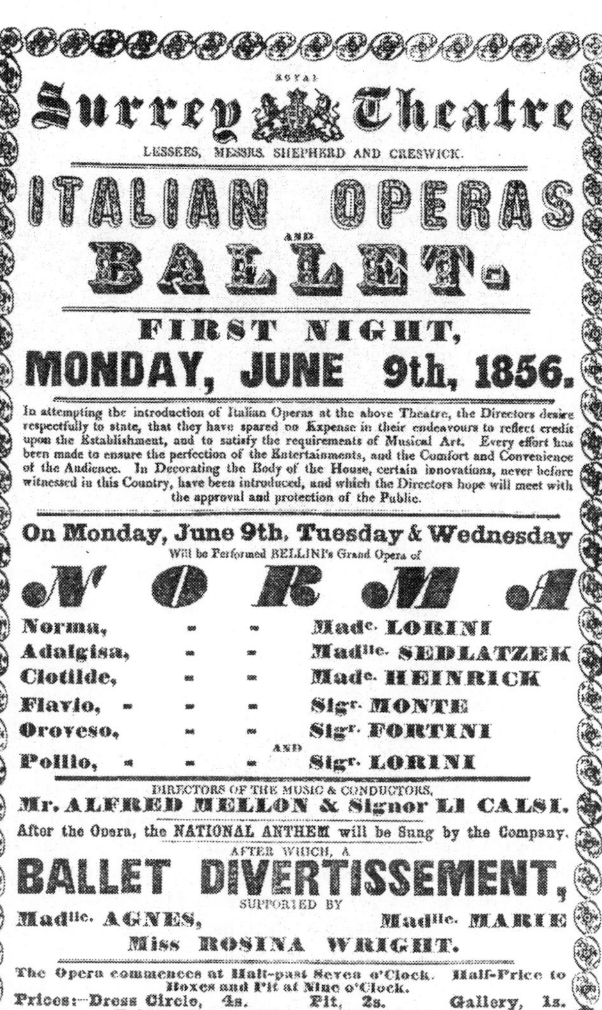

ROYAL

Surrey Theatre

LESSEES, MESSRS. SHEPHERD AND CRESWICK.

ITALIAN OPERAS

AND

BALLET.

FIRST NIGHT,

MONDAY, JUNE 9th, 1856.

In attempting the introduction of Italian Operas at the above Theatre, the Directors desire respectfully to state, that they have spared no Expense in their endeavours to reflect credit upon the Establishment, and to satisfy the requirements of Musical Art. Every effort has been made to ensure the perfection of the Entertainments, and the Comfort and Convenience of the Audience. In Decorating the Body of the House, certain innovations, never before witnessed in this Country, have been introduced, and which the Directors hope will meet with the approval and protection of the Public.

On Monday, June 9th, Tuesday & Wednesday

Will be Performed BELLINI's Grand Opera of

NORMA

Norma, - - Madᵉ. LORINI
Adalgisa, - - Madˡˡᵉ. SEDLATZEK
Clotilde, - - Madᵉ. HEINRICK
Flavio, - - - Sigʳ. MONTE
Oroveso, - - Sigʳ. FORTINI
AND
Pollio, - - - Sigʳ. LORINI

DIRECTORS OF THE MUSIC & CONDUCTORS,

Mr. ALFRED MELLON & Signor LI CALSI.

After the Opera, the NATIONAL ANTHEM will be Sung by the Company.

AFTER WHICH, A

BALLET DIVERTISSEMENT,

SUPPORTED BY

Madˡˡᵉ. AGNES, Madˡˡᵉ. MARIE

Miss ROSINA WRIGHT.

The Opera commences at Half-past Seven o'Clock. Half-Price to Boxes and Pit at Nine o'Clock.

Prices:—Dress Circle, 4s. Pit, 2s. Gallery, 1s.

Private Boxes. £2 10s., £2 2s., & £1 1s.

John K. Chapman and Company, Printers, 5, Shoe Lane, and Peterborough Court, Fleet Street.

to put an exact date on this performance, but it looks like another effort to keep the company in touch and rescue something from the disaster.

For their pre-Christmas season Shepherd and Creswick played safe with four tried-and-true Surrey formulas – Shakespeare, drama translated from the French, blood-and-thunder and farce. Characteristically the blood-and-thunder was by far the most successful.

Their first offering, on 8 September 1856, was *The Half-Caste*. The next day's *Times* mentioned that the 'French original from which the piece is taken was brought out at the Porte St Martin, early in the present year', and that in

> the Surrey version... a comic personage is introduced for the sake of the ever-welcome Widdicomb, who on this occasion represents Lord Adolphus Snooksby, a very strange specimen of the English aristocracy, who is perpetually beginning to tell an anecdote about a certain walk in Regent-street, but is never suffered to bring his tale to a conclusion.

Their next production, on 20 October 1856, was a dramatised version of Mrs Harriet Beecher Stowe's second anti-slavery novel, *Dred,* a best-seller only published that year. The colourful *Times* review makes it clear how the roles of hero and villain were enhanced for the benefit of the Surrey audiences, and is worth quoting at length:

> Whatever impression may be made upon any given reader by Mrs Stowe's last novel, – whether he weeps or yawns, sympathizes or disbelieves – the last thing he will dream of will be the possibility of using the story he has just perused as the plot of a drama producible on the English stage. Dred himself, with his mouth perpetually overflowing with Scriptural phraseology, scarcely utters six lines that would be considered tolerable if spoken within the walls of a theatre. The cholera, which makes a great figure in the book, is a nemesis that does not readily wear a picturesque form, and, though Mademoiselle Piccolomini may render consumption delightful [as La Traviata] and Madame Ristori may confer beauty on the fever caused by malaria [as Auber's Manon], this particular scourge has about it an amount of solid prose that no idealism can dilute. Nina Gordon, charming creature as she is, manifests herself rather in talk than in action, and though her lively rattle is most agreeable in print it is not at all fitted for a stage, where every word should be uttered with some definite purpose. That camp meetings and Presbyterian conferences are theatrical impossibilities is obvious beyond the need of explanation.

The writer sums up the conversion of *Dred* into a play, therefore, as 'a tolerably hard puzzle for the exercise of human ingenuity'. The problem has nonetheless been solved effectively at the Surrey:

> In performing his difficult task the author of the dramatized *Dred* has chiefly employed his energies in making the sable hero a more practical personage than he is in the narrative. The Stowe Dred is a first-rate Biblical scholar, who would answer you with pages from the Hebrew prophets if you only inquired the way to the next inn; but, it must be confessed, his performances fall far short of his predictions. Now the Surrey Dred, precluded from the use of Scriptural language, is the most active creature in the world. His eye is everywhere, and his foot speedily follows his eye; so that if ever a slave is going to be flogged, or a fugitive is about to be apprehended, Dred is sure to be at hand with a rifle and a brace of pistols, and the delivery of the oppressed comes as a matter of course....

As Dred now needs 'some adversary sufficient to call forth his energies', the character of Tom Gordon is also built up:

> Mrs Stowe has drawn that young gentleman as a very unpleasant ruffian, but he is a babe of innocence, a marvel of loving-kindness compared to the Tom Gordon of the Surrey stage. With a huge whip perpetually in his hand, this fine specimen of a planter seems ever on the point of literally 'flogging all creation'. He bullies women, he kicks children, he talks of 'whipping till the blood falls from the back' as a lively operation; 'rubbish' and 'trash' are the civilest words that fall from his lips when addressing the coloured race. Let us add that his opportunities for brutality are considerably more frequent than in the book;... not only is Cora forced to work on Tom Gordon's cotton plantation, but she is literally flogged by his order till the executioner is laid low by the knife of the ever ready Dred....

Old 'Tiff', says the reviewer, is entertainingly transferred to the stage with little change save for bearing pistols to help at Tom Gordon's overthrow. In Tiff the comic actor Widdicomb achieves new fame. Not only does he 'elicit the frequent roars of his audience' but less predictably 'his occasional touches of pathos deserve especial commendation'.

Dred ran for forty-one nights – not as good as *Uncle Tom's Cabin* four years before, but it must have helped the treasury after the opera losses. It was followed by a short season of Shakespeare and French drama, starting with *Othello* on 8 December, and then *Romeo and Juliet.*

Here we see a future *grande dame* of the theatre at the start of her adult success in the girl who played *Dred's* Nina Gordon and Juliet, namely Adelaide Biddles or Bedells (1837-1921). She had been acting professionally since she was six. From the Surrey she went on to command a major position with her husband Charles Calvert, especially in Manchester with their outstanding Shakespearean seasons. Their careers are traced in Richard Foulkes's book *The Calverts: Actors of Some Importance* and in Mrs Calvert's own memoirs. All eight of their children followed them on the stage, Louis Calvert being the best-remembered. The *Times* critic of 18 December 1856, reviewing *Romeo and Juliet* at the Surrey, was prescient in suggesting a good future for Adelaide:

> The revival of *Romeo and Juliet* at this house, while it has advantageously brought forward both the managers, – for Mr Creswick displays all his chivalric gallantry in Romeo, and Mr Shepherd puts forth all his gaiety in Mercutio – exhibits in a new light the talent of Miss Adelaide Biddles, a young lady who, during the early part of the season, did not stray beyond the limits of ordinary melodrama, but whose unaffected and touching representation of Nina Gordon is doubtless still fresh in the memory of transpontine dilettanti. This young actress now plays Juliet and brings with her the physical qualifications of a commanding yet delicate figure, a distinct but not unfeminine voice, and a profusion of raven hair well adapted to the hapless fair one of Verona. In the traditional business of the character she is thoroughly versed, and in pourtraying both the gentler and the stronger emotions she manifests an amount of genuine feeling that may obtain for her a position more generally recognized than that which she at present holds.

The same review presents further interest for us as it looks on to the current productions in the suburbs generally:

> Next week the whole theatrical interest of the metropolis will be immersed in the ocean of pantomime but it is worthy of record that the suburban establishments preserve to the last their veneration for Shakespeare. At the Surrey, *Romeo and Juliet* alternates with Mr Charles Wray's version of the French drama *Les Oiseaux de Proie;* at the Standard the accomplished Miss Glyn plays Lady Macbeth; at the City of London Theatre Mr Rickards becomes 'legitimate', and enacts the Moor of Venice. Nor let us forget the equestrian *Macbeth* at Astley's. Fidelity to the national poet is a lasting virtue in the outposts of London.

And after Shakespeare, the pantomime:

> Nothing save the well-deserved celebrity of this first of transpontine houses for its pantomimes could ever have drawn together such an overflowing audience as was last night seen collected within its walls. An eager throng besieged the doors long before admittance could be obtained, and no sooner was access given than the surging stream rushed in at every inlet with a fearful impetus, filling the building from floor to ceiling with a rapidity almost inconceivable. In the frantic scramble for places that ensued, confusion the most indescribable reigned triumphant; and the blank despair depicted in the looks of the bewildered box-keepers, assailed at one and the same moment by crowds of distracted candidates for front seats, could not astonish, but might excite the pity of the most exigeant spectator.

In short, a typical Boxing-night crowd at the Surrey!

With support from classics like *Virginius* and *A New Way to Pay Old Debts,* the pantomime ran till 7 March 1857. Dickie Flexmore and his wife, Madame Auriol, then had a four-week ballet season, though hardly classic: *The Dumb Savoyard and His Monkey* sounds too much like Monsieur Gouffé! It dates from that period as well, as Davidge had put it on at the Coburg way back in July 1830.

The opera season which followed was sung exclusively in English. The expensive lesson of 1856 had been well learned. The National English Opera Company under the direction of the old Surrey hand, J.H. Tully, presented fifteen operas in its twelve-week season. In the absence of an in-house company Tully brought all his own singers. I cannot trace that any of them had met a Surrey audience before. An advertisement a few weeks earlier had announced:

> The National English Opera Company (from the Theatre Royal, Drury Lane). Last week but one of their provincial tour, owing to the commencement of their London season at the Royal Surrey Theatre, on Whit Monday, June 1 1857. They will give their 333rd representation THIS EVENING, May 11 at the Theatre Royal, Bath. They have also to fulfil engagements at Bristol and Cheltenham. The company comprises the following distinguished artistes; Lucy Escott, Miss Lanza, Miss Dyer, Miss Cronin, Mr Henry Haigh, Mr Manvers, Mr Charles Durand, Mr Ainsley Cooke, Mr Temple and Mr Henry Squires.

They opened at the Surrey with *Maritana* and *The Bohemian Girl* alternating in the first week, and *La Traviata* the whole of the second week. That was an unusual week for London opera-goers. Three houses were staging opera, and one could hear any opera one liked provided it was Verdi! *La Traviata* could be heard in Italian at Covent Garden, the same in English at the Surrey, and *Il Trovatore* in English 'with Equestrian Illustrations' at Astley's. The last contribution cannot be lightly dismissed, as it was under the baton of Meyer Lutz, with many of Emma Romer's old company – Rebecca Isaacs, Augustus Braham, Adam Leffler and Borrani, all old Surrey favourites. And to demonstrate that anything the Surrey could do, so could Astley's on horseback, Astley's followed the Surrey *Maritana* and *La Sonnambula* with equestrian versions. The Surrey retaliated by staging *Il Trovatore* without horses. *The Times* of 20 July reported:

> The travels of *Il Trovatore* have indeed been extensive. When Mr W. Cooke, of Astley's, having made Shakespeare ride on horseback for about two seasons, resolved to furnish the lyrical drama likewise with equestrian support, *Il Trovatore* was the first work selected for his experiment. The operatic season having duly set in at the Surrey, the same work has been produced, under the superintendence of Mr Tully, and is executed in very creditable style.

Though described as a better singer than actor, the young tenor Henry Squires is said to show much promise as Manrico, having 'a chest voice of great compass'. His big moment is 'the famous "Miserere", in which the quality of his organ and his power of expression are displayed to perfection, and which is, of course, encored'. The gesticulating passion of Lucy Estcott as Leonora contrasts with 'the quietitude of Mr Squires' and Charles Durand's 'unruffled' Count di Luna. Acuzena gets the balance right:

> The most finished performance in every respect is the Acuzena of Miss Lanza, who not only sings the music in artist-like style, but acts in a free, unconstrained manner that happily avoids both tameness and exaggeration. The chorusses are executed with great spirit, and the manner in which the whole work is done shows high talent... on the part of the musical director. He finds his reward in the enthusiasm among the audience that is most remarkable considering the warmth of the weather.

These days, the mind boggles at the thought of there being twice as much opera Surrey-side as in the West End; also, at the fact that on the same evening at the Surrey one could see both *Il Trovatore* AND *The*

Daughter of the Regiment or, another evening, *La Traviata* AND *La Sonnambula.*

The Surrey production of *Der Freischutz* opened on 17 June 1857 and is intriguing in that the hero is given the name Rudolph instead of Max. The last time that happened had been thirty years earlier in Elliston's time. Did they dust off some old parts which had been lying in the cellar since then?

Most of the other operas were already familiar to the public – *Lucia di Lammermoor, Norma, Fra Diavolo, Masaniello,* and the home-grown *Waterman, Beggar's Opera* and *The Quaker* – but they heard *Esmeralda,* based on *The Hunchback of Notre Dame,* for the first time. This opera, originally called *Ermilinda,* was written by Battista in 1851, translated into English by C. Jefferys, and premiered at Drury Lane. At the Surrey it played four nights, with Lucy Escott as Esmeralda and Ainsley Cooke as Quasimodo. In this season *La Traviata* was heard at the Surrey for the first time, with Lucy Escott as Violetta, Henry Haigh as Alfred and Charles Durand as Germont. But nothing is sacred. I regretfully have to report that, at the end of the opera season, the Surrey was putting on an operatic burlesque called *Our Traviata.*

The opera season finished on 22 August (*Il Trovatore* AND *Der Freischutz)* and after a three-week holiday the dramatic season started on 14 September 1857 with Shepherd in a new piece, *A Bird in the Hand Worth Two in the Bush.* There was also a new visiting company that autumn, rather late in the day as regards novelty but one to get into the history books – Christy's Minstrels, perhaps the best-known of its type.

The attention of the country was now being attracted towards the east, as reports of the Indian Mutiny began to reach the public consciousness. The Surrey, in what might be called its news-feature capacity, put on *India 1857* with W.H. Eburne as General Havelock and Basil Potter as Nanna Sahib 'the Leader of the Revolt'. It was first staged in three acts on 9 November, but evidently did not 'go', as after a fortnight it was re-staged as 'revised and compressed into Two Acts'. Probably it was outclassed by Astley's *The Storming and Capture of Delhi* which was running at the same time; the stories coming out of India at the time lent themselves well to equestrian treatment. The Surrey piece staggered on for another couple of weeks but disappeared without even the seasonal excuse that all must give way to the pantomime. Creswick filled the gap so successfully with one of his swashbuckling roles that no-one reading the *Times* critic on 30 November would realise that *India 1857* had been performed. The entire review was devoted to its companion piece:

> A four-act drama, entitled *The Wife's Revenge; or, The Masked Riders,* has been produced at this house with considerable success. The action is supposed to take place at the time when Charles I removed his court to Oxford, and the hero, Sir Everard Tracy, is a staunch Cavalier, who, at the head of a party of comrades, called, from the vizards on their faces, the 'masked riders', makes himself the terror of the neighbouring Parliamentarians. Constantly captured, he as often escapes, and it is the general principle of the drama that he appears to be in an inextricable scrape about the middle of each act, but is as free as air at the moment when the drop scene falls....

It sounds just the thing for a radio or television serial. It certainly made a fine starring vehicle. As the *Times* remarks, the hero places himself 'in a position something like that of Arturo in *I Puritani,* where the melodious Cavalier drove his sweetheart mad by aiding the same Royal personage'. The review describes it as 'a good bustling melodrama', though burdened with much ineffective 'poetical' dialogue. Its success is mainly due to Creswick. As Sir Everard he 'becomes for the nonce the perfection of a Cavalier, gay in temperament, gentlemanlike in manner, reckless in time of danger, and gallant always'. Mention is also made of Miss Eburne's 'troublesome wife' and the 'ill-advising Roundhead guardian' of Basil Potter, while Mr Vollaire, 'concealing a fair proportion of his face by an artificial red nose, creates mirth as a debauched and cowardly Parliamentarian'. The conclusion generalises:

> It will be observed that the interest of the drama is altogether on the Royalist side; the brave, the handsome, and the generous espouse the cause of Charles; the cowardly, the ugly, and the grovelling sympathize with the Parliament. All this is in perfect accordance with the system of stage politics, as established for the last two centuries. Whatever may be the political tendency of a particular period, the Cavalier is sure to be the popular figure with a theatrical audience... in opposition to the Puritan.

The pantomime for Boxing Night 1857 was *Queen Mab; or, Harlequin Romeo and Juliet,* with the 'Surrey Buck' as Clown; Miss Willmott was Columbine and Glover the harlequin, with Bradbury as Pantaloon and 'Young Bond' as Sprite. There always had been sprites associated with the Surrey pantomimes, but here was one claiming equal billing with the traditional leads.

It is unusual for one theatre to give unsolicited testimonials to another. In March 1858 the Royal Soho Theatre was advertising 'The

Production of the CELEBRATED SURREY DRAMA called *THE CHARMING POLLY*'. This was one of J.T. Haines's works, commissioned in Davidge's day.

At the Surrey the dramatic season ran until 29 May 1858. The new season commencing on 7 June was given over in its three months' entirety to Benjamin Webster and his company, 'during the re-building of the Adelphi'. Generally this meant that a theatre had been destroyed by fire but in this case it was a planned exercise, reminiscent of the days when Yates brought the Adelphi company to the Surrey year after year. On 2 June 1858 the Adelphi advertised the 'last night of the old popular and pet Adelphi Theatre. Mr B. Webster will address the audience on past successes and future prospects. Notice to Engineers. This Theatre to be rebuilt by Tender...'. Most of the pieces taken to its temporary home had been seen at the Surrey before, though a fortnight's novelty of Irish pieces was provided by Mr and Mrs Barney Williams. *The Flowers of the Forest* was revived with Ira Aldridge and Miss Aldridge, and an old Surrey hand, William Smith, as acting manager. Also in the Adelphi company was someone who had made his name on the Surrey boards twenty-five years earlier, Gallot – but this time there was no dead camel to haunt him. Another old Surrey play, *Jack Sheppard,* was put on with a difference, as the name part was played by Mrs Billington. But then, the Surrey had shown the way by mounting its own production of *Jack Sheppard* two years earlier with Mrs Keeley in the title role.

The playbills then announced that the Surrey Theatre would 'open for the Dramatic Season Under the Management of Messrs. Shepherd & Creswick on Monday, September 27. Doors open at Six O'Clock. Commence at Half Past. During the Recess the Theatre will BE GREATLY IMPROVED and RE-EMBELLISHED. A New & Magnificent Curtain by Dalby'. The 1858 cast list included 'Mrs Hudson Kirby (the Popular Tragic Actress, late of this Theatre, her First Appearance in England since her Return from America)'. She was the widow of J. Hudson Kirby who had been savaged by Osbaldiston and had appeared at the Surrey in Mrs Davidge's time; he died at the early age of twenty-nine.

Praised by *The Times* as Juliet a year previously, Miss Adelaide Biddles now appears as Mrs Charles Calvert, with her husband who was the Surrey's junior leading man. They appeared together in various pieces during the season. I get the impression that the management were running three mini-companies. Time and again one finds in the evening's programme Creswick in something fairly highbrow such as Shakespeare, supported by Mrs Hudson Kirby and Basil Potter; Shepherd in melodrama or comedy, supported by Fernandez; and Widdicomb by himself or in a 'screaming farce'.

On Monday 20 December 1858 there was 'A Grand Extra Night' with Phelps of Sadler's Wells as guest artist playing Othello to Creswick's Iago. The following night brought back a number of favourite pieces including *The Hunchback* and the ballad-opera *The Waterman.* Two other guest artists, Rebecca Isaacs and John Buckstone, came back to their old haunts on the Wednesday. Then the doors were shut for a couple of nights while the pantomime was set up. Its title was *Harlequin Father Thames and the River Queen; or, The Great Lord Mayor of London.* Buck was, of course, Clown. There were some new principals: Mlle Rosine was Columbine and last year's Sprite had bifurcated into the 'brothers Talleen'.

An old favourite, *The Lady of Lyons* by Bulwer Lytton, was revived on 14 March 1859 with the Surrey regulars Potter and Vollaire supporting a guest artist, Miss Agnes Elsworthy, who played the part of Pauline Deschappelles; Creswick was Claude Melnotte. Shepherd's piece that week, *Unknown; or, the Heart of Honour,* also had a French setting in the time of Louis XIV. There were seven scenes in and about the Louvre, providing plenty of opportunity for Dalby, the stage designer, to show his talents. As might be expected, Henry Widdicomb appeared in 'the Screaming Farce' of *Nicodemus; or, A Ghost in Spite of Himself.*

The evening of 23 March 1859 was a benefit for the London Copper-Plate Printers' Benevolent and Pension Fund, when *Money* and *All That Glitters is not Gold* were staged. One trusts that the Benevolent and Pension Fund obtained both money and real gold, because this sounds like the same organisation as the Society of Copper Plate Printers whose benefit night at the Surrey on 13 September 1826, as we saw in chapter six, had caused Charles Dibdin the Younger to record: 'We were disgusted. After that season, we declined giving Charity Benefits'. Perhaps fences had been mended, or memories faded after thirty-odd years.

Shepherd took his own benefit on 4 April 'under the Especial Patronage of Admiral Sir Charles Napier K.C.B. and John Locke, Esq. the Member for the Borough of Southwark'. The bill included *Katherine and Petruchio* and *The Waterman.*

The three mini-companies came together on 19 May 1859 for Basil Potter's benefit night, when *Henry IV Part One* was revived. This had the same cast as that reviewed in the production of September 1855 – Creswick as Hotspur, Shepherd as the Prince, Vollaire as Falstaff and Widdicomb as Francis the pot-boy.

The 1858-59 dramatic season ended on Saturday 28 May. On the Wednesday there was an echo of the Surrey's 'nautical past' when *Black-Eyed Susan* was staged. Mrs Honner was a guest star in her old role of Susan, but it is not easy to imagine how well a new man, Ryder, did in

T.P. Cooke's role of William. On the Saturday there was an even more unlikely combination, with Shepherd as William and Mrs Hudson Kirby as Susan. Was this an occasion for a dramatic letting down of hair?

After two weeks the theatre re-opened, still with Shepherd and Creswick as lessees but otherwise nowhere to be seen, for the place was temporarily 'Under the Sole Management of Mr Charles Calvert'. He had acquired the services for six weeks of Herman Vezin and his wife – their 'first appearance in London' – and they appeared mainly in Shakespearean roles, Macbeth and Lady Macbeth, Hamlet and Ophelia, Shylock and Portia, Othello and Desdemona. Apart from the Calverts, the only Surrey regulars appearing were Miss Cuthbert, Miss Kemble and Vollaire. This 'fill-in' season finished on 23 July 1859. Tradition of the last thirty-odd years called for an opera season – and did not get it. Since its rebuilding in 1806, 1859 was the first year in which no opera whatsoever was staged at the Surrey. When one looks around London that summer there is no opera to be seen anywhere. The Royal Italian Opera Company of Covent Garden was on tour in the provinces; when it did return it was for a farewell performance only. Drury Lane and the Lyceum were 'to be let'. The only bright spot on the horizon was the Royal English Opera Company under the direction of Miss Louisa Pyne and W. Harrison, with Alfred Mellon as conductor. They were currently also on tour, announcing a return to London on 3 October. But not to the Surrey.

I do not know where Shepherd, Creswick and the rest of the Surrey company might be found during this summer. Perhaps they were on tour or appearing separately as guest artists. There were similar gaps in 1860 and 1861, with only the odd sightings of members of the company.

Later in 1859 it was advertised that 'the Royal Surrey will open on Saturday next October 1. The most costly and elegant theatre in London', but it was for drama only. A contemporary classic was re-written and put on under the name of *The Bridal of Beatriz.* After referring to the appearance on the stage of a coach drawn by 'horses with very human knees', *The Times* comments that, of course, 'purely literary judges will be greatly shocked at this profanation; but we are not sure that purely literary judges would be the safest advisers as to the best means of catering for the Surrey public'. In the same programme was yet another troupe of minstrels,

> called the 'Campbell Company'... aspiring to fame by that broad path which has been trod so successfully by Pell and his brethren, and by the Christy's Minstrels. In their part-songs their harmony is correct, their solo vocalists pleasing, their

> spoken jokes are numerous, and in their grotesque songs and dances they are perhaps more grotesque than any of their predecessors, their chief humorist being one 'Charlie Fox', a great celebrity in the United States.

The reviewer cautions the minstrels against 'prolixity' and too much pausing, recalling the Christy company's merit of pace in never allowing the audience 'to stop and think'. The theatre is said to have been re-decorated and 'presents a very light and cheerful appearance, while the costumes in the tragedy bear witness to the taste and liberality of the manager'.

On 25 October 1859 *The Times* again had space for the Surrey with a report that

> Last night Mr Shepherd the joint lessee of this house, made his first appearance for the season in a drama based on and named after Sir E.B. Lytton's novel *What Will He Do With It?* For himself he had chosen the character of Rugge, the itinerant manager and gave great effect to the mixture of slang, pomp and ruffianism that constitutes this social excrescence, his costume being in itself a visible manifestation of brag and insolence....

On 11 November *The Times* reported new pieces at the Surrey, each of the two lessees having chosen a vehicle for his individual talents. Creswick starred in a tragedy, *The Patriot Spy*. Shepherd chose *First Love,* adapted from *Le Chevalier St George,* an old St James's Theatre play under Lafont which furnished the plot for Balfe's opera *The Bondman:*

> The mulatto gentleman... who, in the last century, made such a noise in the fashionable world of Paris,... proficient in fencing, pistol shooting, riding, love-making, and, in short, of all the arts,... is played by Mr Shepherd with a great deal of force and address, and the devoted Countess is acted with much intelligence and earnestness by Miss Edith Heraud. The story of the piece... is both surprising and diverting to an audience not previously acquainted with its ramifications, while... the sentiments are of a kind that appeal to every multitude not trained in Transatlantic prejudice against the negro blood. For *First Love* we may fairly auger a permanent success.

Actually it only ran for three weeks.

The 1859 pantomime was *Harlequin King Holyday; or, the Fairies of the Enchanted Valley and the King that Once Killed a Cat.* As well as the regular evening performances, there was a 'Grand Morning

Performance on Monday January 2 and every succeeding Monday at 2 o'clock'. Matinees had arrived at the Surrey.

On 23 February 1860 the *Times* critic reported on a new piece at the Surrey Theatre with the title *Cause and Effect; or, The Dancing Girl of Marseilles.* The description of the plot goes on for half a column, but let us go straight to the final scene in which the villain, Mantueffel,

> enters the chateau disguised as a prefect of police, on the pretext of taking notes for the purpose of effecting his own apprehension, and Estelle accompanies him attired as his clerk. He carries off the Marchioness, but this is his last exploit, for before he can reach his vessel, Estelle has brought the gendarmerie to the bay, and he is shot in an endeavour to resist.

The piece is viewed as 'a capital specimen of its class' and its effect is heightened by the spirit with which Shepherd and Miss Sarah Thorne play the robber and the dancing girl, 'who stand as the good and evil principles of the story':

> One is the rollicking villain, who shrinks not from the perpetration of any crime, but whose 'pluck' and dexterity are such that he never becomes wholly unpopular; the other, slight in figure, is equally apt and determined, with all the advantages of moral justice on her side. Nor should we omit mention of the very pretty view of the Bay of Marseilles, which is shown by the light, first of the sun, afterwards of the moon.

There was a change of mood for the week beginning 2 April 1860, with 'The Popular Ballads of Old England. Vocalists Miss Poole and Mr Ramsden' set against 'Wood's American Burlesque Opera Company in their entertainment entitled *Ethiopian Life in America*'. Interesting transatlantic comparisons, no doubt!

It sometimes happened at this time for members of the aristocracy to indulge in amateur theatricals for the entertainment of their guests, even to hiring a working theatre for a day. Professional actors and actresses might well be 'invited' to give backbone to the production. At first sight it might appear from the Surrey playbills for the two weeks commencing 9 April 1860 as if – no doubt for a suitable cash contribution – such an opportunity were given to a pair of titled amateurs to play leading roles on the Surrey stage, with suitable support from the regulars, such as Vollaire and Fernandez. Would it seem risible to have T.P. Cooke's role as Long Tom Coffin in *The Pilot* being played by Sir William Don, with Lady Don as Kate Plowden? They also played Bob and Joan Cherry in *Rough and Ready* and Cousin Joe and Margery in *Rough Diamond;*

also the name parts in the farce *The Toodles.* These parts cover a wide range of histrionics, so if I add that Sir William was the seventh baronet, educated at Eton, commissioned in the 5th Dragoon Guards, owner of steeple-chasers, might one doubt that they were able to get the best (or the worst) out of these parts? In fact they were not amateurs at all. Sir William had sold the ancestral estates at Newton, Berwickshire, for £85,000 ten years before his Surrey appearances and gone on the stage, firstly in America for five years and then in Britain. His second wife, Emily Saunders, was a 'charming actress', the daughter of John Saunders of the Adelphi and once of the Queen's Theatre, Dublin.

In its review of 30 April 1860 *The Times* detected some literary piracy:

> A very amusing tale of jealousy and its cure is told at this theatre in the shape of a three act comedy entitled *The Godolphins.* The principal situations and the relations to each other of the chief characters are as nearly as possible those of *Jealous Wife.* Indeed, we may almost surmise that the author took Colman's comedy in hand for the express purpose of so modifying the plot as to render Major Oakley the leading personage.

Certainly it must have been very difficult to find enough different plots to satisfy an audience expecting something new nearly every night. To echo the views of Charles Dibdin the Younger, thirty-five years earlier, it is a wonder that the Surrey ever had any hits, as this implies extended runs. Presumably the regular clientele were then prepared to see the same piece several times in quick succession. The *Times* account concludes:

> A transpontine public cannot be expected to remain satisfied without a liberal allowance of melodramatic horrors, though it may be awed into an occasional worship of Shakspeare; but the success of this piece shows that it is also capable of deriving enjoyment from a picture of life in which crime has no part, and can appreciate a well conducted comedy, even when not influenced by the name of a celebrated author. The present managers of the Surrey are not violent reformers, who would effect such a thorough change as that of Sadler's Wells by Mr Phelps, but they have an evident disposition to elevate their public, and in these decentralizing days we should not be at all surprised if their house – one of the best built in London – became a recognized place for the production of important novelties.

Chapter Twenty-Six

Farewells (1860-62)

The advertisements for Saturday 16 June 1860 announced the 'First Night of the New Season' – but not under Shepherd and Creswick. Although they remained the joint lessees they do not appear in any of that week's productions. Nor do any of their main players: no Vollaire, no Widdicomb, no Basil Potter, no Sarah Thorne. In short it is much as it was at this time in the previous year. Presumably they are making guest appearances somewhere, either individually or as a company, but I have not been able to track them down. However the Surrey theatre was not dark. The clock had been turned back fifteen years. The place was again under the direction of Mrs Davidge's brother-in-law, Joseph Kerschner, after many years of faithful service in the box office 'daily from 11 till 3 o'clock'. The advertisements continue:

> First night of Tully's beautiful English ballad-opera, *WILLIAM AND SUSAN; or, All in the Downs* supported by Messrs. W.M. Parkinson, E. Rosenthal, E. Morrow, J.W. Morgan, O.W. Summers; Miss Rebecca Isaacs, Miss Fanny Huddart. An increased Band, efficient chorus, and augmented Ballet. Conductor, Mr J.H. Tully, who will preside in the orchestra. Leader of the Band, Mr Isaacson. Concluding with Gay's *BEGGAR'S OPERA* in which all the above talented artistes will perform. On Monday next, June 18, the first dramatic night, Mr John Douglass, proprietor of the Royal Standard and Pavilion Theatres, Mrs R. Honner, the great Surrey favourite, and a powerful company will appear in three dramas. N.B. Dramatic Nights, Mondays, Tuesdays, and Wednesdays. Grand Opera Nights, Thursdays, Fridays, and Saturdays.

The new opera, *William and Susan,* was, of course, yet another version of *Black-Eyed Susan* but with more music.

The bills for Monday 18 June announce that 'The Performances will commence with, (by permission of BENJAMIN WEBSTER, Esq.) not acted these 15 years, the impressive and interesting drama, with startling effects, in Three Acts, entitled – *THE ROVER'S SECRET*'. In the cast are those old-timers John Neville and Mrs Honner, and also J.B. Johnstone (who had adapted Henry Mayhew's *London Labour and the*

London Poor for the Surrey) together with his two daughters. The second piece was 'the Popular Nautical Drama, originally produced at this Theatre, entitled *Ben the Boatswain'*. What, nautical drama at the Surrey again? After all these years of French costume melodrama? And opera as well? Yes, Tully's *William and Susan* was to be repeated on 21 and 22 June,while 'Flotow's Opera of *Martha* is in active preparation'. One could not ask for a better helping of nostalgia.

Martha was brought in on 23 June with Miss Annie Long in the title role. *Macbeth* and *Maritana* followed, with musical contributions by Christy's Minstrels to provide variety. With *Martha* on 2 July was *The Spoil'd Child,* the vehicle used nearly forty years earlier to introduce Eliza Vincent, as the Little Pickle, to Surrey audiences. This time, it was for the 'great little child actress Miss Lelia Ross'.

The displayed advertisement in *The Times* of 6 July read:

> Under the direction of Mr J. Kerschner – The new romantic patriotic opera, entitled *Garibaldi, the Italian Liberator* will positively be produced on Monday next. Every care has been employed to render the exploits of the illustrious hero worthy of record. To-Night, a grand operatic performance of *Il Trovatore;* supported by an eminent operatic company, under the direction of Mr J.H. Tully.

A similar insert on 10 July announced the 'Transcendant success of Tully's patriotic English Opera, *Garibaldi, the Italian Liberator,* which was received with every demonstration of approval. Tumultuous acclamations of applause were bestowed throughout the entire opera, and its announcement for repetition elicited prolonged cheers. It will consequently be repeated every evening'. This puff was of course written by the management. The sad truth is that it only ran one week, was not reviewed by *The Times,* is not mentioned in Eric Walter White's *Register of... English Operas* and as far as I can trace is never heard of again.

Other operas in this brief month-long season were *The Waterman* and *The Bohemian Girl* for the home-grown product, and Frances Davidge's English version of *La Sonnambula,* brought out yet again. This was the last link with the Davidge era. Mrs Davidge and her brother-in-law Joseph Kerschner disappear from the story at this point. There are, though, indications that, much later, Joseph's daughter Frances Davidge Kerschner (my grandmother) was translating French plays for the Surrey.

Apart from a farewell benefit on 6 August 1860 for the comedian Henry Widdicomb to mark the end of his twelve-year association with the Surrey, the theatre was dark for two months. The darkness was

Plate IX Thomas Potter Cooke, Paris 1826
(famed in Paris for gothic-horror roles rather than nautical heroes)

Plate X Richard Shepherd
(soley or jointly lessee and manager of the Surrey Theatre, 1848–65)

Plate XI William Creswick
(jointly lessee and manager of the Surrey Theatre, 1849–62)

Plate XII View from the portico of the Royal Surrey Theatre, c. 1840
(note the horse-omnibus)

broken on 15 September by Dalby, the scenic artist, who turned the theatre – according to the advertisements – into 'The Hall of a Thousand Lights, gorgeous and brilliant effect!'

Then *The Times* of 17 September 1860 reported:

> On Saturday night Messrs. Shepherd and Creswick inaugurated their winter season by the production of two long dramas, which for nearly six solid hours afforded vast satisfaction to an audience remarkable alike for its extreme density and for its disposition to burst forth into a thunder of grateful acknowledgment whenever an established favourite came upon the stage. Equally strong was a determination to welcome Mr Charles Rice, a gentleman who has gained a high celebrity for 'fun' at some of the eastern theatres, and who appeared for the first time at the Surrey on Saturday. The cries of 'Bravo Charley' and 'Go a-head Charley' which accompanied his achievements proved that his fame was perfectly familiar to his new public.... Both the dramas gave complete satisfaction to the audience, and the Surrey season has thus commenced amid general good-humour.

Rice was the successor to Henry Widdicomb. The previously-established pattern of an evening's entertainment continued, namely drama featuring Creswick, melodrama with Shepherd and farce built round the 'funny man'. About the only scrap of documentation for this period which survived the fire of 1865 is the'Pay List for the week ending Friday, October 18th 1861', now held by Southwark Local History Library. It shows Rice as the highest-paid employee at £6 a week (say equivalent to £400 in the later 1990s) with James Fernandez and Esther Jacobs at £4, Georgiana Pauncefort at £3:10s (£3-50p) and Vollaire at £3:5s (£3-25p). Seven ladies of the ballet are listed, but no musical or operatic staff. The two scenic artists, Messrs. Brew and Johnson, who succeeded Dalby, received £3:10s and £2:10s respectively. The full list is reproduced in the appendix.

In July 1860 Wilkie Collins finished his novel *The Woman in White*. It had been serialised in Dickens's monthly magazine *All the Year Round* and had proved an outstanding success. Any such success was likely material for conversion to dramatic form, but on this occasion the Surrey management did not keep its plans as well concealed as when *Oliver Twist* had been snatched from under Dickens's nose. In a letter to his publisher Wilkie Collins wrote: 'They are going to dramatise the story at the Surrey Theatre, and I am asked to go to law about that. I will certainly go and hiss unless the manager makes a "previous arrangement" with me'. There is no mention of hissing in the *Times* report of 8 November 1860:

> The production of a dramatic version of Mr Wilkie Collins's *Woman in White,* with Mr Creswick as the famous Count Fosco, has created no small sensation at the Surrey Theatre. Places suited for standing only are occupied as on the occasion of some great holyday.... If once a tale becomes generally popular, a desire to see it in a dramatic form immediately spreads like an epidemic.... Whether a story be fitted for stage purposes or not people do not inquire, nor even care. They only want to see the personages they have read about clothed in a visible form, and turn from the book to the stage as a child turns from letter-press to pictures.

The writer refers to the length of an average novel as being at least eight times that of a play, causing the playwright to cut much that the novelist had deemed necessary. However,

> adapted novels are brought out on the almost expressed assumption that the whole public is already in possession of the story, and can without difficulty fill up lacunæ which would be absolutely fatal were the stage the only available source of knowledge. The correctness of this assumption of course depends on the popularity of the book, and the state of the Surrey audience bears ample testimony to the large circulation of 'All the Year Round'. The audience clearly understand the drift and purpose of Count Fosco before that estimable nobleman has spoken half-a-dozen words, whereas if they had never read Mr Collins's novel, it is very questionable whether they would have completely appreciated the polished villainy even when the curtain had descended.

This is a good summary of the problems of dramatisation in Victorian days. It is instructive to compare how solutions were then found with the methods adopted today when making the 'film of the book' or the television equivalent. I get the impression that today's producers assume that very few people have read the book before seeing the film. Hence we have the modern market in books selling well because of the film, while at the Surrey seats sold well because of the book. The fact that *The Woman in White* was published in instalments made life more difficult for J.R. Ware who adapted it. The review continued:

> Throughout the whole course of the piece it is evident that the novelist and the dramatist are working in opposite directions, the former ever contriving an almost infinite extension, that

ROYAL SURREY THEATRE,

Lessees........Messrs. SHEPHERD and CRESWICK.

Another Hit! Glorious Reception! Splendid Triumph of THE NEW DRAMA founded on the Popular Tale Published in the Celebrated Serial of "ALL THE YEAR ROUND," Edited by **CHAS DICKENS, Esq.**, entitled

THE WOMAN IN WHITE!

Written by **WILKIE COLLINS, Esq.**, and adapted expressly for this Theatre by **J. R. WARE, Esq.**

Produced for the First Time, on Saturday last, to a Crowded anddelighted Audience. Thunders of Applause! Breathless Anxiety! Success! Success!! Success!!!

COUNT FOSCO - - MR. CRESWICK.

"A Bill of Fare of Unrivalled Attraction."—*Vide, Era.*

On MONDAY! November 5th, 1860, and During the Week—The

WOMAN IN WHITE!

Walter Hartright ... (a poor Drawing Master) ... Mr. J. FERNANDEZ

Count Fosco { 'he looked like a man who could tame anything—if he had married a Tigress instead of a woman, he would have tamed the Tigress.' } Mr. CRESWICK

Mr Frederick Fairlie ('a beardless face, pale, but not wrinkled,') Mr. Esser JONES

Sir Percival Glyde | 'a most prepossessing man, but his face somewhat marked and worn.' | Mr. James HOLLOWAY

Spado ('he was a light-haired man, with a mark on his left cheek.') Mr R NORMAN

Laurie Fairlie, afterwards Lady Glyde | 'she had eyes, lovely in colour, lovely in form, and exquisitely tender.' | Miss PAGE

The Woman in White | 'there was nothing wild, nothing immodest in her manner; it was quiet, and self-controlled, a little melancholy, and a little touched with suspicion.' | Miss PAGE

Marian { Laura's Half-sister—' her expression was bright, frank, and intelligent.' } Miss FORESTER

Mrs. Vesey | a family dependent—'she looked the perfection of composure, and female amiability' | Mrs ATKINS

Molly ... (a North Country thick-headed Servant Girl) ... Miss Jenny BELLAIR

THE CHURCHYARD AT LIMMERIDGE

THE COTTAGE AT HAMPSTEAD.

Old Wilmington Church & Vestry

GARDEN AND VILLA OF FOSCO.

The 25th, 26th, 27th, 28th, 29th and 30th Nights of The

GITANILLA!

Pronounced by the Public and the Press to be one of the Very Best Dramas ever produced.

DEVIL'S BRIDGE,

AND MOUNTAIN CATARACT! by Dalby.

TUESDAY & THURSDAY, being Charitable Benefits, the Free List will be Suspended.

Mercer and Gardner, Machine Printers, Kennington Cross.

> the curiosity of his readers may be kept on the stretch for months, while the latter is labouring to effect the greatest possible compression, that his spectators may be put in possession of everything within the space of three hours....

As to the production, 'the semi-supernatural appearance given to Anne Catherick is highly effective', while to achieve the necessary similarity to Lady Glyde 'the two parts are both played (and very well played) by the same actress, Miss Page'. The role of Hartright is performed by Fernandez, a young actor who has 'every appearance of a rising man'. The prominent character, however, is Count Fosco, 'a gentleman, firm of purpose and smooth of exterior, bland when others are boisterous, and collected always, – these peculiarities are excellently portrayed by Mr Creswick'.

The Woman in White overlapped and then displaced another piece which had done quite good business – *Gitanilla*, which ran thirty nights – but Creswick had taken the lead in this, so it had to go.

The Times reviewed the pantomime *Harlequin and Cinderella; or, The Fairy of the Little Glass Slipper* on 27 December 1860. Starting with the customary over-written account of the expectant spectators, the writer postulated the reactions of a foreigner:

> He would carry away some strange notions of this best abused country in Europe with him. Full dress he would report to be an abandonment of coats, an unlimited exposé of dirty shirt sleeves and a violent display of red and other handkerchiefs.... If he were to be unprejudiced he would have to admit that instead of the phlegmatic audiences he had expected to see he had found an enthusiastic, noisy, howling, but withall good-tempered mob.... The curtain rose upon a singular piece of a doubtful tendency, with the uninstructive title of *Old and Young Joe,*... although the audience showed their good taste for some time in making it inaudible.... At last the business of the evening really commenced, and was ushered in with a perfect hurricane of whistles, catcalls, and universal cries of 'Sit down', interspersed with numerous interrogatories to an individual named Bill as to the exact location of his wife at that moment, and why she had not accompanied him.... After this storm had somewhat subsided the overture began, and 'the people' showed their appreciation of its merits by adding a few touches of their own.... The popularity of the 'Young Recruit' provoked the choral powers of the audience.... So charmed were they with their success as to demand for themselves unanimously an encore, which, it is needless to add, was graciously awarded....

The plot of Cinderella is then described for anyone without this knowledge. In conclusion:

> When the curtain fell the applause was deafening, and as that, after all, is the best test of the merits of the piece, we must pronounce it, although with some defects, decidedly good. For children this pantomime is capitally adapted. There is an absence of those perpetual allusions to passing events and of that love of punning, which, although more attractive to children of a larger growth, is only so much Greek to the infantine mind. Add to this that the fairy part of the play is peculiarly well arranged, that the dresses and dances (especially those of a band of juvenile fairies varying from six to 12 years of age) are particularly graceful, and we need say nothing further to induce parents who care more for their children's amusement than their own to see this pantomime....

The Surrey helped parents to this end by having a 'morning' performance at half past one on Boxing Day, and 'Juvenile Nights' running from half past six till nine on Wednesdays and Fridays.

There is a touching disclaimer on the bills for 25 February 1861 advertising *Ambition* – 'This statement is respectfully made as an apology for all anachronisms'. It does not inspire much faith in the playwright.

For Easter Monday, the bills announced the 'Engagement of those eminent artistes Mr and Mrs Charles Mathews for 12 nights only'. Mr Charles Mathews and the Surrey Company appeared in *The Pirates of the Savannah.* There was also a comedy 'supported by Mr and Mrs Charles Mathews'. In earlier appearances at the Surrey 'Mrs Charles Mathews' meant Madame Vestris but she had died in August 1855. Charles had set his eyes on a clever actress, born Lizzie Weston, for his second wife. Unfortunately her husband, A.H. Davenport, objected. There was a punch-up at the stage door, a messy divorce, and a gap before she thought it wise to appear on stage again. It may even be that the Surrey was the place chosen to re-introduce her to the public, April 1861 the date, and *The Adventures of a Love Letter* the piece. Sherson's researches into this did not find anything relevant before December 1866. Mr and Mrs Mathews also revived *Paul Pry* while Charles resurrected *Patter v. Clatter,* a virtuoso piece in which he played five parts and which he performed throughout his long career.

The Surrey put on 'A Great Shakesperian Treat' in April 1861 when Phelps of Sadler's Wells paid another visit to alternate with Creswick the parts of Brutus and Cassius, Othello and Iago, and King John and Faulconbridge. On this occasion the next generation was introduced, with Edmund Phelps appearing in, for example, *Werner.*

The season ended on 27 May 1861 with a benefit for Creswick. Several Surrey old-timers came back to support him – Phelps, Buckstone, Miss Atkinson and Paul Bedford (with a song 'Jolly Nose'). The theatre was dark again until 7 September. If the company was on tour I have not been able to trace it, though Creswick on his own did three weeks at the Great National Standard Theatre, Shoreditch, 'in the Surrey drama of *Ambition'*.

As the Surrey Theatre had, on a number of occasions, provided its patrons with 'news-reel' type representations of current events, one might expect to find something on the American civil war which had started in April 1861. This apparently was not yet considered of interest to Surrey-siders. Instead they were given more melodrama from the French:

> The Theatre will OPEN for the season on Saturday September 7, with a double company, Dramatic and Operatic, forming an unprecedented combination of talent and novelty.
>
> A new drama, THE IDIOT OF THE MOUNTAIN; Mr Creswick, Mr Shepherd, Mr J. Fernandez, Mr Vollaire, Mr G. Vincent, Mr Maclean, Miss Georgiana Pouncefort, Mrs E.Webster, Miss E. Johnstone etc.
>
> An original opera SHAKESPEARE'S DREAM; Mr Maurice de Solla, Mr Wallworth, Miss Camille Chipp, Miss Fanny Thirlwall.
>
> Boxes 2s. Pit 1s. Gallery 6d.

The plot of *The Idiot of the Mountain* is – idiotic. It has one great moment, though, as *The Times* described:

> Here we have one of those curious scenes in which the art of the painter becomes all-important in carrying out the intention of the author; and the managers of the Surrey are fortunate in owning an artist of such ability as Mr Charles Brew. The proposed interview between Caussade and Ravel is held in the cottage of the latter, and while they are endeavouring to overreach each other their conversation is overheard by Jeanne, who, hoping to gain some intelligence useful to her father, is suspended from the branches of a tree which grows on the opposite side of the chasm, and almost reaches the rude dwelling. While she is thus suspended, the branch is struck by lightning, and she falls into the abyss, and clambering wounded into the cottage, she finds herself in the power of the smuggler, who has long been an unsuccessful suitor for her hand. The idiot Claude, however, who is her

> guardian genius throughout the piece, ascends the crags to save her, and Ravel is defeated. It should be remarked that the interior of the cottage and the exterior landscape are both shown at once, and that a complicated action is carried on with immense skill and with excellent effect.

The handbills have a woodcut of this scene, with the heroine, wearing a neat pinafore over her dress, swinging from a twig above the chasm, while the two men in the cottage strike dramatic poses at one another. This complex scene brings to mind the sensational multiple setting portrayed on the bills for Fitzball's *Jonathan Bradford,* which had opened at the Surrey on 12 June 1833.

The operatic talent on call was able to mount the world première of an English opera, even though it might escape the eyes of such experts as Eric Walter White. *The Times* of 9 September 1861 recorded that

> the opera, entitled *Shakespeare's Dream,* is a neat translation by Miss Maynard of the short dramatic poem by the late Ludwig Tieck which represents the boy Shakespeare falling into the company of Oberon and Titania.... It is gracefully set to music by Mr Bennett Gilbert, whose memory is laudably tenacious of Mendelssohn, and sung by a compact company, of which the most remarkable member is Miss Chipp, a soprano of very fluent execution. With new and beautiful scenery by the Messrs. Brew [and Johnson], and with the attraction of an effective corps de ballet, the little opera agreeably varies the evening's entertainment.

The reviewer, though, counsels the audience not to encore every single piece: 'If they wish to hear it twice through, they had better demand a repetition of the whole work after the fall of the curtain, and thus allow those to retire who are less greedy of enjoyment'.

The new opera was displaced after two weeks by Shield's *Rosina,* which can still find a place on stage today, and which in turn was superseded by 'a new Operatic Burlesque Extravaganza' called *Cooleen Drawn; or, The Great Sensation Diving Belle.* This was a skit on Dion Boucicault's *Colleen Bawn,* produced a year earlier, which had a scene in a cave where the colleen is rescued from drowning. For a skit it was remarkably well got up. There were seven scenes, including 'The Great Whiskey and Water Scene' and fifteen musical numbers. Every single principal member of the cast – six male, three female and one 'pantomime dame' character – sang, and there was a chorus and a ballet. The playbills suggest it used every 'stage-Irishman' joke in the book. Unlike most skits, it ran and ran, and although there are clearly problems of definition,

HAVE YOU SEEN

THE

IDIOT OF THE MOUNTAIN

AT THE

SURREY THEATRE?

GO & SEE IT

" **Drew down loud applause.**" —*Telegraph.*
" **Abounds with interest.**" —*Morning Herald.*
" **The idea is admirable, and its construction most ingenious.**" —*Morning Star.*
" **A most Powerful Drama.**" —*Standard.*
" **The gratification to the Management must be considerable, and the SUCCESS was UNMISTAKEABLE.**" —*Era.*

& GARDNER, Machine Printers, Kennington Cross.

it may have been the first genuine musical comedy on the London stage. If from musical comedy one expects music interspersed with spoken dialogue, with comedy and a happy ending , then Mozart's *Seraglio* would qualify. As a vernacular piece the *Cooleen Drawn* is a musical comedy by most printed definitions, as are the Gilbert and Sullivan pieces which turn up a decade or more later. This is a debatable area in which it seems that most people would exclude the burlesques of James Robinson Planché and, although musical comedy is not required to be British, the Spanish *sainetes* (already seen at the Surrey), the French imports such as *Les Cloches de Corneville* (first seen in London in 1878) and the works of Johann Strauss such as *The Gipsy Baron*. They would in general await the English shows of George Edwardes with the Gaiety Girls of the 1890s before recognising true musical comedy.

However, on reading what the critic of *The Era* had to say on 20 October 1861 one gets the impression that the general understanding of musical comedy is met, or at least closely approached. Beginning 'The Management of the Surrey have achieved a hit – a most legitimate and unequivocal hit', the reviewer first notes of this season that the addition of opera and 'still more recently, Burlesque' to the repertory gives the Surrey a 'tout ensemble... unique in the character of the metropolis'. Then:

> The title of the Operatic Burlesque produced at this Theatre is *The Cooleen Drawn*... a parody on the successful Drama of *The Colleen Bawn* in which every salient incident of that well-known story is seized upon, and in manner at once grotesque and amusing, twisted and most ingeniously converted into a form of individuality to suit the new phase of dramatic personæ required for the unity and sequence of the piece. We have already said that the present Burlesque is a great success, and one of the best we have ever seen within the walls of the Surrey Theatre.

For this success various 'special reasons' are adduced:

> First of all, though abounding in jokes and humour, and revelling in a perfect shower of puns, it is in dialogue and insinuation singularly free from all vulgarity and slang phrases – an objection so universally prevalent in all, or nearly all, of our modern Burlesques. The same commendable refinement runs through all the songs and duets of which there is even a larger proportion than usually falls to the share of such pieces. Next in importance to the chasteness of the composition, and the intrinsic merit of the Burlesque,

> ranks the acting of the piece; and here, without one exception, we must accord unqualified praise to every lady and gentleman engaged in its representation. The care and taste with which the Burlesque has been put on the Stage, and, finally, the music and scenery that accompanies and appertains to it, give the last links to those several causes that conspire to stamp the Surrey Burlesque as a great and triumphant hit, and imparts to it that completeness, vivacity and neatness that leaves so gratified and pleasing a sense on the imagination.

Both the printed definitions and the normal perception of the genre emphasise tastefulness. I suggest that the Surrey's 'Operatic Burlesque Extravaganza' *Cooleen Drawn* deserves consideration as the first English musical comedy.

The 1861 Christmas pantomime had about the longest title ever – *Harlequin Hey Diddle Diddle, The Cat and the Fiddle and the Cow that Jumped over the Moon; or, Oranges and Lemons and the Twelve Dancing Princesses.* There was a long review in *The Times* of 27 December 1861. Although the Surrey is not mentioned until a third of the way through, and this particular pantomime has to wait more column inches before it is named, the comments are valuable as a very perceptive report on the 'political correctness' of the day. The Surrey, unlike other theatres, kept its fairy tale basis for an adult audience. It introduced matinees and Juvenile Nights specifically for the children, leaving out the adult drama or melodrama which usually preceded the pantomime. The *Times* man, taking a wide view, wrote:

> The world is characteristically censorious, and not less so in the present century than at any former period of its history.... Some few years ago, a well-known philanthropist made a deadly onslaught with his pen against the fairy tales of our youth. Taking high moral ground, he argued that they were palpable falsehoods, and that we were guilty of inconsistency, if not of something worse, in permitting them to remain on the shelves of nursery libraries while we taught our children that commandment which prohibits lying. Happily, this attempt to deprive us of all that is poetic and imaginative was a simple failure, and did not drive out of circulation a single copy of Jack the Giant-killer or of the Arabian Nights' Entertainment.

The reviewer also complains of those who seem to delight in depriving 'historic characters of all those associations with which we love to connect them', referring to the denial of a cat to Dick Whittington by 'a studious author' who supposes us misled by 'achat' – medieval corruption of the French for merchandise. No such theories 'will ever find favour at the Surrey':

> Faith in the literature of our childhood is there pure. No such heresy as that which would dispute that a beanstalk grew up to the skies in one night would be tolerated there if its effect were to rob the audience of its interest in the hero, and hence the manager who adheres to the uncorrupted text of the story-book is sure of sympathetic friends in boxes, pit and gallery. Extravaganzas at proper times meet with applause and success in the Surrey, but at Christmas there must be no compromise. The extravaganza will never supersede the Christmas pantomime in Blackfriars-road.

The remainder of the critic's report concerns the behaviour of a Surrey audience on the day, and it is clear that this has not changed over fifty years or more. It seems almost hereditary! With less purple irony than usual the writer describes the crowded and good-humoured spectators and provides a new insight:

> Notwithstanding the usual architectural distinctions between various parts of this theatre, there is the best understanding between the pit and the gallery; and the manner in which the boxes fraternise with both without, at the same time, sinking their own dignity, is admirable. Though the house was an overflowing one in all parts last night, the drama which preceded the pantomime was allowed to proceed with but little interruption, and even the interval that followed it was not marked by more than the ordinary demonstrations of impatience. At one time, matters looked a little threatening; but a call of order from the gallery, directed to the boxes, and a song, the chorus of which was given by the whole house, restored all parties to their previous good temper.

The reporter then details the story-line, which is 'more than usually hazy',

> but to make up for this there is more than the average number of ogres of gigantic height and with mammoth heads.... There are bad spirits and good spirits innumerable in the opening business, if that can be called an opening which consumes considerably more than two hours. Anywhere else but in the Surrey some of the scenes would be regarded as insufferably tedious; but the audience did not seem to think them so. On the contrary, the Cat and the Cow were encored in several of their gambols; and as for the men with the goggle eyes and the bottle noses, they elicited as much applause as the most graceful of the dancing fairies.

There is one aspect of the production not mentioned by the critic: no slap-dash chorus line for the Surrey! Instead, we have 'The Military Evolutions by Sergeant-Major Wallis, 7th Surrey Volunteers'. There is a story of Queen Victoria's disgust with the sloppy chorus of Egyptian soldiers when she saw *Aida* at Covent Garden, following which she volunteered her Guards for future productions, but that was getting on for twenty years after Sergeant-Major Wallis had knocked the Surrey chorus into shape. *The Era* of 29 December 1861 gives an indication of the Sergeant-Major's evolutions:

> In the scene of the Ruby Castle, in order to recover possession of the Princess Pirouette, was a Corps of Volunteer Amazons in a French grey or light blue uniform, who not only charged and stormed this Castle with success, but in their previous excellent and well-conducted military manoeuvres elicited the most enthusiastic applause....

The attraction of French plays to the Surrey management can be seen in yet another review of one in *The Times* of 5 April 1862. This was *Four Stages of Life* 'in which blindness is used both as a provocative of sympathy and as an agent for the production of dramatic effects'. Several of the characters are 'not remarkably thankful' and owe their success to the acting of Creswick (hero), Miss Pauncefort (Mathilde) and Vincent (villain). There is one 'real character', though,

> the hump-backed physician, with his kind heart and the imperturbable good humour to which his own deformity furnishes perpetual aliment. Mr Shepherd was never more thoroughly at home than in this showy part, visibly marked out to the eye by an admirable make-up and a beard of formidable dimensions, supposed to have been grown during the sojourn in the Crimea. The hilarity of the doctor diffuses itself all over the house, and he is as welcome an apparition to the audience as to the afflicted personages of the story.

Vollaire, who translated the piece, also played the part of the man who sets the story in motion in the first place. But who is this George Vincent in the role of the villain? Could he, by any chance, be the son of Miss Eliza Vincent, reputedly fathered by Osbaldiston in 1834?

Now we come to the end of a partnership era. It was announced that on 26 September 1862,

> *A New Way to Pay Old Debts* will be repeated, and Mr Creswick will appear for the last time. On Saturday next (October 4) the house will re-open for the winter season, under

> the sole management of Mr Shepherd, and a version of the celebrated French drama, *La Bouquetière des Innocents,* will be produced.

The parting seems genuinely to have been friendly. Within five years Richard Shepherd and William Creswick were again in partnership at the Surrey. If one may guess at the reason for their temporary split, it would be that Creswick saw more opportunity for classical roles north of the Thames than the Surrey could carry at the time.

The Times of 27 September 1862 chronicled it thus:

> The joint management of Messrs. Shepherd and Creswick – which has now lasted nearly 14 years – and under which the Surrey has become perhaps the most respectable of suburban theatres, terminates with the present week. Their work in elevating the theatre has not been exactly the same as that of Mr Phelps at Sadler's Wells, but nevertheless they have laboured strenuously to uphold a taste for the old poetic drama; and, while they have still adhered to melodrama as the most permanent form of transpontine entertainment, they have avoided the old transpontine vulgarities, and many of their pieces have been put upon the stage in a style that would have awakened legitimate admiration at any house in London. Their pantomimes have been always brilliant, and last year, when the town abounded with 'sensation scenes', they produced a scenic effect in *The Idiot of the Mountain* which challenged comparison with the most triumphant cispontine achievements.

For his farewell benefit William Creswick performed Sir Giles Overreach in *A New Way to Pay Old Debts*. His curtain-speech to the crowded house was reported in full. It has several points of interest. Creswick either predates or ignores his profession's superstitious dread of quoting *Macbeth,* he feels free to joke with his paying customers about his profits, and in the most gentlemanly terms he can thank the press as well as his Surrey public for their support:

> Ladies and Gentlemen, – Although somewhat fatigued by my exertions in the play, I cannot help making an effort to express, however feebly, my sincere appreciation of your kindness this evening. There are moments in our lives when to interpret feelings words are but weak agents, and of the fact I am now myself most painfully conscious. What can I say? How can I thank you not only for this night's sympathy and approbation, but for so many nights – nay, years, of the

most constant, unvarying, and liberal encouragement? Under such a pressure of pleasant obligations I have only left to say, – more is thy due than more than all can pay.

As I am not about to leave the country or retire from my profession, nor in all probability from management, I am spared the pain which I must otherwise have felt at the present moment. In truth, I have resolved to regard this farewell as a leave-taking of friends – friends who have assembled to compliment me and do me honour, and therefore I may be pardoned, I hope, if I briefly allude to the cause which has led to my having issued such numerous invitations. In two short nights from this I shall close the labours of nearly 14 years within these walls; labours conscientiously directed, and I trust not altogether fruitless. I don't mean as far as my purse is concerned; I refer to that fruit which a well-conducted theatre devoted to the true interests of the drama should produce. But on that point, perhaps, it may not become me to speak; the public are the judges, and it is they who must decide that question. In any case, I feel I owe to that public and to our liberal press a lasting debt of gratitude for their generous recognition of my humble exertions.

To stop the tongue of idle rumour, and satisfy those who take any interest in my leaving this theatre, I beg simply to state that my contract with my excellent partner, Mr Shepherd, will expire on Monday, and believing it would prove mutually advantageous not to extend the term, we have resolved to sever our business connexion. Whether our sanguine expectations will be realised is a matter in the womb of time; but be that as it may, I have the present satisfaction, and to me a most gratifying one, of knowing that we part with the most friendly feelings and, I believe, sincerely wishing each other prosperity and happiness.

Now, ladies and gentlemen, permit me to extend those wishes to each and all of you, and with reiterated thanks to rest your grateful debtor, and, for the present, respectfully and regretfully bid you Farewell.

Chapter Twenty-Seven

Shepherd and Anderson (1862-64)

Shepherd, now the sole manager of the Surrey, opened in the autumn of 1862 as he meant to go on, concentrating above all on spectacular effects. *The Times* reported on 6 October that though the theatre had been closed for a week only,

> the indefatigable lessee had found time in that short interval to paint and renovate the salle in every part, to put on the stage a long drama, abounding with the most elaborate scenic effects, and, in addition to all this, to mount a looking-glass curtain, measuring 1,000 feet square. His exertions were not unrewarded, for the house was crowded in every part by one of those eager, expectant, sympathetic audiences which appear so strange to those who are only accustomed to the colder public on the north bank of the Thames.

The long drama was *The Medal of Bronze,* adapted from Bourgeois and Dugue's Ambigu-Comique piece *La Bouquetière des Innocents.* For once, the English version (translated by the Surrey actor, Vollaire, and made fit for the stage by H.P. Grattan) is less blood-thirsty than the original in that the lady least deserving of popularity is merely banished, rather than beheaded and burnt on a charge of witchcraft. Perhaps the audience slowly became aware of what it had missed, for after the conclusion of the drama,

> the looking-glass curtain was exhibited, but at so long an interval that the spectators became obstreperously impatient. An address from Mr Shepherd, who bade them reflect how much had been prepared for their amusement within the short space of six days, quieted them in a moment, so perfectly were they convinced of the justice of the reproof. The marvellous curtain, manufactured by Mr Villars, of the London-road, consists of eight large plates of glass, and its effect is enhanced by a divertissement executed before it by the three Misses Morgan and a corps de ballet. Middle-aged sight-seers will possibly recollect the looking-glass curtain exhibited years ago at the Coburg (the present Victoria), but they may be informed that that early wonder was composed of much smaller pieces than Mr Villars's work now shown at the Surrey.

In its acclaim, finally, for 'a new drop scene by Messrs. Telbin and Grieve', the report shows Shepherd commissioning work from members of the two families who, after Clarkson Stansfield, embodied the most illustrious scene-painters of the nineteenth century.

Perhaps as a 'thank you' for the assistance given by Sergeant-Major Wallis in drilling the chorus for the 1861 pantomime, a benefit night was given to the 7th Surrey Volunteers on the last night of the season, 22 December 1862. Phelps came down from Sadler's Wells, as he had done many times before, and played Shylock, with Georgiana Pauncefort as Portia and Shepherd as Gratiano – a rare event for him to appear in Shakespeare!

The special effects in the 1862 pantomime were arranged by Charles Brew, whose name features prominently in the playbills as a known box-office draw – 'If You Want To See The Only Great and Gorgeous Pantomime You Must Go to The Surrey – Four Magnificent & Matchless Scenes!!! The Only Great Transformation Scene is Brew's!!' The pantomime was written

> By Mr MARTIN DUTNALL, Author of *Hey Diddle Diddle, Cooleen Drawn,* &c. being a New Version of that most favourite and famous Pantomimic Nursery Tales, entitled *HARLEQUIN AND MOTHER GOOSE; OR, THE QUEEN OF HEARTS AND THE WONDERFUL TARTS.*

That is, a rewrite of the pantomime which made Grimaldi's name in 1808. One can still see traces of the original version. There is Colin, who becomes Harlequin, but played by Miss Julia St George – the Principal Boy/Girl is now established. Columbine in the opening scenes is now named Bluebelle rather than Colinette,

> A pretty country maiden, with basket brimming o'er,
> Whom every one who sees her is certain to adore,

and is the daughter rather than the proposed bride of the Squire, who becomes Sprite rather than Clown. Regardless of amendments a good time was had by one and all.

On 7 February 1863 the pantomime was joined by *Effie Deans,* 'First Time on any Stage'. On 9 February 1863 *The Times* reported:

> Mr Shepherd's announcement that on Saturday last he was about to produce a freshly-dramatized version of Sir Walter Scott's *Heart of Midlothian,* called *Effie Deans, the Lily of St Leonard's* brought together one of those vast, dense, turbulent throngs that are by no means unusual on the other side of the

> river, but to which a parallel can rarely be found on the northern bank, save perhaps at Drury Lane on the nights immediately following Christmas. We do not mean to say that central London cannot frequently show crowded theatres, for Lord Dundreary [a character in *Our American Cousin,* remembered for his long whiskers] is a standing witness to the contrary. But in a transpontine public there is a wild anticipation of enjoyment, a determination to be amused, and to find a tumultuous expression for gratification which seems peculiar to the Southern atmosphere. The heartiest laugh of a West-end audience is a faint smile compared with the hilarious roar of the Surrey gallery.

An interesting distinction is then drawn between the technique of the Surrey's adapter and that of Dion Boucicault, whose own play (first produced at New York in 1860 as *Jeanie Deans; or, The Heart of Midlothian*) had opened on 26 January 1863 at the Westminster Theatre (that is, Astley's) re-titled *The Trial of Effie Deans:*

> The principle adopted by the author of the Surrey drama is diametrically opposite to that pursued at the Westminster. While Mr Boucicault has endeavoured to construct a drama that will create an interest independent of its connexion with the novel, altering the original course of action at his pleasure, and sometimes bringing in his strongest effects where little or nothing has been done for him by the novelist, it is the boast of Mr Shepherd that he has closely followed in the footsteps of Sir Walter. A play founded on the *Heart of Midlothian* is to be seen at the Westminster; *The Heart of Midlothian* itself, reduced to a dramatic shape, is professedly exhibited at the Surrey.

The production evidently gave a lot of scope for effects. *The Times* continued:

> The first act is chiefly occupied with the Porteous Riot and forms a kind of prologue to the rest. The unfortunate Captain is himself brought on the stage, and, after being much knocked about by his turbulent persecutors, seems in imminent danger of being hanged before the very eyes of the audience. However, the drop-scene descends in time to save him from this novel ignominy, and the execution of the mob's sentence takes place in the imagination only. The tumult and the forcible entrance into the Tolbooth are capitally managed, and produced much excitement.

And to show that the Surrey maintained one of its oldest traditions:

> The escape takes place across a huge cataract of real water, which falls from nearly the top of the stage and really breaks against the craggy rocks at the bottom. This scene is the work of Mr Charles Brew, whose fame has been kept alive in the memory of the Surrey audience by his brilliant decorations of the pantomime, which is even now as attractive as it was at Christmas. It is the custom when a remarkable picturesque effect is produced on the stage to call both the artist and the manager who has paid for it, and Mr Shepherd and Mr Brew received the customary honours.

Most of the cast received individual mention, such as:

> For the Laird of Dumbiedikes we have a Mr Gourlay, a real Scot, who discourses in pure Doric, and is endowed with a dry humour which has gained him a high reputation on the other side of the Tweed.... With wondrous self-denial Mr Shepherd has elected for himself the unthankful part of Argyle, and Miss Elizabeth Webster bestows upon Queen Caroline an amount of personal attraction greater than is awarded her by the historical record.

The poor author, J.B. Johnstone, is not cited. Unusually, though, the audience gets a second mention:

> The mass of humanity that crowded every part of the theatre burst out into an uproarious demonstration of satisfaction at the termination of the drama. Occasionally its temper had been ruffled by such delays as inevitably ensue on the first night of a piece illustrated by elaborate scenery, and it was addressed from the stage sometimes of entreaty, once of reproof; but the little hitches were all forgotten long before Effie had received her pardon, and the justly delighted manager had only to express his satisfaction at the obvious pleasure which his numberless patrons had derived from his labours....

Shepherd had moved house once more and was at 7, Terrace, Kennington Park, a little nearer the theatre. He now took a new partner. On 16 September 1863 *The Times* recorded that 'Mr James Anderson, the well-known tragedian, is now associated with Mr Shepherd in the lesseeship of the Surrey Theatre', their style in the opening production auguring well:

> The enterprise is inaugurated by a five-act drama entitled *The Scottish Chief,* and traceable mediately to Miss Porter's novel,

> but immediately to a tragedy written by a gentleman named Walker, and produced at Covent-garden in the year 1820, under the title of *Wallace.* This tragedy was played for about 16 nights, but since its withdrawal it has been little thought of, save in connection with the early career of Mr Macready, by whom the 'hero of Scotland' was represented.

Anderson evidently saw eye to eye with Shepherd's policy for the Surrey and helped to continue it. As the *Times* article proceeds we learn that Anderson (who had 'taken this subject in hand') caused such effects and visual splendours to be introduced by the scenic artists Brew and Johnson as turned 'a by no means inviting tragedy into a very exciting sensation piece'.

Johnson's scenes are said to include Stirling Castle courtyard, its banqueting-hall (reminiscent of Charles Kean's *Macbeth* both for its design and the 'primitive Scotch festival' enacted within it) and views of the Carron and Glenfilas. 'Tableaux', costumes, and 'skilfulness of the grouping' are also praised before the reviewer moves on to the cast:

> There are also points depending on the actor by which much excitement is occasioned. Such are the leap taken, not by a 'dummy', but by Mr Anderson himself from a high window to a rustic bridge, with the aid of a rope, and his defeat of the traitor Monteith in single combat, when his hands are loaded with chains. On the first night of performance the head of Wallace was held up for inspection after the execution, but some of the audience found this dose of the horrible somewhat too strong for their stomachs. Hence the fate of the patriot is now simply indicated by the heavy sound of the axe upon the block, which is of itself quite enough to cause a titillation of the nerves....

Wallace is performed by Anderson, doing the play 'incalculable service',

> with a degree of effectiveness which probably no other living actor could attain in this particular part. Strong of limb, commanding in figure, powerful of voice, thoroughly accomplished in all the athletic branches of his profession, and withal capable of assuming a tone of the deepest tenderness, he is just the man to represent the stalwart hero of a rude country in a rude age, and to soften him down with that amount of sentimentality which the play requires, without utterly destroying his historical, or rather legendary, individuality.

Anderson was not the only Surrey performer ready to risk life and limb as his own stunt-man if it could make a striking effect. *Ashore and Afloat* has one of the most ridiculous plots imaginable but it provides splendid opportunities for stunts and for another popular Surrey sensation, as *The Times* of 18 February 1864 reported:

> With the demonstration of Joshua's guilt, and consequently of Newton's innocence, the story virtually comes to an end, but not the piece. The most important 'effect' is still looming in the future. For the sake of committing one crime more, the old rascal has let Ruth down into the mine, where she hopes to find Newton, and drawing up the basket has left her to perish. The situation of the poor girl is horrible. Alone in the subterranean region she perceives that the waters are pouring into the mine, and that she must soon be drowned or crushed by the falling rocks. But she is rescued by the gallant Hal, under circumstances that raise the audience to a frenzy of excitement. Descending in the basket he takes her in half-insensible, and as the frail-looking vehicle is reascending to the top of the stage its progress is stopped by the fall of a beam, while a torrent of water (real water) is falling in the background.

(Certainly real water – this is the Surrey!) The writer continues:

> What is to be done now the basket has become a fixture? Hal cuts a cord, allows the basket to fall from beneath his feet, and rises with his companion by the aid of the rope alone, the curtain falling as they approach the surface of the earth. It is this new 'sensation', admirably contrived, that will make the fortune of the piece;... it is when the figures of Mr Shepherd and Miss Pauncefort are seen ascending by the rope that the grand distinctive 'hit' is made, of which people will talk when the intricacies of the plot have faded from their memory.

In 1864 two innovations appeared at the Surrey which modern playgoers take for granted: programmes; and stall seats replacing part of the pit. The growing middle-class audience took comfort and literacy for granted, and expected to be so catered for in the theatre. On 6 September 1864 *The Times* reported upon the refurbishment at the start of the winter season in Shepherd's and Anderson's second year: 'Upwards of 100 cushioned stalls now front the pit,...[and] a double row of balcony box-stalls has been constructed'. There is also a new drop-curtain, 'in which a medallion-view of Stratford Church is the chief object'. The opening play was *The Savage and Civilisation,*

> a work which was written some years ago by a young dramatist, now deceased, named Wilkins, and brought out at the City of London Theatre. At the date of its production... literary critics who travelled to Norton-folgate were surprised, when... they discovered a drama with a moral purpose, consistently and gravely worked out, and evidently intended to depend not a little on the 'writing', which was in blank verse. The plot, moreover, had been taken from Voltaire's well-known romance, the *Huron,* and this alone was sufficient to give the work a literary stamp....

The reader is informed that the play had been written for Anderson, whose 'portrait in the Huron costume is a familiar object to all who take interest in theatrical prints'. An instructive point is made about the merits of the piece itself:

> Whether it will attain a lasting popularity may reasonably be doubted. The preponderance of dialogue over action which commanded admiration, when the belief that poetry would soon vanquish melodrama was current among literary enthusiasts, is scarcely an advantage when the soundness of that belief becomes daily more questionable.... *The Savage and Civilisation* may now be looked upon as a monument of that particular state of mind which prevailed among literary critics at the time when it was thought that the abolition of the old patents would result in a broad cropping-up of dramatic poetry.

Included in the bill to support the saga of the noble Huron was the burlesque (not the opera) of *Fra Diavolo.* The *Times* critic took a double swipe at the Surrey and its rival up the road by remarking that Felix Rogers played Beppo 'in mock bombast of the old Coburg kind'.

Later in the month the Surrey was back to its tried-and-true reliance on scenic effects. The *Times* critic on 22 September 1864 approved the efforts made:

> If the manager of the Princess's can boast that he has the best stage street in London, the managers of the Surrey may be proud of their shipwreck. The destruction of Her Majesty's ship *Minerva,* that occurs in the course of a new drama, entitled *A Fight with Fate,* is one of the best things of its kind ever effected by theatrical means. First the deck is shown, covered with persons whose general tranquillity is interrupted by an alarm of 'Fire!' Almost immediately afterwards flames are seen to issue from various apertures, and there is a bustle consequent on the endeavour of a party to escape by the life-

> raft. Then comes a tremendous explosion, supposed to arise from the ignition of the powder magazine, and the ship splits in two and sinks, leaving nothing but a vast billowy sea, which covers the entire stage. On this the life-raft appears manned by four favoured personages, who are, however, tossed about with as much violence as if they were really floating on rough waters, – altogether a most complete exhibition.

It is a bit of a let-down after such an introduction to learn that 'the drama is not very remarkable'.

Subsequent to making the long-established playbill available to audiences, the Surrey was now providing its patrons with programmes. One of the earliest surviving ones, held by Southwark Local History Library, is dated 24 October 1864. It announces 'The First Night of a New Drama, *The Orange Girl,* by Leslie and Rose', with scenery commissioned from William and Albert Callcott, scientific illusions by Darby and machinery by Mather. A large portion of the programme was, as today, given over to advertising. Surrey-siders were offered 'Messrs. Gabriel's Teeth without Springs' and 'Old Dr Jacob Townsend's Sarsaparilla'; they were asked 'Why go to Brighton, when you can have a SEA BATH in your own room? – Send for a Bag of Tidman's SEA SALT!' and 'Do you want Instant Relief for Gout, Bunions & Corns? – Try Toms Pannus Corium Boots!'

The *Times* review of *The Orange Girl* appeared on 27 October:

> For some days past the walls of our streets have been decorated with a remarkable wood engraving representing a young lady's head placed in the centre of a large yellow disc. This does not, as might be supposed, indicate the theory of any innovating astronomer who has substituted a Woman in the Moon for the 'Man' revered in childhood, but symbolizes the production at the Surrey Theatre of a new drama entitled *The Orange Girl.* Symbols are not too literally interpreted. The orange girl on the stage does not appear in the middle of one of her own oranges, but, what is much better, she is the focus of one of the most stirring and effective melodramas that have been seen for some time on either side of the water.

The critic goes on to analyse the distinct approaches to dramatic writing by the French and by the English, adding that 'it is one of the inborn rights of man to make as many years as he pleases separate his play from his prologue'. He makes another telling point by asking, 'If we insist too strongly on probability, what will become of melodrama?' All the regular company was involved in *The Orange Girl:* Shepherd as 'the wily villain'; Anderson as 'the good-humoured artisan'; Miss Pauncefort as 'the distressed wife'; Vollaire as 'an irascible old gentleman with a kind heart'; Felix Rogers and Miss Webster as the 'funny man' and his wife – all the stock characters of melodrama.

And so to Christmas and the pantomime season, the offering being reported by *The Times* of 27 December 1864 thus:

> There is a bewildering mixture of history and romance in the introduction to the pantomime here, and, in describing the plot and passion of which it is full, the only thing certain must be the uncertainty of your narrative. *Harlequin King Pumpkin* is the title, and the alternative epithet of *Richarde Ye Lion Hearte* discloses that the story has something to do with the mighty monarch. From the fact that more or less gallant red-cross knights appear at intervals on the scene, it is also fair to conclude that the period of the Crusades is that chosen for the leading incidents.... But history on the Surrey side of the water differs from that commonly accepted elsewhere....

Certainly the actions given to Saladin are quite out of character, but then, this is pantomime!

> The proud Paynim and the imperious Lion-heart both fix their attentions on the same object, being a young lady of the name of Beauty (Mlle. Constance). At length the King and the lady are made happy, and the event is celebrated in a transformation scene, which for novel arrangement and for brilliancy can seldom have been surpassed in or out of the Surrey. As a spectacle the pantomime was a great success, and the prismatic effects and blaze of light in which fairydom becomes merged in Clown and Pantaloon produced so great and so legitimate furore that Mr Shepherd, the manager, and Mr W. Callcott, the inventor and painter of all these marvels, were constrained to appear before the scene shifted, in spite of the palpable incongruities. It would be unjust to omit mention of the costumes, and particularly of a vegetable series, in which the courtiers of a certain King Pumpkin are equipped in the guise of melons, gourds, carrots and other sightly esculents.

The review, perhaps less enthusiastic than in earlier years, summed up by saying that it 'furnished plenty of entertainment to a house not a nook of which was left unoccupied'.

Pantomimes usually ran for two if not three months at the Surrey. This one did not. The reason follows in our final chapter, as recorded in detail at the time in the public press.

ROYAL SURREY THEATRE

Chapter Twenty-Eight

The End (1865-Style)

'DESTRUCTION OF THE ROYAL SURREY THEATRE'
(*The Times,* 31 January 1865)

Last night, shortly before 12 o'clock, a fire broke out in the Surrey Theatre, and in less than half an hour the whole fabric was wrapped in flames, which soon reduced it to a mass of ruins, with all the multifarious properties and scenery which it contained. Fortunately, when the fire first made its appearance the audience had thinned considerably, and those that remained are understood to have been prevailed upon to leave the place in a quiet, orderly manner, so that, as far as could be ascertained in the confusion that afterwards prevailed, no loss of life and but few injuries appear to have occurred from panic or otherwise.

In the earlier part of the evening the company had played *The Tradesman's Son,* which was followed in due course by what the lessees call 'the gorgeous pantomime' of *Harlequin King Pumpkin.* The audience was an ordinary one in point of numbers, and by no means so large as those that had flocked to the theatre, which has always been famous for its pantomimes during the Christmas holydays.

The last scene of the pantomime was being performed when, it is said, a part of the ceiling immediately over the large chandelier by which the building was principally lighted, caught fire, and a feeling of alarm immediately took possession of the whole of the audience that remained. At this crisis Mr. Green, the stage manager, presented himself in front of the proscenium, and implored the people for their own sakes to remain as quiet as possible, and to leave the theatre in an orderly manner. They could see for themselves that it was the ceiling alone which had at that time caught fire, and he appealed to their reason that it must burn upwards, and that there was ample time for them to leave the building uninjured, if they only did so in a calm and collected manner. The audience, on the whole, it is said, followed this very sensible advice, and were so enabled to leave the place unhurt. Such, at least, was the result of inquiries made on the spot while the fire was raging, of persons connected with the theatre, and who might be presumed to be best acquainted with the circumstances.

Immediately over the ceiling was the carpenter's shop, and this, with its inflammable contents, having caught fire, the whole building was speedily in a blaze. Though the night was calm the flames raged with amazing fury, defying all efforts to arrest them. Most metropolitan readers will know that the theatre was situated at the southern end of the Blackfriars-road, near the point at which that great thoroughfare and the Waterloo, the Borough, and the St. George's roads all converge, and within a quarter of a mile of the Elephant and Castle. Externally it was a modest, unassuming structure, not calculated to attract much attention, and could accommodate probably from about 2,000 to 2,500 people. As a suburban place of entertainment it has always had a respectable reputation, especially under the management of the present lessees, Messrs. Shepherd and Anderson; and the best pantomime of the present season in London is said to have been produced there.

Mr. Shepherd, the manager, is said to have left the theatre before the fire broke out, and to have gone home, but he was brought back, and witnessed the destruction of the place. Mr. Green, the stage manager, having succeeded in abating the alarm among the audience, applied himself with great energy in collecting all the persons engaged in the pantomime, many of them young ballet girls, and seeing them safe out of the building, he himself being among the last to leave. Most of the pantomimists made their escape in the grotesque costumes in which they had been performing, and took refuge in a house opposite. Little, if any, of the movable property in the building could have been saved, so rapid was the progress of the fire. When the roof fell in, which it did shortly after midnight, the flames shot into the air to a great height, lighting up the metropolis for miles round, and attracting people to the spot from all directions. Steam fire engines and others were soon at work, but to no purpose except to save some of the adjoining property.

Two public houses – the Flowers of the Forest and the Equestrian – which abutted on each side of the theatre were long in great jeopardy, and at half-past 1 o'clock this morning the engines were still at work beating back the fire from them. The police kept a clear open space for some distance immediately in front of the theatre, and so enabled the firemen to work without interruption. This was a necessary

> precaution for the safety of the crowd itself, for at times the burning material, as it was carried into the air, fell in red hot showers all about the immediate neighbourhood. Huge jets of gas liberated by the fire from time to time in its progress swelled the volume of flame, rendering it irresistible so far as the theatre itself was concerned, and the efforts of the firemen were at length chiefly directed to save the adjoining houses. At 2 o'clock this morning the fire was still raging, but with diminished fury, and the theatre itself had been reduced to complete ruin.

The Times followed up this report the next day with a further example of journalism at its most impressive under the headline:

> BURNING OF THE SURREY THEATRE
>
> For the second time the old Surrey Theatre has been totally destroyed by fire. When we have said this we have said the gist of all that is really known about the matter. At 20 minutes to 12 on Monday night the alarm of 'Fire!' was given – and not a second too soon – at a quarter to 12 the building was empty, and at 12 it was a red-hot shell. The cause of the disaster is only dimly conjectured, and is, in fact, a matter of very secondary importance. With such a host of combustible influences always at work in a theatre, and at no time more than during the performance of a pantomime, it is superfluous to imagine which of the leading dangers proved fatal on this occasion. The whole building, which was a very old one, and built mainly of wood, burnt up in a few minutes like a tar barrel.
>
> Inquiries yesterday show that most happily, or, as we may term it, most providentially, no lives were lost. That the result was not very much worse is due to a very wet night and a very thin house. The pantomime was nearly over, many of the audience had left, and even the attendance in the pit and gallery was thinning, when Mr. Rowella, the clown, coming on the stage, was alarmed by the peculiar dullish glare proceeding downwards from the opening in the ceiling to which the great chandelier was suspended. He at once left the stage and told his fears to Mr. Green, the stage manager, who instantly despatched some men to ascertain the cause of such an ominous appearance. Before they could reach the spot, however, the glare had so much increased that the audience noticed it. A cry of 'Fire!' was raised in many parts of the house, followed instantly by a rush of smoke through the opening in the ceiling, mixed with long white flames. Mr.

Green at once rushed to the front of the stage and implored the audience not to be unnecessarily alarmed, but to go out quietly, as there was no cause for immediate fear. This sensible advice was followed, as it usually is on such occasions, by a regular stampede. Women screamed and rushed about to any means of egress, others who sought to restore order only added to the confusion by their inarticulate shouting. The gallery stairs seemed, for a moment, blocked, and men slid down the columns into the dress-circle and pit. Even the coolest, and those most likely to see the value of Mr. Green's advice, were also those who best knew the appalling rapidity with which theatres burn, and that the loss of a few seconds might leave them helplessly face to face with the most terrible form in which death can come upon humanity.

Some of these who were most collected made their way upon the stage, the curtain of which had been lowered. Behind, however, confusion was for a time worse confounded, for the gas had been turned off at the first alarm, and the poor ballet girls were running about screaming, and not unnaturally terrified at the knowledge that the sparks which others less dangerously clad might face with impunity would bring certain death to them.

At that time there was not a moment to lose, the ceiling, composed of light timber and painted canvas, began to buckle up, the flames broke through in several places, and within five minutes after the alarm great flakes of burning canvas were falling in a thick fiery shower over all parts of pit and gallery. In another minute a great sweep of flame licked up the curtain, which seemed to disappear before it, and, pouring over the stage, flies, wings, and flats, they were set fire to instantaneously, and the whole theatre – gallery, boxes, roof, and stage – became one mass of bright flame. Fortunately, before this the chief pantomimists, Mr. Rowella, the clown, Mr. Evans, the pantaloon, Mr. Vivian, the sprite, Mr. Green, the stage-manager, and others behind the scenes, had dragged out as fast as they could find them all the ballet girls, children, and supernumeraries that assist in the performance of the pantomime, and who in their light thin dresses as fairies were huddled miserably together in the half-thawed snow and sleet till they were kindly sheltered in adjoining houses.

Hardly were the last clear of the theatre when the whole interior became a mass of flame, in which nobody could have lived for a single instant. So rapid – so almost instantaneous was the spread of the fire that not a single thing was saved in the way of properties; not an article of dress belonging to the company – not even, so we are informed, the money taken during the evening. But for the exertions of the actors we have spoken of, the loss of life behind the scenes would almost certainly have been terrible. Even as it was they had little more than time to save themselves, and they got out at last grimed with smoke and dirt in the dresses in which they had been performing, not having had an instant's opportunity to get even a coat or cloak for themselves.

The theatre was all ablaze from top to bottom, and the fierce glare of flame lit up the sky half over London. There were soon plenty of engines, and plenty of police on the spot, but, as the public is accustomed to hear on these occasions, all the efforts of firemen and engines were fruitless to save the building, and, indeed, could only feebly tend to check the spread of the flames to other houses. From the first the case of the theatre was hopeless, and in less than an hour after the first alarm it had ceased to exist....

The lessees of the late theatre, Messrs. Shepherd and Anderson, are, of course, great sufferers by the fire. Mr. Shepherd estimates the value of the theatre and its contents at about £12,000, and the insurance effected upon it, owing to the heavy duty charged upon property of this description, was little more than £2,000, thus entailing a heavy direct loss on the lessees. The loss will be much heavier when the sacrifice of a season in the height of its prosperity is taken into account. Mr. Shepherd, however, is a man of energy, and, undaunted by his misfortune, is already talking of his intention to build a new and splendid theatre upon the site of the late building. This is not the first time Mr. Shepherd has been a severe sufferer by fire. He was the leading performer under the late Andrew Ducrow, at the period when Astley's Theatre was destroyed by fire, and on that occasion he lost a valuable wardrobe and a lucrative engagement.

The late Surrey Theatre was one of the old-fashioned buildings to which the exits and entrances for the audience were many and wide. Yet, with all these means of escape from such a terribly rapid fire, one cannot think without a shudder of what the result must have been if the calamity had happened during the first week of the pantomime, when the house was thronged from basement to ceiling and every available avenue behind the boxes blocked up with eager spectators. What would be the effect of such an accident at

> several of our metropolitan theatres, which have only one or two long narrow entrances between shops? Yet the theatres, bad as they are in this respect, are on the whole infinitely better than most of the music-halls, which, as a rule, have only one narrow entrance. It would be folly to suppose that we can always have such lucky accidents as to time as that which the other night saved a vast audience from being roasted alive at Edinburgh. The public have had ample warnings, and unless the lessons which they teach are acted upon all England will sooner or later be appalled by some fiery calamity which will approach the horrors even of the Santiago tragedy.
>
> It may be that the majority of people hug themselves with the notion that they at least would be safe in such a scene, as they would never yield to the panic-stricken terrors of a crowd. But a panic-stricken crowd is a kind of human inundation, with about the same amount of reason in it as any other torrent. It is very unwise to join in a panic rush, but in most cases no alternative is left but going with it or being trampled to death by it. Once in the struggle, all is chance, and the coolest, strongest, and most active have not a whit more hope than the most timid or most feeble. In the slaughter which lately happened at Dundee there were more young men killed than young women, and in a somewhat similar accident on the gallery stairs of the Victoria Theatre some years ago the sufferers who then met their deaths were all without exception lads or young men, though there were plenty of girls and young women in the same crowd. A crowd never thinks that there is no proper means of escape from a burning building, or a building supposed to be falling, until the fact is forced on their notice by the crush and the inability to escape. It is then only that the majority become as frantic as a flock of wild animals, and in the midst of this frenzy the coolness and courage of the minority who might save all is paralyzed and helpless, and the same doom falls on all indiscriminately.

The last few sentences are just as painfully true today. What is also unchanged is the reaction of the British public to such disasters. *The Times* reported a week later:

> The committee of the 'Surrey Relief Fund' were able to announce on Monday that the subscriptions received had been sufficient to pay the salaries of every person employed in the late Surrey Theatre and to meet the most pressing cases of compensation for loss of clothes. At various theatres

> performances are about to take place for the benefit of the sufferers – viz. at Drury Lane on the morning of Thursday the 16th; at Covent Garden on the morning of Saturday, the 25th; at Astley's this morning (Wednesday) and at Sadler's Wells tomorrow evening, when Mr. J. Anderson will play Macbeth. A collection amounting to £232 has been made on the Stock-Exchange for the relief of the sufferers.

The Surrey was rebuilt in time for the next year's pantomime – but that is another story.

Appendix:

Surrey Theatre Pay-list
for week ending Friday 18 October 1861

ROYAL SURREY THEATRE.

PAY LIST FOR THE WEEK ENDING FRIDAY, October 18th 1861

MEN PERFORMERS.	£	s.	d.
Messrs. ~~Shepherd~~			
" ~~Creswick~~			
" C. Rice	6	"	"
" G. Vincent ...	2	10	
" Vollaire	3	5	
" Fernandez	4	"	"
" Maclean	2	"	"
" Stretton	[illegible]	18	
" Butler	1	15	
" Tapping	1	10	
" Hummerston ...	1	18	
" Hellier	1	5	
" Wright	1	5	
" Allbrook	1	15	
" Howard	"	12	
" Leonard ...	"	12	
	27	5	

WOMEN PERFORMERS.	£	s.
Mesds. G. Pauncefort	3	10
" E. Webster	2	"
" Johnstone	2	10
" Edwards	1	15
" Atkins	1	11
" Mazoni	2	"
" Ferguson	"	18
" Jacobs ...	4	"
	18	4

BALLET.

	£	s.
Mesds. Inms	"	12
" Rhodes	"	12
" Coleman	"	12
" Box	"	12
" Howard	"	18
" Johnstone		
" Lee		

SERVANTS.

	£	s.	d.
Money and Check Takers	3	18	
Cleaners	1	4	
Hall Keeper	"	18	
Messenger	"	5	

OFFICERS.	£	s.	d.
Stage Manager	"	"	
Treasurer	2	5	
Mr. Braw	3	10	
Mr. Johnson	2	10	
Master Carpenter ...	2	5	
Master Tailor	2	2	
Master Property Man ...	1	10	
Prompter	1	15	
Bill Inspector	1	5	
Officer ... { Policeman / pit man	1	4	6
Painter's Labourer ...	1	1	
Call Boy	"	10	
	19	18	

INCIDENTALS.	£	s.	d.
License for [illegible]	16	10	
[illegible]			
[illegible]	2	10	
[illegible]	"		
[illegible]	"	5	
[illegible]	"	10	
[illegible]	1		
[illegible]	4		

EXPENSES.	£	s.	d.
Washing Bill	.	6	1½
Fireworks	.	7	9
Stamps	.	2	.
Carpenter's Bill	10	10	3
Property Bill	1	17	3
Wardrobe	1	16	10
Bill Deliverers & Boardmen	5	18	3
Bill Posters			
Advertisements	55	2	6
Gas ...	13	16	3
Painting Room ...			
Printing	9	10	8
Colours ...			
Ropes ...			
Linen Drapers ... Lomfry	2	3	5
Drapers			
Ironmongers	.	7	5½
~~Tinman~~ Tinker ...	.	2	6
Coals and Coke ...			
Timber			
Hosier			
Laceman Bousquet ...	2	11	.
Shoe Maker			
Stationer Grundlyer ...	.	1	4
Rent	45	.	.
Taxes Do	12	.	.
Authors Johnson (" Brain")	1	10	.
	116	2	7

List of Sources

Primary Sources

Most of the detailed information in this book is drawn from playbills (especially) and from letters and other documents held either in the author's own collection or in the archives acknowledged in the Introduction. Works consulted include the following.

Books and Articles

Ackermann, Rudolph. *The Microcosm of London* (1808-11).

Bingham, Madeleine. *Sheridan: the Track of the Comet* (1972).

Blanchard, E.L. See Scott, Clement and Howard, Cecil.

Blom, Eric. *The New Everyman Dictionary of Music* (1988).

Calvert, Mrs Charles (Adelaide Biddles). *Sixty-eight Years on the Stage* (1911).

Cooper, F. Renad. *Nothing Extenuate: the Life of Frederick Fox Cooper* (1964).

Decastro, Jacob. *The Memoirs of J. Decastro, Comedian* (1824).

Dibdin, Charles, the Younger. *Memoirs,* edited by George Speaight (1956).

Dibdin, Thomas. *Reminiscences* (1827).

Downer, Alan S. *The Eminent Tragedian William Charles Macready* (1966).

Fagg, Edwin. *The old 'Old Vic'* (1936).

Fitzball, Edward. *Thirty-Five Years of a Dramatic Author's Life* (1859).

Forster, John. *Life of Charles Dickens* (1874).

Foulkes, Richard. *The Calverts: Actors of Some Importance* (1992).

Freedley, George and Reeves, John A. *A History of the Theatre* (1941).

Frost, Thomas. *Circus Life and Circus celebrities* (1875).

Grimaldi, Joseph. *Memoirs,* edited by 'Boz' (Charles Dickens), revised by Charles Whitehead (1846).

Hartnoll, Phyllis (ed.). *The Concise Oxford Companion to the Theatre* (1969).

Highfill, Philip H. 'Edmund Simpson's Talent Raid on England in 1818', *Theatre Notebook XII* (1958).

Hogan, Charles Beecher (ed.). *The London Stage Part 5: 1776-1800* (1968).

Irving, Laurence. *Henry Irving: the Actor and his World* (1951).

Jerrold, Douglas. *Black-Eyed Susan* and introduction (1829).

Lockhart, J.G. *Memoirs of the Life of Sir Walter Scott* (1838).

Moore, Robert E. 'The Music to Macbeth', *Musical Quarterly XLVII* (1961).

Nicoll, Allardyce. *A History of Nineteenth-Century Drama: 1800-1850* and *1850-1900* (1930).

Odell, G.C.D. *Shakespeare from Betterton to Irving* (1966).

Rees, Terence. *Theatre Lighting in the Age of Gas* (1978).

Rice, Charles. *The London Theatre in the Eighteen-thirties,* edited by Arthur Colby Sprague and Bertram Shuttleworth (1950).

Roberts, Peter. *The Old Vic Story* (1976).

Robinson, Kenneth. *Wilkie Collins: a Biography* (1951).

Sadie, Stanley (ed.). *The New Grove Dictionary of Music and Musicians* (1980).

Sala, George A. *Life and Adventures* (1895)

Saxon, A.H. *The Life and Art of Andrew Ducrow* (1978).

Scott, Clement and Howard, Cecil. *The Life and Reminiscences of E.L. Blanchard* (1891).
Sherson, Errol. *London's Lost Theatres of the Nineteenth Century* (1925).
Spencer, Christopher. *Five Restoration Adaptations of Shakespeare* (1965).
Sprague, Arthur Colby. *The Doubling of Parts in Shakespeare's Plays* (1966).
Stirling, Edward. *Old Drury Lane* (1881).
Tomlins, Frederick G. *A Brief View of the English Drama* (1840).
Trewin, J.C. *Mr Macready* (1955).
Trewin, Wendy. *The Royal General Theatrical Fund* (1989).
White, Eric Walter. *A Register of First Performances of English Operas* (1983).
Wilson, Harriette. *Memoirs,* edited by James Laver (1930).
Winston, James. *A Drury Lane Journal: Selections from James Winston's Diaries 1819-1827,* edited by A.L. Nelson and G.B. Cross ((1974).
Yates, Edmund. *His Recollections and Experiences* (1884).

Journals

Age, The
Dispatch, The [Weekly]
Dramatic Censor, The
Entr'acte Almanack, The
Figaro, The
Figaro in London, The
Illustrated London News, The
Morning Chronicle, The
Musical Quarterly, The
New Monthly Magazine and Literary Journal, The
Satirist, The
Strand Magazine, The
Theatre Notebook
Theatrical Inquisitor, The
Theatrical Observer, The
Theatrical Times, The
Times, The

Dissertation

Ryan, Thomas R. *The Surrey Theatre under the management of Thomas Dibdin, 1816-1822* (PhD. thesis, University of Wisconson at Madison, 1974).

Index of People

A

B

C

D

R

S

Y

Index of Pieces

A

B

C

N

O

P

Q

R

S

List of Pantomimes

Compiled by Audrey Knight

1806 The Sorceress of Strozzi; or, Harlequin Wanderer
1806 The Flying Island of Laputa; or, Harlequin Gulliver
1811 Harlequin and Padmanaba; or, the Golden Fish (Covent Garden)
1816 The Dog and Duck; or, Harlequin in the Obelisk
1817 Pedlar's Acre; or, Harlequin in Lambeth
1817 The Magic Grape; or, Harlequin Wine-Merchant
1817 The Touchstone; or, Harlequin Traveller
1818 Sea Serpent; or, Harlequin Yankee
1821 Harlequin Hoax; or, a Pantomime Proposed
1821 Three of Them; or, Harlequin Hum, Strum and Mum
1822 Mother Goose
1822 Three Fishermen; or, the Box, the Fish and the Genii
1822 Death of Harlequin
1823 Fox and Goose; or, Harlequin, the White Knight of Chess
1824 Three Gifts; or, the Farmer and the Puddings
1826 The Monster of the Glen; or, Harlequin and the Fairy Fanciful
1827 Jack and the Beanstalk
1827 Harlequin and the Astrologer of Stepney; or, the Enchanted Fish and the Fated Ring
1829 Tibby and Tabby; or, Harlequin and Poor Puss
1830 A Apple Pie
1831 Old King Cole; or, Harlequin and the Fiddlers Three
1832 The Elfie's Son; or, Harlequin and the Magic Horn
1832 The Valkyrae; or, Harlequin, the Patriotic Pole and the Maid of Muscovy
1832 Harlequin and Oberon
1833 One-Two, Come Buckle My Shoe; or, Harlequin and the Fairy Queen
1834 Harlequin and Little King Pippin
1835 Old Daddy Long Legs; or, Mary, Mary, Quite Contrary
1836 Boys and Girls Come Out To Play; or, Harlequin Hunt the Slipper
1836 Harlequin and the Lady's Bower; or, Cock-a-doodle-do
1837 Harlequin and Old Dame Trot
1838 Harlequin and the Enchanted Figs; or, the Little Yellow Man of the Golden Mountains
1839 Queen Bee; or, Harlequin and Little Goody Two-Shoes

1840 Harlequin and My Lady Lee; or, Goosey Gander and the Spell-bound Goslings
1841 Harlequin and the Ice Queen; or, Jack Frost and King Thaw
1842 Harlequin Puck; or, the Elfin Changeling and the Enchanted Statue of the Crystal Fountain
1844 Pounds, Shillings and Pence; or, Harlequin L.s.d.
1845 Harlequin and the Old Witch of Teddington
1846 King of the Castle; or, Harlequin in the Land of Dreams
1847 Battledore and Shuttlecock; or, Harlequin Trap, Bat and Ball
1848 Cinderella and the Fairy Queen; or, Harlequin and the Little Glass Slipper
1848 Harlequin Lord Lovell; or, Lady Nancy Bell and the Fairies of the Silver Oak
1849 Mother Goose; or, Harlequin and the Golden Egg
1849 Moon Queen and King Night; or, Harlequin Twilight
1850 The Merry Wives of Windsor; or, Harlequin and Sir John Falstaff and the Demon Hunter of the Enchanted Oak
1851 Harlequin Bluecap and the King of the Golden Waters; or, the Three Kingdoms, Animal, Vegetable and Mineral
1852 Harlequin and the Land of Flowers; or, the Fairy of the Rose and the Sprite of the Silver Star
1853 King Muffin; or, Harlequin Heartcake and the Fairies of the Glow-worm Glade
1854 Harlequin and Little-One-Eye, Little-Two-Eyes and Little-Three-Eyes; or, Beasts and Beauties
1855 A Prince of Pearls; or, Harlequin and Jane Shore
1856 Harlequin and the Summer Queen; or, King Winter and the Fairies of the Silver Willow
1857 Queen Mab; or, Harlequin Romeo and Juliet
1858 Harlequin Father Thames and the River Queen; or, The Great Lord Mayor of London
1859 Harlequin King Holyday; or, the Fairies of the Enchanted Valley and the King that Once Killed a Cat
1860 Harlequin and Cinderella; or, The Fairy of the Little Glass Slipper
1861 Harlequin Hey Diddle, The Cat and the Fiddle and the Cow that Jumped over the Moon; or, Oranges and Lemons and the Twelve Dancing Princesses
1862 Harlequin and Mother Goose; or, the Queen of Hearts and the Wonderful Tarts
1863 Harlequin Old King Cole and the Frog That would A-Wooing Go; or, Ride a Cock Horse to Banbury Cross
1864 Harlequin King Pumpkin; or, Richarde Ye Lion Hearte

andson & Pugin del.t et sculp.t

ROYA